At the Crossroads

The Arts of Spanish America & Early Global Trade 1492–1850

Papers from the 2010 Mayer Center Symposium
at the Denver Art Museum

Edited by Donna Pierce & Ronald Otsuka

A publication of the Frederick and Jan Mayer Center
for Pre-Columbian and Spanish Colonial Art
at the Denver Art Museum

Frederick + Jan MAYER CENTER Pre-Columbian + Spanish Colonial ART

DENVER ART MUSEUM

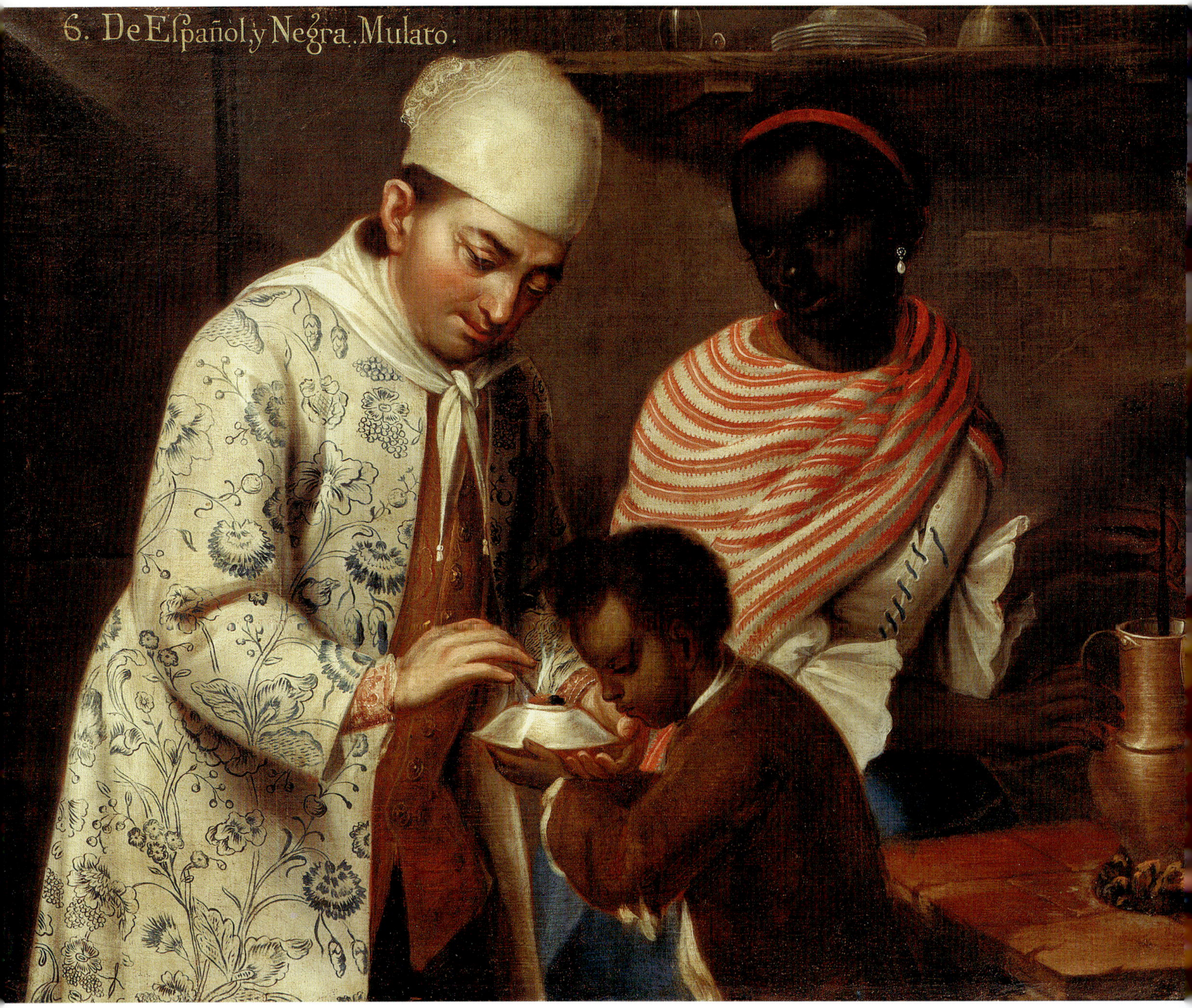
6. De Español, y Negra, Mulato.

Dedicated with affection and gratitude
to Jan Mayer and to the memory of Frederick Mayer
for their vision, passion, and generosity.

Published by the Mayer Center for Pre-Columbian & Spanish Colonial Art at the Denver Art Museum

Library of Congress Cataloging-in-Publication Data

Mayer Center Symposium (10th : 2010 : Denver Art Museum)
At the crossroads : the arts of Spanish America & early global trade, 1492-1850 : papers from the 2010 Mayer Center Symposium at the Denver Art Museum / edited by Donna Pierce & Ronald Otsuka.
p. cm.
This volume presents revised and expanded versions of papers presented at the 2010 symposium. A publication of the Frederick and Jan Mayer Center for Pre-Columbian and Spanish Colonial Art at the Denver Art Museum.
Includes bibliographical references.
ISBN 978-0-914738-80-0 (pbk.)
1. Art, Spanish colonial--Congresses. 2. International trade--History--Congresses. I. Pierce, Donna, 1950- editor of compilation. II. Otsuka, Ronald Y., editor of compilation. III. Frederick and Jan Mayer Center for Pre-Columbian and Spanish Colonial Art, issuing body. IV. Title.
N6502.2.M39 2012
709.8--dc23
2012014591

Mayer Center for Pre-Columbian & Spanish Colonial Art at the Denver Art Museum
100 West 14th Avenue Parkway
Denver, CO 80204
http://mayercenter.denverartmuseum.org
www.denverartmuseum.org

Editor: Donna Pierce and Ronald Otsuka, with the assistance of Nancy Mann
Project coordination, design, and production: Julie Wilson Frick

Cover illustrations: pp. 26–27, fig. 7
Frontispiece: p. 148, fig. 18

Printed and bound by CS Graphics Sdn Bhd. Malaysia
Distributed by the University of Oklahoma Press, www.oupress.com

CONTRIBUTORS
María Bonta de la Pezuela — *Sotheby's | New York, NY*
James M. Córdova and Claire Farago — *University of Colorado | Boulder, CO*
Dana Leibsohn — *Smith College | Northampton, MA*
Jaime Mariazza F. — *Universidad de San Marcos | Lima, Peru*
Donna Pierce — *Denver Art Museum | Denver, CO*
Sara Ryu — *Yale University | New Haven, CT*
William R. Sargent — *Peabody Essex Museum | Salem, MA*
Suzanne Stratton-Pruitt — *Independent Scholar | New York, NY*

Contents

Foreword

The Denver Art Museum strives to collect, display, and interpret the art of the whole world. The scope of the Denver Art Museum collection can be largely credited to Otto Karl Bach, who began his tenure as the museum's director in 1944. Ignoring the advice of eastern colleagues to carve out a special niche in regional art, Bach boldly set out to build an encyclopedic collection of world art. The museum counts among its greatest resources a Spanish Colonial collection rich in art from all over Latin America and an outstanding collection of art from all areas of Asia. As a result, the Denver Art Museum is perfectly poised to engage in an exploration of the global connections between Europe, Asia, and Latin America during the early modern era.

The museum's Spanish Colonial collection began in 1936 with a gift of *santos* from southern Colorado and northern New Mexico. In 1968, Bach established a New World Department that brought Pre-Columbian and Spanish Colonial objects from Latin America together. Today it is the best collection of its type in the United States and, in many areas, it is the most comprehensive collection outside of country of origin. The growth of the New World collections and programs received a major boost with the enlightened endowment gift of the late Frederick Mayer and his wife Jan. This gift made it possible to establish separate curatorial positions in Pre-Columbian and Spanish colonial art. The Mayers also founded the Frederick and Jan Mayer Center for Pre-Columbian and Spanish Colonial Art at the Denver Art Museum, dedicated to increasing awareness and promoting scholarship in these fields by sponsoring scholarly activities including annual symposia, fellowships, study trips, and publications, such as this volume.

Originating in 1915 with a donation of Chinese and Japanese art objects, the museum's Asian art collection now includes works from the entire Asian continent. Spanning a period from the fourth millennium B.C. to the present, these objects illustrate the wide-ranging achievements of Asian artists and artisans. The Asian art collection has grown principally through the generosity of donors. In 2001 the William Sharpless Jackson Jr. Endowment Fund for Curator's Circle was created to ensure the continuation of the Curator's Circle lecture series, whose goal is to engender mutual understanding and esteem among all peoples and nations through the appreciation and enjoyment of Asian art. With his generous support, William Jackson enabled the museum to bring friends from near and far to share their knowledge, appreciation, and enjoyment of Asian art.

In 2006, Donna Pierce of the New World Department partnered with Ronald Otsuka of the Asian Art Department to host "Asia and Spanish America: Trans-Pacific Artistic and Cultural Exchange, 1500–1850," co-sponsored by the Mayer Center and the Jackson Endowment for Curator's Circle. Those papers were published by the Mayer Center in 2009. As a continuation of the theme, the two departments partnered in 2010, again with the support of the Mayer Center and the Jackson Endowment, to organize a symposium titled "At the Crossroads: The Arts of Spanish America and Early Global Trade, 1492–1850." Those papers are presented in this volume.

Over the years, Jackson and the Mayers have generously supported the museum's mission in many ways. All three of them attended the first collaborative symposium in 2006. Sadly, it was Frederick Mayer's last symposium; his untimely death in 2007 was a great loss to the community. We are blessed to have the ongoing support of his wife, Jan, and of William Jackson, and we offer warm thanks for their long-term and ongoing dedication to the museum.

Christoph Heinrich
Frederick and Jan Mayer Director
Denver Art Museum

Introduction and Acknowledgments

The Jan and Frederick Mayer Center for Pre-Columbian and Spanish Colonial Art at the Denver Art Museum sponsors annual symposia alternating between these fields of art. Held in November 2010, the tenth symposium in the series was titled "At the Crossroads: The Arts of Spanish America and Early Global Trade, 1492–1850" and was co-sponsored by the Asian Art Department's William Sharpless Jackson Jr. Endowment for Curator's Circle at the Denver Art Museum. Following up on our 2006 joint symposium, "Asia and Spanish America: Trans-Pacific Artistic and Cultural Exchange, 1500–1850" (published in 2009), we assembled an international group of eleven scholars specializing in the art, culture, and history of Asia, Europe, or Latin America to present recent research on global connections in the arts during the early modern era. Topics ranged from architecture, painting, and sculpture to engravings, ceramics, clothing, and decorative arts of the period. The discussions covered art from the geographic areas of modern-day Ecuador, Colombia, Venezuela, Peru, Bolivia, Mexico, Spain, Italy, the Netherlands, the Canary Islands, the Philippines, China, and India, among others. The Mayer Center sponsors publication of the proceedings of the symposia. This volume presents revised and expanded versions of papers presented at the 2010 symposium.

Dana Liebsohn, Priscilla van der Poel Professor of Art History, Smith College, opens the volume with a thought-provoking discussion of the reception and reinterpretation of Asian motifs in the various art forms of viceregal New Spain (Mexico) and the complexities of interpreting those today. María Bonta de la Pezuela, Vice President and Director of the Latin American Art Department at Sotheby's, New York, follows with a detailed analysis of shipping records and what these reveal about the exportation of Chinese porcelain to the Americas. William Sargent, former H. A. Crosby Forbes Curator of Asian Export Art at the Peabody Essex Museum, examines specific examples of Chinese porcelain produced for export, possibly commissioned for an Augustinian establishment in Mexico.

Jaime Mariazza, Professor of Art History at the Universidad de San Marcos in Lima, Peru, describes the importation of funerary traditions from Europe to Peru via books and engravings and their implementation there by local artists, while independent curator and scholar Suzanne Stratton-Pruitt analyzes the exportation of paintings "by the dozens" from Spain to Peru, including examples by Zurbarán, and examines their impact on Peruvian colonial painting traditions.

Two papers address the exportation of distinctively American objects to Europe. Sara Ryu, Ph.D. candidate at Yale University, presents the results of recent research on corn-paste sculptures from Mexico sent to Europe and the Canary Islands, their reception there, and their relationship to lightweight sculpture production in Europe. The unique genre of *casta* (caste) paintings, invented in New Spain and exported to Europe, and the intellectual motivation of the Mexican artists who invented them, is discussed by Claire Farago, Professor of Renaissance Art, Theory, and Criticism at the University of Colorado, and James Córdova, Assistant Professor of Art History, University of Colorado. Donna Pierce, Frederick and Jan Mayer Curator of Spanish Colonial Art at the Denver Art Museum, closes the volume with a case study on the extent of the geographic range of trade objects by presenting documentary and archaeological evidence for the presence of Asian trade goods in New Mexico, the northernmost province of the Spanish Americas.

Two papers presented at the symposium are not included in this publication. Karina Corrigan, H. A. Crosby Forbes Curator of Asian Export Art at the Peabody Essex Museum, spoke on Chinese export silver and its exportation to the Americas. Charlene Villaseñor Black, Associate Professor of Art History at University of California, Los Angeles, presented a paper titled "Saints' Cults and Conversion in the Global Hispanic World," which addressed the transfer of imagery of saints from Europe to the Americas, and in some cases, from the Americas back to Europe. It is slated for publication elsewhere.

We are grateful to these scholars for their participation in the symposium and their contributions to this publication. As an interdisciplinary study bringing together new research on an understudied era and area, we hope this volume will be an important resource for scholars and enthusiasts of early modern history in general and Asian and Latin American art and history in particular.

We would also like to acknowledge the staff of the New World and Asian Art departments for their efforts in organizing the symposium: Julie Wilson Frick, Mayer Center Program Coordinator; Trish Tomlinson, Curatorial Assistant in the New World Department; Douglas Wagner, Curatorial Assistant in the Asian Art Department; Michael Brown, Mayer Center Spanish Colonial Fellow; Anne Tennant, New World Research Associate; Kealey Boyd, former Curator's Circle Assistant in the Asian Art Department; and Jana Gottshalk, New World Research Intern and current Curator's Circle Assistant. Denver Art Museum events and audio-visual staff, particularly Daniel Fonken and Ron Wilcox, and the security staff led by Tony Fortunato and Terri Cross, provided significant and cheerful support. As always, we thank our New World Department colleague, Margaret Young-Sánchez, Frederick and Jan Mayer Curator of Pre-Columbian Art, for her support.

In addition, we want to thank our respective support groups, Alianza de las Artes Americanas and the Asian Art Association, for their support of the symposium, and we want to acknowledge our first Mayer Center Gold Circle members, Holly Arnold Kinney of the Tesoro Foundation and Jackie Winter.

In the preparation of this publication, we are grateful to Nancy Mann of the University of Colorado for her superb editing skills. Anne Tennant applied her outstanding translation skills to Jaime Mariazza's essay, in addition to providing valuable bibliographic and editing assistance. Michael Brown and Jana Gottshalk contributed bibliographic research as well. Thanks are due to Laura Caruso, former Director of the Publications Department, for ongoing advice and editing. Jeff Wells, Denver Art Museum photographer, was always quick to provide his expert services. Digital mapmaker Fabrice Weexsteen enthusiastically offered his technical and scholarly knowledge in his creation of the enclosed maps, developed in collaboration with the New World Department. We are grateful to CS Graphics for printing the volume and to the University of Oklahoma Press for distribution.

Our profound gratitude goes to Julie Wilson Frick, Mayer Center Program Coordinator, for book coordination, image gathering, compilation, research, contract negotiation, and most importantly, for the elegant and clean design of this and all Mayer Center symposia publications.

On behalf of all of us at the Denver Art Museum and those who participated in the symposium, we want to express our deepest gratitude to the late Frederick Mayer and his wife, Jan, and to William Jackson for providing the opportunity to bring such a distinguished group of scholars together from many parts of the world to share ideas. Creating an ongoing forum for this type of scholarly exchange, along with the ability to publish the results, was a major part of the Mayers' vision and formed the basis of the founding of the Mayer Center for Pre-Columbian and Spanish Colonial Art and its programming. The Mayers and William Jackson represent the ideal supporters, interested in all aspects of museums and the scholarship behind them. The Denver Art Museum in general and the New World and Asian Art departments in particular have been blessed to have them as our guardian angels.

Donna Pierce
Frederick and Jan Mayer Curator of
Spanish Colonial Art /
Head of the New World Department
Denver Art Museum

Ronald Otsuka
Dr. Joseph de Heer Curator of Asian Art /
Head of the Asian Art Department
Denver Art Museum

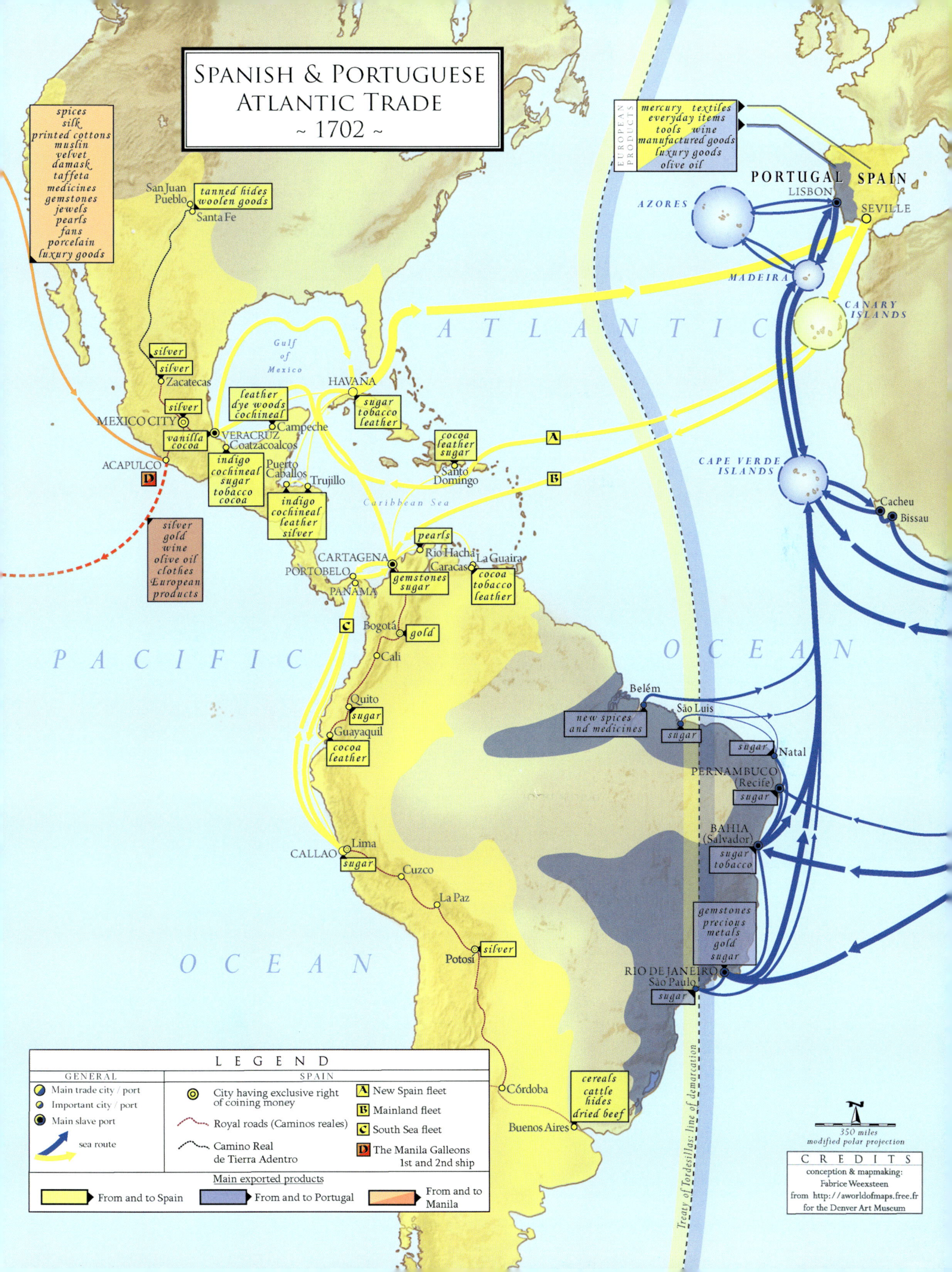
SPANISH & PORTUGUESE
ATLANTIC TRADE
~ 1702 ~
spices
silk
printed cottons
muslin
velvet
damask
taffeta
medicines
gemstones
jewels
pearls
fans
porcelain
luxury goods
San Juan Pueblo
tanned hides
woolen goods
Santa Fe
silver
silver
Zacatecas
silver
MEXICO CITY
vanilla
cocoa
VERACRUZ
Coatzacoalcos
ACAPULCO
D
silver
gold
wine
olive oil
clothes
European products
Gulf of Mexico
feather
dye woods
cochineal
Campeche
indigo
cochineal
sugar
tobacco
cocoa
Puerto Caballos
Trujillo
indigo
cochineal
feather
silver
HAVANA
sugar
tobacco
feather
cocoa
feather
sugar
Santo Domingo
A
B
Caribbean Sea
pearls
Rio Hacha
La Guaira
Caracas
CARTAGENA
PORTOBELO
PANAMA
gemstones
sugar
cocoa
tobacco
feather
C
Bogotá
gold
Cali
Quito
sugar
Guayaquil
cocoa
feather
PACIFIC
OCEAN
CALLAO
Lima
sugar
Cuzco
La Paz
Potosí
silver
Córdoba
Buenos Aires
cereals
cattle
hides
dried beef
ATLANTIC
OCEAN
EUROPEAN PRODUCTS
mercury textiles
everyday items
tools wine
manufactured goods
luxury goods
olive oil
PORTUGAL
SPAIN
LISBON
SEVILLE
AZORES
MADEIRA
CANARY ISLANDS
CAPE VERDE ISLANDS
Cacheu
Bissau
Belém
new spices
and medicines
São Luís
sugar
sugar
Natal
PERNAMBUCO
(Recife)
sugar
BAHIA
(Salvador)
sugar
tobacco
gemstones
precious metals
gold
sugar
RIO DE JANEIRO
São Paulo
sugar
Treaty of Tordesillas: line of demarcation
350 miles
modified polar projection
LEGEND
GENERAL
Main trade city / port
Important city / port
Main slave port
sea route
SPAIN
City having exclusive right of coining money
Royal roads (Caminos reales)
Camino Real de Tierra Adentro
A New Spain fleet
B Mainland fleet
C South Sea fleet
D The Manila Galleons 1st and 2nd ship
Main exported products
From and to Spain
From and to Portugal
From and to Manila
CREDITS
conception & mapmaking:
Fabrice Weexsteen
from http://aworldofmaps.free.fr
for the Denver Art Museum

Made in China, Made in Mexico

Dana Leibsohn

Visual culture, global trade, early modernity. To speak of these things is to raise the specter of money—especially silver from Spanish America and what it could buy. Across the early modern period, the urban centers of viceregal New Spain and Peru became sites of extravagant display and exuberant consumption. In the seventeenth century, for instance, Mexico City was legendary for its markets and promenades, its public festivals. Women in luxurious silks strolled through shady parks, and perched upon imported velvet cushions as their coaches bumped along rutted streets. Home décor could require lavish spending, although people of humble means also desired and purchased foreign imports. The city might be muddy with floodwater, but for festivals and official celebrations its main streets were decorated with pomp and pride. Yet in spite of such showiness, most modern accounts of global trade in the early modern world focus upon European habits of consumption.[1] The role of Spanish America, when it figures at all, tends to center upon silver, particularly as a prime driver of cross-cultural competition and trade. The webs of exchange that bound Manila to Mexico City, Batavia to Amsterdam, and Havana to Seville were, for many, spun from dreams of silver.

We sense the allure of American wealth from "The History of the West Indies" (*Tari-i Hind-i garbî veya Hadís-i nev*), a manuscript created in Ottoman Turkey in the late sixteenth century. This work draws upon a mix of sources, including accounts of the Americas published in Spanish and Italian, and its images feature the flora and fauna of Spanish America.[2] The manuscript also includes one urban scene, a depiction of Potosí, the city nestled high in the Andes at the base of extraordinarily rich silver mines (today in Bolivia). While silver itself is not pictured, the site of the mines, Cerro Rico, looms in the background and a canal, part of the water management system for working silver, slices through the center of the painting (Fig. 1). The buildings that compose Potosí are neither particularly "Spanish" nor especially "Andean" in architectural form. Yet the image conveys both compression and dense clustering at the base of Cerro Rico, features that parallel the actual layout of the city. The human figures—one pale, one dark—hint at the city's ethnic diversity: indigenous people, mestizos, Spaniards, and Creoles, as well as Africans and African Americans, lived in this mining boomtown.[3]

The text beneath the painting says nothing about the city or the setting of the scene. Nor does it discuss the history of Spanish America. Rather, it explains methods for extracting silver ore. Within the context of the manuscript, then, the painting of Potosí functions as an image of desire, inviting contemplation of the geographic origins of silver, and, by implication, the wealth that silver might bring. Giancarlo Casale has recently argued that this manuscript was deeply implicated in Ottoman ambitions to compete with the Portuguese for access to Indian markets.[4] Seen from this perspective, the image figures in what today might be called global politics and anxieties over transnational markets; it reinforces (and becomes constituent of) the trope that casts Spanish America as the place where money is made. Cerro Rico is both metaphor and metonym for wealth—evocative of the monetary value of silver, but also the ambitions it could inspire, the lust it might satisfy.

Formed in the sixteenth century, the trope binding Spanish America to silver production still circulates today. In various forms, it can be found in histories of trade, analyses of consumption in early modern Europe, and writings on modern globalization. Ann McCants, one of the most sensitive students of wealth, poverty, and the role of trade objects in early modernity, maintains that "the Americas cannot be left out of the picture, not only because chocolate and tobacco were found there, but more importantly still, the metallic

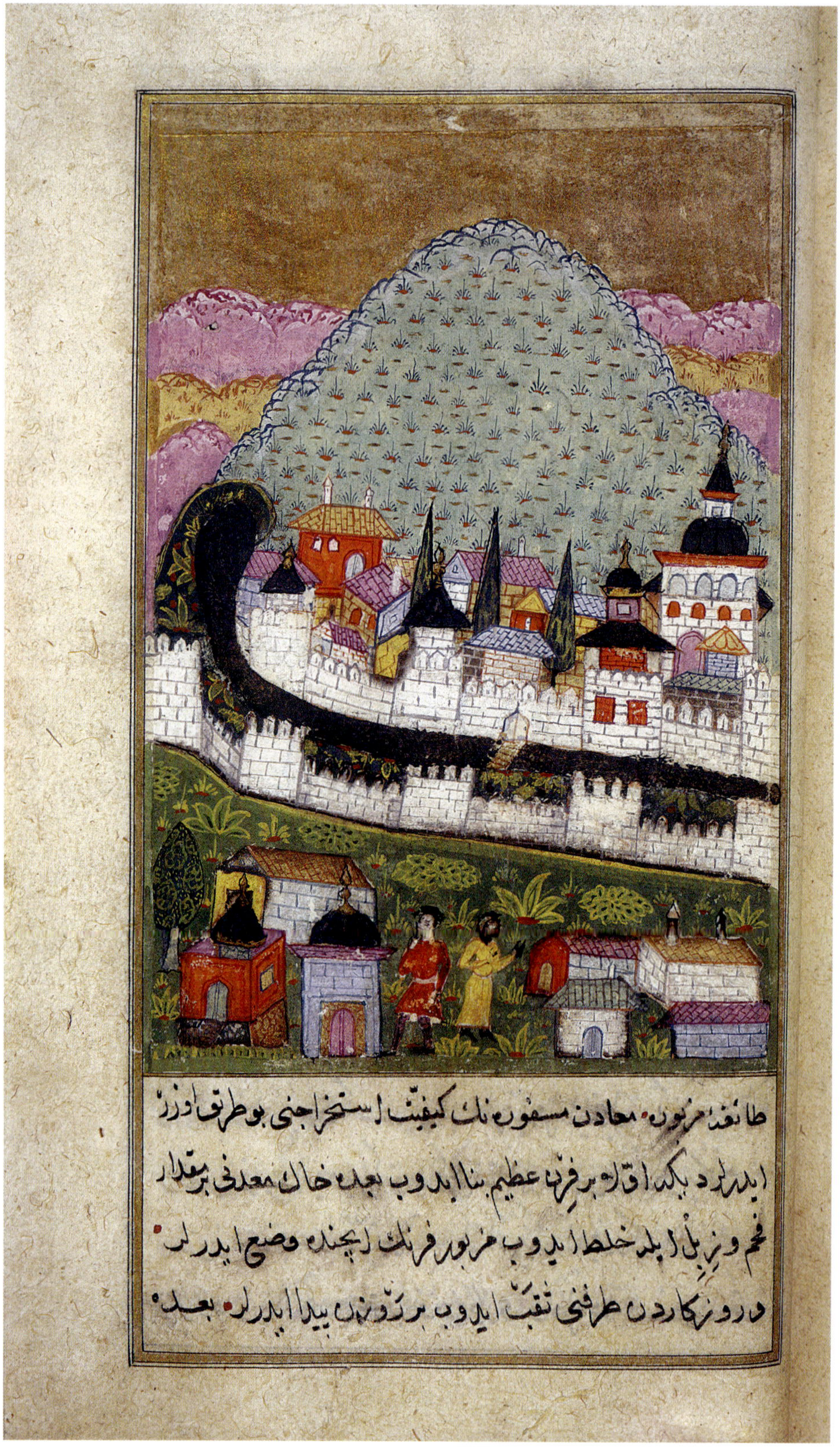

Fig. 1. *View of Potosí*, from *Tarih-i Hind-i garbî veya Hadîs-i nev* (The History of the West Indies). Turkey, late 16th century. Colored and black inks, gold leaf, paper. The Edward E. Ayer Collection, Newberry Library, Chicago.

commodity, silver, which greased the wheels of the entire global trade edifice, was located there in prodigious quantities."[5] She is not wrong, and her position helps to explain the power of money in the early modern period; it also renders Spanish America indispensable to any discussion of global trade. Yet to those who study Spanish America today, such claims are also disconcerting. For viewing New Spain and Peru as important solely (or even largely) because they produced silver for others renews those deep-rooted perspectives wherein "good colonies" supplied raw materials for high-end, cosmopolitan consumption elsewhere.

Without doubt, silver extracted from mines in Spanish America shaped the history of early modern exchange in fundamental ways. This point has been argued well. [6] Yet the trope of America-as-the-land-of-silver has also skewed understandings of visual and material culture, for it reveals very little about what it meant to covet or value things in Mexico or Peru, Guatemala or Bolivia. In this essay, then, I wish to ask what we might learn by viewing Spanish America as a place of trade and exchange, consumption and creativity and not, primarily, as the land from whence silver came. I take as my point of entry trans-Pacific trade and the ways in which visual culture connected China to New Spain in the seventeenth century. More specifically, this essay explores how chains of meaning were formed for and with Chinese things that came to Mexico. Certainly other important perspectives on global trade exist—many of which surface in this volume—but I am interested in historical geographies that often, still, remain at the margins of current debates.[7] And so I turn towards the Pacific as a way to understand both histories of early modern exchange and how people in Spanish America made sense of imports from afar.

Local Tastes and Consuming Passions

Archival documents and travel writing of the seventeenth century point to deep and abject poverty in the urban centers of New Spain. Yet the glitz of Mexico City also caught observers' eyes. Bernardo de Balbuena's 1604 poem *Grandeza mexicana* is unabashedly focused on luxury.[8] For him, Mexico City seems charged with magnetic energy, pulling into its orbit a dazzling array of people and things. His description of imports from across the Pacific emphasizes the sumptuous—precious stones and metals, silken cloth—implying that opulence was not one choice among many, but an inevitable condition of urban life. Stephanie Merrim has called *Grandeza* "a paean to mercantile capitalism," suggesting that "Balbuena waxes poetic but does not fictionalize...New Spain had indeed become a hub of international commerce, a global city in economic terms."[9] Trade networks crossed vast oceans and traversed the Valley of Mexico, shunting an impressive array of goods into the city. Nevertheless, Balbuena's depiction of trans-Pacific trade (as well as trans-Atlantic and more local trade) discloses relatively little about the texture of lived experience. For histories of trade and consumption, his descriptions are resonant less for their scope and veracity than for their pride and ambition. Goods may have been on offer from India and China, but it was not the geographic origin, in and of itself, that mattered most; foreign imports were valued because they spoke to desires among elites that were cosmopolitan, not simply colonial.[10] The range of evocative meanings created by the "pull" of local demand in Mexico turned upon aspirations formed in the Americas, but also those that extended well beyond.[11]

To be sure, Baroque strategies of expression and stylized excess color Balbuena's view of Mexico City. Yet Balbuena is not the only one in New Spain struck by residents' consuming passions. A number of travelers and moralists condemn such lavish taste: all that lace, so many layers of silk, and even servants in pearls—the expectation was for less flash, less bling. Rebecca Earle has persuasively argued that the discourse of luxury in Spanish America is sewn through with racial and political undertones,[12] a point underscored by sumptuary laws issued in New Spain stipulating who could appear in public wearing luxury materials, and who could not.[13] Such regulations were issued multiple times, suggesting an intractable desire for lovely things that touched an anxious nerve. This is hardly unique to Mexico; civic and moral

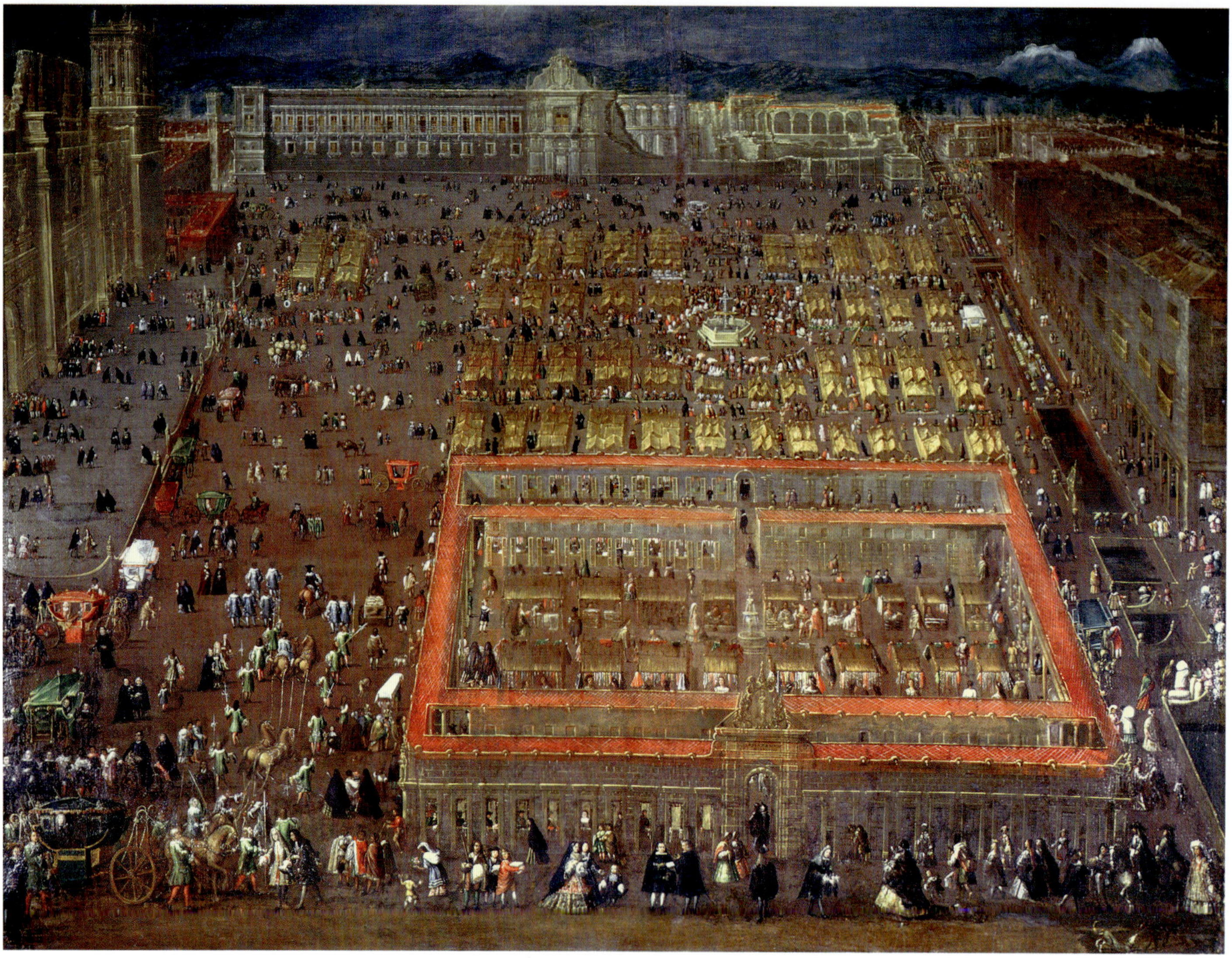

Fig. 2. Cristóbal Villalpando, *Main Plaza of Mexico City*. Mexico, c. 1695–1700. Oil on canvas. Private collection, Corsham Court. Courtesy Bridgman Art Library International.

anxieties about luxury are known from many places in the early modern world.[14] Distinctive here, however, is the complexion of these anxieties, and how they turned on perceptions and practices linked to global trade.[15] This is because Mexico City, unlike many places, was both metropole and, in the context of early modern world politics, a colonial setting.

An image of Mexico City painted on the cusp of the eighteenth century by Cristóbal Villalpando sharpens this point. As with the Balbuena poem, this painting surfaces frequently in discussions of visual culture and trade in Spanish America (Fig. 2), in no small part because it, too, highlights local habits of consumption. Towards the back of the painting, on the right, the volcanic mountains of Iztaccihuatl and Popocatepetl anchor the scene in central Mexico. On the left stands the cathedral, and across the back of the plaza is the viceregal palace, partially ruined from riots in 1692. Coaches, grooms, and men upon horseback dot the plaza. Women meander through open spaces with children in tow. The walled Parián occupies the center of the painting, with men and women consulting shop-owners and comparing wares. Spilling out behind the walled market, indigenous women perch under umbrellas selling goods. Dozens more shoppers hover near tents, on the hunt for ever-better merchandise. This is a partially imagined view,[16] although the evocative power of the painting rests, in part, upon an investment in realism. The viceregal palace had been burned, the cathedral does occupy the northern flank of the plaza at the heart of Mexico City, and the Parián once stood at the plaza's center. Moreover, it is not hard to imagine people strolling along market stalls, surrounded by elegant women and well-dressed men ambling the streets, or humble water carriers and porters hunched under bundles. Although much later than *Grandeza mexicana*, this image can be read through a similar lens: it is not the artist's realism that matters most, but his emphasis. Villalpando has all but filled the center of his painting with the possibility of shopping. This city—his work seems to say—is one that takes very seriously the opportunity to buy things.[17]

For all its local color, this painting also beckons across the Pacific. The Parián in Mexico City was known as a place where imported goods were sold, especially products of the Pacific trade. This connection was intentionally cultivated, for the Parián in Mexico City carried the same name as the Chinese enclave in Manila. In the eyes of Manila's Spanish residents, the Parián was always a place of foreigners; this resonance was also familiar to people in Mexico City, be they wealthy or poor.[18] In crossing the Pacific, the term Parián created an evocative but imaginary parallel between Chinese bodies and labor over there (in Manila) and foreign things over here (in Mexico City). Seen in this light, the Villalpando painting constructs a civic center that embraces but does not domesticate the foreign. The image illuminates one way that China and its exports, in material and symbolic form, occupied a public space in the center of Mexico City.

Set alongside Balbuena's poem, this painting complicates the trope evoked by the *Tari-i Hind-i garbî veya Hadís-i nev*. For *Grandeza* and Villalpando's scene invite—indeed, encourage—viewers to see Mexico City as a place where buying, not only producing, mattered greatly. That is, the silvery wealth produced in Spanish America fueled diverse and vibrant habits of consumption in New Spain, not just abroad. This may seem an obvious point, but the spending enabled by silver in New Spain raises a fundamental question for any discussion of global trade: to what extent were local tastes and preferences exceptional, and to what extent did they parallel those of other early modern settings? Arif Dirlik rightly notes that the global can embrace the local (and vice versa), but the homogenizing tendencies of global cosmopolitanism cannot be overlooked.[19] How, then, to understand the role of global trade in the visual culture of seventeenth-century cities in New Spain, especially since these settings differed in so many ways from metropolitan centers in Asia and Western Europe, and from contemporary colonial settlements in Southeast Asia, Africa, and North America?

It is tempting to address the question of distinctiveness by isolating instances in which New

Spain was "first on the scene"; that is, by identifying those instances when residents of Mexico embraced foreign imports or developed habits of consumption before others. Craig Clunas has described this historical approach as one of inversion.[20] Such arguments underscore the conversation between metropoles and their colonies, yet search out those moments in which the colonies were leaders, not followers. While this interpretative position has its adherents, I would argue that its usefulness is limited. In part this is because this way of thinking depends upon a model of colonial relations that ultimately pits metropoles against peripheries; yet we know such relationships were mutually constitutive and rarely dyadic. Moreover, for an argument of this type to be meaningful—that is, an argument of originary exceptionalism—"being first" must also have some inherent value. History, however, rarely bears this out.[21] And so, instead of looking for where New Spain "fits" into the early modern world of trade, or even "how distinctive" its visual culture is, I propose a different line of inquiry. That is, I suggest we ask what the visual culture of New Spain might teach us about the meaning of foreign consumption. Are its lessons primarily local and regional, or do they have broader implications?

Trans-Pacific

The galleons that sailed the Pacific provide a good entry into this query, for they contributed to both specific qualities of visual culture and broader patterns of exchange in the seventeenth century. Beyond this, the galleon trade has become increasingly well documented, and our knowledge of the ways in which it created value—for objects and consumers, merchants and makers—has deepened in recent years.[22] Geographically and conceptually Manila and Acapulco tethered the Pacific trade. The excursion west, out of Acapulco, was considered the easy one, requiring about three months of travel. On this trip much of America's silver began its odyssey into China, although it did not travel alone. Friars, cochineal, paper, officials, letters, and legal documents also made this journey towards Asia. The voyage east was considered more brutal, in part because it took twice as long—from Manila to Acapulco could be six or seven months without landfall, and some years, even longer. This was the trip of imports: porcelain, lacquer furniture, ivory carving, beeswax, silk and more silk. This was also a "journey of return" for official paperwork, colonial officials, and friars, and a trip of dislocation (and, at times, relocation) for Asian slaves and shipmen. Economic historians have pointed out that the taking of profits in Spanish America was no simple affair. Financial gains could be impressive, but trans-Pacific trade carried serious risks.[23] The meanings for Chinese objects—be they luxuries or mundane commodities—were created, then, in a crucible where chancy business ventures mixed with the lure of hefty profit.

The inflection of imports from Asia was also fluid in New Spain. As porcelains and furniture traveled ever farther from China, and ever deeper into Spanish America, their connotative value—what scholars of consumption tend to call the semiotic capacity of material objects—shifted and changed. This is no less true of imports today, for the cultural resonance of an object is never fully fixed at its site of manufacture. Unfortunately for historians, few texts survive from Spanish America explicitly commenting upon the meanings invested in Asian objects. Even Antonio de Morga, the seventeenth-century official stationed in Manila who wrote one of the fullest descriptions known of the exotica flowing into the port city, disappoints on this theme. He says almost nothing about the pleasures of encountering particular materials or designs. Instead it is the quantity and kind of commodities that capture his attention, as if the sheer amount of merchandise and its diversity was what mattered most. His point of view should not be hastily dismissed; yet, certainly, there was more to consumer desire than he lets on.[24] If we cast a wide net, across official reports, inventories, maps, and objects, it becomes possible to glean something of the evocative power and signifying limits of Chinese imports.

For both commodities and merchants, Manila was often a prime destination east out of China. A city firmly tied into East Asian and Southeast

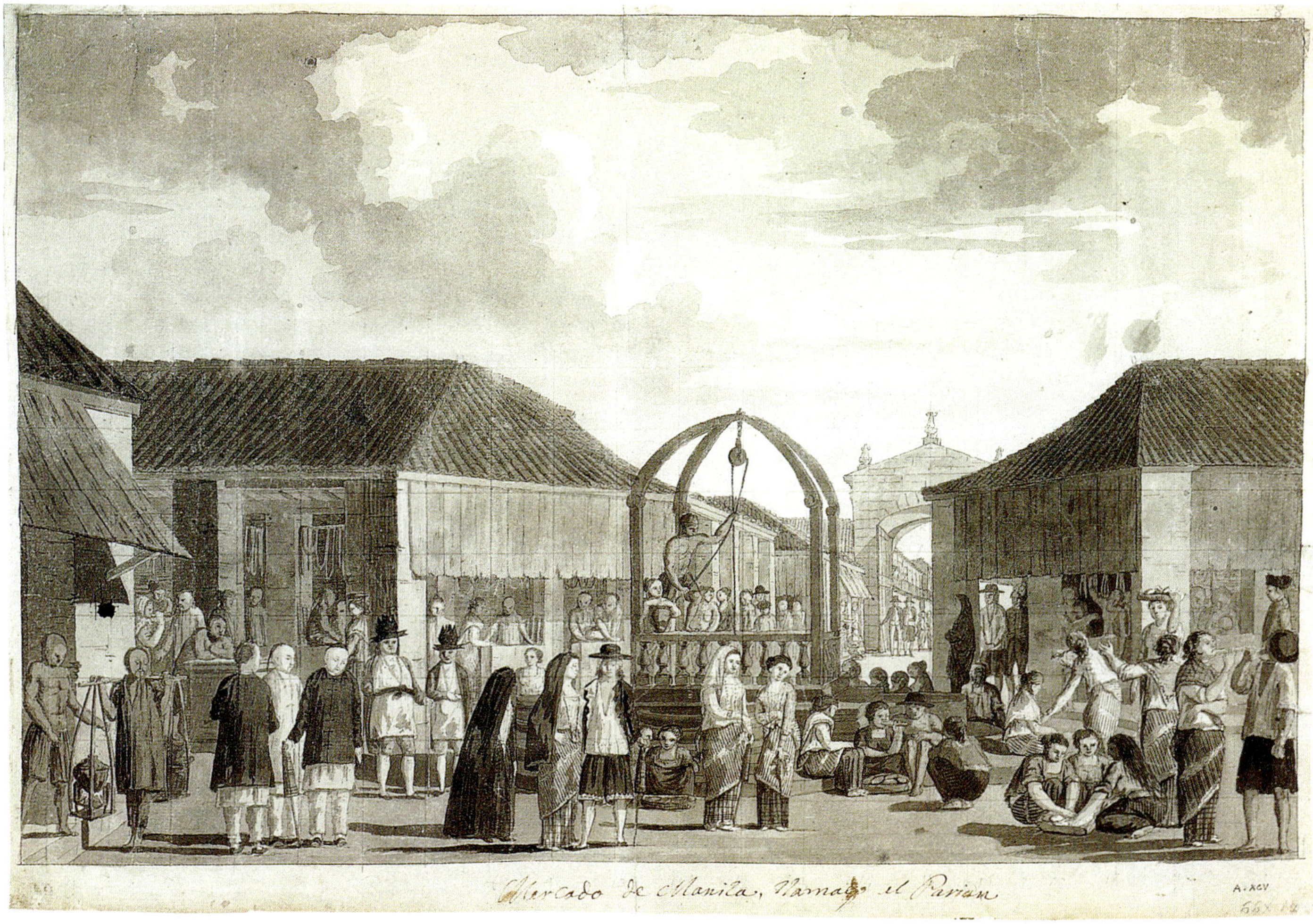

Fig. 3. Juan Ravenet, *View of the Parián, Manila*. 1792. Ink, sepia wash on paper. Museo Naval, Madrid.

Asian trade networks before the arrival of Europeans, Manila thrived as a way station under Spanish rule. Before—but especially after the arrival of Spanish settlers—it became known for its cultural and linguistic heterogeneity.[25] The balance of power in Manila was uneasy, with only a few hundred Spanish, indigenous, and Japanese residents, but thousands of Chinese. This produced an urban environment riven by deep tension. Even Manila's urban plan makes this clear. Dominating the center of town were the private residences of Spaniards, the cathedral and monastic complexes, the palace of the archbishop, and the hall of the Audiencia. This was Intramuros, a region Juan Grau y Monfalcón described in 1637 as "very sightly in its buildings and plan," with many structures made of stone.[26] While Chinese and Japanese people also lived in Intramuros, the majority resided outside the walls, in neighborhoods nearby. The proximity made daily trips to the center of Manila feasible, but Chinese workers and merchants, in particular, were to live separately. Ideally they could be locked out of town at night.[27]

The Parián, a center of Chinese life, had houses built of straw for the very poorest residents, tile and brick for the more established.[28] In contrast to the Parián of Mexico City, the Manila Parián was a bustling hub of immigrant life. Signs and banners hung outside shops advertising in Chinese characters bakeries, restaurants, pharmacies. Estimates are unreliable, but at its most vigorous, the Parián of Manila was home to thousands of Chinese residents. Only a few images of the Parián are known today; Figure 3 offers a late-eighteenth-century view. Painted by Juan Ravenet, the scene is one of several made of Manila during the Malaspina Expedition (1789–1792). Today, we might call the image ethnographic in its ambition, for it depicts not only market stalls and a central fountain, but also people of many ethnicities. Ravenet has attended to distinct modes of dress and diverse body postures, and in the original, one can see small faint numbers sketched onto figures in the foreground—a key to the "ethnic types" depicted in the scene.

While the Parián may have seemed an exotic setting in Spanish eyes, it was no paradise. Across the seventeenth century, the enclave was burned repeatedly; in particularly arduous years, massacres of Chinese residents were devastating.[29] Spanish-language documents rarely discuss the feelings or sentiments of anyone in Manila, but reports describing raids in the Parián suggest something of Chinese anxieties (if not also strategies of self-preservation). When officials appear, people scatter and hide; Chinese craftsmen and shop owners who are caught might hastily express a readiness to convert to Christianity rather than face expulsion. Spaniards, too, preferred that the Parián not be abandoned: they relied upon Chinese people to bake their bread, supply the galleons, provide fish and vegetables for dinner, make their shoes, cut their hair, and repair broken things. Indeed, numerous documents describe how unimaginable life in Manila would be without Chinese goods and services. Yet the Spanish fear of rebellion ran strong. This tension—between anxiety and dependence—gave rise to an implicit policy in which Spanish consumers both summoned and repulsed Chinese people and their commodities.[30] This classic friction of cross-cultural exchange mattered in Manila because precious few Chinese goods arrived in Mexico uncolored by or immune from what transpired in the Parían, and, as Igor Kopytoff has reminded us, the social construction of things often depends upon the social construction of people.[31]

One recurrent theme in this vein is Spanish disappointment in the quality of silk brought to Manila by Chinese merchants. There are complaints about too many sticks adhering to silk fibers, and cloth having been cut into uneven sizes. From a Spanish point of view, Chinese merchants seemed indifferent to reasonable laws about product purity; from a Chinese perspective, Spanish legalities were beside the point, as long as their imported merchandise would sell. These differences were not argued only in alphabetic prose. They were also enacted through bodily movements and speech acts. In June and July of 1609, for instance, a Spanish official and a Chinese-Spanish interpreter visited the Parián, and, standing at a corner of its four main streets explained their expectations for high-quality merchandise. The pair then headed out to the docks, where, day after day, they marched onto Chinese boats, describing to merchants and boat captains the regulations and expectations for future silk shipments.[32] There is no way of knowing whether, upon their return to China, the merchants at the docks told anyone about the quality of silk requested by Spanish officials. The repetition of legislation on this topic suggests not. Nevertheless, I have not found Spanish reports of silk being sent back because the quality was unsatisfactory.[33] Nor does there exist much indication that Chinese commodities went without buyers.[34] If silks were stacked in storehouses moldering as they awaited customers, the records on such things are scant from the seventeenth century. The documentary trail implies that whatever Chinese merchants brought to Manila, they could sell.[35] This opens the very real possibility that in Manila (and elsewhere in New Spain) Spanish consumers were not the full masters of their own purchasing power. There were, more than likely, real limits to the influence and sway of Spanish American taste and desire.

We must imagine, then, that Spanish consumers, at least on occasion, learned to covet what they could buy.[36] This may seem disempowering—and perhaps for some in seventeenth-century New Spain it was—but basic economics teaches us that producers never determine the full meaning of the goods they sell. The evocative range of imported commodities also develops on local terms. In Manila, this relationship turned on events and conditions that involved hundreds of Chinese people, and daily encounters in the Parián. As commodities made their way across the Pacific, the relationships among Chinese commodities, Chinese people, and Spanish consumers shifted. Anxiety still formed part of the equation, but in many ways, objects opened their fields of reference.

In Acapulco, the first port of call in the Americas, some of this elasticity becomes palpable. If all went well, galleons would land in December or January and an annual fair to disperse imported goods was held soon after. From Acapulco objects traveled northeast along what was called the "China Road," an appellation that both responded to and reinscribed the Asian ancestry of imports in New Spain. Other merchandise traveled along different paths. Some passed overland to the port of Veracruz, where it was reloaded upon ships and sent to Spain; some made its way south to Ecuador and Peru. Yet other commodities moved north into what is now Northern Mexico, New Mexico, New Orleans, Virginia, and Florida.[37] The sheer distribution of Chinese objects in seventeenth-century America suggests their appeal. What remains less clear is whether these commodities resonated along the same connotative axes when purchased in Florida and in Mexico City. New Spain was culturally varied, and the experiences of "China" in Acapulco were hardly identical to those in Manila or Mexico City, leave alone Zacatecas or Santa Fe.

Perhaps the best-known description of Acapulco and its bay is a visual one, created in 1615 by Adrian Boot, the engineer responsible for the reconstruction and fortification of Acapulco (Fig. 4). While some seventeenth-century writers praised the port and its protective landscape, it was also known as a scrappy town that sprang to life when the galleons arrived, only to fall into languor after the fair closed.[38] In Boot's image, the town—virtually deserted and dwarfed by the port and surrounding landscape—stretches along the bottom of the scene. Only three figures appear; two are laborers, the third rides a prancing steed. This well-dressed man peers over the hill into the city from the left, as if directing our gaze less to Acapulco than across the bay and out to the horizon. Through iconography and composition, Boot's image highlights oceanic trade, giving pride of place to the placid expanse of ocean and embrace of coastline that frames the bay. It also includes several ships, situating one at the center of the scene. The pentagonal fort perched upon the promontory jutting into the bay, built as defense against pirate attacks, further reminds viewers of the intense competition over goods and profits in which Acapulco was involved.

How "Asian" was Acapulco in the seventeenth century? This is difficult to answer. Surely it had

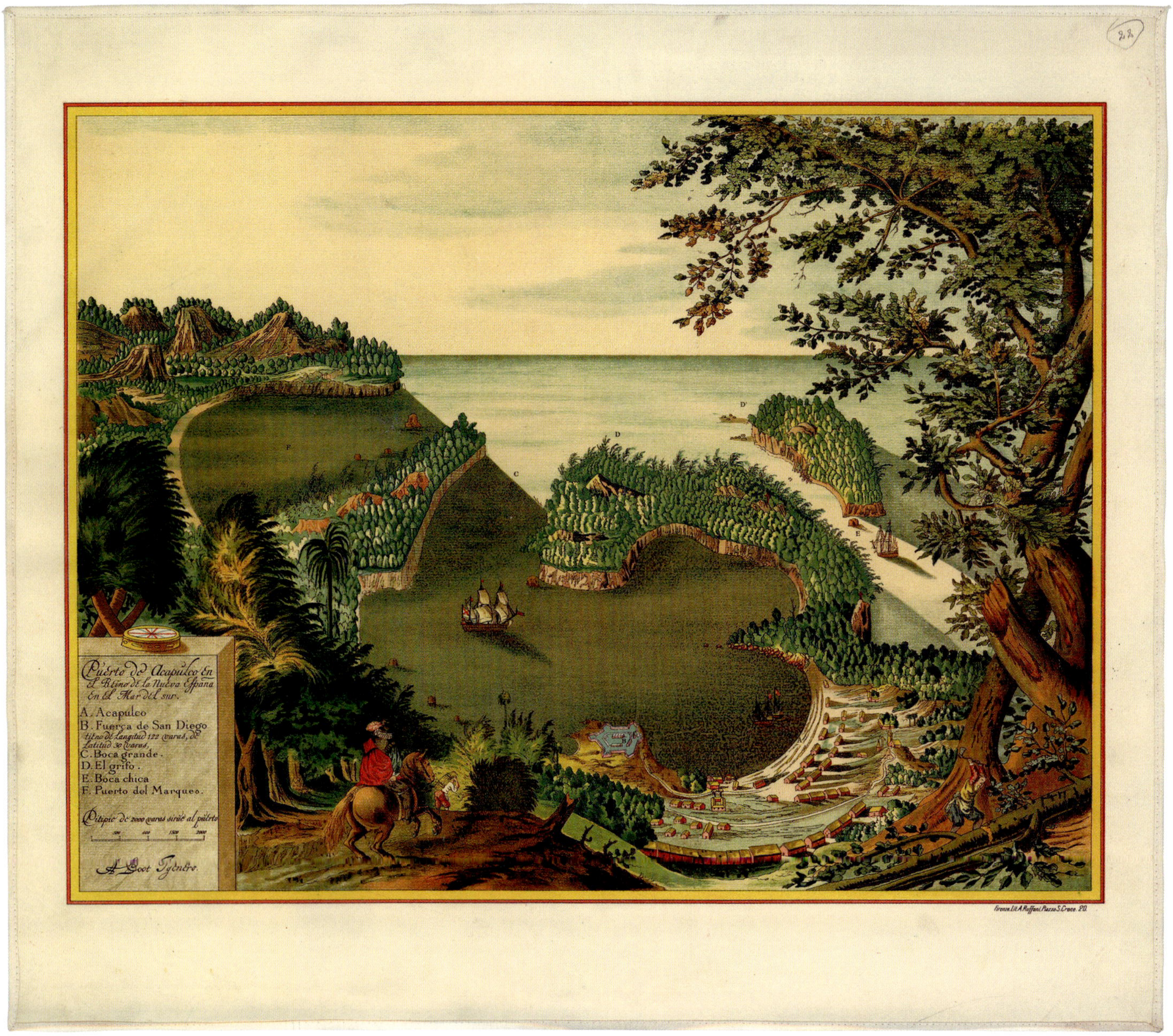

Fig. 4. Adrian Boot, *Puerto de Acapulco en el Reino de la Nueva España en el Mar del Sur, Litog.* Ruffoni, 1628. Colored inks on paper. Nettie Lee Benson Latin American Collection, University of Texas, Austin.

fewer Chinese and Japanese residents than Manila, and so direct knowledge of either place would have been more restricted. Yet how thoroughly Asia infused local culture remains an open question. Boot, for instance, purchased imports from the galleon trade,[39] although José Antonio Calderón Quijano's interpretation of his Acapulco scene as having been inspired by Asian imagery probably stretches too far.[40] We do know that, on an annual basis, Chinese things and their promise of profit animated Acapulco's shores, drawing merchants and their mules into town, some from hundreds of miles away. This ephemeral transformation represented one significant way that China became tangible to those who lived in New Spain. In contrast to the daily give and take in Manila, though, the Acapulco fair was an annual ritual of cross-cultural contact, one largely negotiated through the mobility of objects.

It is true that people of Asian descent came to New Spain in no small number in the seventeenth century, weaving themselves into the fabric of daily life in Acapulco and other communities—sometimes as slaves, sometimes as independent merchants.[41] Ed Slack, for instance, has argued that the Chinese who settled in Acapulco in the seventeenth and eighteenth centuries were primarily sailors, slaves, and servants; others, who moved inland to Mexico City and Puebla, worked in occupations as diverse as harp playing and tailoring, cobbling and coach driving, although he found that barbering and vending (especially of textiles and foods) were among the most common vocations.[42] This all suggests that for some residents of the Americas, the connection with China—forged through contact with people and not only things—would have been close and familiar. Yet for many, in Acapulco and elsewhere across New Spain, the relationship between Asia and home was more imaginary than lived.

For instance, anxieties—over the taking of profits from the Pacific trade, the quality of merchandise, and the safekeeping of goods before they could be sold—were keenly felt each year in Acapulco. Financial plans and worries therefore inflected the phrase and concept "de China" (from China). Beyond this, relationships between Chinese people and Chinese things in Acapulco were often highly attenuated—so much so that "de China" could describe imports actually created in China by Chinese craftsmen, but also objects from Japan and Southeast Asia.[43] Passage across multiple bodies of water, then, played a fundamental role in shaping the symbolic value of Chinese things in New Spain.[44] China did not appear everywhere in Spanish America, nor did the number or kind of Chinese commodities outstrip European imports. Nevertheless in the seventeenth century Chinese objects became quintessential signifiers of desired things from elsewhere, alluring for their scarcity but also for their evocation of far away worlds, and, at times, their affordability or the financial returns they promised. The value of Chinese things drew sustenance from their site of origin, but no less so from the ways in which they traveled and took up residence in American homes.

Chinese Things, Mexican Homes

Today, surviving material objects that speak directly of China's trade with Mexico in the seventeenth century are relatively rare, although the porcelain vessel in Figure 5 represents an example of works that were once relatively common. Created in the kilns of Jingdezhen just before 1600, this porcelain vessel was sent to Manila, where it was slated for a Pacific journey to Mexico. Its shape and design, neither of which was exceptional for porcelain exported from China at the time, offer a glimpse of the tastes that Chinese objects would have satisfied in Mexico. Because the vase was salvaged from a shipwreck—a ship that de Morga himself lost at sea—it is impossible to know where the curling dragon might have settled in the Americas. That pleasure might have been taken from its iconography and cool surface can be imagined, but there is little in the historical record to anchor to this vessel any unambiguous, evocative meaning. This is, in fact, the case for most objects that have survived from this period. In contrast to objects, inventories from the seventeenth century are plentiful. Both because of and despite their patterned emphases and silences, inventories open onto

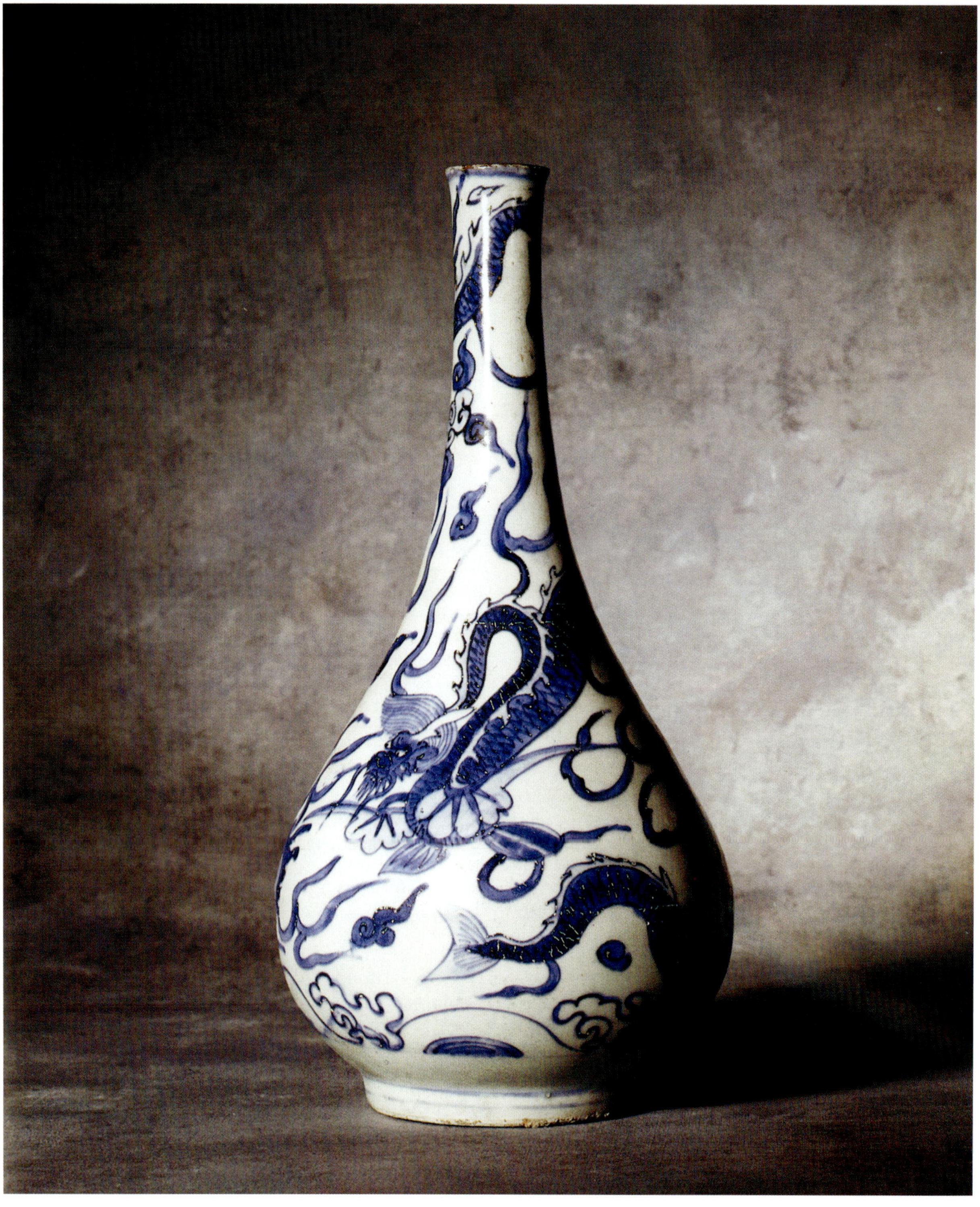

Fig. 5. Jar with curling dragon. Jingdezhen, China, c. 1600. Porcelain, excavated from the *San Diego*. Museo Naval, Madrid.

elements of perception and daily practices that few other sources can. And so, to understand some of the ways in which Chinese objects were known in Mexico, I turn to one distinctively large set of inventories that dates from 1622 and describes the possessions of colonial officials in Mexico.[45]

Alessandra Russo observes that certain kinds of inventories stress mobility, others stasis.[46] The 1622 examples imply both. Along with an awareness of the transitory nature of wealth, the officials' lists suggest how people used objects to stabilize their place in the world. Some documents, for instance, explain that what a person owns now does not match what he once owned in the past, or hoped to own in the future. Since these documents capture a moment that for many men was "mid-career," the sense of *in medias res*, and a keen awareness of the possibility of shifting fortune, not just shifting value, is often quite poignant. It is also clear that those who owned imported things were often rich men—not people scraping together funds to purchase from afar now and then. From this we sense how geography, consumer pleasures, and economic investment overlapped.[47]

Among those who study Spanish America, the objects most highly valued in the 1622 documents will be unsurprising.[48] They include land, silver, tapestries, bed linens and canopies, table linens, cushions for *estrados*, guns and swords, coaches and animals to pull them, clothing, writing desks and other furniture, jewelry, and, the most consistently expensive of all objects, slaves. Francisco Figueroa Venegas, who served the Crown in multiple settings in Mexico, offers one good example. He owned two slaves, one he calls "China" (Chinese), although she was likely from Macao, the other from Angola (also suggesting Portuguese traders). Further down the economic scale, yet still highly valued, were paintings and books, furniture imported from Europe, and many Chinese textiles, including silks of green, orange, and blue, and velvets of deep red and black. Figueroa Venegas also owned things from the Americas, including feather paintings he explicitly describes as made by indigenous hands.[49] While the point is never articulated explicitly, Figueroa Venegas—and others whose possessions were cataloged in 1622—clearly participated in a world of trade. Not all of the officials' inventories mention imported goods or identify sites of origin for household objects, but multiple references are made, implicitly and explicitly, to Africa, Asia, Europe, and the Americas.[50]

And yet, even as these documents imply a global reach among consumers in New Spain, the world did not really come to Mexico. Relatively consistent patterns connected commodities and geographies: Flanders is the source of many paintings and images, and the Germanies of writing cabinets (*escritorios*).[51] Other sites in Europe, apart from Castille, are mentioned more rarely. A few men owned tapestries from Brussels or Ottoman Turkey; by and large, however, the places that surface most often are China and Spain (Castilla).[52] Not all of the inventories identify the sources of household imports, but of those that do, China—especially in reference to silks and other textiles—seems to surface more frequently than any other geographic setting. This is not to say that Chinese objects dominated the homes of New Spain. Although inventories never open directly onto lived reality, these imply that registering the Chinese-ness of certain things was a way to stress their value.[53]

While all inventories are basically lists, the 1622 documents also suggest how objects shaped lived experiences. Color was clearly of interest to wealthy residents of New Spain. In high-end houses, one might find silk textiles of carmine and black, but also purple, tangerine, green, yellow, turquoise, white, brown, orange, and gold, some of them striped. Further research is needed to say whether these fabrics were remnants, left over from Asia—as some scholars have suggested—or the choices of Mexican consumers, made known to Chinese merchants through middlemen in Manila. The chromatic array may have included some of both. Either way, a willingness to clothe one's body and home in vibrant hues represents an important part of the aesthetic story in seventeenth-century New Spain. The feel of silk against the skin and the way it shone when it caught the light would have contrasted with other fabrics at hand: heavy velvets, raised brocades of gold and silver thread, and raspy wools. This may seem incidental today, but in the past ephemeral bodily experiences created subtle yet tangible, and at times quite personal conduits for encountering China in Mexico.

On a more conceptual level, it is possible to trace in these inventories an interest in "doubled foreignness,"[54] with Chinese things serving as complements to objects imported from Europe. This, of course, raises the specter of import substitution, but the evidence I draw from these documents does not point firmly in this direction. Import substitution may have existed in New Spain (see below). Many of the colonial officials who registered their valuables in 1622, however, were not purchasing Chinese silks simply because they could not afford, or otherwise procure, silk or velvet from Europe. Rather, a close reading of the inventories reveals a taste for pairing imported things, including sets of *estrado* cushions. For instance, one often reads of six cushions of silk from China, six of silk from Castile.[55] The pricing suggests this pairing is not driven in any obvious way by economics: Chinese pillows are not consistently "cheaper," in any sense of the word, nor do split sets frequently appear (that is, ten pillows from China and two from Castile). What mattered, it seems, was the doubling itself.[56]

This interest in color and in pairing different kinds of imports opens onto the possibility that, in New Spain, the intersection of global trade and material consumption differed from that in other settings. Thinking comparatively, we know that in Western Europe, collecting and pairing foreign objects was at times in vogue. Yet even if Mexicans wished to "emulate" Europeans (itself an open question), recent work in the history of colonialism teaches us that mimicry is complicated, and cannot easily explain habits of consumption. Neither can we assume any simple aspiration for global cosmopolitanism.[57] Local tastes and predilections, along with even smaller-scale, family and personal metaphors and webs of association also played their role. For this reason the purchase of Chinese and Castilian pillows in Mexico City could not "mean the same thing" as the purchase of such objects in Madrid or Amsterdam, or even Manila. Wealth and desire aside, the geography and politics of colonialism rendered Mexico a distinct case. For those who see colonial practices as a stepping-stone to nationalist traditions, this position holds its appeal.[58] While I take this point, my sense of the doubling leads down another path.

Admittedly, several dozen pillows and colored silks are not enough to sustain a broad theory of colonial consumption. Yet the ways in which imported objects were valued as household things is evocative. For it implies that in some settings in the seventeenth century, at some level of conceptual abstraction and material juxtaposition, certain imports from China could be construed as parallel to imports from Castile, and not as fundamentally different. This, of course, could never happen in Europe, nor could it happen in China, which suggests that the particular hybridity created in Spanish America may be its most distinctive contribution to narratives of global trade. This fact is not insignificant, particularly for the scholarship on the Americas, yet there is more to this than Spanish America as a "middle ground," where things from Asia, Europe, Africa, and the Americas mixed in distinctive ways. No less important is the question of what the particular patterns of mixing and juxtaposition in New Spain allow us to see about imported objects more generally and the trade networks that shuttled them around the world.

Colonial Distinctions

While the taste for porcelain would never dwarf the desire for silver, blue-and-white wares from the late Ming and early Qing kilns held enormous appeal for the residents of New Spain.[59] In the seventeenth century, imported wares were familiar objects in churches and convents, and in elegant urban townhouses. Nuns who had not forsaken worldly goods would eat from porcelain dishes, as would wealthy miners' families. Across New Spain, from Mexico City to Manila, porcelain appeared along many tiers of the social and economic scale: the glassy surfaces and cobalt

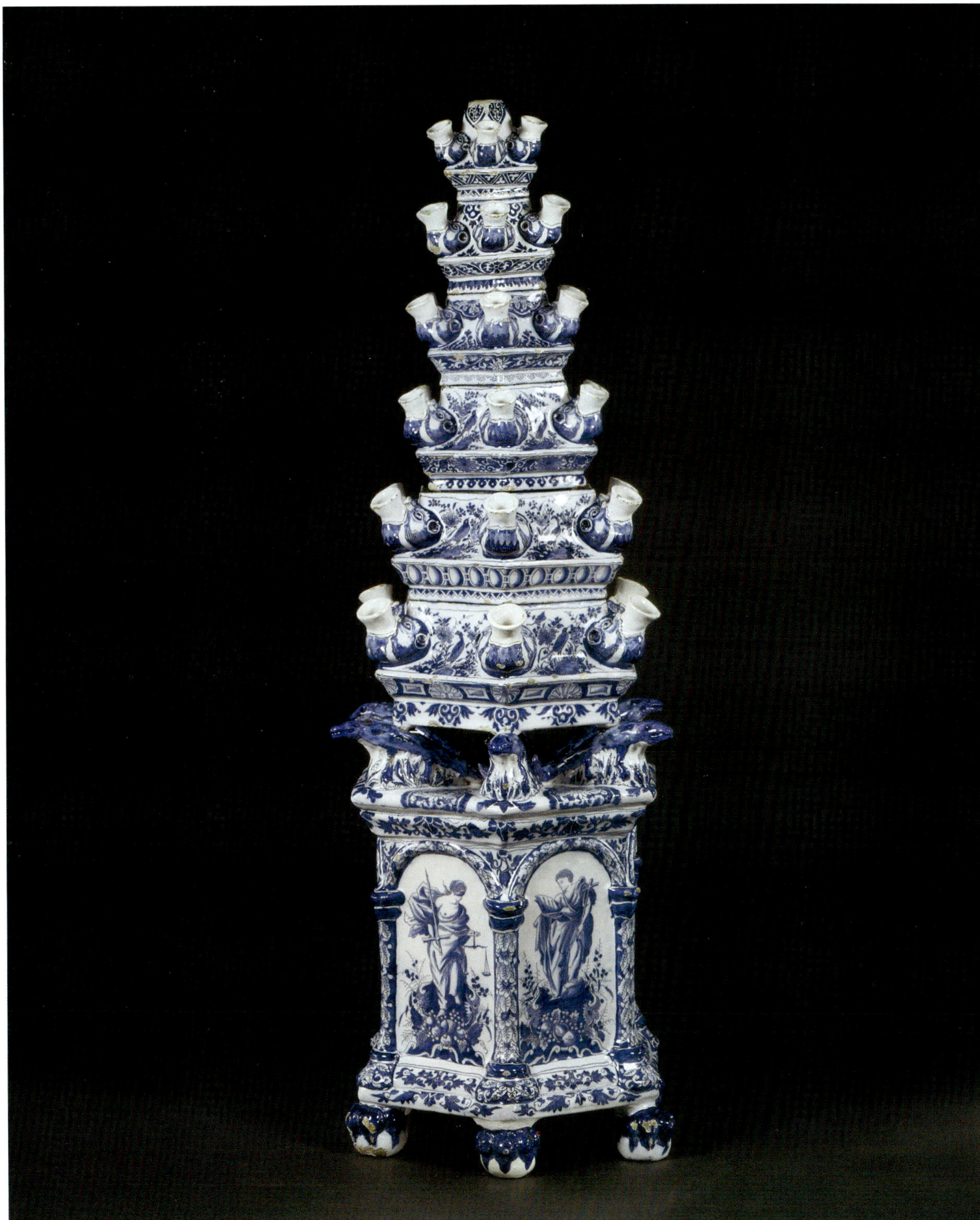

Fig. 6. Flower pyramid, "Greek A" factory. Delft, Holland, c. 1695. Tin-glazed earthenware. Victoria & Albert Museum, London.

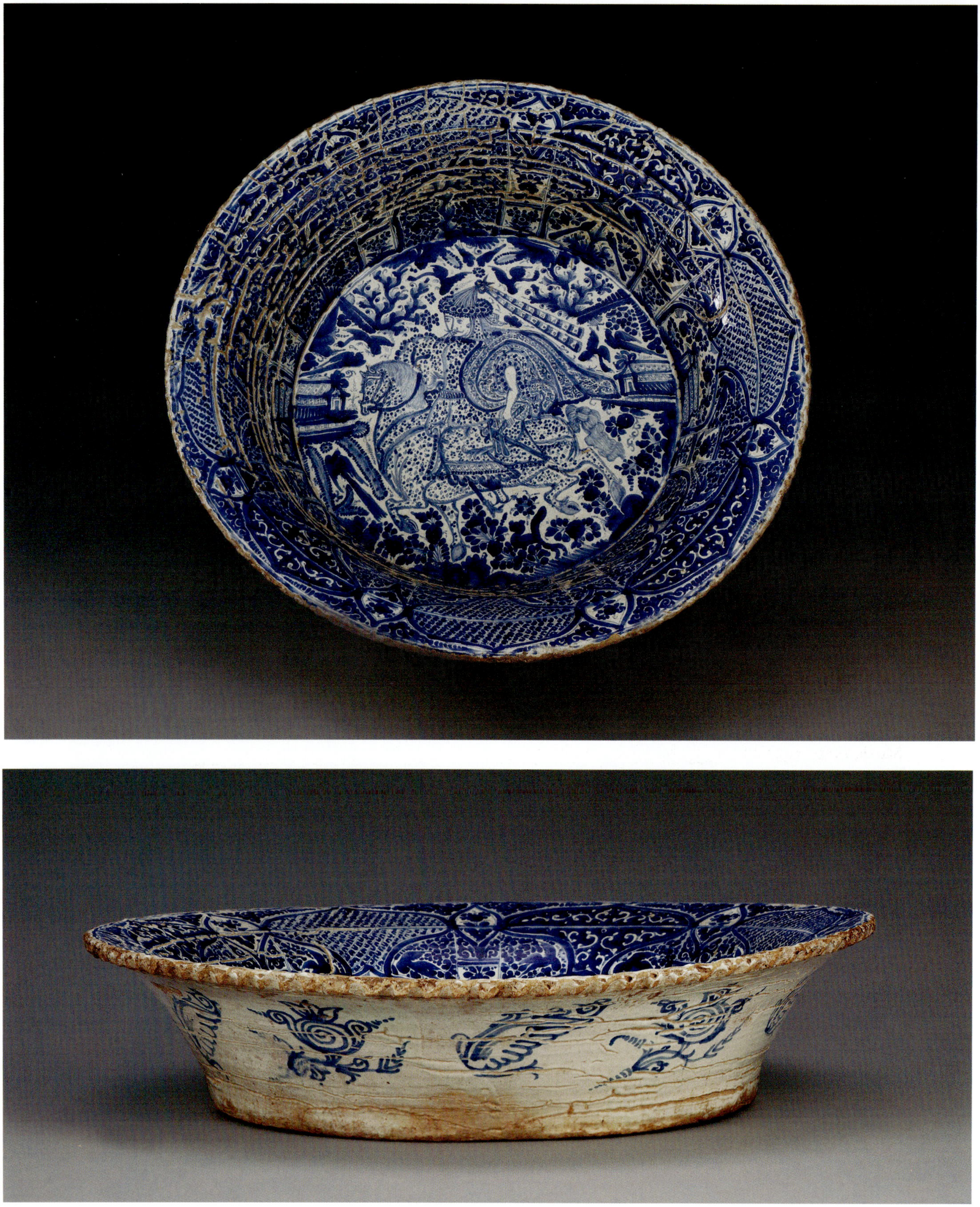

Fig. 7. (above, opposite) Basin *(lebrillo)*. Puebla, Mexico, late 1600s. Earthenware, lead/tin glaze, cobalt in-glaze paint. 6 x 26 in. Denver Art Museum, Funds from 2001 Collector's Choice; 2001.314.

blue designs of Chinese ceramics were known to many besides the very rich and highly privileged. This aligns with habits of consumption also developing in metropolitan centers in Europe and Asia, and although the patterns were not identical, porcelain was drawn into trading centers in Africa and across Southeast Asia.[60] As one of the most coveted materials in the early modern world, Chinese porcelain raises questions of global cosmopolitanism and cultural distinctiveness with a force not shared by other imports. Jingdezhen porcelain did not elicit the same meanings across the whole of the early modern period. Nor did the widespread emulation of Chinese porcelain follow a single path, as tulip stands, a characteristically Dutch form often created in Delftware, make clear (Fig. 6). Current research on these differences is suggestive,[61] though, because it invites new thinking about how the colonial context of Mexico might reshape local responses to Chinese imports. With this in mind I wish to consider the relationship between porcelain and the blue-and-white wares of Puebla—wares, I will argue, that have the potential to complicate traditional ideas about emulation, creativity, and porcelain itself.

Today the blue-and-white ceramics of Puebla, Mexico represent one of the best-known object types created in New Spain. These were popular ceramics in their day, a point confirmed by their presence in private homes and religious settings across the Americas.[62] Created in large numbers in the latter part of the seventeenth century and the early years of the eighteenth, blue-and-white ceramics from Puebla were rarely shipped across the Atlantic to Europe. Nor were they often sent west, to the Philippines or Asia. Rather, objects such as those in Figures 7, 8, and 9 were very much "of the Americas." The Puebla vessels drew inspiration from multiple sources, including Spanish majolica (with its own debt to Hispano-Muslim ceramics), Chinese porcelain, and local Mexican traditions. We sense this from the coloring and décor of the *lebrillo* in Figure 7. The blue-and-white of the basin is perhaps the most obvious link to Chinese ceramics, although the iconography derives from an array of models—some themes reinterpret images from other ceramics, others owe their origin to prints or textiles. Beyond iconography, the *lebrillo* displays elements typical of many surviving Puebla ceramics: the flaring shape of the basin and ragged lip were familiar forms; so, too, the use of both dark and pale blue, applied in thick pools or, alternately, sketched with a loose brush; and the riot of pattern.[63] This visual language also prizes energetic design. Here, for instance, a horse steps lively through a landscape abuzz with birds and dense with plants; the rider wears clothing so voluminous it curls over one shoulder, and his hat ribbons flap as if blown by a breeze.

It is impossible to know whether people in New Spain viewed such works as art historians are today tempted to do, by parsing the "Chinese" and "European" features from those that seem more

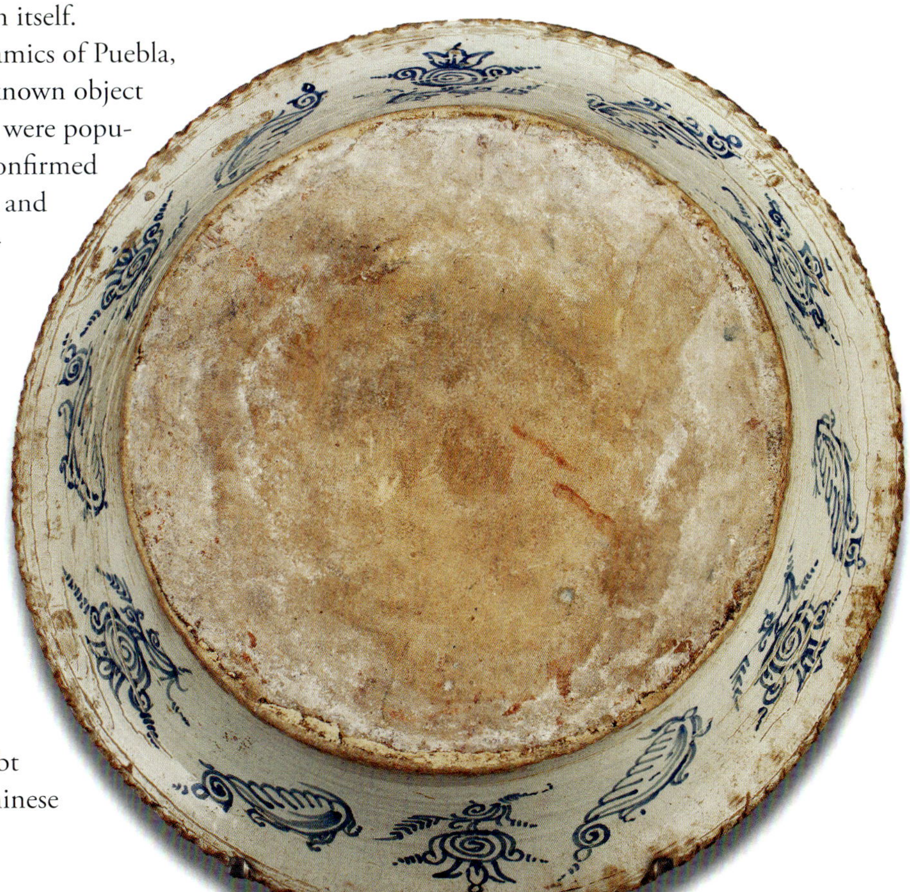

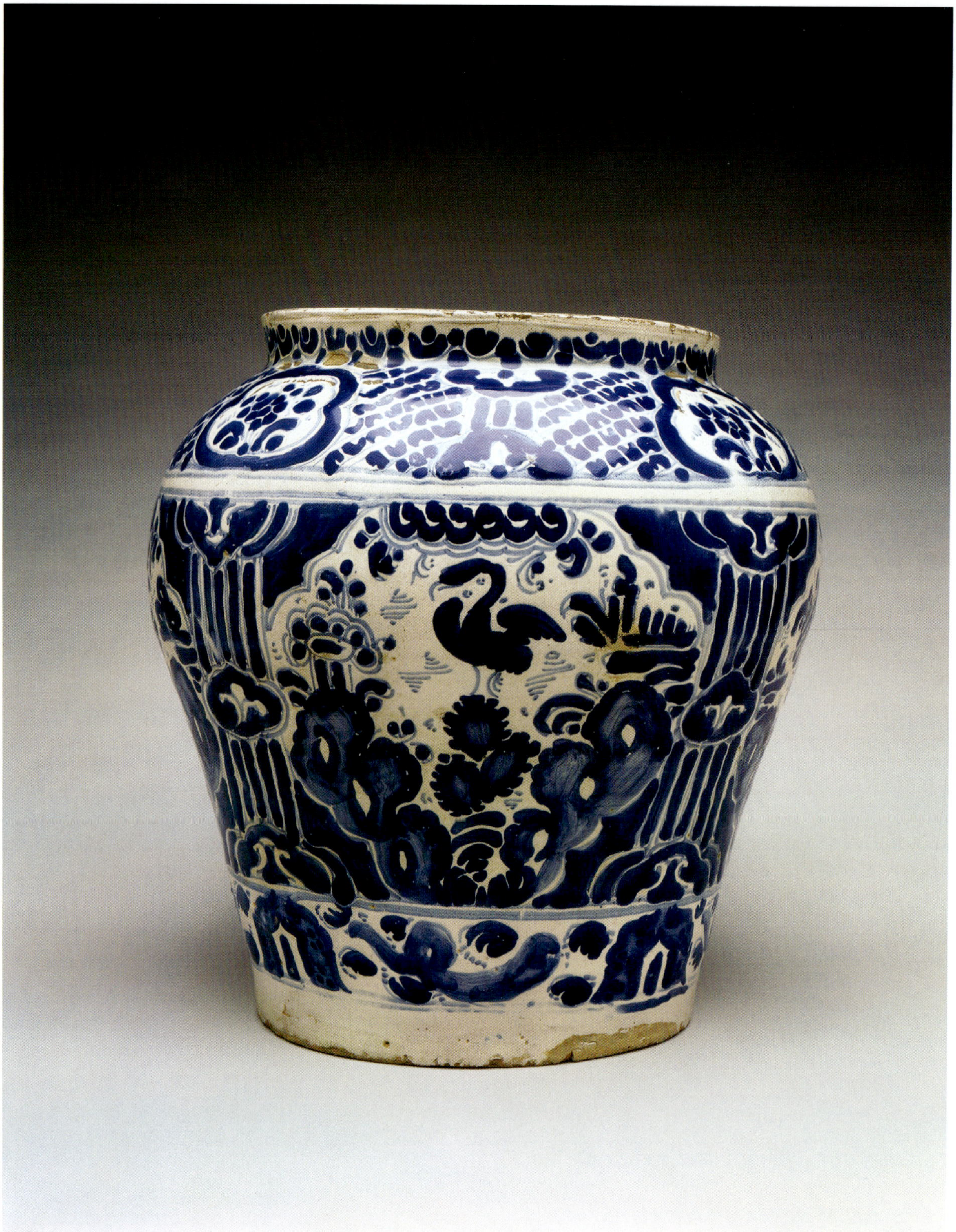

Fig. 8. Jar. Puebla, Mexico, c. 1700. Tin-glazed earthenware. Hispanic Society of America, New York.

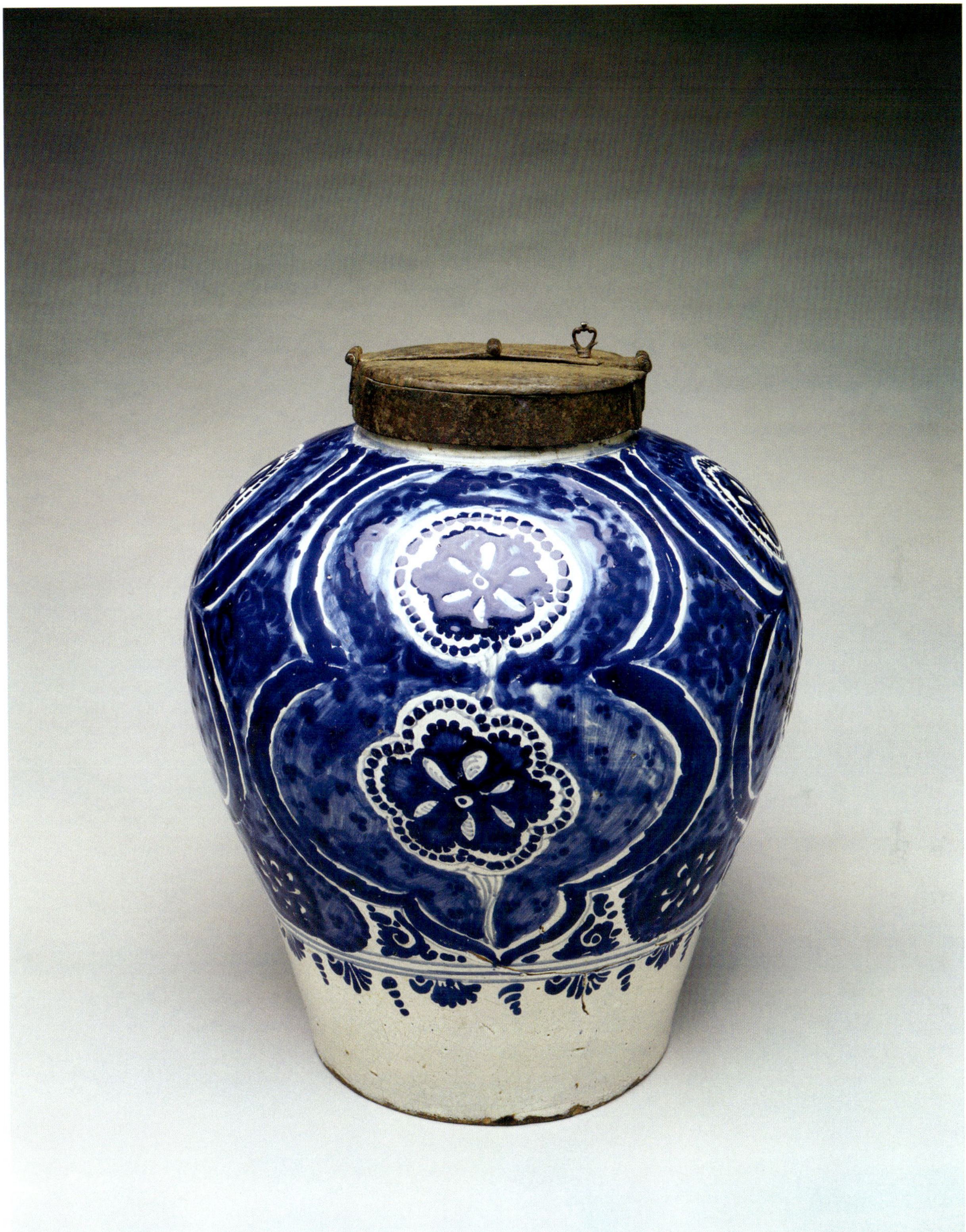

Fig. 9. Jar with iron lid. Puebla, Mexico, c. 1700. Tin-glazed earthenware. Hispanic Society of America, New York.

truly "local." More certain is that in the late seventeenth century the Chinese resonance of Puebla ceramics was intentionally honed through guild rules stipulating that one class of fine ceramic wares (*loza fina)* should emulate the porcelains of China.[64] Of crucial importance to the guild was not the shape of the pot, the thinness of the walls, the translucence of the glaze—all material properties of great interest among Europeans seeking to emulate Chinese porcelain, and, certainly, among people in China who made and used porcelain. Rather, among the things that mattered greatly in Puebla was color. While modern eyes might home in on a Chinese-inspired crane (perched upon a prickly pear cactus), one necessary "Chinese" feature of the vessel in Figure 8, at least in the eyes of the Puebla guild and its patrons, would have been the use of blue—which was to be very dark and used quite liberally.

This jar would not have looked much like porcelain to anyone living in China late in the second half of the seventeenth century. And no one in Puebla would have mistaken such vessels for porcelain, either. Porcelain from China was a separate and lovely thing, and not easily "confused" or "mistaken" for *loza fina* from Puebla.[65] This point may seem obvious, but in discussions of colonial copies and emulations, "confusion" is still cited as a reason why local ceramics are so different from foreign and metropolitan models. For instance, across the last several decades, the ceramics of Puebla have been described as "a misunderstood mix of Chinese, Aztec and Spanish motifs that is almost lunatic in style," and as "ersatz Orientalism" with an "irrepressible independent spirit."[66] To see the Puebla works as misunderstandings is to view them through a lens clouded by connoisseurship which, when followed to its logical conclusion, implies that Puebla ceramics were "good enough" for local settings, but ultimately missed the mark of high quality set by porcelains made in China. This argument, mutatis mutandis, has a long history in the scholarship on colonialism. It is certainly true that the vessels from Puebla are inventive, but they are also heavily potted and often hastily painted and glazed. The bumps and hollows created by pooled glaze hardly evoke the visual or tactile vocabulary of fine porcelain from Jingdezhen.[67] The vessel in Figure 9 offered its owners a fundamentally different material experience of clay and glaze than would a porcelain jar: to hold this Puebla vessel would be to embrace a heavier pot, with a rougher surface and a warmer touch to the skin. No ceramics are ever unitary or homogenous in their evocative range, yet documents from seventeenth-century New Spain reveal very little about how the *lebrillo* or jars illustrated here compared to porcelains from China. It seems impossible that the differences went unnoticed, and evidence from the early eighteenth century suggests that the gap between Puebla ceramics and porcelain did, indeed, register. Admittedly, the written evidence is slim, but we sense something along these lines from Diego de Santa Cruz Oyanguren Espíndola, who not only claims to have invented ceramics in the Chinese style, but also describes his creations as so well executed no one could tell the difference between the model and the emulation.[68] Regardless of "how close" the Puebla and Jingdezhen ceramics were, his assertion suggests that differences between porcelain and Puebla blue-and-white ceramics were indeed noticeable in New Spain—at least in the eighteenth century. But whether people in Mexico City and Puebla found pleasure in the qualities that separated porcelain from *loza fina*—whether the differences produced more delight than dilemma—it is difficult to say.

What then to make of the Puebla ceramics? Some seek to align these wares with European ceramic-making traditions, and so invoke the vocabulary associated with Chinoiserie and its concomitant traditions. The color scheme and date of the Puebla ceramics have led others, working along a similar vein, to view these vessels as a mode of import substitution. This perspective casts the blue-and-white *loza fina* as parallel, at least in basic ambition, to Talavera wares created in Spain in the seventeenth century,[69] Delftware from Holland, and other European porcelain-like but less expensive ceramics. Yet other scholars argue emphatically against the substitution model, stressing instead the creativity of the Puebla wares and their relationship to new forms of Creole taste and identity. Seen from this angle, parallels between *loza fina* and other blue-and-white emulative traditions are more coincidental than not.[70]

To my eye the crux of the issue is slightly different, and it turns on the notion of an artifactual conversation. The issue is not strictly "how Chinese" nor "how European" are the Puebla ceramics. Nor, on the other hand, is it "how autochthonous" these works may be. Rather, what I find important is that these vessels speak in a productive way to traditions introduced from afar, in particular, calling attention to the elasticity of the imports as models.[71] What potters in Puebla and consumers in Mexico City expected from their ceramics we cannot know. It is clear, however, that these objects created a visual and haptic experience that was valued and cultivated. These experiences also differed from those created by both porcelain imported from China and import substitutions created in western Europe and Japan.[72] And this, I suggest, is a crucial point. This compound difference—the distance of Puebla ceramics from both Chinese models and other cultural emulations—is what allows Spanish America's distinctive habits of consumption and production to impinge upon the world of early modern trade more broadly.[73] My point is subtle yet I hope compelling. One of the achievements of Puebla blue-and-white ceramics is that they shift the traditional parameters and significance of "Chinese porcelain" into a register of form and tactile qualities that other ceramic traditions did not pursue. These wares also teach us that "porcelain" (rather like the term "Chinese") became more porous and negotiable through China's trade with New Spain. Apart from the wealth of its silver, then, another contribution of Spanish America to the history of global trade derives from the material and visual properties of Puebla ceramics, ceramics that invite (if not insist upon) broader thinking about the imagined boundaries of two influential entities in the early modern world: China and porcelain.

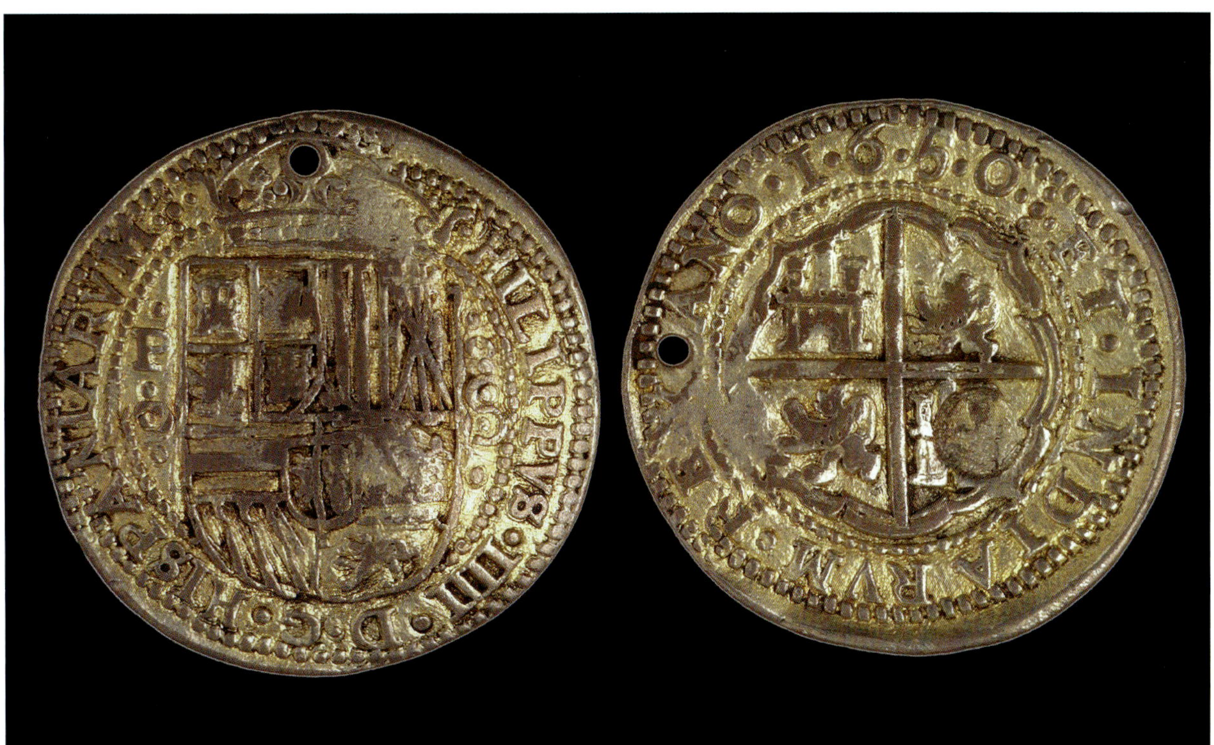

Fig. 10. Eight-*real* coin. Minted in Potosí, Bolivia, 1650. Silver. American Numismatic Society, New York City.

Trading Histories

It seems unlikely that any ceramicists in seventeenth-century Puebla set out to encourage new ways of imagining the early modern world. Yet historical effects are never guided in full by human intention. This is one point of connection between the history of Spanish America's silver and objects fashioned of Chinese silk or Mexican clay. Pieces of eight, such as the coin in Figure 10—minted in 1650 in Potosí, Bolivia—traveled the world along paths of coincidence and need. No Spanish official, colonial bureaucrat, or indigenous miner purposely aimed to make Spanish coinage one of the world's most desired currencies. This is not to say that things in the seventeenth century had lives of their own, but the mobility of silks, ceramics, and coinage drew the residents of New Spain into a history of trade and consumption that was only partially of their own making. Daily experiences in townhouses, markets, and churches in Mexico City, Puebla, and Manila were surely influential, but the material and evocative meanings of things could not be forged strictly on local terms. We may never know how much Chinese merchandise any single coin from Potosí might purchase; moreover, the Ottoman painting of the Bolivian mine site, discussed at this essay's opening, makes it clear that however much the exchange value of Potosí silver, it was of interest in settings most people in Spanish America would never see or know. I would suggest in closing, however, that this does not render such practices irrelevant to Spanish America's visual culture, which, as a field of study, has a history of privileging local and trans-Atlantic histories.[74] Why then seek to read trans-Pacific trade through lenses focused upon both the history of early modern exchange and the specificity of New Spain and its habits of art-making?

An image painted in New Spain by Pedro Calderón early in the eighteenth century offers one path into this query. An imposing yet local scene, the painting portrays the crucified Christ of Chalma and offerings set upon his altar (Fig. 11). Today the church remains in worship, although the altar no longer takes this form.[75] The heterogeneity of the assemblage—the wood and wax, the porcelain and silver, the arrangement of sacred with unholy things—was hardly unfamiliar in New Spain, suggesting little anxiety over the conjoining of imports and locally made things. This Christ was deeply bound to Chalma, a site in central Mexico important in pre-Hispanic times, and the ore for the silver candlesticks would also have been mined and cast in the Americas. The wax of the elegant tapers is more ambiguous, since candles were made of imported beeswax (from across the Pacific, but also from across the Atlantic), as well as wax from New Spain.[76] For worshippers at this altar, and viewers of this scene, the porcelain vases derived value and appeal from their status as imports from China. Puebla blue-and-white wares would have been well known in this town, but the vessels here signal trans-Pacific trade more explicitly. The painted flowers, like the wax, point toward both local and foreign geographies—although actual imported porcelain vases were sometimes filled with silk flowers fashioned in Mexico of Chinese imported threads. In Spanish America, few other images show the sacred and local mingling so seamlessly with the import and the commodity. Calderón's painting makes it clear that such compositing could be central to both image-making and its evocation of a site of reverence in the Americas. Recently, Thomas daCosta Kaufmann has pointed out how difficult it is "to describe and give a coherent and convincing account for the creation and consumption of forms, subjects, and types of art that are not originally indigenous to cultures in which they are found."[77] This painting makes a case for juxtaposition and balance. Its mood is one of quiet and benignity.

To respect Calderón's creation—especially its ease with the world of trade—is no easy task. Yet if we could take his point, and see the visual culture of Spanish America as more worldly, we might know more about the past. As all of the essays in this volume show, the circulation of foreign things in Spanish America clearly impinged upon broader histories of consumption and exchange. Taking this process ever more seriously leads in many useful directions. It would, for instance, allow for more nuanced understandings of how wealth was

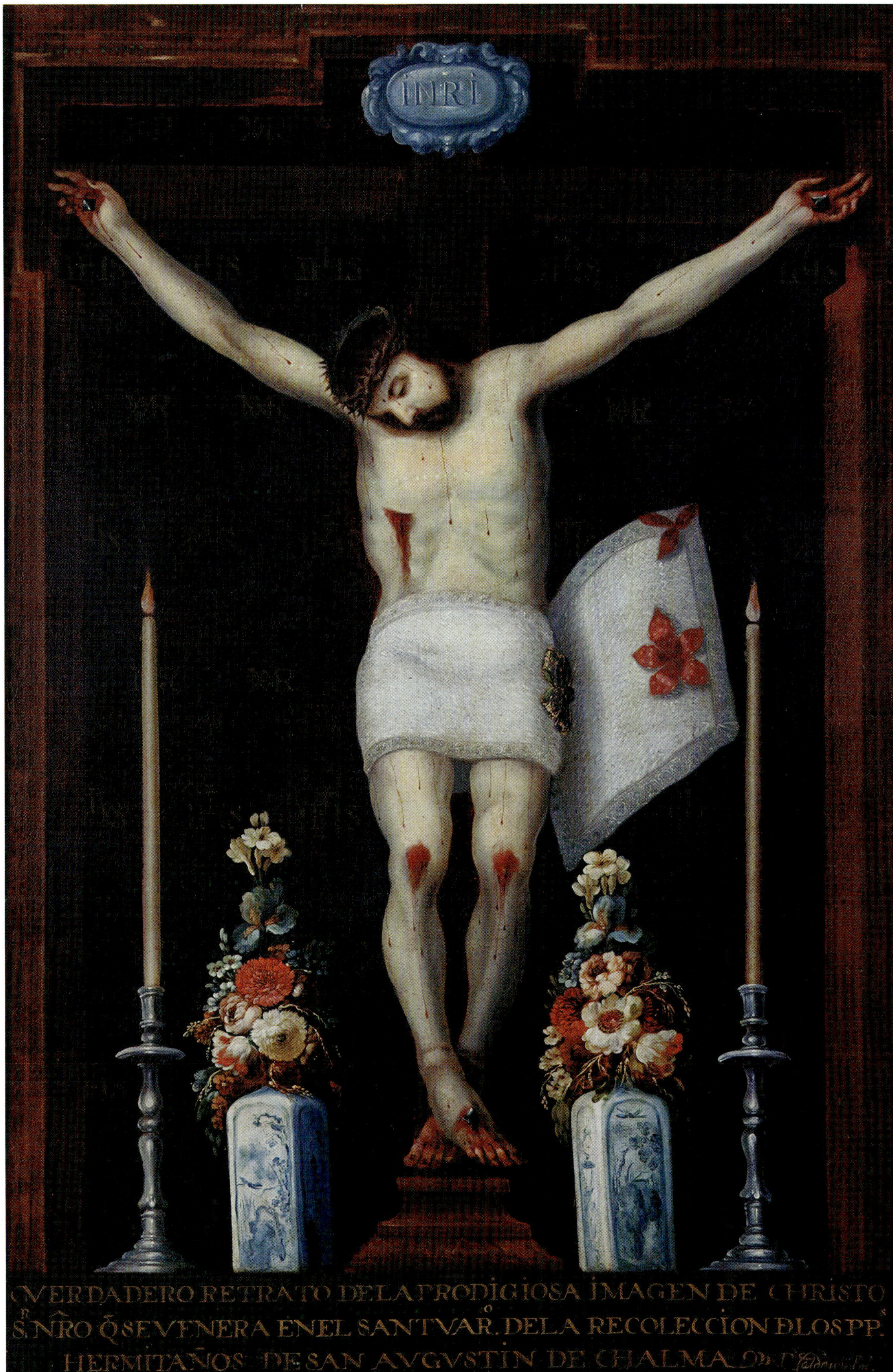

Fig. 11. Pedro Calderón, *Christ of Chalma*. Mexico, 18th century. Oil on canvas. Museo Nacional de Historia, Mexico City.

expressed in the seventeenth century, not only in London or Amsterdam, but in places too long considered marginal to the history of exchange. Examining practices that bound Spanish America to China—both lived and imagined—should also stretch our view beyond the lives of the wealthy, opening a window onto the complexity of colonial interactions. The relationships among Spain, New Spain, and China differed from those forged by other European powers, suggesting that metropole, periphery, and colony were categories more complex in early modernity than is usually presumed. Such work also makes it possible to strengthen and broaden what is known about the affective power of materials. Blue-and-white ceramics inspired by Chinese porcelain were created in so many settings, yet they did not follow just one route into meaning. The Puebla ceramics may not have often left the Americas, but they color our understanding of porcelain and shift the range of its symbolic weight.[78] To acknowledge all this is a modern ambition, not one proposed by Calderón. His painting, though, invites us to look behind the scenes, to see how the foreign became familiar. If we accept his gesture, and I suggest that we should, we can glimpse how the worshippers in Chalma who filled Chinese porcelain vases with flowers depended upon people and places they may never have visited or even imagined—people and places that nevertheless made possible their rituals of faith and belief in glorious worlds.

Notes

For a larger project on this theme, I am grateful for the research support of a New Directions Fellowship from the Andrew W. Mellon Foundation and a Harnish Fellowship from Smith College. I also owe a debt to colleagues who have graciously discussed portions of this essay with me, shared references, and helped sharpen my thinking with difficult questions, including Byron Hamann, Barbara Kellum, Barbara Mundy, Jeanette Peterson, and the graduate student and faculty participants in seminars at the Institute of Fine Arts in New York, the School of Oriental and African Studies, the University of Minnesota, the University of Southern California, and the Victoria & Albert Museum.

[1] See Craig Clunas on the implications of Europe's privilege in studies of early modern consumption, in "Modernity Global and Local: Consumption and the Rise of the West," *American Historical Review* 104, no. 5 (December 1999): 1497–1511.

[2] The manuscript is known today as the "first major work in Ottoman Turkish about the Spanish exploration and conquest of the New World." See Giancarlo Casale, *The Ottoman Age of Exploration* (New York and Oxford: Oxford University Press, 2010), 160. Useful descriptions appear in *Tarih-i Hind-i garbî veya, Hadís-i nev: A History of the Discovery of America* (Istanbul: Historical Research Foundation, Istanbul Research Center, 1987) and Thomas Goodrich, *The Ottoman Turks and the New World: A Study of the Tarih-i Hind-i garbî and Sixteenth-Century Ottoman Americana* (Wiesbaden: O. Harrassowitz, 1990).

[3] On the ethnic and social complexity of Potosí, see Bartolomé Arzáns de Orsúa y Vela, *Historia de la villa imperial de Potosí* (Providence: Brown University Press, 1965); Peter Bakewell, *Miners of the Red Mountain: Indian Labor in Potosi, 1545–1650* (Albuquerque: University of New Mexico Press, 1984); and Jane Mangan, *Trading Roles: Gender, Ethnicity and the Urban Economy in Colonial Potosí* (Durham: Duke University Press, 2005). For comparative images of Potosí, especially those created in Spain and Spanish America, see *Potosí: Catalogación de su patrimonio urbano y arquitectónico* (La Paz: Instituto Boliviano de Cultura, 1990); Pedro Querejazu and Elizabeth Ferrer, eds., *Potosí: Colonial Treasures and the Bolivian City of Silver* (New York: Americas Society, 1997); and Richard Kagan, *Urban Images of the Hispanic World, 1493–1793* (New Haven: Yale University Press, 2000).

[4] Casale, *The Ottoman Age*, 152–179.

[5] Anne McCants, "Exotic Goods, Popular Consumption, and the Standard of Living: Thinking about Globalization in the Early Modern World," *Journal of World History* 18, no. 4 (2007): 433–462, 438.

[6] See, for instance, Dennis Flynn and Arturo Giraldez, "Born with a 'Silver Spoon': The Origin of World Trade in 1571," *Journal of World History* 6, no. 2 (1995): 201–221 and "Path Dependence, Time Lags and the Birth of Globalization: A Critique of O'Rourke and Williamson," *European Review of Economic History* 8 (2004): 81–108. Other helpful work on this theme, especially by scholars of Spain and Spanish America, includes the early, but now much debated study of Earl Jefferson Hamilton, *American Treasure and the Price Revolution in Spain, 1501–1650* (Cambridge: Harvard University Press, 1934); and more recently, Vera Valdés Lakowsky, *De minas al mar. Historia de la plata Mexicana en Asia, 1565–1834* (Mexico City: Fondo de Cultura Ecónomica, 1987); Hang-Sheng Chuan, "Trade between China, the Philippines, and the Americas during the Sixteenth and Seventeenth Centuries," in *Metals and Monies in an Emerging Global Economy*, edited by D. O. Flynn and A. Giraldez, 281–285 (Aldershot: Ashgate, 1997); and Marina Alfonso Mola and Carlos Martínez Shaw, "La era de la plata española en Extremo Oriente (1550–1700)," in *España y el Pacífico/Legazpi*, Tomo II, edited by Leoncio Cabrero, 527–542 (Madrid: Sociedad Estatal de Conmemoración Culturales, 2004).

[7] Research on Asia and the Americas is more vibrant than it was even twenty years ago, with compelling new work being done on decorative arts and patterns of daily life, slaves and other immigrants, silver, and economies of trade. In the notes that follow, I have tried to cite a reasonable sampling of this work. Even so, the history and visual culture of trans-Atlantic trade remains far better studied than that of the Pacific. Moreover, studies of the visual and material culture of the sixteenth and eighteenth centuries are still more numerous than those focused on seventeenth-century practices.

[8] The literature on Balbuena is extensive, but I have found useful the perspectives of Christian Chester, "Poetic and Prosaic Descriptions of Colonial Mexico City," *Exploration* 9 (1981): 1–21; Madrigal Luis Iñigo, "*Grandeza mexicana* de Bernardo de Balbuena o 'El interés, señor de las naciones,'" *Versants: Revue Suisse de Litteratures Romanes* 22 (1992): 23–38; Osvoldo Pardo, "Giovanni Botero and Bernardo de Balbuena: Art and Economy in *La grandeza mexicana*," *Journal of Latin American Cultural Studies* 10 (2001): 103–117; Veronika Ryjik, "El mito de la nueva Arcadia: La *Grandeza mexicana* de Bernardo de Balbuena y la revaloración de los tópicos pastoriles," *Bulletin of Spanish Studies* 83 (2005): 539–614; and Stephanie Merrim, *The Spectacular City: Mexico and Colonial Hispanic Literary Culture* (Austin: University of Texas Press, 2010).

[9] Merrim, *The Spectacular City,* 92, 121. The mercantilism of Balbuena is a theme Merrim pursues emphatically, arguing that the exoticism of "the Orient" displaces the exoticism of indigeneity in Balbuena's poem.

[10] While "foreign" is not a term that surfaces in seventeenth-century documents, I find it helpful for thinking about imports into Mexico from disparate and distant settings, which would have been understood, collectively, as having come from afar. For a different perspective on this, however, see Gustavo Curiel, "Al remedo de la China: El lenguaje achinado y la formación de un gusto dentro de las casas novohispanas," in *Orientes y Occidentes: El arte y la mirada del otro*, edited by Gustavo Curiel, 299–317 (Mexico City: Instituto de Investigaciones Estéticas, 2007).

[11] In the scholarship on visual culture, the degree to which people in New Spain substantively shaped or set parameters for the kinds of foreign goods to be imported, especially in the seventeenth century, remains understudied. It is generally presumed that consumer desire and purchasing opportunity aligned more often than not. This may have been the case, but the point warrants further examination. Also poorly understood is the extent to which demand for imported commodities—be they paintings or porcelains—was answered satisfactorily by the supply of foreign objects available in New Spain, although an interesting perspective can be found in Neil de Marchi and Hans van Miegroet, "Exploring Markets for Netherlandish Paintings in Spain and Nueva España," *Nederlands Kunsthistorisch Jaarboek* 50 (1999): 80–111.

[12] Rebecca Earle, "Consumption and Excess in Spanish America (1700–1830)," Working Paper (April), Centre for Latin American Cultural Studies, University of Manchester, 2003. While her research focuses on the eighteenth century, her broader point holds. For instance, merchant letters written on the cusp of the seventeenth century encourage the use of Chinese silks in indigenous communities, while others discourage the practice. Regardless of the writer's position, key arguments turn upon the intersection of financial and moral reasoning. See, for example, Emma Blair and James Robertson, *The Philippine Islands, 1493–1898*, vol. 11, "Letter of Hieronimo de Salazar y Salcedo" and vol. 12, "Letter of Conde de Monterrey."

[13] The *Ordenanzas de la Real Audiencia de Nueva España sobre las juntas y trajes de los negros y mulatos*, an example from 1612, forbade black and mulatto women to wear pearls, gold or silver jewelry, and shawls or dresses of imported Castilian silk. The document is transcribed and published in Richard Konetzke, *Colección de documentos para la historia de la formación social de Hispanoamérica, 1493–1810* (Madrid: Consejo Superior de Investigaciones Científicas, 1953–1962).

[14] See, for instance, Juan Sempere y Guariños, *Historia de luxo, y de las leyes suntuarias de España* (Madrid: Lope de Vega, 1973 [1788]), or, for comparative perspectives from outside the Hispanic world, Craig Clunas, *Superfluous Things: Material Culture and Social States in Early Modern China* (Honolulu: University of Hawaii Press, 2004) and Evelyn Welch, *Shopping in the Renaissance: Consumer Cultures in Italy, 1400–1600* (New Haven: Yale University Press, 2005). Of course, anxieties about consumption, especially luxury consumption, also surface well before and well after the early modern period.

[15] In this essay I do not take up the question of how fully "global"—as opposed to "cross-cultural" or "long-distance"—were the seventeenth-century trade networks in which Spanish America participated. For a considered and very useful discussion of both the strength and the fragility of far-flung trade connections involving Spanish America, see Frederick Cooper, *Colonialism in Question: Theory, Knowledge, History* (Berkeley: University of California Press, 2005).

[16] On the faithfulness of the image, Francisco de la Maza, *El pintor Cristóbal de Villalpando* (Mexico City: INAH, 1964); María Josefa Martínez de Río de Redo, "La Plaza Mayor," in *Mexico en el mundo, de las colecciones de arte*, vol. 2, Nueva España, 9–11 (Mexico City: El Gobierno de la República, 1994); *Cristóbal de Villalpando, ca. 1694–1714, Catálogo Razonado* (Mexico City: Fomeno Cultural Banamex, 1997); Kagan, *Urban Images*, 160–162, and Michael Schreffler, *The Art of Allegiance: Visual Culture and Imperial Power in Baroque New Spain* (University Park: Pennsylvania State University Press, 2007), 32–35. On the form of the Parián, see María Rebeca Yoma Medina and Luis Alberto Martos López, *Dos mercados en la historia de la ciudad de México: El Volador y La Merced* (Mexico City: INAH, 1990), 57ff.

[17] Much of the merchandise in Villalpando's Parián and elsewhere in the plaza has been sketched (in oil paint) rather than carefully delineated. Yet in many passages of the painting, he has taken considerable care in his depiction of figures and their clothing. The impression of viewing the original, then, is that the commodities on offer matter less than the spectacle and display of public space, in which sites of shopping are central.

[18] Silvia Arrom, "Popular Politics in Mexico City: The Parian Riot, 1828," *Hispanic American Historical Review* 68, no. 2 (1988): 245–268.

[19] Arif Dirlik, "The Global in the Local," in *Global/Local: Cultural Production and the Trans-national Imaginary*, edited by R. Wilson and W. Dissanayake, 21–45 (Durham: Duke University Press, 1996). The homogenizing impulses of globalization have been well debated, especially among scholars of the late twentieth and early twenty-first centuries. For interesting, but distinct perspectives on the tension between globalization and cultural distinctiveness, see, for instance, Andreas Wimmer, "Globalizations *Avant la Lettre*: A Comparative View of Isomorphization and Heteromorphization in an Inter-Connecting World," *Comparative Studies in Society and History* 43, no. 3 (2001): 435–466 and Anna Tsing, *Friction: An Ethnography of Global Connection* (Princeton: Princeton University Press, 2005). Among scholars of Spanish America and its visual culture, explicit discussion of the topic is not common, although

Gauvin Bailey's *Art on the Jesuit Missions in Asia and Latin America, 1542–1773* (Toronto: University of Toronto Press, 1999) and Serge Gruzinski's *Les Quatre Parties du Monde: Histoire d'une Mondialisation* (Paris: La Martiniere, 2004) represent examples drawn from quite different intellectual traditions.

[20] Clunas, "Modernity Global and Local," 1507.

[21] To take two well-known examples: paper and gunpowder were first used in China; what has rendered these materials so influential and historically transformative was not the simple fact of "first use," but rather their diffusion over time, their varied uses, and the range of different cultural values invested in them.

[22] For research in this field William Schurz, *The Manila Galleon* (New York: E. P. Dutton, 1939) and Pierre Chaunu, *Les Philippines et le Pacifique des Ibériques XIVe, XVIIe, XVIIIe siècles* (Paris: SEVPEN, 1960) are still influential. Other, more recent studies—especially on the mechanics and economies of the galleon trade—include Katharine Bjork, "The Link That Kept the Philippines Spanish: Mexican Merchant Interest and the Manila Trade, 1571–1815," *Journal of World History* 9, no. 1 (1998): 25–50; *El Galeón de Manila* (Mexico City: Aldeasa, Ministerio de Educación, Cultura y Deporte, 2000); Ostwald Sales Colín, "Les cargazones del galleon de la carrera de poniente: Primera mitad del siglo XVII," *Revista de Historia Económica, Año XVIII* 3 (2000, Otoño-inverno): 629–660; Antonio-Miguel Bernal, "La 'Carrera del Pácifico': Filipinas en el sistema colonial de la Carrera de Indias," in *España y el Pacífico/Legazpi,* Tomo II, edited by Leoncio Cabrero, 485–525 (Madrid: Sociedad Estatal de Conmemoración Culturales, 2004); Carlos Martínez Shaw and Marina Alfonso Mola, *La ruta española a China* (Madrid: El Viso, 2007); and Shirley Fish, *The Manila-Acapulco Galleons: The Treasure Ships of the Pacific* (Central Milton Keyes: Authorhouse, 2011).

[23] Antonio-Miguel Bernal cites examples of merchant profits of over 1000 percent ("La 'Carrera del Pácifico,'" 517), although this was the exception, not the rule. Lisa Schell Hoberman has traced a diminution in the number of Mexican merchants—both shippers and investors—involved in trans-Pacific trade from the late sixteenth to the middle of the seventeenth century, although as with trans-Atlantic trade of the same period, the number of investors shrank more rapidly than the value of cargoes, so that over the seventeenth century "fewer people shipped more money." See *Mexico's Merchant Elite, 1590–1660* (Durham: Duke University Press, 1991), 39–41, 266–267. Schurz discusses many of the risks of the trans-Pacific trade, although largely for the eighteenth century (*The Manila Galleon*, 154–190), and Jeremy Baskes, while focused on the Atlantic trade, offers astute observations about risk relevant for the Pacific in "Risky Ventures: Reconsidering Mexico's Colonial Trade System," *Colonial Latin American Review* 14, no. 1 (June 2005): 27–54.

[24] Antonio de Morga, *Sucesos de las Islas Filipinas* (Mexico City, 1609) [*History of the Philippine Islands*, translated by E. H. Blair and J. A. Robertson (Cleveland, 1907)]. While his account may fairly speak to Spanish impressions of foreign goods arriving in Manila, it also resonates, particularly in its description of excess, with the "inexpressibility topos" developed in early modern travel writing about Spanish colonial settings, especially the Americas. For a brief discussion of this in relation to de Morga, see Dana Leibsohn, "Response to the Global Renaissance," in *Global Design History*, edited by Glenn Adamson, et al., 21–24 (Abingdon: Oxford University Press, 2011). The topos, more broadly, surfaces in a wide range of interdisciplinary scholarship; recent examples pointing to this range would include, Naomi Mandel, *Against the Unspeakable: Complicity, the Holocaust and Slavery in America* (Charlottesville, University of Virginia Press, 2006) and Page Richards, "The Topos of the Inexpressible and Self-Critique," *GRAAT-Online* 8 (August 2010).

[25] On this diversity and its implications for urban and civic life, see Robert Reed, *Colonial Manila: The Context of Hispanic Urbanism and Process of Morphogenesis* (Berkeley: University of California Press, 1978) and Inmaculada Alva Rodríguez, *Vida Municipal en Manila (Siglos XVI–XVII)* (Córdoba: Universidad de Córdoba, 1997). For an analysis of Spanish perceptions of Manila see also, Antonio García-Abásolo, "Filipinas. Una Frontera Más Allá de la Frontera." In *Fronteras del mundo hispánico: Filipinas en el contexto de las regiones liminares novohispanas,* edited by Marta María Manchado López and Miguel Luque Talaván, 71–88 (Córdoba: Servicio de Publicaciones de la Universidad, 2011). On distinct aspects of Spanish American culture in the Philippines as opposed to Mexico, see Russell Skowronek, "The Spanish Philippines: Archaeological Perspectives on Colonial Economics and Society," *International Journal of Historical Archaeology* 2, no. 1 (1998): 45–71.

[26] "Grau y Monfalcón's Informatory Memorial of 1637," in *The Philippine Islands*, vol. 27, 77–79. Intramuros may have been considered the heart of the city, but wealthy Spaniards also had "country houses" outside the walls and along the banks of the Pasig River (Reed, *Colonial Manila*, 49). This suggests a certain porousness to the walled city. In addition, as Alva Rodríguez notes, colonial officials stationed in Manila may have praised the city, but it was not a place most wanted to live out their lives (*Vida municipal*, 25–26).

[27] Binondo and the Parián were dominated by Chinese residents, while Dilao, to the east of Intramuros, was the residential district for Japanese people. Indigenous Filipino neighborhoods also burgeoned outside the city walls.

[28] There existed several successive versions of the Parián in Manila. Early on, the Parián was located within the walls of the city; after 1595, it was transferred outside the city walls, although even then it did not occupy just one site. See Alberto Santamaría, "The Chinese Parián (El Parián de los Sangleyes)," in *The Chinese in the Philippines*, edited by Alfonso Felix, Jr., 67–118 (Manila: Solidaridad Publishing, 1966).

[29] In the seventeenth century, massacres of Chinese in Manila occurred in 1603, 1639, 1662, and 1686. See Santamaría, "The Chinese Parián," 78.

[30] This dependence was in many ways felt daily. For instance, wheat, a food so important to Spaniards, was not cultivated in the environs of Manila until late in the seventeenth century. Before that, it was imported from China by Chinese merchants (Alva Rodríguez, *Vida Municipal*, 38–39). On the history of tensions involving the Chinese in the Parián specifically, see Rafael Bernal, "The Chinese Colony in Manila, 1550–1770," in *The Chinese in the Philippines*, edited by Alfonso Felix, Jr., 40–66 (Manila: Solidaridad Publishing, 1966). A more recent account that captures the drama of Chinese-Spanish relations appears in Timothy Brook, "Weighing Silver," in *Vermeer's Hat*, 152–184 (New

York: Bloomsbury Press, 2009). For a summary of Spanish strategies for living with (and managing) Chinese people in Manila, see Antonio García-Abásolo, "The Spanish Image of the Chinese in the Philippines," *Revista Española del Pacífico* 21/22 (2008–2009): 67–75.

[31] See "The Cultural Biography of Things: Commoditization as Process," in *The Social Life of Things*, edited by Arjun Appadurai, 64–94 (Cambridge: Cambridge University Press, 1986).

[32] Archivo General de las Indias (AGI), Filipinas, 128, 8 (Carta de Domingo de Zabalburu sobre géneros chinos). The account, which appears amidst documents of a later date, does not reveal what dialects were spoken by the interpreter; the scribe's phrase is simply "en lengua china y española" (in Chinese and Spanish). Interestingly, and presumably as part of a broader interest in identifying individuals who came to Manila to trade, the names of the Chinese boat captains were dutifully transcribed into the Spanish record.

[33] It would be overreaching to say it never happened, but my research to date suggests that "returning" Chinese merchandise was not considered a viable response for consumers or merchants in Manila.

[34] A point underscored by de Morga, who notes, with a bit of ironic disdain, that Spaniards will buy even "gewgaws and ornaments of little value." *Sucesos de las Islas Filipinas*, 408.

[35] Future research will help hone our view of this. There nevertheless exists one oft-cited anecdote about Manila consumers rejecting Chinese merchandise. It focuses upon a Chinese carver who once made a wooden nose for a Spaniard in need; the next year, Chinese merchants returned to Manila with a multitude of noses they could not sell. Usually invoked as a quaint tale of cross-cultural misunderstanding, the anecdote, in its singularity, implies that merchandise from China tended to find buyers in Manila. Diego de Bobadilla registered the story in *Relación de las gloriosas…* (Mexico City, 1638), and it has circulated widely, including, for instance, in Bernal's 1966 "The Chinese Colony" and Fish's 2011 *The Manila-Acapulco Galleons*.

[36] This would certainly have been the case at the time of the Ming-Qing transition, when shifts in patterns and levels of kiln production affected porcelain shipments to Manila (and of course elsewhere).

[37] See Donna Pierce, this volume, but also Donna Pierce and Cordelia Snow, "A Harp for Playing: Domestic Goods Transported over the Camino Real," and Patricia Fournier, "Ceramic Production and Trade," both in *El Camino Real de Tierra Adentro, 2*, compiled by Gabrielle G. Palmer and Stephen L. Fosberg, 71–86 and 153–175, Cultural Resources Series, no. 13 (Santa Fe: Bureau of Land Management, 1999); and Linda Shulsky, "Chinese Porcelain at Old Mobile," *Historical Archaeology* 36, no. 1 (2002): 97–104. For the eighteenth century in northern Mexico, see Gustavo Curiel, *Los bienes del mayorazgo de los Cortés del Rey en 1729* (Mexico City: Instituto de Investigaciones Estéticas, UNAM, 1993) and Clara Bargellini, "Asia at the Missions of Northern New Spain," in *Asia and Spanish America: Trans-Pacific Artistic and Cultural Exchange, 1500–1850*, edited by Donna Pierce and Ronald Otsuka, 190–199 (Denver: Denver Art Museum, 2009).

[38] See, for instance, José Antonio Calderón Quijano, *Historia de las fortificaciones en Nueva España* (Sevilla: Publicaciones de la Escuela de Estudios Hispano-Americanos de Sevilla, 1953).

[39] An inventory of Boot's possessions, made when he faced charges by the Inquisition in 1637 in Mexico City, lists a few imports from Asia, including an inkwell, writing set, and writing cabinet identified as Japanese in origin ("del Japon") (AGI, Audiencia de México, 28). We do not know where he purchased these things, although it was likely in Acapulco or in markets in Mexico City. The inventory also registers an impressive number of books, as well as clothing of silk, velvet, and damask, and household items similar to those listed by officials in their inventories of 1622 (see below). I thank John Fabian López for help in obtaining a copy of Boot's inventory.

[40] He sees this influence in the strongly angled perspective and treatment of the landscape, *Historia de las fortificaciones*, 230 (the point is also made in *El Galeón de Manila*, 80). Unfortunately, the history of Boot's image making is not well known. A Dutch engineer who came to Mexico City to work on water drainage in 1614, Boot was in Acapulco from 1615 to 1617, then later in Veracruz. This image clearly owes much to European prototypes, and Roberto Mayer notes that Boot's original views of all three cities—Mexico City, Acapulco, and Veracruz—were in Holland as early as 1632. See "Trasmonte y Boot: Sus vistas de tres ciudades mexicanas en el siglo XVII," *Anales del Instituto de Investigaciones Estéticas* 87 (2005): 177–198. Kagan discusses the seventeenth-century "after life" of these images in Amsterdam and beyond in *Urban Images*, 82, 153.

[41] See, for instance, Tatiana Seijas, "The Portuguese Slave Trade to Spanish Manila, 1580–1640," *Itinerario: International Journal on the History of European Expansion and Global Interaction* 32, no. 1 (2008): 19–38; Melba E. Falck Reyes and Héctor Palacios, *El japonés que conquistó Guadalajara. La historia de Juan de Páez en la Guadalajara del siglo XVII* (Guadalajara and Jalisco: Universidad de Guadalajara and Biblioteca Pública del Estado de Jalisco Juan José Arreola, 2009); and Edward Slack, Jr., "The *Chinos* in New Spain: A Corrective Lens for a Distorted Image," *Journal of World History* 20, no. 1 (2009): 35–67.

[42] Edward R. Slack, Jr. "Sinifying New Spain: Cathay's Influence on Colonial Mexico via the *Nao de China*," in *The Chinese in Latin America and the Caribbean*, edited by Walton Look Lai and Tan Chee-Beng, 7–34, (Leiden: Brill, 2010).

[43] A similar, although not identical process can be charted for Asian people—many more of whom were considered (and labeled) "Chinese" than actually came from China. See, for instance, Tatiana Seijas, "Transpacific Servitude: The Asian Slaves of Mexico, 1580–1700," Ph.D. dissertation, Yale University, 2008; on the evocative resonance of Chinese things in Mexico as compared to Chinese people, see Dana Leibsohn, "Trading Histories: Foreign Things in Manila and Mexico," Paper presented in the Silberberg Lecture Series, Institute of Fine Arts, New York, April 2011.

[44] This has been noted by several scholars, and is discussed in a particularly useful way, especially for the eighteenth century, by Gustavo Curiel, "Al remedo de la China." Recently Sonia Ocaña Ruiz has argued that the use of the term "Chinese" to refer to Asian imports—be they people or objects—"suggests a lack of interest in their precise origins" ("*Enconchado* Frames: The Use of Japanese Ornamental Models in New Spanish Painting," in *Asia & Spanish America: Trans-Pacific Artistic and Cultural Exchange*, edited by Donna Pierce and Ronald Otsuka, 129–149 (Denver: Denver Art Museum, 2009), 129. She may be correct; however, it is clear that in

some cases what came from China, in particular, did matter.

[45] This group of *inventarios de bienes* is today housed in the Archivo General de Indias, Audiencia de México, 259–263, and is composed of several hundred inventories. The inventories respond to a royal request and so register only certain kinds of objects of value, not the full gamut of valued possessions known from contemporary testaments or house inventories. Nevertheless, the range of wealth described here is striking. Viceroy don Diego Carrillo de Mendoza y Pimental and rich men who owned houses in the center of Mexico City represent one end of the spectrum; at the other are poorer ex-officials—often men serving in regions with large indigenous populations—who had (or said they had) very few possessions of value. These are also highly gendered accounts, revealing the assets of men, although some describe their wives' belongings, or what came to them through dowries.

[46] Alessandra Russo, "Cortés's Objects and the Idea of New Spain," *Journal of the History of Collections* 23, no. 2 (November 2011): 1–24.

[47] This intersection is well discussed in the literature on early modern luxury and consumption, particularly among Europeanists. See, for instance, Lisa Jardine, *Worldly Goods: A New History of the Renaissance* (New York: Doubleday, 1996), who notes that early modern consumption was complicated precisely because it represented both investment and pleasure. Other helpful voices on this theme include Jan de Vries, "Between Purchasing Power and the World of Goods: Understanding the Household Economy in Early Modern Europe," in *Consumption and the World of Goods*, edited by John Brewer and Roy Porter, 85–132 (New York and London: Routledge, 1993) and chapters in *Consumers and Luxury in Europe, 1650–1850*, edited by Maxine Berg and Helen Clifford (Manchester: Manchester University Press, 1999).

[48] For comparison, see Gustavo Curiel, "El efímero caudal de una joven noble. Inventario y aprecio de los bienes de la marquesa Doña Teresa Francisca María de Guadalupe Retes Paz Vera (Ciudad de México, 1695)," *Anales del Museo de América* 8 (2000): 65–101.

[49] AGI, Audiencia de México 259, No. 91, ff. 253–273. I thank Tatiana Seijas for insights into the Portuguese connections in his inventory and in these documents more generally.

[50] For example, Castile, the Germanies, Japan, and China are frequently named as the origin site of specfic objects. In contrast, Portuguese trade networks and sites in Africa tend to be signaled through the names and descriptive language used for slaves. North-South networks, across the Americas, seem to figure less prominently than either trans-Atlantic or trans-Pacific routes, although explicit references to objects made in New Spain—primarily textiles and furniture—surface with some consistency. Examples of the latter include beds from Campeche, chests from Michoacán, and writing cabinets from Tlaxcala.

[51] In their basic outline these patterns bound New Spain to a broad range of early modern tastes and purchasing practices forged through European and trans-Atlantic trade.

[52] Japan is mentioned in several of the inventories, largely in connection with furniture such as writing cabinets and cases (*escritorios, bufetillos)* and elaborate chests (*baules*). Painted screens (*biombos)* surface only rarely. It is possible screens were not seen as valuable enough to warrant explicit mention, or that 1622 is simply too early for *biombos* to be widespread, even in wealthy homes. Sofia Sanabrais has also found relatively few *biombos* mentioned in inventories before the 1630s; by midcentury, though, they appear with more frequency (personal communication, April 2011).

[53] Although these inventories map trans-Pacific imports in quite consistent patterns, with textiles more consistently described as "de China" and furniture items as "de Japón," it would be a mistake to presume that either phrase referred strictly to an actual place in Asia. Sometimes this was the case, but "de China" and "de Japón" were also imagined geographies, and the affective power of Asian imports rested, in no small way, upon the blurred boundaries among actual and imagined entities.

[54] This is my phrase, not one that emerges from the inventories.

[55] Not all the inventories mention color or details about the fabric, although a number of them indicate that the pillows of Chinese silk match the color of those made from Spanish silk.

[56] While my research on the point is still nascent, gender also inflects this habit. Many of the silk objects "doubled" in these inventories would have been used in household settings dominated by women or that had strong female connotations. This opens onto the complicated topic of the gendering of Asia in Spanish America, a theme as yet understudied, especially in comparison to early modern Europe, where China was often, although not always, feminized.

[57] On cosmopolitan ambitions and colonialism in Spanish America, see, for instance, Serge Gruzinski, *The Mestizo Mind: The Intellectual Dynamics of Colonization and Globalization* (New York: Routledge, 2002) and Walter Mignolo, *The Darker Side of the Renaissance: Literacy, Territoriality and Coloniality* (Ann Arbor: University of Michigan Press, 1995). For comparative perspectives, Tsing's *Friction* and Cooper's *Colonialism in Question* are both useful.

[58] Ocaña Ruiz, for instance, claims that Asian works figured among the elements used to construct the New Spanish identity ("*Enconchado* Frames," 145); and Curiel, in several essays, has argued that purchasing from afar, and particularly from Asia, was instrumental in the creation of Creole identities. See, for instance, "Al remedo de la China" and 'Perceptions of the Other and the Language of 'Chinese Mimicry' in the Decorative Arts of New Spain," in *Asia and Spanish America: Trans-Pacific Artistic and Cultural Exchange, 1500–1800*, edited by Donna Pierce and Ronald Otsuka, 19–36 (Denver: Denver Art Museum, 2009).

[59] See María Bonta this volume, but also the very useful work, all of which draws upon archaeological evidence, by Patricia Fournier-García, *Evidencias arqueológicas de la importación de cerámica en México, con base en los materiales del Ex-convento de San Jerónimo* (Mexico City: INAH, 1990); George Kuwayama, *Chinese Ceramics in Colonial Mexico* (Los Angeles: Los Angeles County Museum of Art, 1997); and Etsuko Miyata Rodríguez, "The Early Manila Galleon Trade: Merchants' Networks and Markets in 16th- and 17th-century Mexico," in *Asia and Spanish America: Trans-Pacific Artistic and Cultural Exchange, 1500–1800*, edited by Donna Pierce and Ronald Otsuka, 37–58 (Denver: Denver Art Museum, 2009). For a perspective that emphasizes trade with Spain and other European empires but clearly implicates New Spain, see Teresa Canepa, *Zhangzhou Export Ceramics: The So-called Swatow Wares* (London and Lisbon: Jorge Welsh, 2006) and "Portuguese and Spanish Trade in Kraak Porcelain in the Late

16th and Early 17th Centuries" (dissertation excerpt, shared by the author in March 2011).

[60] See, for instance, Robert Batchelor, "On the Movement of Porcelains: Rethinking the Birth of Consumer Society as Interactions of Exchange Networks, 1600–1750," in *Consuming Cultures, Global Perspectives: Historical Trajectories, Transnational Exchanges*, edited by John Brewer and Frank Trentmann, 95–122 (New York: Berg Books, 2006).

[61] Julia Curtis, *Trade, Taste and Transformation: Jingdezhen Porcelain for Japan, 1620–1645* (New York: China Institute Gallery, 2006); Rita C. Tan, et al., *Zhangzhou Ware Found in the Philippines: "Swatow" Export Ceramics from Fujian 16th-17th Centuries* (Manila: Yuchengco Museum, 2007); Luísa Vinhais and Jorge Welsh, eds., *Kraak Porcelain: The Rise of a Global Trade in the Late 16th and Early 17th Centuries* (London: Jorge Welsh, 2008), and Canepa, cited above (n. 59). The most numerous studies, however, are those focused on eighteenth-century European practices. Examples of quite recent work in this area include Stacey Sloboda, "Porcelain Bodies: Acquisitiveness, Gender and Taste in 18th-century England," in *Material Cultures, 1740–1920: The Meanings and Pleasures of Collecting*, edited by John Potvin and Alla Myzelev, 19–36 (Burlington: Ashgate, 2009); David Porter, *The Chinese Taste in Eighteenth-century England* (Cambridge and New York: Cambridge University Press, 2010); and Alden Cavanaugh and Michael Yonan, eds., *The Cultural Aesthetics of 18th-century Porcelain* (Surrey and Burlington: Ashgate, 2010).

[62] For early, but still important work on Puebla ceramics, see Edwin Barber's works, *The Maiolica of Mexico* (Philadelphia: Pennsylvania Museum and School of Industrial Art, 1908) and *The Catalog of Mexican Maiolica Belonging to Mrs. Robert de Forest* (New York: Hispanic Society of America, 1911), as well as Enrique Cervantes, *Loza blanca y azulejo de Puebla* (Mexico: privately printed, 1939). More recently, Margaret Connors McQuade has published significant research in a series of exhibition catalogues, including *Talavera Poblana: Four Centuries of a Mexican Ceramic Tradition* (New York City: Americas Society Gallery, 1999) and *The Grandeur of Viceregal Mexico: Treasures from the Museo Franz Mayer*, edited by Hector Rivero Borrell Miranda, et al., 208–248 (Houston: Museum of Fine Art, 2002). For more on the Spanish influence, as it mixed with Chinese and local traditions, see also the essays in *Cerámica y Cultura: The Story of Spanish and Mexican Mayólica*, edited by Robin Gavin, Donna Pierce, and Alfonso Pleguezuela (Albuquerque: University of New Mexico Press, 2003).

[63] Guild rules in Puebla dating from 1653, and then revised in 1682, account for some of the consistency in the genre, although Margaret Connors McQuade links the dot pattern so prevalent on Puebla blue-and-white ceramics and the affinity for horror vacui to Hispano-Muslim ceramic practices adopted by Puebla painters. See *The Grandeur of Mexico*.

[64] Although the guild rules date to1682, the "Chinese-ness" of Puebla ceramics remained unresolved—at least in some eyes—well into the eighteenth century. In 1720, for instance, Diego de Santa Cruz Oyanguren Espíndola described himself as the "inventor" of Chinese-style ceramics in Puebla. Cervantes, *Loza blanca y azulejo*, 42. See also discussion below.

[65] While he focuses more explicitly on the eighteenth century, see Curiel, "Perceptions of the Other," for a summary of the differences between Puebla wares and Chinese porcelains imported into Mexico.

[66] John Carswell, *Blue and White: Chinese Porcelain around the World* (London: British Museum Press, 2000), 142, and Florence Lister and Robert Lister, *Spanish and Mexican Maiolica: An Annotated Catalogue of the Collections of the Museum of International Folk Art, Santa Fe, New Mexico*, 2 vols. (1976), 5, 82.

[67] Across the Ming and early Qing periods, as different kilns in Jingdezhen served disparate markets and patrons, standards and expectations varied considerably. There was, then, no single "Jingdezhen style." Moreover, the porcelain made in Chinese kilns and sent to European and Mexican markets often shows the signs of hasty production. Even so, for those familiar with Chinese ceramics, the Puebla wares represent a wholly other kind of pottery.

[68] Cervantes, *Loza blanca y azulejo*, 42.

[69] This includes, for instance, blue-and-white Talavera ceramics with butterfly and geometric designs framing large, single animals (known as "Serie de las mariposas") or bird and flower patterns ("Serie de helechos y golondrinas"). See *Recorridos: Guía de las colecciones del siglo XVII del Museo Nacional de Artes Decorativas* (Madrid: Ministerio de Cultura, 2007).

[70] For a recent advocate of import substitution, see Slack, "Sinifying New Spain." Curiel falls decidedly on the other side of the argument: "It is necessary to undo, once and for all, the general and erroneous idea that blue-and-white ceramics of Puebla were simple copies of Chinese porcelain produced as an affordable response to the high prices commanded by imported Chinese porcelain" ("Perception of the Other," 34, n. 8). Clearly there is more work to be done on this theme. While Curiel is correct that Puebla ceramics are not simply local versions of Chinese porcelain, the relationships among Puebla's blue-and-white industry, shifts in production in Chinese kilns across the mid-to-late seventeenth century, and the rise in production of European and Japanese emulations of Chinese porcelain in this period leave many questions as yet unanswered.

[71] This idea—of a productive engagement among colonial images and objects and those of metropolitan or foreign origins, in which no original is left unchanged—has been explored in many studies of cross-cultural contact. I have found particularly useful Greg Dening, *Islands and Beaches: Discourse on a Silent Land, Marquesas, 1774–1880* (Honolulu: University of Hawaii Press, 1980); Homi Bhabha, "Signs Taken for Wonders," in *Location of Culture* (London and New York: Routledge, 1994), 102–122; and Gruzinski, *Mestizo Mind*.

[72] While the wares of western Europe and Japan were hardly identical, the makers shared certain interests in replicating the surface and texture of porcelain (among other things), which did not seem to drive the Puebla ceramicists or their patrons.

[73] To date, more scholarship focuses on how the Puebla ceramics figure in the history of Mexican visual culture and taste. This, too, is an important topic, but it is the frames of reference offered by early modern history writ large that interest me here.

[74] Scholarship among Latin Americanists, especially over the last three decades, has placed considerable emphasis on indigenous contributions to early modern visual culture as well as to Creole tastes and their imprint upon Mexican art history. Although I have not done so here (and some may

well fault the essay for this), I see bringing these themes into conversation, and engaging them with broad narratives of trade and visual culture, as worthy but not insignificant challenges.

[75] While there is much to be said about how meaning accrues in an image crafted explicitly to commemorate another object, for the purposes of this essay I wish only to note that, over the years, this painting has been seen largely as material testimony to a place (Chalma), a practice (Christian worship), and a symmetrical disposition of things (the Chalma Christ and a suite of offerings).

[76] María José Esparza Liberal and Isabel Fernández de García Lascurain, *La cera en México: Arte e historia*, Prólogo de Teresa Castelló Yturbide (Mexico City: Fomento Cultural Banamex, 1994).

[77] Thomas DaCosta Kaufmann, "Interpreting Cultural Transfer and the Consequences of Markets and Exchange: Reconsidering *Fumi-e*," in *Artistic and Cultural Exchanges between Europe and Asia, 1400–1900*, edited by Michael North, 135–162 (Surrey, UK: Ashgate, 2010), 138.

[78] This is not a point that has been sufficiently argued in the literature. For instance, Robert Finlay, in the widely cited essay, "The Pilgrim's Art: The Culture of Porcelain in World History" (*Journal of World History* 9 [1998]: 141–188), does admirable work discussing the "enthusiasm of blue-and-white porcelain in places as different as Japan, Borneo, Mombasa, Istanbul and Amsterdam" (169); Spanish America, however, barely registers in his survey.

The Perils of Porcelain

Chinese Export Porcelain for the Mexican Colonial Market

María Bonta de la Pezuela

In the seventeenth and eighteenth centuries, "everybody who was anybody" had a service of Chinese porcelain. The noble class had Chinese porcelain services with their coat of arms emblazoned on them, while those of less nobility had services decorated with their monogram (Fig. 1). This was true not only in Europe but throughout the world, even in the Spanish colonies of America. Indeed, the fashion for all things Chinese was no different in New Spain than it was in New England.

Between 1573 and 1823 the Manila galleon (or Nao de China, as it was also called) ensured the delivery of these services and other exotic goods to the colonial elite of New Spain. These objects were cultural, ideological, and political ambassadors. They give testimony about two open cultures that adapted to each other's requirements and needs—just as the Western cultures acquired objects of Chinese form and decoration in the early seventeenth century, incorporating them into their homes and daily lives, in time Asian craftsmen responded by learning to produce objects that satisfied a Western aesthetic sensibility.

The market for Chinese export porcelain in colonial Mexico must be studied through a global lens, since the porcelain made for the colonial Mexican market is closely related and in many cases identical to the porcelain made for the colonial French, Dutch, and English markets. The porcelain services and vases that arrived in New Spain were produced in the same kilns and sold in the same markets as the wares being made for the rest of the world, making them subject to the same market forces that would eventually determine the evolution of style and price (Fig. 2).[1]

During the 250 years that the galleon sailed, there were three main commercial markets for Chinese porcelain in the world (aside from Canton): the *rua nova dos mercadores* in Lisbon, the East India Company auctions in Amsterdam, and the commercial fair in Acapulco that took place every year upon the arrival of the galleon from Manila. Our focus here will be on the porcelain that traded hands in Acapulco: how it arrived, who acquired it, and at what prices.

The Spanish Outpost in Manila

After the Treaty of Tordesillas (1494) forced Spain to find an alternate route to the Indies, New Spain became the main link between the mother country and its highly prized colony in the Philippines, placing it at the very center of the Spanish empire. The Manila galleon became the primary vehicle of administrative, economic, and commercial communication between the Philippine colony and the Viceroyalty of New Spain.[2] Every year it carried the *situado* (an annual stipend of silver used to fund operations in the Philippines), government officials, merchants, missionaries, slaves, and precious trade goods between the two colonies.

The Philippines' strategic geographical location made it the focal point for Spanish trade in the Indies. It was accessible from the American colonies and was equidistant from the important production areas of Asia: Java, India, Malacca, and China. The Portuguese base in Macao ensured proximity to the silks of China, and the Dutch in Batavia (Jakarta today) were close to the spices of the Moluccas, but Manila was centrally located, facilitating the acquisition of all the commodities the East had to offer.

It was also an attractive magnet for Chinese, Japanese, and Portuguese merchants, who gladly made the trip to the Philippines in search of the highly sought-after Mexican silver pieces of eight. Even when the Spaniards traveled to China or Macao, the Chinese were often more disposed to sell to them than to merchants of other nationalities who offered goods instead of silver in exchange. In 1699, while the English trading vessel *Macclesfield* was anchored in Canton, a ship from Manila laden

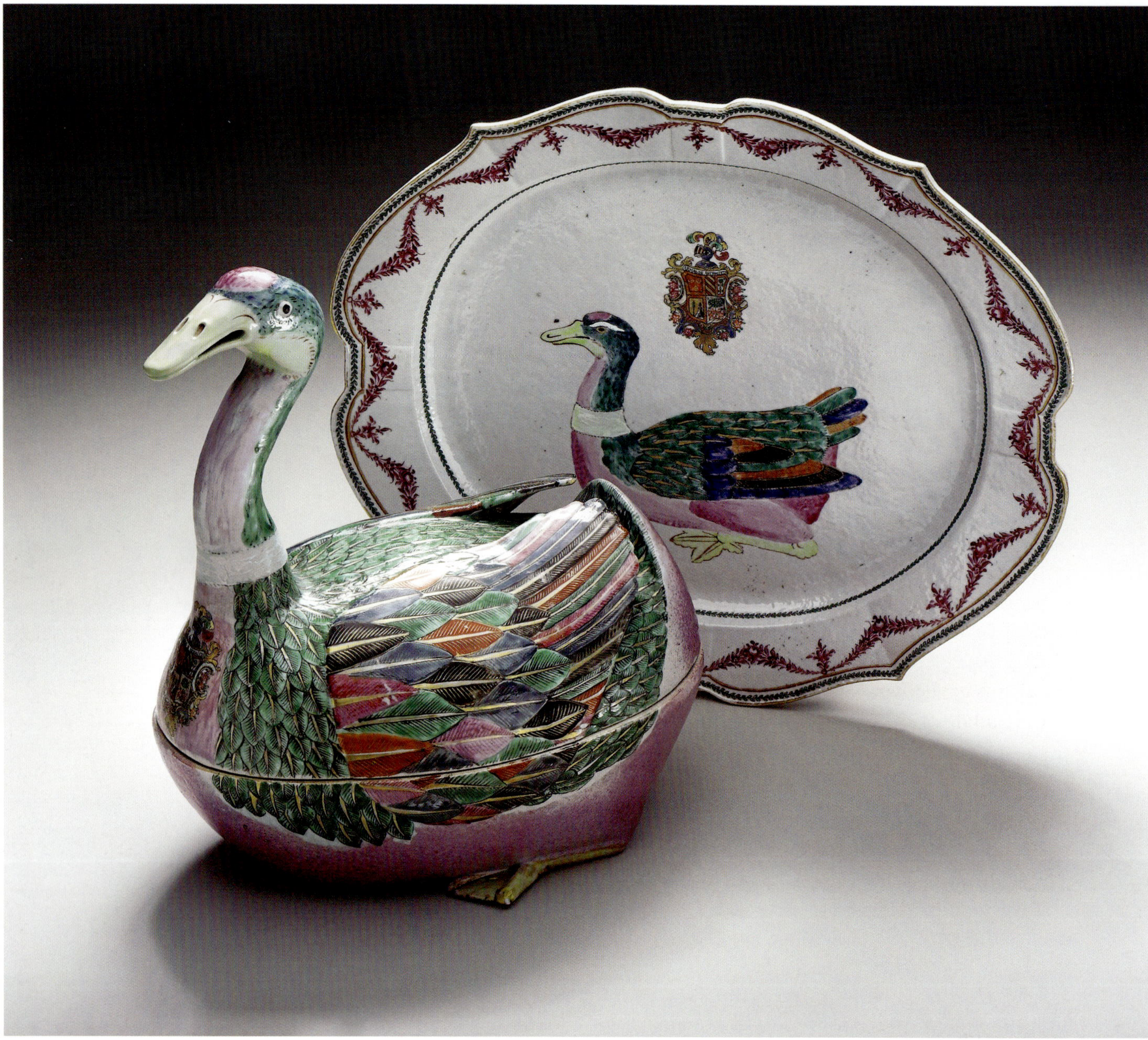

Fig. 1. Tureen and Platter. China, c. 1770. Porcelain. Courtesy of the Peabody Essex Museum, Salem, Massachusetts; The Copeland Collection, 2001.

with Spanish silver arrived in Macao, causing prices to rise dramatically.[3]

Manila was home to "a cosmopolitan society, more racially and ethnically diverse than any in the Spanish Indies."[4] There were Spanish government administrators and missionaries, Chinese workers, Mexican Indians, Japanese, Javanese, and Portuguese traders, African slaves, and criminals who had been expelled from New Spain. Outside the walled city across the Pasig River was the market known as the *Parián*, the central marketplace where Chinese merchants lived and sold their wares (see p. 17, fig. 3). It held a labyrinth of small, dark stalls, with narrow aisles that scarcely fit two people side by side.[5] Although the items on offer in the *Parián* included teas, lacquerware, bronze objects, ivories, and porcelain, most of the business done there involved the silk trade. In 1755 only 15 out of a total of 627 stalls sold porcelain (in contrast to 107 that sold silk), representing only 2 percent of the overall marketplace.[6] Only 1 percent of the total number of registered merchants at the *Parián* in Manila sold porcelain in the middle of the eighteenth century.

The Manila Galleon

The majority of the ships employed in the Spanish transpacific trade were built in the royal shipyards at Cavite on the southern shores of Manila Bay, using raw materials that were mostly available locally.[7] In order to avoid the summer monsoons and take advantage of favorable tradewinds, the galleon had to leave the Philippines between June and July. By the eighteenth century an annual commercial fair in June gave one last opportunity for Chinese junks to arrive in Manila laden with silks, lacquerware, teas, and porcelain bound for the Americas.[8]

Space aboard the galleon was limited and therefore at a premium. A complex system of allotment was managed by the governor and the archbishop, who naturally favored their families, rich commercial merchants, and powerful members of the religious orders.[9] Fueled by the potential profits available, a secondary market developed as receipts were handed out to various members of

Fig. 2. Chinese dynasties and reigns as they correspond to the Manila galleon trade (in red).

Manila Galleon (1573–1823)

Ming Dynasty (1368–1644)	
Hongwu	1368–1398
Jianwen	1399–1402
Yongle	1403–1424
Hongxi	1425–1426
Xuande	1426–1435
Zhengton	1436–1449
Jingtain	1450–1456
Tianshun	1457–1464
Chenghua	1465–1487
Hongzhi	1488–1505
Zhengde	1506–1521
Jiajing	1522–1566
Longqing	1567–1572
Wanli	1573–1620
Taichang	1620–1621
Tianqui	1621–1627
Chongzhen	1628–1644

Qing Dynasty (1644-1911)	
Shunzhi	1644–1661
Kangxi	1662–1722
Yongzheng	1722–1734
Qianlong	1736–1795
Jia Qing	1796–1821
Daoguang	1821–1850
Xianfeng	1851–1861
Tongzhu	1862–1873
Guangxu	1874–1908
Xuantong	1909–1911

the community, who in turn used them to barter with merchants anxious for a greater share of the cargo space.

This created hazardous conditions aboard the galleon, which was usually overloaded with commercial merchandise packed in every available corner of the ship, making it heavy and cumbersome to navigate. Sometimes in the frenzy of a storm or to improve the maneuverability of the ship, cargo was tossed overboard. Such was the case aboard the *San José* in 1696, when, in an effort to lighten the load of the ship, "several [jars] were cast into the sea full of pepper, purcelane (porcelain) and other goods of value."[10] Indeed, throughout the 250 years that the Manila galleon sailed, the Philippine Sea and the Pacific Ocean were the scene of many shipwrecks where entire cargoes and crews were lost and buried.[11]

Aside from jars, porcelain was transported mostly in *balsas* or cylindrical wooden crates that had been packed by Chinese workers in Manila.[12] These were densely packed with the pieces of inferior quality on the outside, hiding the more valuable finer pieces of porcelain deeper in the crate. The objective was not only to pack as much porcelain as possible in each crate, but—should the package be opened for inspection either at departure in Cavite or upon arrival in Acapulco—to contrive that duties would be charged on a lower perceived value of cheaper wares.[13] Each crate was marked with an emblem that corresponded to its registration and listing in the ship's manifest. These emblems were usually monograms made up of the merchant's initials that made the crate readily identifiable (Fig. 3).

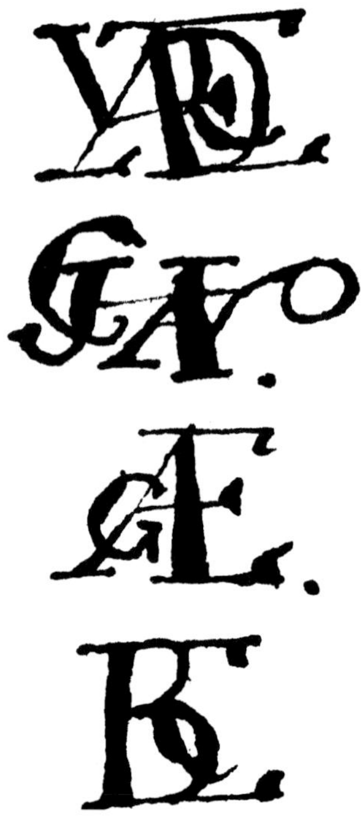

Fig. 3. Monograms used by merchants in Manila to identify their cargo. Archivo General de la Nación (AGN), Mexico, Filipinas, vol. 25, exp. 1, "Expediente que trata de la descarga de la fragata *Joseph de Gracia*, 1779," fs. 1r–59v.

By the seventeenth century Manila lived exclusively from the galleon trade. The fleet sent one year carrying an entire community's consignments for sale in New Spain would return with the proceeds the following year, completing the commercial cycle. It is therefore understandable that the entire community was invested in the preparation and success of each voyage. Tremendous fanfare preceded each departure, including masses, confessions, communion, and an elaborate procession through the city with the image of the Virgin Mary and the patron saint of the ship, amid gun salutes and ringing church bells, and culminating in the blessing of the ship by the archbishop.

This was understandably an important motivational ritual for the departing crew and passengers, who were faced with an average of seven months' worth of terrible storms, diseases, and hunger—all with the ever-present risk of dying at sea. In 1730 the captain of the galleon *Nuestra Señora de Guía* implored the Virgin of la Soledad to save the ship from the storm and promised an ex-voto in return. His prayers were clearly answered, as the ship arrived safely in Acapulco on February 21, 1731, and today the ex-voto made in gratitude hangs at the basilica dedicated to Nuestra Señora de la Soledad in Oaxaca.

Because of the transpacific currents that aided in the galleon's voyage, the American coastline was usually sighted in northern California. The galleon would then follow the coast heading south to Acapulco, with a brief stop in the port of San Blas, where a messenger was dispatched to Mexico City announcing the arrival of the Nao de China. This set the country in motion to prepare Acapulco for its reception. *Te Deums* were prayed, church bells were rung, gun salutes were fired, and administrative personnel and merchants started making their way to the port city.

Acapulco: The Sale and Distribution of Chinese Porcelain in New Spain

As Manila lived for the galleon trade, so did Acapulco, and during the two to three months that the Nao de China was in port, the town swelled with activity, its population doubling or tripling with the added inhabitants who had flocked there in order to participate in the galleon trade (p. 20, fig. 4). From within New Spain came administrative personnel sent to guard against contraband cargo and ensure complete payment of all taxes as well as the preparation of the *situado*; merchants hoping to buy Asian porcelains, silks, and spices; clergy preparing for their new missions; troop regiments going to reinforce the Philippine garrisons; delinquents condemned to forced labor in the remote archipelago; and shippers and handlers expecting assignments to carry the goods back into the country after the fair that would be held once the galleon had cleared arrival procedures.

The galleon also brought its share: mostly merchants hoping to sell their cargo and a crew who needed to prepare the ship for its return trip. To these should be added a third, distinct group of merchants and crew from Peru, who often made the trip in search of Asian merchandise, which was unavailable from any other source.

Every ship carried a document with a detailed account of the crew, the passengers (including who had died or been born aboard), the cargo, the weather, and the food rations (rice, meat, fish, pork, salt, flour, sugar, sweets, wine, oil, chickens) as well as how much silver was sent for the *situado*. A shipping manifest known as the *libro de sobordo* detailed the commercial property aboard and was kept by the silver master of the ship. Upon arrival in Acapulco, it was the *libro de sobordo* that was used to register the cargo (Fig. 4).

As was the case in Manila, visual inspection of the merchandise was almost never required. There were a few surprise inspections, though. In the middle of the seventeenth century, don Pedro de Quiroga, a *visitador* who was sent to Acapulco to oversee the disembarking procedures, wrought havoc in the commercial relations between the Philippines and New Spain.[14] After a thorough examination of the galleon cargo, which made the illegal practices that had been the custom up to

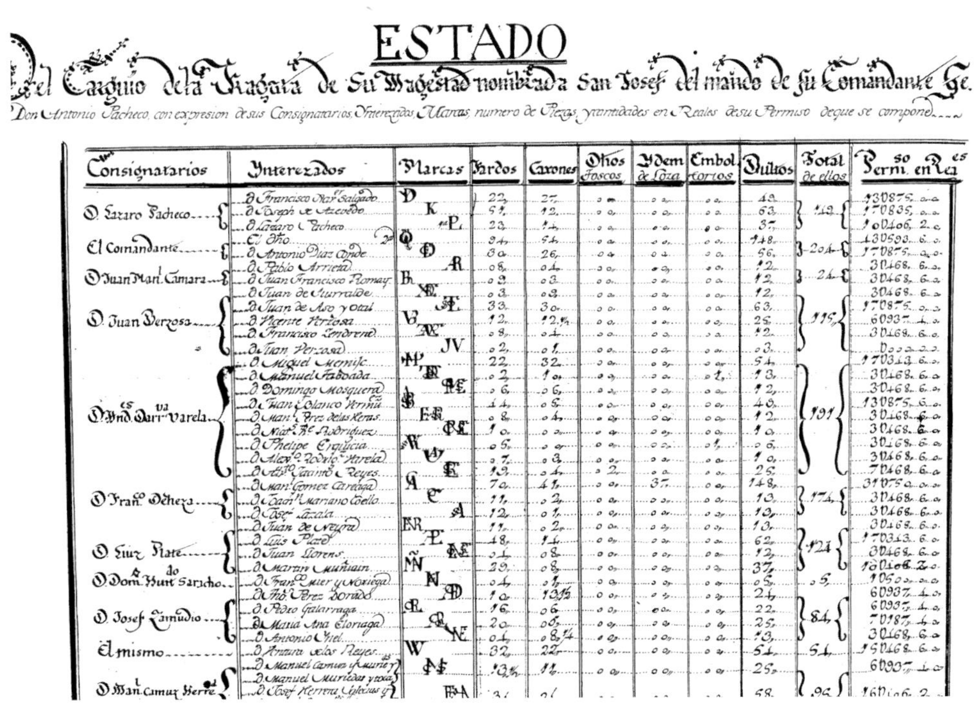

Fig. 4. Detail of *Libro de sobordo*, 1779. AGN Mexico, Filipinas, vol. 25, exp. 1, "Expediente que trata de la descarga de la fragata *Joseph de Gracia*, 1779", fs. 1r–59v.

Fig. 5. Chart of porcelain in Manila galleon cargo.

Year	Name of Vessel	Total Cargo
1729	Sagrada Familia	-
1730	Ntra. Sra. de Guía	3,996 pieces
1732	Ntra. Sra. de Guía	3,973 pieces
1735	Ntra. Sra. de Guía	3,946 pieces
1736	Ntra. Sra. de Covadonga	1,801 pieces
1737	Ntra. Sra. de Guía	3,003 pieces
1738	Ntra. Sra. del Pilar de Zaragoza	2,619 pieces
1741	Ntra. Sra. del Pilar de Zaragoza	2,050 pieces
1751	La Santísima Trinidad & Ntra. Sra. del Buen Fin	-
1753	**La Santísima Trinidad & Ntra. Sra. del Buen Fin**	**-**
1757	Ntra. Sra. de la Portería	376 pieces
1759	Ntra. Sra. del Rosario and San Juan Bautista	1,004 pieces
1760	La Santísima Trinidad and Ntra. Sra. del Buen Fin	2,469 pieces
1761	Ntra. Sra. del Rosario and San Juan Bautista	997 pieces
1764	Santa Rosa	389 $^{1}/_{2}$ pieces
1766	San Carlos Borromeo	1,058 pieces
1772	San Carlos	1,000 pieces
1773	**San José de Gracia**	**-**
1774	Ntra. Sra. de la Concepción	1,311 pieces
1775	San José de Gracia	1,722 packages
1779	San José de Gracia	1,918 packages
1781	San José [de Gracia]	1,266 packages
1783	San José de Gracia	2,343 crates & bales
1784	San Felipe	1,001 crates & bales
1785	San José de Gracia	1,534 crates & bales
1786	San Andrés	2,135 crates & bales
1787	San José de Gracia	1,975 crates & bales
1789	San Andrés	2,740 crates & bales
1791	San Andrés	2,026 packages
1794	**San Fernando Magallanes**	**2,561 bales & crates**
1796	San Andrés	2,414 crates & bales
1797	Magallanes	3,004 crates & bales
1798	San Andrés	-
1800	Magallanes	2,944 packages
1800	Santa Potenciana	698 bales
1800	San Rafael	975 bales
1801	El Montañes	1,277 bales
1801	Rey Carlos	2,555 bales
1802	Ntra. Sra. de Guía	1,651 packages
1804	Magallanes	3,376 crates & bales
1805	Arcángel	537 crates & bales
1807	Magallanes	3,103 bales
1809	San Fernando Magallanes	3,328 packages
1811	Rey Fernando	3,536 packages

Porcelain

120 bales with porcelain
51 bales with porcelain
61 bales with porcelain
16 bales with porcelain, 2 jars
78 bales with porcelain, 2 jars
35 bales with porcelain
1 bale with porcelain
10 bales with porcelain
2 jars
4 porcelain vases, Marqués de Ovando
-
243 crates of porcelain, 61 bales with porcelain, 2 jars
-
-
-
-
-
coffee service for viceroy Bucareli
one small green porcelain jar, one crate with porcelain
37 crates of porcelain
6 jars
-
-
48 dozen cups, 10 dozen plates, 18 crates (huacales)
41 crates (*huacales*) of porcelain
6 crates of porcelain, 3 jars
53 crates (*huacales*) of porcelain
-
-
service for viceroy, conde de Revillagigedo
43 crates (*huacales*) of porcelain
36 crates (*huacales*) of porcelain
14 crates of porcelain cups
-
-
5 crates of porcelain
-
one small crate with 26 little pieces of porcelain, tea service, box with porcelain toys
3 crates of porcelain
-
4,800 small cups, 3 tea services, 2 coffee services, 1,564 cups wth handle
-
-
-

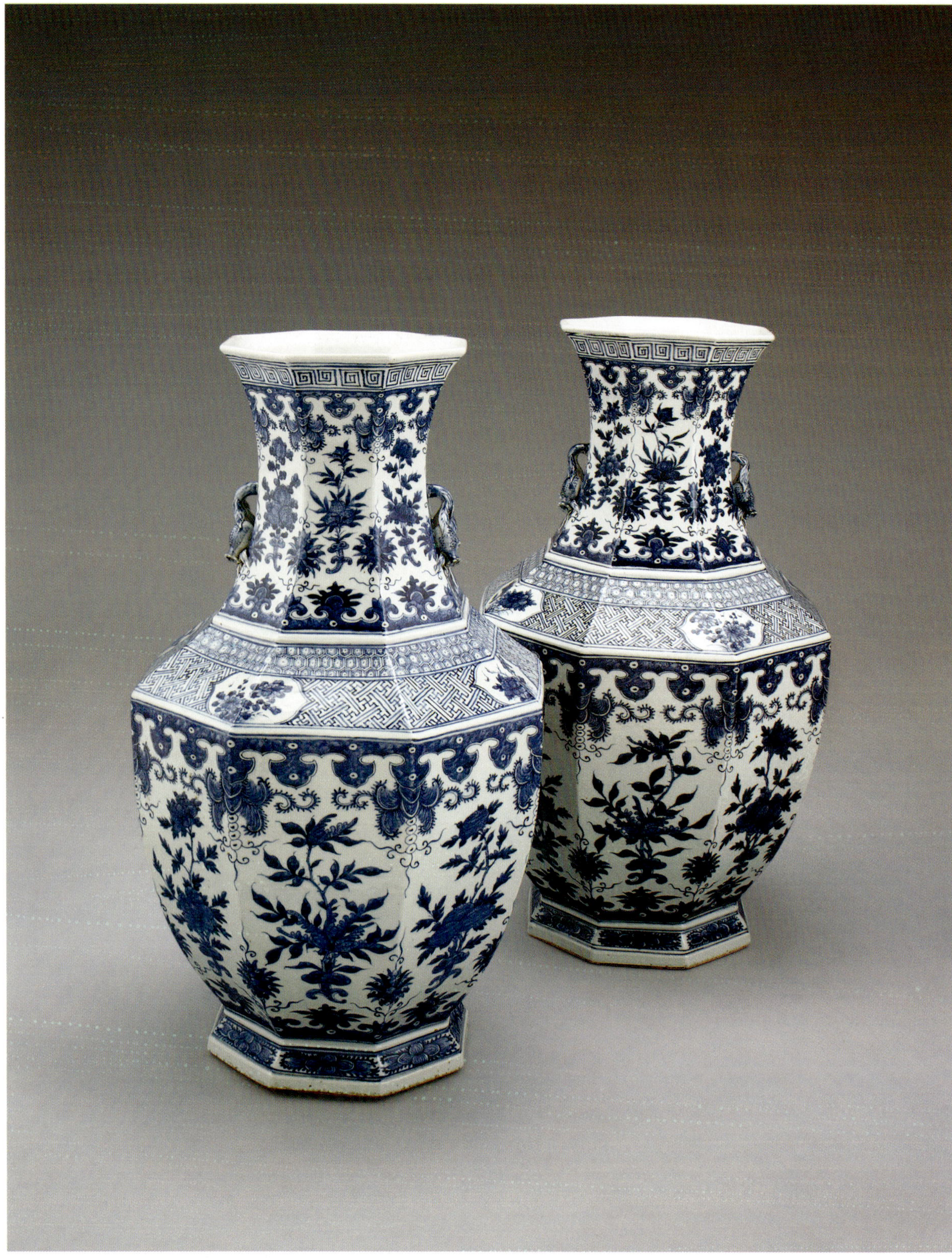

Fig. 6. Pair of octagonal vases. China, Qing dynasty, Qianlong period (1736–1795). Porcelain. 23.5 in. Denver Art Museum, Gift of May Wilfley in memory of her parents, A. R. Wilfley and Addie M. Wilfley; 1974.27.

that point evident, he charged the Manila merchants exorbitant fines.[15] During the eighteenth century, galleon cargo was occasionally spot-checked, meaning that a few pieces from the cargo were chosen at random to be opened and the contents verified against the *libro de sobordo*. This was, however, done rather hastily and superficially. As an example, for a cargo of almost two thousand pieces in 1779, only five packages were opened.[16]

It is virtually impossible to know how much or what type of porcelain arrived on any given galleon, and as a result, how much porcelain reached Mexican territory during the Spanish Colonial period. The sloppy manner in which administrative procedures were carried out at both ports makes it difficult to arrive at even an approximate figure. However, from the very general figures collected from the shipping manifests and the few mentions of porcelains which they contain, Chinese porcelain rarely accounted for more than 2 percent of any given shipment (Fig. 5).

This, of course, does not take into consideration what must have reached New Spain as contraband. The landing in San Blas of a courier to announce the galleon's arrival was a prime opportunity to unload contraband cargo. With the excuse of needing water, jugs filled with porcelain were lowered ashore and returned to the ship refilled with water. As has already been mentioned, ships left the Philippines already loaded with porcelain-filled water jugs.

Gifts could be sent from the Philippines to New Spain aboard the galleon "fuera de registro," meaning that they were not considered part of the registered cargo and as such did not pay taxes (but still had to pay the *alcabala* tax in Mexico City). This created a generous loophole for the merchants of Manila, who took great advantage of it. As a result, in 1774 Viceroy Antonio de Bucareli y Ursúa wrote to the governor of the Philippines stating that gifts were permitted, but insisting that they come registered in the *libro de sobordo* and within all the limits of the law.[17]

This is the more interesting as the viceroy himself had received a service, decorated with his coat of arms, as a gift from his nephew in Manila the year before.[18] Four years later, in 1778, Bucareli attempted to crack down on the clandestine importation of "gifts" by ordering that they pay double duty.[19] It appears to have been mostly large jars and vases (known as *tibores*) that were sent as gifts, as their size and shape made it difficult to disguise them as anything else (Fig. 6). These were also among the most expensive porcelain objects, making it attractive to send them as tax-free gifts, even though they would have been intended for sale. A great amount of merchandise surely arrived in Acapulco hidden under the label of gifts. On the *San Fernando Magallanes* in 1794, 10,007 pesos were sent in gifts, more than on any other ship between 1781 and 1801.[20]

Yet another example is that of don Juan Vicente de Güemes Pacheco de Padilla, known as the second count of Revillagigedo, viceroy of New Spain from 1789 to 1794. Just like Bucareli before him, he sent numerous letters to the officials in Acapulco, asking them to be especially vigilant in finding contraband and sanctioning merchants who attemped to import property without paying taxes.[21] What appeared on paper to be zealous adherence to the regulations resulted in the opposite at the end of his term, when the *San Fernando Magallanes* arrived in Acapulco with several pieces of unregistered merchandise. Included in these was an entire porcelain service composed of 1,242 pieces being sent by don Diego García Herreros to "His Excellency, Señor conde de Revillagigedo."[22]

From the moment the galleon arrived in New Spain, an extensive distribution network was put into place that ensured the wide dispersion of these exotic, beautifully painted, imported objects. Archeological sites as far north as present-day New Mexico and Arizona have revealed the extent to which Chinese porcelain was distributed in the New World. After the fair in Acapulco, the porcelain destined for the commercial market was transported to and resold at the *Parián* in Mexico City, in the southwestern corner of the plaza mayor, along the arcade known as the Portal de Mercaderes (p. 14, fig. 2). Named after its Philippine counterpart, it held within its walls a great variety of local, European, and Asian merchandise (Fig. 7).

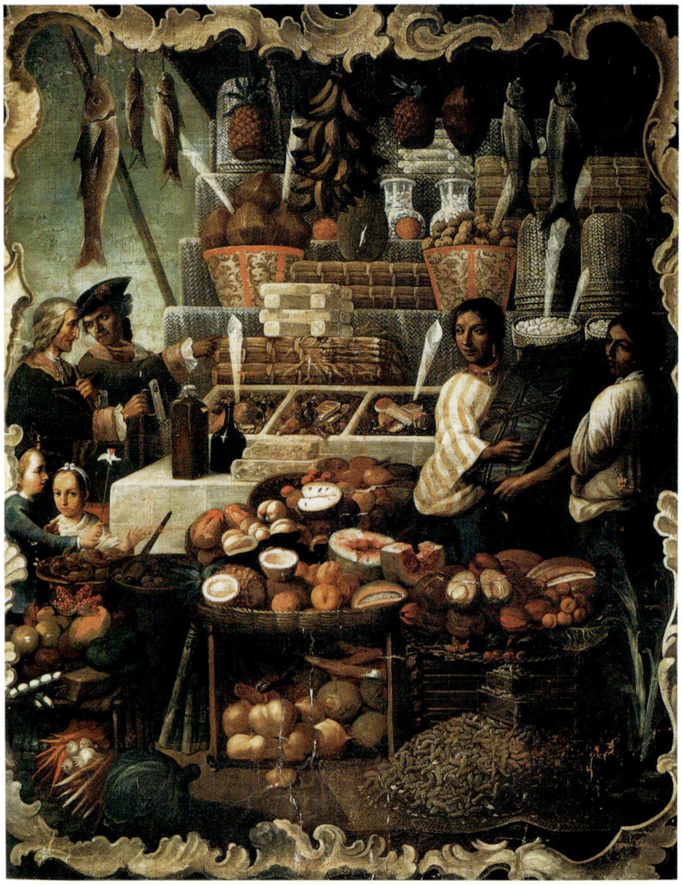

Fig. 7. Anonymous, *Parián Market Scene.* Mexico, c. 1775. Oil on canvas. Courtesy of Museo Nacional de Historia, Chapultepec Castle, Mexico City (IHAH).

As Chinese porcelain reached a wide geographical territory, so too did it grow to cover many social classes. Particularly during the second half of the seventeenth century, Chinese porcelain was predominantly an exotic, luxurious material that became highly fashionable among the affluent upper classes. Most, if not all, of the noble families of Europe had entire services of porcelain made to order with the family arms painted prominently on each piece. These services, which were only fractional parts of greater, lavish collections, were prominently displayed in the castles of Europe.

With the European and Spanish nobility setting the standard of taste for the American colonies, it is not surprising that similar Chinese armorial porcelain services would find their way into the homes of the colonial nobility. Services belonging to significant colonial individuals such as the conde de Gálvez, conde de la Cortina, conde de Santiago de Calimaya, and to the Ahedo and Ovando families all survive at least in some fraction today (Fig. 8).

Prices

The value of a Chinese porcelain plate in colonial Mexico was determined by a number of factors, each of which contributed to the final price paid by the end-user. Price varied extensively depending on where and when the object was purchased. At each stage of the process, from the original purchase in China, to its resale in Manila, through the transpacific voyage and arrival at the fair in Acapulco, until the final sale at the *Parián* or store in the colonial capital, a myriad of elements could seriously affect the final price, including technical problems at the kilns in Jingdezhen or in the sale and delivery schedule to Canton. For example, the floods of 1784 and ensuing drought and famine raised the price of rice in China, thereby causing wages to rise. This was reflected in an increase of 8–10 percent in the purchase price of porcelain at Canton.[23]

Pirates and shipwrecks that delayed or even cancelled the arrival of the galleon in Acapulco caused a scarcity of Chinese goods on the market, increasing the demand for them the following year. In the 1780s the Philippine merchants found themselves in tight straits owing to English incursions in the Pacific. Having survived the English siege of Manila in 1780 and having paid the Chinese merchants the inflated prices caused by the war, the officials of the *San José de Gracia* arrived in Acapulco in 1784 to learn that the war had ended. Naturally, with the end of the war came a drop in the market. Merchants in New Spain would not agree to the high prices that had been paid in Manila and were offering only about 50 percent of value.[24]

In the middle of the eighteenth century, the Marqués de Ovando, who was stationed in Manila as its governor, ordered two services and four vases from don Joseph Azevedo to be purchased at Canton.[25] Above the price of 220 pesos for one of the services and 65 pesos for each pair of *tibores*, Azevedo charged an extra 7½ percent commission, plus transportation charges, which were 42 pesos from Canton to Manila, 6½ percent for shipping, and an extra 8 pesos per vase for shipping.[26] Once in Acapulco, the Marquesa de Ovando (who had been widowed and also had a baby boy onboard the ship) hired don Antonio Balda to transport her husband's belongings to Puebla.[27] He charged 40 pesos per vase, with the condition that if one were to break, he would receive its mate and would indemnify the Marquesa at 400 pesos per vase. The inventory of the Marqués's belongings made a few months later lists six pairs of vases at 200 pesos each pair, which still amounts to over 300 percent above the original purchase price (Fig. 9).[28]

In sum, though the Chinese export porcelain that can be accounted for as having arrived in New Spain during the sixteenth, seventeenth, and eighteenth centuries represents a small fraction of the overall market for Asian goods, its impact was far greater. Starting with the Chinese merchant who sought the Spanish buyer for his wares, via the Manila galleon that carried the goods to New Spain, and the fair in Acapulco, the porcelain that arrived in New Spain stands as testimony to a shifting balance of power.

Fig. 8. Chinese export armorial porcelain in Mexico.

Individuals or families
- Cervantes family
- Selva Nevada family
- Viceroy don Antonio Bucareli y Ursúa
- Viceroy 2nd conde de Revillagigedo
- Ovando family
- Marqués de Ovando
- Ahedo family
- Viceroy don Matías de Gálvez y Gallardo
- Conde de la Cortina
- Conde de la Torre de Cosío
- Marqués de Prado Alegre
- Marqués del Jaral de Berrio
- don Isidro Antonio de Icaza y Capparossa
- Agreda family
- Oquendo family
- don José María Loreto de la Canal

Proclamation services or commissioned for public institutions
- Consulado de México
- The city of Puebla
- The city of México
- The city of Los Angeles
- The city of Valladolid
- Real Academia de San Carlos
- Carlos IV, commissioned by the Real Tribunal Novohispano

Fig. 9. El Marqués de Ovando's porcelain order (1755).

	Price in pesos
2 porcelain services	220 each
2 pairs of Chinese porcelain vases	
purchase price in Canton (per pair)	65
don Joseph Azevedo's commission (7½%)	4.88
tranportation Canton-Manila	42
transportation Manila-Acapulco (6½%)	4.23
extra shipping charge (8 pesos per vase)	16
subtotal	*132.11*
transportation Acapulco-Mexico City	80
Total for vases	212.11
Insurance value in Acapulco, February 1756	800
Fair market appraisal, November 1756	200

Notes

This article is taken from information already published by me in *Porcelana China de Exportación para el mercado novohispano: La colección del Museo Nacional del Virreinato* (Mexico City: Universidad Nacional Autónoma de México, Instituto de Investigaciones Estéticas, 2008).

[1] In the first years of the China trade, galleons sent from the West carried almost any Chinese porcelain that was available. Purchasers chose from the wares that were made available by the Chinese merchants, which were generally the popular blue-and-white wares of the Ming period, as well as celadon and *blanc-de-chine* pieces of the sixteenth century (see Fig. 1).

[2] The governor of the Philippines fell under the command of the Viceroyalty of New Spain.

[3] David S. Howard, *The Choice of the Private Trader: The Private Market in Chinese Export Porcelain Illustrated from the Hodroff Collection* (London: Zwemmer, 1994), 24.

[4] Catherine Lugar, "The History of the Manila Galleon Trade," in *Archeological Report: The Recovery of the Manila Galleon, Nuestra Señora de la Concepción*, edited by William Mathers (Sutton Pacific Sea Resources, 1990), 15.

[5] Archivo General de la Nación (AGN), Mexico, *Filipinas*, vol. 5, expediente 5, "Relación de la quema acontecida en el antiguo Parián de Sangleyes en que residieron los infieles hasta la total expulsión ejecutada en año pasado de 1755, en los extramuros de la ciudad de Manila, capital de las Islas Philipinas, la noche del día 17 de 1756," folios 220r–226r.

[6] AGN, Mexico, *Filipinas*, vol. 3, exp. 16, "Año de 1755. Testimonio de las diligencias de reconocimiento, hechas en la Alcayzería Parián de esta ciudad, en que se verifica la total.

[7] The iron anchor and bells were likely made in China and imported to Manila. See Bonta, *Porcelana China*, 36–39.

[8] William L. Schurz, *The Manila Galleon* (New York: E. P. Dutton, 1959), 78.

[9] For more details see Bonta, *Porcelana China*, 83–87.

[10] John Francis Gemelli Careri, *A Voyage Round the World*, in A. and J. Churchill, eds., *A Collection of Voyages and Travels*, 4 vols. (London: Awnsham and John Churchill, 1704), 479.

[11] The transpacific trade was vulnerable not only to inclement weather but also to constant piracy, especially from the English. For instance, between 1576 and 1602, at least eleven out of fifteen vessels sank at sea. See Bonta, *Porcelana China*, Appendix 1.

[12] The shipping manifests consulted for this study include mentions of *balsas* as well as *cajones* and *huacales*.

[13] Time and again regulations and decrees were issued insisting that the trade truthfully declare the quality of merchandise in each crate. An example is found in AGN, Mexico, *Filipinas*, vol. 3, exp. 18, "Año de 1755. Providencia gobernadora sobre que los mercaderes de uno y otro sexo procedan arreglar sus mercaderías y cargamentos por clases de fardos y distinción de géneros y lo de más que incluye," f. 317r. Of course the frequency with which these declarations were made reveals their absolute lack of enforcement.

[14] Schurz, *The Manila Galleon*, 188.

[15] Carmen Yuste López, *El comercio de la Nueva España con Filipinas, 1590–1785* (Mexico: Instituto Nacional de Antropología e Historia—Departamento de Investigaciones Históricas, 1984), 14.

[16] AGN, Mexico, *Filipinas*, vol. 25, exp. 1, *op. cit.*, f. 57v.

[17] AGN, Mexico, *Filipinas*, vol. 8, exp. 4, "1774, Índice de las cartas que comprenden la correspondencia de oficio del Excelentísimo Señor Virrey, gobernador y capitán general de esta Nueva España, con el Ilustrísimo Señor don Simón de Anda y Salazar, gobernador y capitán general de las Islas Filipinas…," f. 156v.

[18] AGN, Mexico, *Filipinas*, vol. 8, exp. 3, fs. 81r–82r. After the viceroy died in 1779, the coffee service was purchased at auction by the conde de San Bartolomé de Xala; it is today in one of the most imporant private collections of Chinese export porcelain in Mexico.

[19] Yuste López, *El comercio de la Nueva España*, 52; also see AGN, Mexico, *Filipinas*, vol. 13, exp. 10, fs. 228r–228v.

[20] AGN, Mexico, *Filipinas*, vol. 35, exp. 1, "Demostración de los cargamentos hechos por el comercio de Filipinas…," f. 49r.

[21] One such letter was written in 1791 from the viceroy to don José de Rozas in Acapulco. AGN, Mexico, *Filipinas*, vol. 31, exp. 3, f. 56r.

[22] AGN, Mexico, *Filipinas*, vol. 35, exp. 1, "Resultas de efectos que se hallaron sin avaluar ni cargar en el registro de la fragata de S.M. nombrada Fernando de Magallanes," f. 18r.

[23] C. J. A. Jörg, *Porcelain and the Dutch China Trade* (The Hague: Martinus Nijhoff, 1982), 117.

[24] AGN, Mexico, *Filipinas*, vol. 15, letter from don Gabriel Gutiérrez de Terán to the viceroy, fs. 140r–145r.

[25] AGN, Mexico, *Vínculos y Mayorazgos*, vol. 126, exp. 1, "Inventario de biens del Muy Ilustre Señor don Francisco Joseph de Ovando y Solís, Marqués de Ovando, Presidente, Gobernador y Capitán General que fue de las Islas Filipinas," f. 83r.

[26] *Ibid.*, fs. 57r–57v.

[27] *Ibid.*, f. 14r.

[28] AGN, Mexico, *Vínculos y Mayorazgos*, vol. 127, exp. 4, "Inventario de las propiedades de don Francisco Joseph de Ovando y Solís, Marqués de Ovando, de su casa en la ciudad de Puebla, hecha el 18 de noviembre de 1756," n/p.

Porcelains with the Arms of the Order of Saint Augustine

For New Spain? A Theory

William R. Sargent

The Peabody Essex Museum (PEM), Salem, Massachusetts, has the only published charger with a combination of patterns more often associated with a series of ten or twelve well known Chinese export jars, including one in the collection at the PEM.[1] In the center of the charger (Fig. 1) is the emblem of the Augustinians, while on the wide flaring rim is a structure, shown twice. A rich array of patterns and motifs covers the surface: scrolls, sacred fungus, chimes, flower blossoms, peaches, lotus, rabbits, birds, cranes, phoenix, boys on water buffaloes, people, and box forms surmounted by dragons. In contrast, the underside has two simple and quickly executed motifs of a bird on a branch, descending from the lip of the dish on opposite sides. The base is unglazed. Jars with the Augustinian motif have been dated from c. 1575 to 1620, but a sherd of a jar with a rim identical to that on the PEM jar (Fig. 2) was recovered from the 1638 wreck of the *Nuestra Señora de la Concepción*.[2] There are intriguing clues to consider these porcelains as possibly associated with Macau,

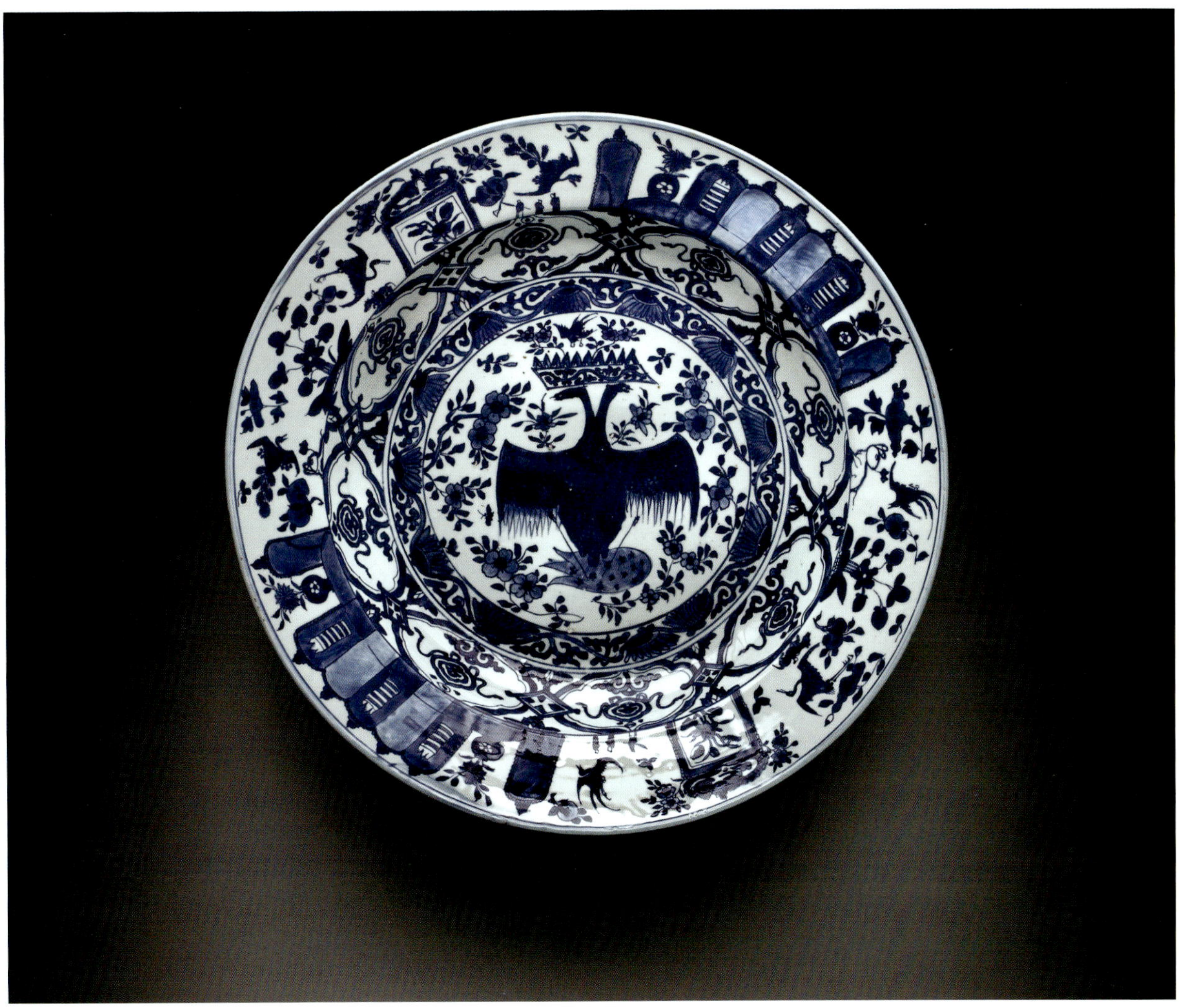

Fig. 1. Charger. Ming dynasty, Wanli period (1590–1635). 20 in. diam. Peabody Essex Museum, Salem, MA: Museum Purchase, and with funds donated by the AEA Visiting Committee in memory of Joseph Hinkle, 1998, AE85571.

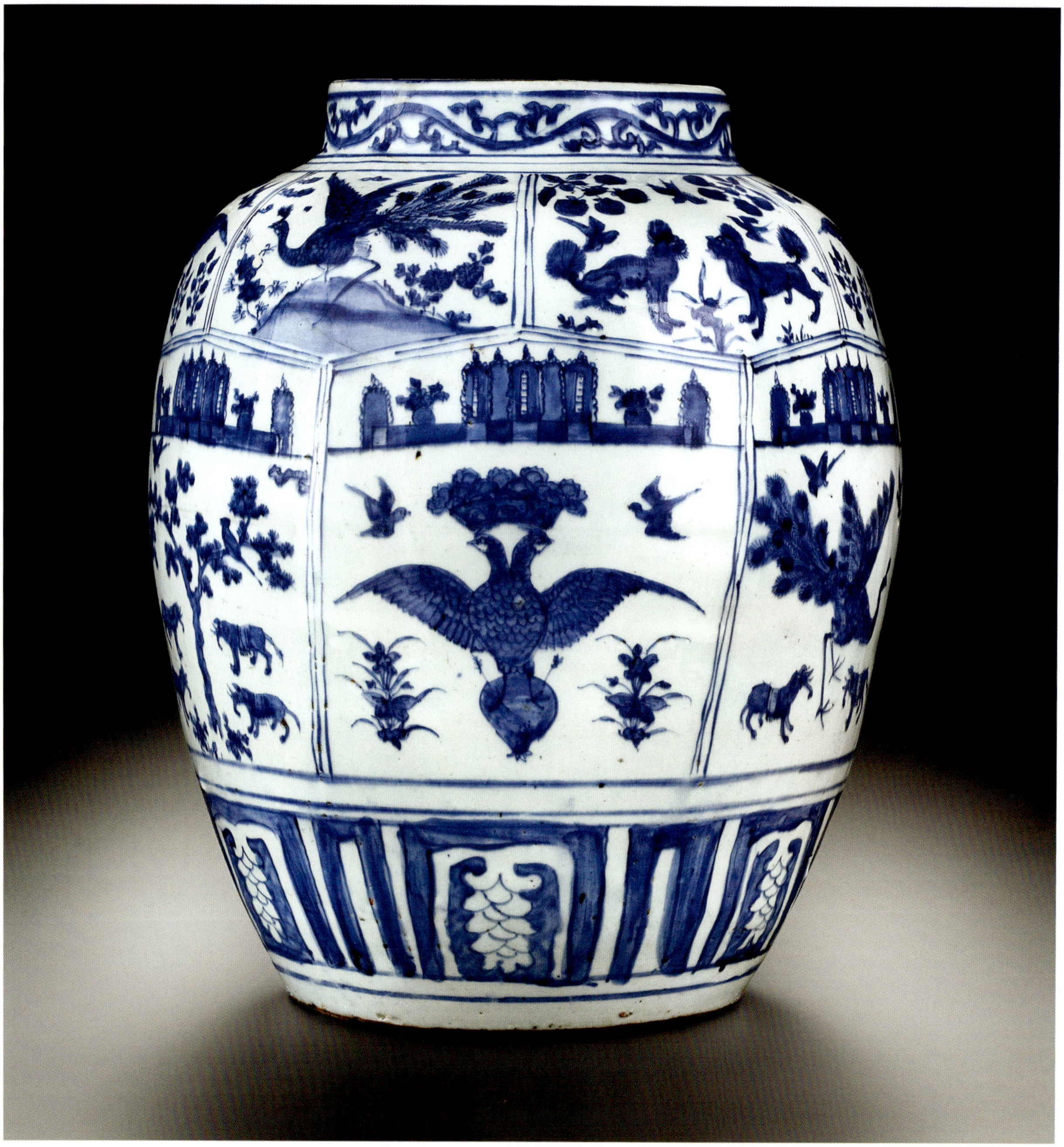

Fig. 2. Jar. Ming dynasty, Wanli period (1590–1635). 15½ in. h. x 13 in. diam. Peabody Essex Museum, Salem, MA: Museum Purchase, 1990, E83015.

and substantial arguments to be made for a Manila church, but there are also interesting cases—such as the one proposed here—for Mexico as the country for which the pieces were intended.

Philip II of Spain (reigned 1556–1598) granted the privilege to the Augustinians in the Philippines to use the heraldic device in the center of the charger as the emblem for their society. That device is the double-headed or bifacial eagle, surmounted by a coronet, and astride a heart pierced with arrows that symbolizes love and charity.[3] The motif has been associated with the Spanish market in the Philippines,[4] as it was previously with Macau[5] and Mexico.[6] The Augustinians had established monasteries in Mexico, the Philippines, Macau, and India, and it is unclear which monastery, or monasteries, ordered this charger and the associated jars and plates. There are no extant records to indicate the source of the order for these porcelains, and no sherds have been found *in situ* to indicate a specific destination.

Spanish Augustinians arrived in Macau on November 1, 1586, and established the Nossa Senhora da Graça monastery, but in 1589 the monastery was handed over to the Portuguese by order of King Philip II, who also ruled then as king of Portugal.[7] The frequently stated late Ming dating of these porcelains lent credence to the assumption that they were made to order for Macau, if it was not the founding date of the monastery that inspired the dating of the jars.[8] However, the evidence for that market and dating is far from conclusive.

The first Catholic missionaries in the Philippines were from Mexico and under the leadership of Augustinians, led by the conquistador Miguel López de Legazpi (1502–1572) and Andrés de Urdañeta (1508–1568), the navigator and Augustinian friar. They arrived on April 27, 1565, establishing the first Augustinian houses there that year, and founding the city of Manila on May 19, 1568. The Province of the Most Holy Name of Jesus of the Philippines of the Religious Order of St. Augustine was officially formed on March 7, 1575. Philip II granted the Augustinians the right to use the crowned double-headed eagle as an emblem after they purportedly rediscovered the Niño de Cebú, a Flemish carved wood figure of the Christ Child that had been given by Ferdinand Magellan (c. 1480–1521) to the wife of the chieftain of Cebú, Rajah Tupaz, after her conversion to Catholicism in 1521. The association of these porcelains with the Philippines rests on this connection.[9]

If these porcelains were made for Manila it might be logical to think they were either for the church at Cebú or for San Agustín in Manila, although they could have been for any Augustinian church. The church at Cebú was constructed soon after arrival of the Augustinians, but the existing basilica is the fifth constructed on that site and dates to about 1739. If these porcelains were made for that first church, then they would have had to survive the fires that destroyed it and two subsequent buildings. The convent and church of San Agustín (previously called San Pablo) was completed in 1607 and is the oldest still standing in the Philippines. In 1762, during the Seven Years' War, British troops under Admiral Samuel Cornish (c. 1715–1770) pillaged the church and monastery. After the Philippine Revolution of 1898, many of the Augustinians who had administered the more than 400 schools and other churches on the islands left for Mexico and other Latin American countries. If the porcelains were in Manila and survived fires, pillaging, earthquakes, and the revolution in 1898, could they have found their way to Latin America or Europe with the dispersal of friars?

Manila did become a great and important city, described by the Jesuit historian Padre Francisco Colín (1592–1660) as the new Venice, with a healthy trade route between China, Japan, Macau, Sulawesi, Saigon, and Siam, and through Portuguese traders in Goa, Cochin, Bengal, Nagapatam, Cananor, and Ormuz.[10] At the end of the sixteenth century Francesco Carletti (1574–1636?), a Florentine merchant who wrote of his travels to Mexico, Manila, and beyond, bought in Manila a "full set" of "white [porcelain] with blue decoration…by the intermediation of the fathers of

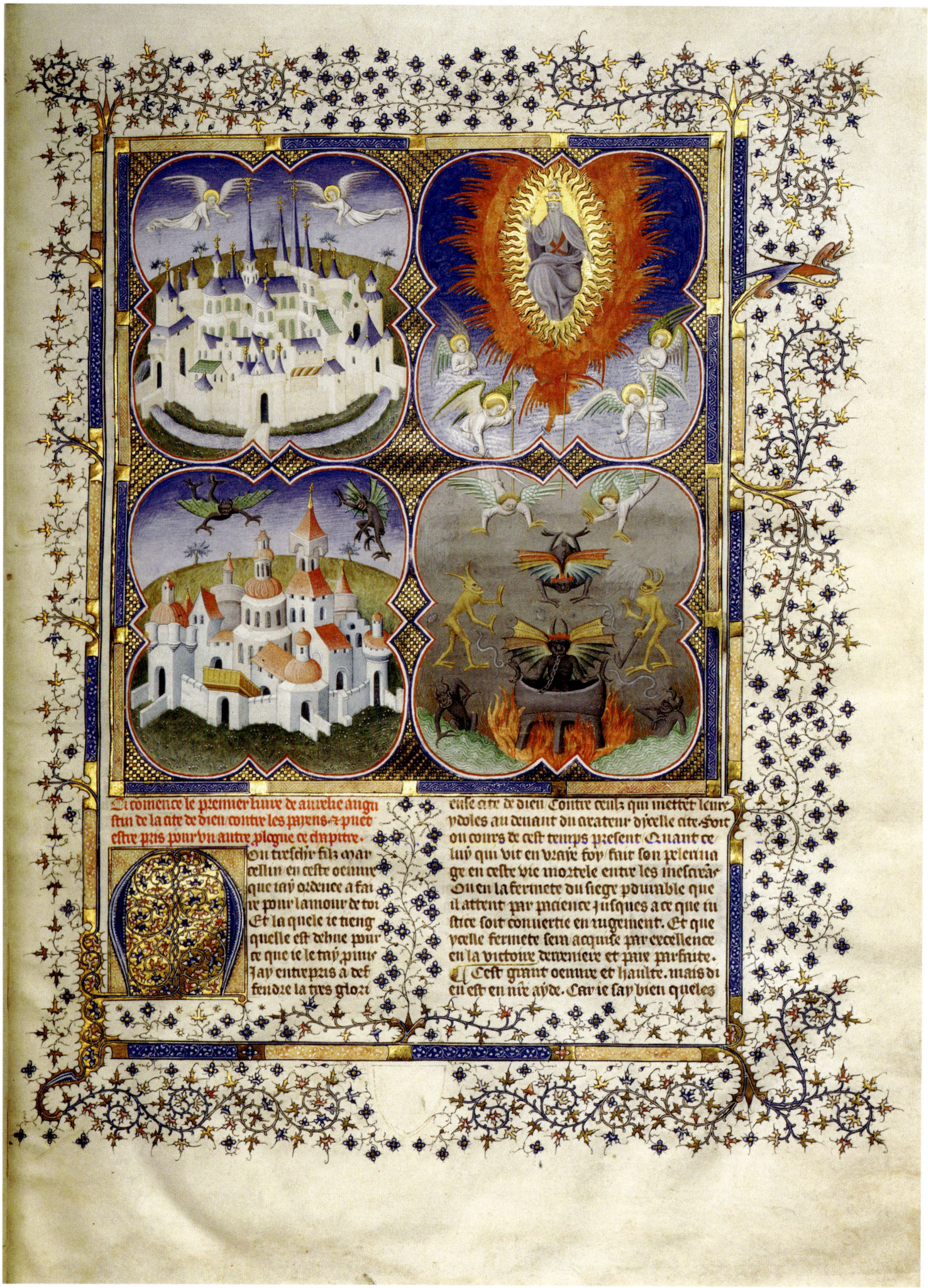

Fig. 3. Orosius Master and Assistants, *The City of God*. Paris, France, 1408–10. Vellum with gold leaf, ink, and paints. 17 1/8 x 12 3/8 in. Philadelphia Museum of Art: The Philip S. Collins Collection, gift of Mrs. Philip S. Collins in memory of her husband, 1945-65-1.

the *Compañia de Jesus*, who also intermediated to buy five jars."[11] He also recorded that the city of Manila was built as a fortress because of the many nearby enemies and that the Spaniards who lived there were comfortable and "with many conveniences." He reported that "added to the profit from the merchandise that they send to New Spain, they soon are made rich," and "from the merchandise brought there by the Chinese and then transported to Mexico they earn 150 and 200 percent."[12] Further, he noted the "porcelain, and very many other sorts of merchandise, from all of which they make very noble trade with the Spaniards, who buy it from them to take it to Mexico in New Spain."[13] He does not remark on any Asian goods kept in Manila for the use of the Spaniards living there (although that most certainly must have been the case), but he implied that most goods were reshipped for the benefit of trade.

The *Caja de Filipinas (Contaduría)*—the inventories of ships from 1565 to 1576 between Manila and Acapulco—list porcelain on a regular basis.[14] Otherwise the records of porcelains shipped to the Philippines for that market appear thin: of twenty ships entering and leaving Cavite, the main port, in 1657, not one listed porcelain as a cargo; instead, the cargoes were silver, gold, textiles, spices, metals, and wine.[15] There is the possibility that porcelains such as we are describing were private trade and would not have appeared in ships' official records. The trade route, from the Philippines to Acapulco, passing through Mexico City, then Puebla and sailing from Veracruz to Seville or Cádiz, is well known. So too is the plentiful evidence of the existence of Chinese export porcelain in New Spain and the Caribbean and its influence on local pottery production.[16] Less well understood is the history of collecting porcelain and other Chinese export arts in the Philippines.[17]

The heart is a prominent motif for the Augustinians, but the double-headed Habsburg eagle is a seldom-used adjunct.[18] The eagle did become synonymous with St. Augustine, who was called "the eagle of Hippo" (the town in North Africa, now Algeria, where he was bishop).[19] More often, each motif is found on its own. There is, in fact, no single emblem of the Augustinian order. There are multiple versions, including the heart, the heart with a book, the bishop's miter with a book, the heart with the crosier and shepherd's pastoral, a belt and bishop's miter with book, the bifacial eagle, the bifacial eagle over the heart, and the bifacial eagle with the heart in the center and the bishop's miter superimposed.[20] While the eagle and heart emblems are much discussed in the literature on these porcelains, little is said about the other major motif, the architectural structure included in alternate panels on the charger, jars, and associated plates.[21]

The architectural motif has been associated by some with the city of God,[22] as discussed by St. Augustine in *De Civitate Dei* (City of God), written between 413 and 427 A.D., in which he describes the character of two cities, that of God and that of man. In book 14, chapter 28, he describes the heavenly city created by the love of God. St. Augustine wanted to create a community on earth predicated upon principles of order, justice, and faith, and thus closely identified with the Church.[23]

The city of God and city of man were often depicted in manuscripts and prints, among which are those in a miniature from the Bohemian artist called the Orosius Master (active c. 1394–c. 1418) and his workshop (Fig. 3). The miniature, painted in Paris between 1408 and 1410, depicts the city of God filled with church spires and angels, and the city of man inhabited by flying demons and onion-domed structures. The same iconography was used for the 1701–1702 choir stalls of the former church of San Agustín, Mexico City, one back panel of which is carved with the city of man, over which seven angels are pouring out "the seven bowls of the wrath of God."[24] The city of God occasionally appears in Spanish Colonial paintings such as *The Mystical City of God* (Fig. 4) by Cristóbal de Villalpando (c. 1649–1714), the iconography for which was borrowed from the frontispiece of *La mística ciudad de Dios* (1620) by Sor María de Jesús de Agreda (1602–1665). In Villalpando's painting the city is represented as large and complex, with parallel streets surrounded

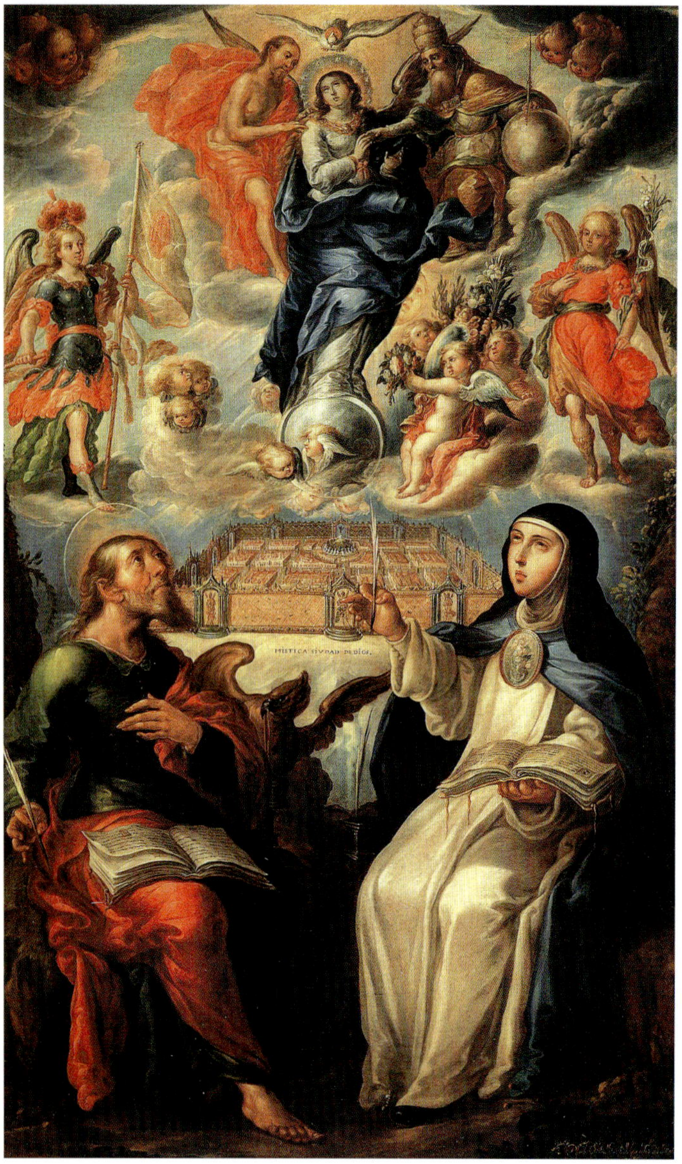

Fig. 4. Cristóbal de Villalpando, *The Mystical City of God*. Mexico, 1706. Oil on canvas. Museo de Guadalupe, Zacatecas, Mexico. From Juana Gutiérrez Haces, et al., *Cristóbal de Villalpando*. Mexico D.F.: Fomento Cultural Banamex, A.C., 1997.

by a high square wall with three niches on each side containing statues.[25]

But the understanding that the Church represented the City of God on earth, or that a fortified compound was "the perfect realization of the Church Militant,"[26] does not preclude the possibility that the structure depicted on the porcelains was meant to represent a specific church. The building motif on the porcelains discussed here does not follow the Renaissance approach to depicting the cities, which seems to have been the standard for over three centuries, nor does it follow the iconography of the formal walled city found in the painting. Instead it bears a striking resemblance to what could be an architectural elevation of the major form of colonial church architecture in New Spain: a church surrounded by a walled compound (*atrio*), at the corners of which are towers or chapels (*posas*), as depicted in an engraving from *Rhetorica Christiana* by Fray Diego de Valadés (Fig. 5). This layout and construction was common to Augustinians (who had arrived in Veracruz May 22, 1533), Franciscans, and Dominicans in Mexico. By 1562 there were fifty Augustinian priories in Mexico, including the sixteenth-century monasteries in Malinalco and Metztitlán, which today retain their walled *atrio* (Fig. 6).[27] The muddled depiction of the building on the porcelains might suggest a hand-drawn image of a church used as a source, rather than a print that would have been copied faithfully.

There are at least twenty-one Augustinian monasteries extant in Mexico,[28] and the heart motif is common on many of the church façades. At least one sixteenth-century monastery, in Cuitzeo, Michoacán, uses both the bifacial eagle and the heart.[29] Another sixteenth-century building, the Capilla Real de Indios, now the Palace of Justice, Tlaxcala, has a bas-relief stone armorial that includes the crowned double-headed eagle with the emblem of Aragón in the center.

If we look at the image on the porcelains as an elevation of a church compound, the central edifice could be a church with its *espadaña* (the pierced vertical wall-belfry of the façade) and merlons (a crenelation used more often for decorative

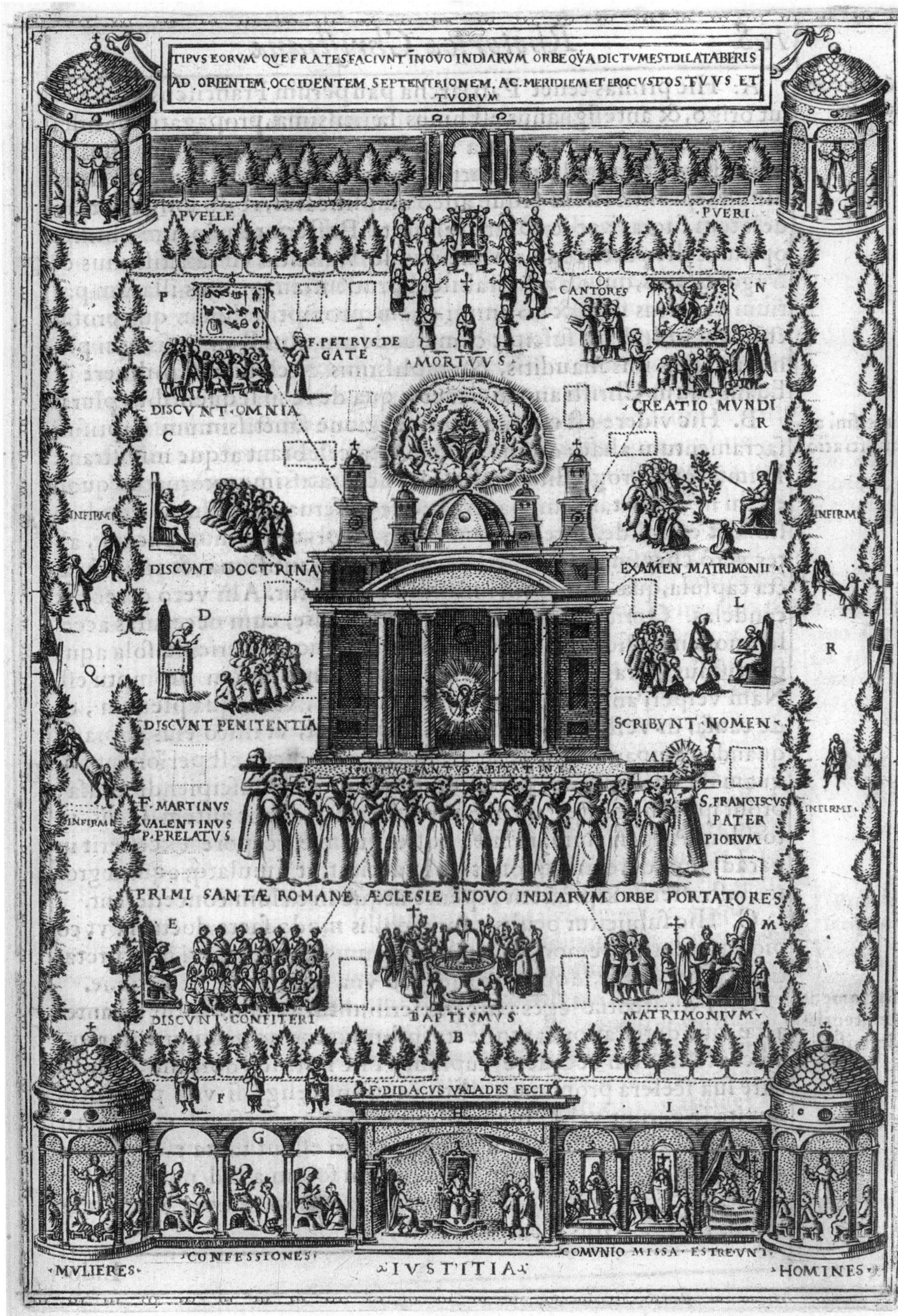

Fig. 5. Diagram of the *atrio* of the Mexican Church in the 16th century. Engraving from the *Rhetorica Christiana* by Fray Diego de Valadés (Perugia, 1579). Courtesy of the Benson Latin American Collection, General Libraries, University of Texas at Austin.

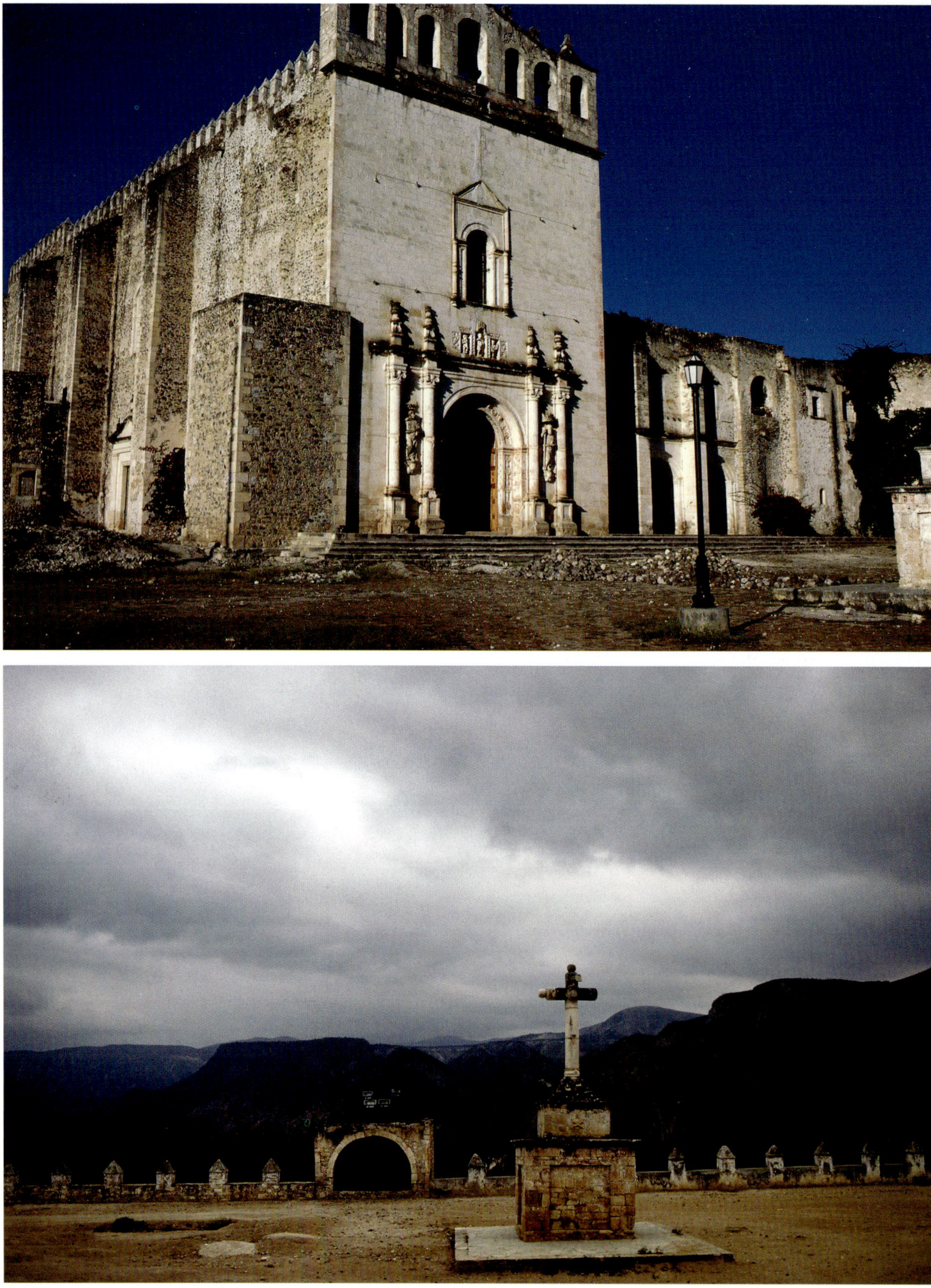

Fig. 6. Mission church and *convento* (top) and *atrio* (bottom). Metztitlán, Hidalgo, Mexico, circa 1560. Photos: D. Pierce.

purposes than for defensive ones) adorning the roofline. The merlons, in fact, were singled out as not only beautiful but giving "authority to the immense and massive" church and cloister of Cuitzeo, Michoacán.[30] Extending to either side would be the walls of the *atrio*, or patio, the walled churchyard, and at each end the roofs of two corner shelters (*posas*), or chapels. The four chapels were assigned separately to girls, boys, women, and men, according to the 1579 *Rhetorica Christiana*.[31] The *atrio* was a distinctive answer to the need in New Spain for a space to contain the crowds of local converts who could not fit into the churches themselves. The porcelains depict what appear to be jars of flowers on the top of the wall, but may be a decorator's misinterpretation of trees within the wall.

This type of church architecture was common in New Spain, regardless of the religious order, although the *espadaña* is most often associated with the Augustinians.[32] The *atrio* is known throughout the Spanish world, especially along the coast and open plains of Mexico, but does not seem to be used in the construction of Portuguese colonial churches.[33] The arrangements of contiguous parts of these complexes were unique to Mexico,[34] so if the structure is meant to depict a church surrounded by an *atrio*, that would be further evidence that the porcelain order did not come from Macau.

The shelters (*posas*) also echo the traditional fortifications found in almost all Spanish Colonial forts. Seacoast towns were fortified throughout the Spanish colonies, as they were by every other colonizing European power. Churches could and did serve as forts: it was suggested in 1536 that the cathedral in Puebla could double as a fortress, and when inhabitants of Oaxaca requested that a fortress be built, the viceroy told them all they had to do was close the door of the *atrio* of the church.[35] Octavio Paz notes that other than the seaports, "the only fortified aspect of most New World towns became the mission churches which had defendable walls and doors, and symbolized the idea that the Christian religion provided the ultimate protection."[36] But most of these walls were not constructed as true fortresses; they served more mundane purposes, such as ensuring privacy for the gardens of the monasteries, containing livestock, functioning as cemeteries, and constructing a formal space for religious processions and ceremonies.[37] A number of scholars have said that all religious compounds in Macau were walled, as was that of San Paulo,[38] but the walled forecourts found in Macau and other Spanish colonial sites outside Mexico do not follow what is a depiction of the ideal convento patio concept by Fray Diego de Valadés.

Churches constructed in sixteenth-century New Spain were described even at that time as "exceedingly sumptuous and ostentatious," and the Augustinians were the most predisposed to this extravagance;[39] they were the leaders in grandiose construction.[40] Their dedication to the decoration and enrichment of their churches and convents followed the sentiment expressed in Psalms 26:8: "Oh Lord, I love the habitation of thy house, and the place where thy glory dwells."

One monk wrote to Philip II from New Spain, "We have founded a large number of monasteries, which reflect our tastes and customs, our rule and manner of life. The churches are adorned with bells, statues, and retablos, and have [musical] instruments and organs in the choirs. The sacristies are filled with jewels, silver, and ornaments; they are clean and well cared for, offered and consecrated to the King of Heaven, to honor Him in divine worship."[41] Another letter to Philip II, by Dr. Anguis, complained about "the excesses that are here evident in the buildings that are too sumptuous."[42] Francesco Carletti wrote, "the City of Mexico is an earthly paradise, full of every good thing and of all sorts of delights. It enjoys everything that comes from Spain, from China, and from other provinces of those lands."[43] And of the churches in Mexico City he said, "Also, there are very beautiful churches and convents, in particular of the Augustinian monks."[44] It is not difficult to imagine the use of extraordinary porcelains in these surroundings.

The property of the Church in Mexico was secularized in 1834, after which many of the

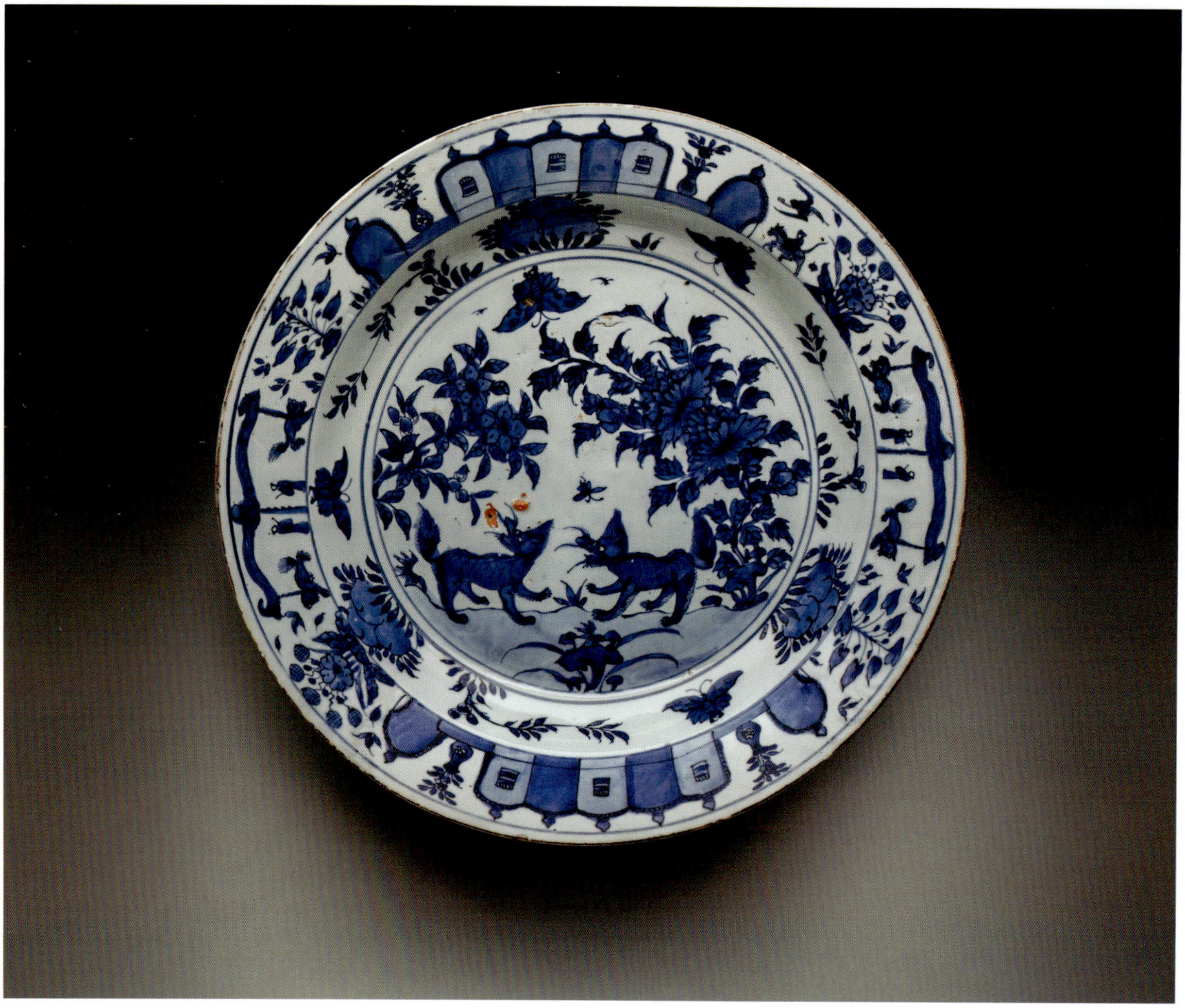

Fig. 7. Plate. Ming dynasty, Wanli period (1590–1635, or later). 14 ¾ in. diam. Peabody Essex Museum, Salem, MA: Museum purchase, 2006, AE86539.

churches were stripped of most of their treasures, possibly explaining the lack of documentation for the history of these porcelains in Mexico.[45] However, four jars with the Augustinian motif may have a Mexican provenance, while none of the others have a provenance that either substantiates or refutes any theory of a possible market.

The many works of Chinese and Mexican origin, in various media, decorated with variations of the different Augustinian motifs add to the complexity of identifying the original market for these porcelains. There are *tibors de tonalá* (a large Chinese-inspired earthenware jar from Tonalá, Jalisco, Mexico) dating to the seventeenth century, with the eagle over a heart and under an architectural arch flanked by rampant lions.[46] A tin-glazed earthenware *lebrillo* (basin) dating to 1680–1700, probably made in Puebla, Mexico, is decorated in the Chinese manner with the double-headed eagle,[47] while two more versions are in the Franz Mayer Museum, Mexico City. Other artifacts with Augustinian motifs include a Mexican silver missal stand made between 1700 and 1750 decorated with the double-headed eagle with a large heart-shaped reserve on its breast,[48] and a cope, late sixteenth or early seventeenth century, made of Chinese export silk brocade with a repeating pattern of the emblem with the heart misinterpreted as a jar.[49] Fragments of a Chinese porcelain cup, 1662–1722, decorated with a double-headed eagle and a partially remaining cross in Imari colors, were recovered from the Zócalo area, Mexico City.[50]

In Manila, the early Augustinian church was considered one of the most grandiose and sumptuous in the world.[51] There were numerous Augustinian churches in the Philippines; the most famous extant example is San Agustín, in the Intramuros district of Manila.[52] That church now holds a number of pieces decorated with the double-headed eagle, among which is an elaborately carved eighteenth-century wood bench, possibly of Asian manufacture, with two bifacial eagles in the deeply carved back panel.[53] Many more artifacts of Asian origin are published, such as a series of eighteenth-century liturgical silk capes with the double-headed eagle, but their histories are unclear.[54]

Another clue rests in the motifs found on a series of associated plates that have recently been on the market, one example of which is in the Peabody Essex Museum (Fig. 7). This plate lacks the Augustinian motif, but the border incorporates the same building as that on the jar and charger. The Buddha lions facing each other under flowering branches in the center are taken from details found on the jars but not on the charger. The same lion motifs are also found on a series of Peruvian textiles dated from the late seventeenth to the early eighteenth centuries.[55] The associated elements of design on the plate tie it to the Augustinian examples, but add to the complexity of the issue of history and provenance for this group of porcelains.

While many of the related motifs found depicted on Chinese and viceregal arts postdate the charger, jars, and associated plates, the continued use of the emblems associated with the Augustinians demands further research to confirm their histories. The number (ten to twelve), the variety in sizes and quality of the porcelain jars, and the inconsistencies of decoration between them suggest not one single order for a single client, but possibly multiple orders, perhaps made over a wider period than we assumed and for multiple markets and clients. Some of the jars may have been made on speculation after an initial order. Documentary evidence regarding early orders and their markets is really required before a definitive statement can be made about them. Until such documentary or archaeological evidence is uncovered, the histories of these intriguing pieces remain a mystery.[56]

Notes

1 Two unpublished chargers are known in private collections in Spain. Two jars are in a private collection in Mexico; one in a private collection in Portugal (see Mudge, *Chinese Export Porcelain*, 47); and one jar is in a private collection in California (see Kuwayama, *Chinese Ceramics*, 28–29).

2 Mathers, Parker, and Copus, *Archaeological Report*, 419, pl. 21a.

3 I thank Fr. Blas Sierra de la Calle for identifying the symbolism behind the heart.

4 Diez de Rivera, "The Spanish Market," 38–39.

5 Pinto de Matos, *Chinese Export Porcelain*, 125.

6 Kuwayama, *Chinese Ceramics*, 28–29; Mudge, *Chinese Export Porcelain*, 47, where the example cited is in a private collection

in Mexico and is discussed under the heading "Mexican Forms."

[7] Gutiérrez, *The Augustinians after the Counter-Reformation*, 226.

[8] Dias et al., *Reflections*, 68–69, nos. 7–8. Howard, *The Choice of the Private Trader*, 231, stated, "it is recorded that a number were at the Convent of the Order founded at Macao," but this has not been documented.

[9] Galende, *Angels in Stone*; Galende, *San Agustín: Noble Stone Shrine*; Galende and Jose, *San Agustín: Art & History*.

[10] Rodríguez, "Early Manila Galleon Trade," 37.

[11] Rodríguez, "Early Manila Galleon Trade," 45, citing Carletti, *Razonamientos de mi viaje*.

[12] Pierce and Otsuka, eds., *Asia & Spanish America*, 82.

[13] Ibid., 89.

[14] Rodríguez, "Early Manila Galleon Trade," citing Archivo General de Indias, Sevilla, *Caja de Filipinas*, 943–956.

[15] Rodríguez, "Early Manila Galleon Trade," 41.

[16] Rodríguez, "Early Manila Galleon Trade," 36–58.

[17] In December 2007 Laura Levesque met with the author to discuss her Ph.D. dissertation on this subject for Hong Kong University.

[18] Correspondence from Fr. Blas Sierra de la Calle, Museo-Oriental, Valladolid, Spain, March 16, 2008.

[19] For a description of symbols of the order of St. Augustine, see Dr. Miguel Metelo de Seixas, "Ecclesiastical Heraldry on Chinese Porcelain Imported by the Portuguese," in Santos, *Portugal in Porcelain from China*, 453–457.

[20] Fr. Blas Sierra de la Calle, O.S.A., "Sedas de Oriente para Dios," 111–112. I thank Fr. Blas Sierra de la Calle for sharing this article with me (the translation is this author's). Also, Christie's London, November 6, 2007, lot 245, where Antonio Diez de Rivera is said to have confirmed, through the head priest of the Augustinian monastery in Manila and Fr. Blas Sierra de la Calle, that the order used several versions of the emblems including the eagle without the heart.

[21] Pinto de Matos, *Azul e Branco da China*, 68, describes this building as "architectural ruins."

[22] Fr. Blas Sierra suggested that it represents "the City of God," and with the other motifs together creates three united decorative elements; correspondence with the author, March 16, 2008.

[23] Saint Augustine, *The City of God*, 594; see also translation by Marcus Dods, New York, 1950, 477.

[24] The stalls were carved by Salvador de Ocampo and workshop, and are now in the Hall of the "Generalito," Escuela Nacional Preparatoria, Dirección General del Patrimonio, Universidad Nacional Autónoma de México, Mexico City; see Metropolitan Museum of Art, *Mexico: Splendors of Thirty Centuries*, 327–331.

[25] Museo Regional de Guadalupe, in Bargellini and Komanecky, *The Arts of the Missions*, 274–275.

[26] Lara, *City, Temple, Stage*, 39, and 45, where it is explained that Augustine used architectural terms such as "house" or "temple" to describe what he meant by "city," as he wrote, "The House for the Lord, the City of God, is the Holy Church that is being built all over the earth."

[27] Peterson, *The Paradise Garden Murals of Malinalco*.

[28] There are two Augustinian provinces in Mexico. *Provincia Michoacanensis* (Mexico) has ten convents, sixteen vicariates or parishes, and one chaplaincy; *Provincia Mexicana SS. Nominis Jesu* (Mexico) has six convents and seven vicariates. See "Hermits of St. Augustine," *Original Catholic Encyclopedia* (1914), 281.

[29] Weismann, *Art and Time in Mexico*, 30, no. 22.

[30] Escobar, *Americana Tebaida*, 358.

[31] Fray Diego de Valadés, *Rhetorica Christiana*, Perugia, 1579. I thank Matthew DelGrosso for sharing the information on this source.

[32] Mullen, *Architecture and Its Sculpture*, 44.

[33] Luís António Durão suggested that there are examples of churches inside forts associated with Portugal, including a very large church called S. João Baptista in the fortress with the same name in Angra do Heroismo, Terceira Island, Azores. The fortress was built during the sixty years of domination by the Philips (1582–1640), although the church itself was built after 1640. E-mail correspondence with the author, September 7, 2002.

[34] Edgerton, *The Spiritual Conquest of Mexico*, 5.

[35] Weismann, *Art and Time in Mexico*, 76–77; Ricard, *The Spiritual Conquest of Mexico*, 164.

[36] Metropolitan Museum of Art, *Mexico: Splendors of Thirty Centuries*, 247.

[37] Weismann, *Art and Time in Mexico*, 76–77.

[38] Pinheiro, Yagi, and Koreaga, "The Role of Iberian Institutions," 292.

[39] Edgerton, *The Spiritual Conquest of Mexico*, 23; Mullen, *Architecture and Its Sculpture*, 44; and Peterson, *The Paradise Garden Murals of Malinalco*, 17, where it is stated that the missionaries were not required to take the vow of poverty, a claim disputed by Fr. Blas Sierra de la Calle in e-mail correspondence with this author.

[40] Metropolitan Museum of Art, *Mexico: Splendors of Thirty Centuries*, 327.

[41] Ricard 1982, 169.

[42] Peterson, *The Paradise Garden Murals of Malinalco*, 17.

[43] Ibid., 66.

[44] Francesco Carletti, *My Voyages around the World*, 58.

[45] One jar is in the Royal Collection, Windsor Castle, and was inventoried in 1866. I have been unable to confirm how or when it came into the collection.

[46] Offered by Christie's, New York, November 18, 2007, lots 61 and 61A. Two other Tonalá examples with the bifacial eagle, but without the heart motif are in the collection of the Museo de America in Madrid. A later example with a double-headed eagle over a heart can be found in the Museum of International Folk Art, Santa Fe.

[47] Barber, *The Emily Johnston de Forest Collection*, 21, no. 61, acc. no. 11.87.35; and Metropolitan Museum of Art, *Mexico: Splendors of Thirty Centuries*, 464–466.

[48] Rivero Borrell et al., *The Grandeur of Viceregal Mexico*, 222–223; the missal stand, silver, c. 1700–1750, 268–269. A similar motif is found in stone in the entrance hall of the Senate Building in Macao, and has been published by Teresa Canepa in "The Portuguese and Spanish Trade in Kraak Porcelain," Fig. 10. The double-headed eagle seems to have a bishop's miter rather than a crown and holds in its claws the sun and the moon; the heart is held on a chalice with a shield on the eagle's breast.

[49] Royal Ontario Museum, Toronto, Canada, cat. no. 973.422; also an example in the Metropolitan Museum of Art, Rogers Fund, 1912, in Dorothy G. Shepherd, "Iran between East and West," in T. Bowie, ed., *East and West in Art*, Bloomington-London: Indiana University Press, 1966, 84–105.

[50] Rodríguez and Yajima, "The Pacific Route of Ceramic Trade," 7.
[51] Gaspar de San Agustín, O.S.A., *Conquistas de las Islas Filipinas 1565–1615*, first printed in the seventeenth century, and reprinted by C.S.I.C., Madrid, 1975, 107; I thank Antonio Diez de Rivera for sharing this, and for many additional thoughts on my theory.
[52] Galende, *Angels in Stone*.
[53] Galende, *San Agustín: Noble Stone Shrine*, 116; Galende and Regalado Trota, *San Agustín: Art & History*, 61. I thank Fr. Blas Sierra de la Calle, Director of the Museo Oriental, for sharing this information.
[54] See Sierra de la Calle, "Sedas de Oriente para Dios," 140–141, noted as Filipino manufacture but possibly Chinese, and again in Blas Sierra de la Calle, *Museo Oriental China, Japón, Filipinos: Obras Selectas* (Valladolid, 2004), 506–507, with the same notation for a nearly identical example, p. 509, as well as another example identified as Filipino, but possibly European.
[55] Museum of Fine Arts, Boston, 11.1264, and Textile Museum, Washington, DC, 91.504.
[56] I particularly want to thank Antonio Diez de Rivera, Madrid, who has shared his conviction that these porcelains were made for the church in Manila, for his exchange of thoughts on my theory and for sharing correspondence he has had on this subject with Fr. Blas Sierra de la Calle, Valladolid, and to thank Fr. Blas Sierra for corresponding directly with me on this subject as well.

Bibliography

Augustine, Saint, *The City of God*. Edited by Betty Radice and translated by Henry Bettenson. London: Penguin Books, 2003.

Baird, Joseph Armstrong Jr. *The Churches of Mexico 1530–1810*. Berkeley: University of California, 1962.

Barber, Edwin Atlee. *The Emily Johnston de Forest Collection of Mexican Maiolica: The Metropolitan Museum of Art*. New York: Metropolitan Museum of Art, 1922.

Bargellini, Clara, and Michael K. Komanecky. *The Arts of the Missions of Northern New Spain 1600–1821*. Mexico City: Antiguo Colegio de San Ildefonso, 2009.

Canepa, Teresa. "The Portuguese and Spanish Trade in Kraak Porcelain in the Late 16th and Early 17th Centuries." *Transactions of the Oriental Ceramics Society* (London) 73 (2008–2009): 61–78.

Carletti, Francesco. *My Voyages around the World*. Translated by Herbert Weinstock. New York: Pantheon Books, 1964.

Carletti, Francesco. *Mi viaje alrededor del mundo (1594–1606)*. Barcelona: Noray, 2006.

Dias, Pedro, et al. *Reflections: Symbols and Images of Christianity on Chinese Porcelain*. Lisbon, 1997.

Diez de Rivera, Antonio. "The Spanish Market." *Oriental Art* 45, no. 1 (1999).

Edgerton, Samuel Y. *Theaters of Conversion: Religious Architecture and Indian Artisans in Colonial Mexico*. Albuquerque: University of New Mexico Press, 2001.

Escobar, Matías. *Americana Tebaida*. 2d ed. Morelia, Mexico: Balsal Editores, 1970.

Galende, Pedro G. *Angels in Stone: Architecture of Augustinian Churches in the Philippines*. Manila: G.A. Formoso Pubs., 1987.

Galende, Pedro G. *San Agustín: Noble Stone Shrine*. Manila: G.A. Formoso Pubs., 1989.

Galende, Pedro G., and José Regalado Trota. *San Agustín: Art & History 1571–2000*. Manila: San Agustín Museum, 2000.

Gutiérrez, D. *The Augustinians after the Counter-Reformation*. Villanova, 1983.

Howard, David Sanctuary. *The Choice of the Private Trader: The Private Market in Chinese Export Porcelain Illustrated from the Hodroff Collection*. Minneapolis: Zwemmer, 1994.

Kubler, George. *Mexican Architecture of the Sixteenth Century*. New Haven, CT: Yale University Press, 1948.

Kuwayama, George. *Chinese Ceramics in Colonial Mexico*. Los Angeles: Los Angeles County Museum of Art, 1997.

Lara, Jaime. *City, Temple, Stage: Eschatological Architecture and Liturgical Theatrics in New Spain*. Notre Dame, IN: Notre Dame University Press, 2004.

Mathers, William M., Henry S. Parker II, and Kathleen A. Copus. *Archaeological Report, The Recovery of the Manila Galleon Nuestra Señora de la Concepción*. Sutton, VT, 1990.

McAndrew, John. *The Open-Air Churches of Sixteenth-Century Mexico: Atrios, Posas, Open Chapels and Other Studies*. Cambridge, MA: Harvard University Press, 1965.

Mudge, Jean McClure. *Chinese Export Porcelain in North America*. New York: Clarkson N. Potter, 1986.

Mullen, Robert J. *Architecture and Its Sculpture in Viceregal Mexico*. Austin: University of Texas Press, 1977.

Metropolitan Museum of Art. *Mexico: Splendors of Thirty Centuries*, exh. cat. New York: Metropolitan Museum of Art and Bulfinch, 1990.

Peterson, Jeanette Favrot. *The Paradise Garden Murals of Malinalco: Utopia and Empire in Sixteenth-Century Mexico*. Austin: University of Texas Press, 1993.

Pierce, Donna, and Ronald Otsuka. *Asia & Spanish America: Trans-Pacific Artistic & Cultural Exchange, 1500–1850: Papers from the 2006 Mayer Center Symposium*. Denver: Denver Art Museum, 2009.

Pinheiro, Francisco Vizeu, Kogi Yagi, and Miki Koreaga. "The Role of Iberian Institutions in the Evolution of Macao." *Journal of Asian Architecture and Building Engineering* 4 (November 2005): 285–292.

Pinto de Matos, Maria Antónia. *Chinese Export Porcelain from the Museum of Anastácio Gonçalves, Lisbon*. Lisbon: Philip Wilson Pubs., 1996.

Pinto de Matos, Maria Antónia. *Azul e Branco da China: Porcelana ao tempo dos descobrimentos, Colecçao Amaral Cabral*. Lisbon: Instituto Português de Museus, 1997.

Ricard, Robert. *The Spiritual Conquest of Mexico: An Essay on the Apostolate and the Evangelizing Methods of the Mendicant Orders in New Spain, 1523–1572*. Los Angeles: University of California Press, 1966.

Rivero Borrell M., Héctor, et al. *The Grandeur of Viceregal Mexico: Treasures from the Museo Franz Mayer*. Houston: Museum of Fine Arts, Houston and Museo Franz Mayer, Mexico City, 2002.

Rodriguez, Etsuko Miyata, and Ritsuko Yajima. "The Pacific Route of Ceramic Trade: The Commercial Flow of Oriental Ceramics between Asia and Latin America."

The Oriental Ceramic Society of the Philippines (June 2007): 5–8.

Rodriguez, Etsuko Miyata. "Early Manila Galleon Trade: Merchants' Network and Market in 16th- and 17th-Century Mexico." In *Asia & Spanish America: Trans-Pacific Artistic & Cultural Exchange, 1500–1850*, edited by Donna Pierce and Ronald Otsuka. Denver: Denver Art Museum, 2009.

Santos, Alberto, ed. *Portugal in Porcelain from China: 500 Years of Trade.* Vol. 2. Lisbon, 2008.

Shepherd, Dorothy G. "Iran between East and West." In *East-West in Art: Patterns of Cultural and Aesthetic Relationships*, edited by Theodore Bowie. Bloomington: Indiana University Press, 1966, 84–105.

Sierra de la Calle, Fr. Blas. *Museo Oriental Arte: Chino y Filipino.* Valladolid: Publicaciones del Museo Oriental, 1990.

Sierra de la Calle, Fr. Blas, O.S.A. "Sedas de Oriente para Dios. Ornamentos Liturgicos del Real Colegio de PP. Agustinos. Valladolid." *X Jornadas del Patrimonio Cultural de los religiosos españoles*, Madrid, 2002.

Valadés, Fray Diego de. *Rhetorica Christiana.* Perugia, 1579.

Weismann, Elizabeth Wilder. *Art and Time in Mexico from the Conquest to the Revolution.* New York: Harper and Row, 1985.

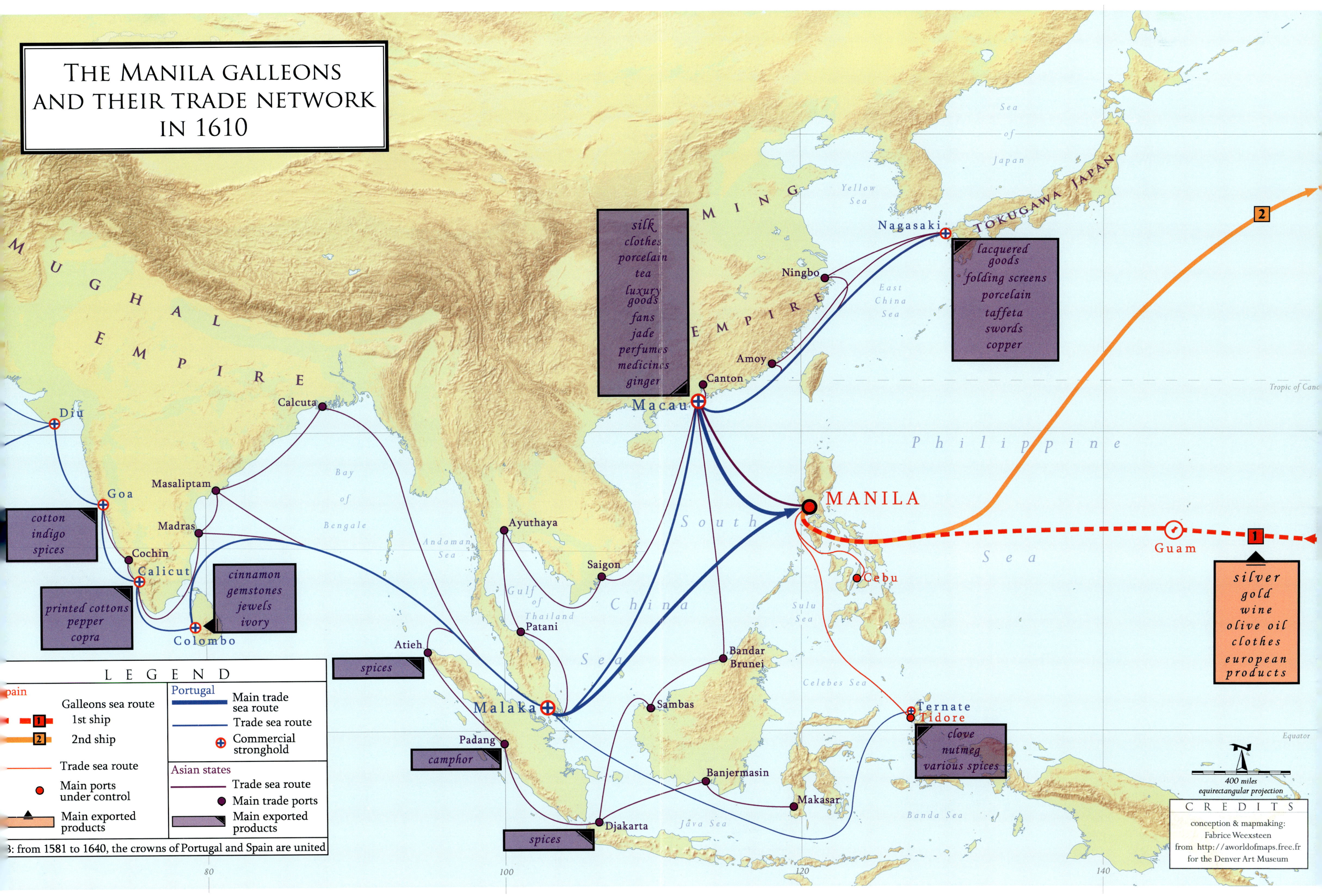
THE MANILA GALLEONS AND THEIR TRADE NETWORK IN 1610
MUGHAL EMPIRE
MING EMPIRE
TOKUGAWA JAPAN
Sea of Japan
Yellow Sea
East China Sea
Philippine Sea
South China Sea
Bay of Bengale
Andaman Sea
Gulf of Thailand
Sulu Sea
Celebes Sea
Java Sea
Banda Sea
Tropic of Cancer
Equator
Nagasaki
Ningbo
Amoy
Canton
Macau
MANILA
Cebu
Guam
Ternate
Tidore
Diu
Goa
Cochin
Calicut
Colombo
Madras
Masaliptam
Calcuta
Ayuthaya
Saigon
Patani
Atieh
Malaka
Padang
Djakarta
Sambas
Bandar Brunei
Banjermasin
Makasar
silk clothes porcelain tea luxury goods fans jade perfumes medicines ginger
lacquered goods folding screens porcelain taffeta swords copper
cotton indigo spices
printed cottons pepper copra
cinnamon gemstones jewels ivory
spices
camphor
spices
clove nutmeg various spices
silver gold wine olive oil clothes european products
1
2
LEGEND
Spain
Galleons sea route
1st ship
2nd ship
Trade sea route
Main ports under control
Main exported products
Portugal
Main trade sea route
Trade sea route
Commercial stronghold
Asian states
Trade sea route
Main trade ports
Main exported products
NB: from 1581 to 1640, the crowns of Portugal and Spain are united
80
100
120
140
400 miles
equirectangular projection
CREDITS
conception & mapmaking:
Fabrice Weexsteen
from http://aworldofmaps.free.fr
for the Denver Art Museum

Overleaf:

The Manila Galleons and their Trade Network in 1610

Fabrice Weexsteen for the Denver Art Museum

References

Chaunu, Pierre. "Le Galion de Manille" in *Annales. Economie, Sociétés, Civilisations*. Paris: 1951, V. 6, N. 4, 447-462, 1951.

Hoberman, Louisa S. and Susan M. Socolow, eds. *The Countryside in Colonial Latin America*. Albuquerque: University of New Mexico Press, 1996.

Spate, Oskar Hermann Khristian. *The Pacific since Magellan, volume 1, The Spanish lake*. Canberra: Australian National University Press, 2004. (1st edition: 1979).

From Spain to the Viceroyalty of Peru
Paintings by the Dozen

Suzanne Stratton-Pruitt

The fortified harbor of Portobelo, on the Caribbean coast of Panama, was the point of convergence for two trade routes, one from Lima carrying huge quantities of gold and silver, and the other from Spain. Between 1560 and 1650 the ships from Spain set out from Seville (Fig. 1), but after the silting up of the Guadalquivir River in the mid-seventeenth century the actual port of embarkation for the Americas was moved to Cádiz. When the galleons arrived in Portobelo the town bustled with trade fairs that could last ten or twelve days even in difficult times, and up to forty days.[1] Goods for the South American market were transported from Portobelo across the isthmus of Panama by mule or riverboat, and then trans-shipped to the port of Callao near Lima. There merchandise was loaded onto mules and sent over the long routes to Potosí, Chile, Tucumán, and the Río de la Plata area. Among these goods were many paintings and innumerable engravings.[2]

The requirements of this trade—salability on the colonial market and portability—influenced subject matter and style in ways that subsequently carried over into art created in Spanish South America. In particular, the trade reinforced a tendency to work in series: not only matched sets of angels, saints, martyrs, patriarchs, and apostles, but also sibyls, heroes of antiquity or of popular literature, and stories told in twelve episodes.

There is documentary evidence of a number of artists in seventeenth-century Seville whose business apparently depended entirely on shipping

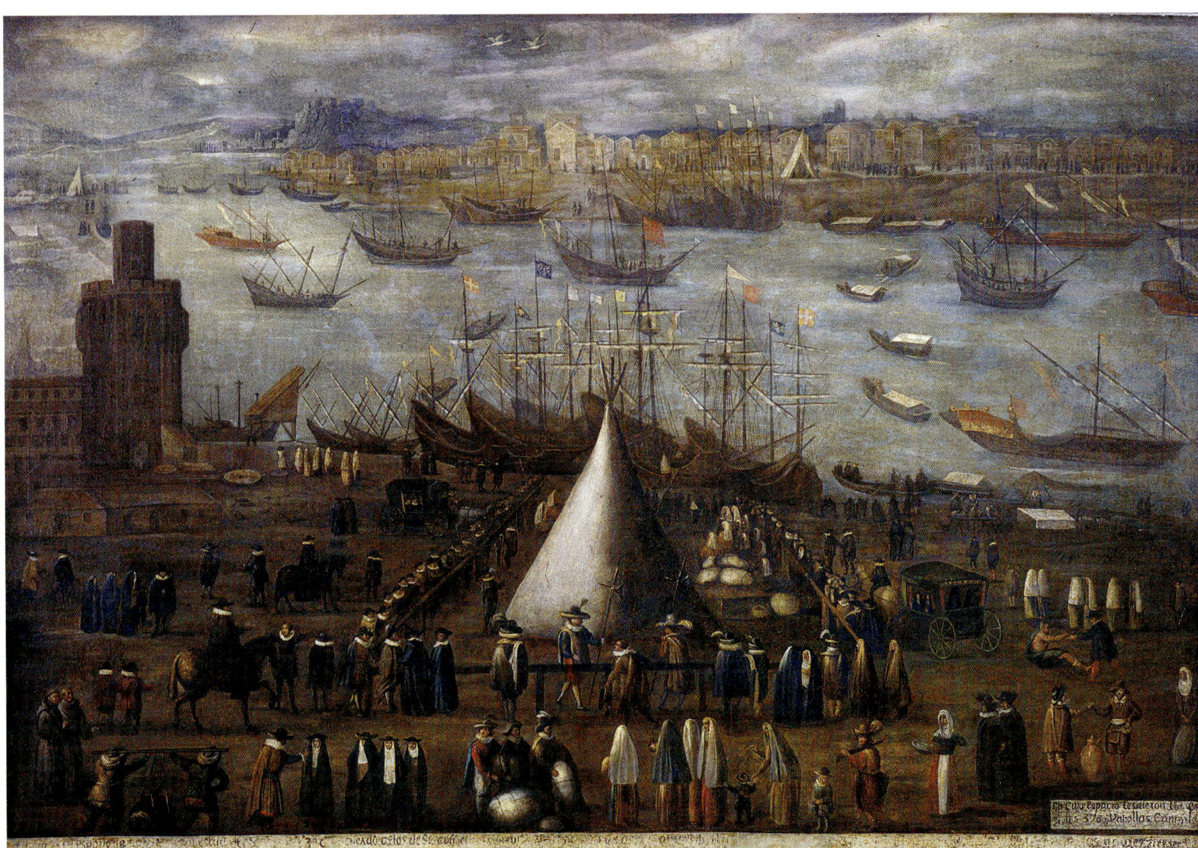

Fig. 1. *The Arenal at Seville*. Spain, circa 1600–1620. Oil on canvas. 143.7 x 100.4 cm. Courtesy of The Hispanic Society of America, New York.

paintings to the New World.[3] Miguel Guëlles was one of them, but there were also Juan de Luzón, Juan Fajardo, and Juan López de Carrasco, who are known to us only by name. At least one artist who had come from Spain to work in the Viceroyalty of Peru was also engaged in the art trade to some extent. A document of February 17, 1595, records that the Spanish/Italian painter Mateo Pérez de Alesio owed Francisco López for the purchase of fifty *retablos* with figures and persons that he brought from Spain (*cinquenta retablos de figuras y personas que truxo de España*).[4]

It was a risky business. The cargo carried by the fleets was vulnerable to storms and pirates, as well as human error. In 1640, Francisco de Zurbarán sued captain Diego de Mirafuentes for payment for some canvases that the artist had consigned to be sold at Portobelo. The paintings arrived in such deteriorated condition that the artist could never have earned the promised three times their worth in Seville. One of Zurbarán's assistants testified that he had heard from many witnesses that the ship's captain had used the paintings to decorate the ship for a party, probably causing the damage (*y esa causa le pudo suceder el maltratarse*).[5] The documentary record of Zurbarán's case brought before the court of the Casa de la Contratación in Seville states that the paintings were of very good quality painted by Francisco de Zurburán and other of the best painters of Seville.[6] In any event, Zurbarán seems never again to have sent works by his own hand across the Atlantic. Any painting in Latin America ever considered as a "Zurbarán" is in fact by his workshop.

Despite the difficulties, however, the great majority of paintings that were sent to South America from Spain arrived unharmed.[7] The method of shipping was quickly established. Paintings were sent in rolls, in cases made to fit the preordained dimensions and numbers of the canvases. Contracts state that all the paintings should measure, for example, two *varas* by two and a half *varas,* and were to be delivered without stretchers.

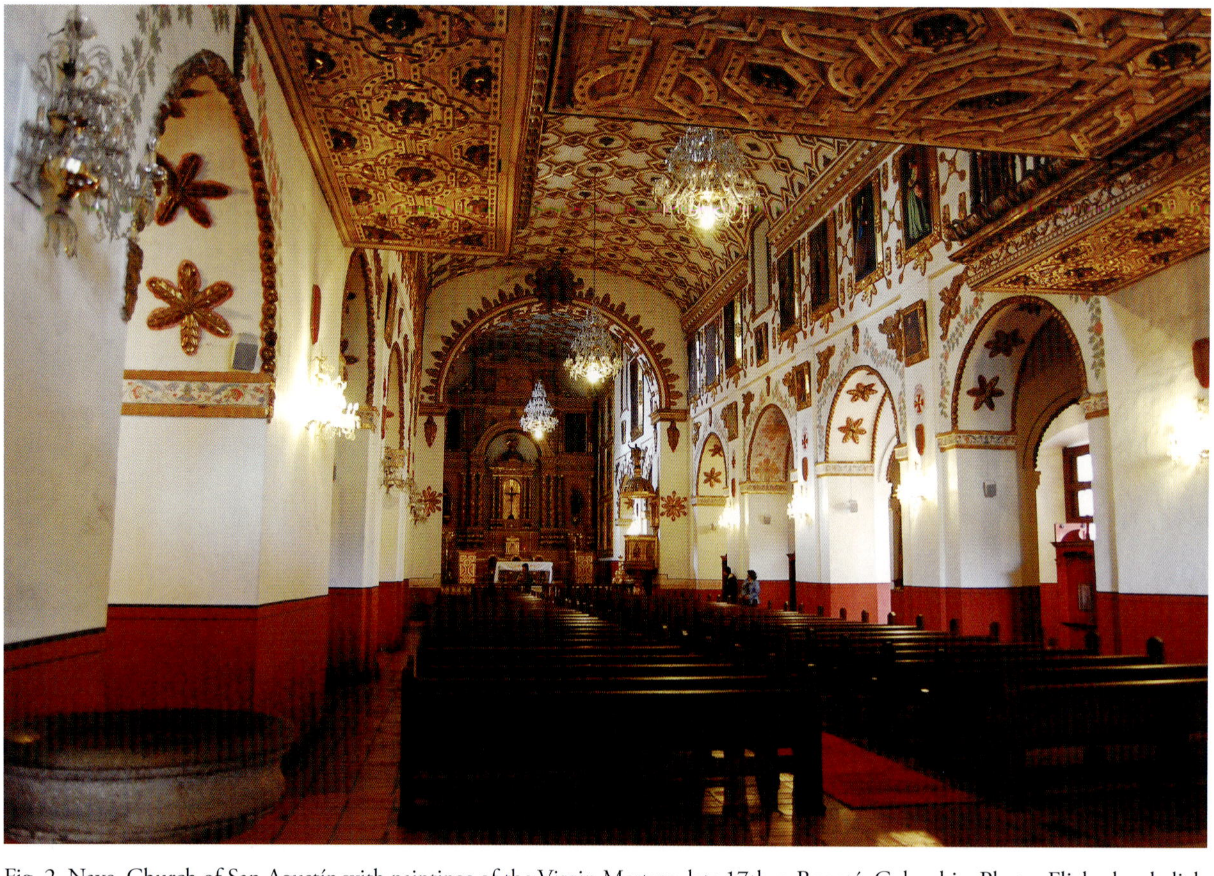

Fig. 2. Nave. Church of San Agustín with paintings of the Virgin Martyrs, late 17th c. Bogotá, Colombia. Photo: Flickr, herrbelial.

Documents attest that the art trade with Peru was well established by the late sixteenth century. In his last will and testament dated 1594, the Seville artist Pedro de Villegas mentioned paintings that he had sent to Lima.[8] In 1614 Francisco Pacheco sent 25 canvases to be sold in Cartagena de Indias, and in 1627 he sent another batch of paintings for sale in Lima.[9] These paintings from Seville supplemented the actual presence of European artists in the Viceroyalty of Peru, and the style and iconography of these works influenced both collectors and painters working in colonial South America.

In Friar Juan Meléndez's history of the Dominican order in Peru, published in 1681, he describes the painted decoration of the nave of the Dominican church in Lima. The vaults over the family chapels of the Agüero and Aliaga families, the presbytery, and the crossing were decorated with "*celestes Paraninfos*" (angels) and the length of the nave to the choir with prophets, sibyls, personifications of the virtues, and virgin saints.[10] Paintings of these subjects were imported from Spain in considerable numbers, and had a decisive influence on South American colonial art.

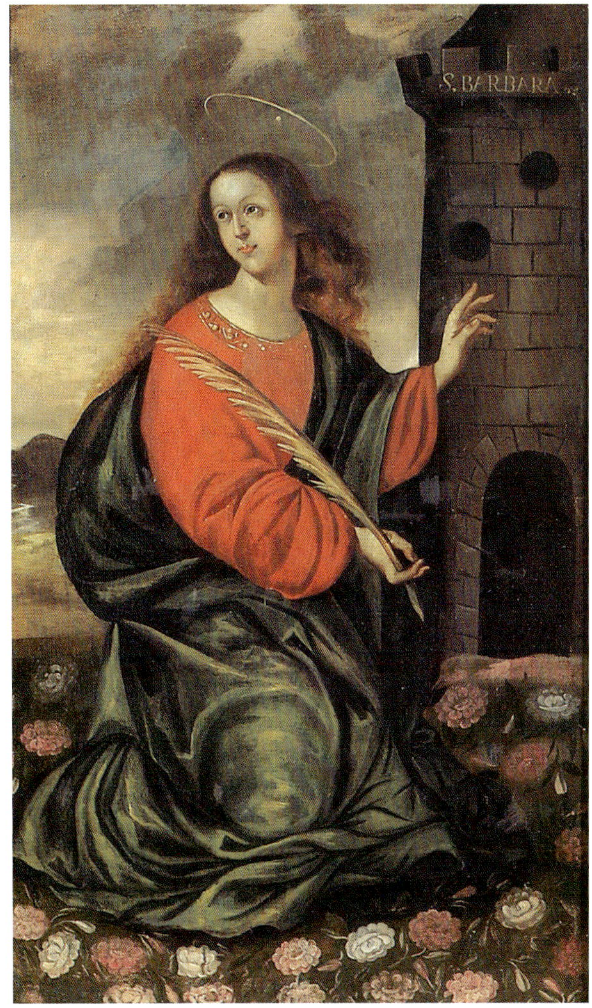

Fig. 3. *Saint Barbara*. Colombia, 17th century. Oil on canvas. 182 x 105 cm. Church of San Agustín Bogotá, Colombia. Photo: Ernesto Monsalve.

Sibyls

The sibyls, the oracles of antiquity, had come to be considered the prophetesses of the coming of Christ, and therefore took their places in a Christian context. Sibyls appeared in groups of nine or ten or twelve, with their attributes. A series of twelve sibyls by Zurbarán, inventoried in 1837 in the Sevillian collection of Antonio and Aniceto Bravo, were perhaps based on the full-length figures in engravings by Pieter de Jode.[11] It is reasonable to suppose that these were reproduced by his workshop both for Spanish collectors and for export. And Zurbarán's workshop was not unique in turning out paintings of the sibyls. In the 1651 inventory of the artist Francisco Polanco, for example, were twelve paintings of angels and twelve of sibyls, possibly created for the American market.[12] Colonial painters also painted sibyls for churches and other religious institutions. A set of thirteen paintings of the sibyls was created

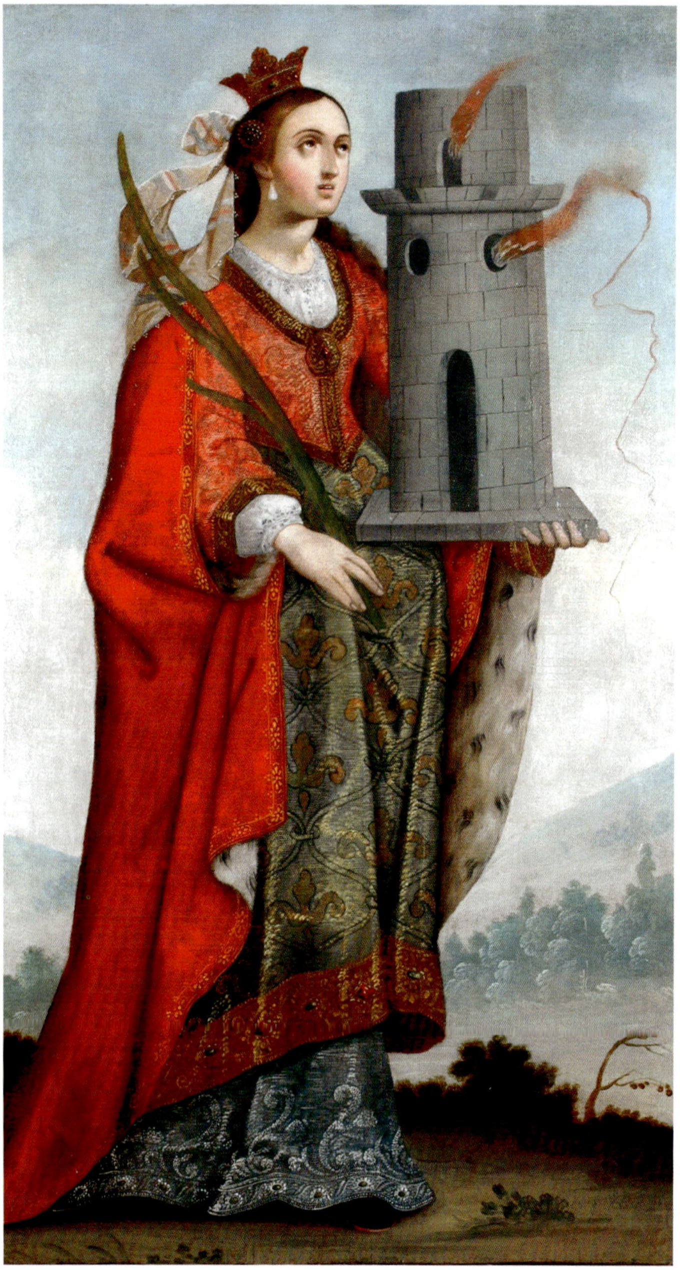

Fig. 4. *Saint Barbara*. Bolivia, late 17th or 18th century. Oil on canvas. $45^{3}/_{8}$ x $25^{1}/_{4}$ in. Courtesy of Saint Joseph's University, Philadelphia.

for the interior of the church of San Francisco, Potosí around 1640,[13] and there is a set of sibyls in the collection of the Seminario de San Antonio Abad in Cuzco.[14] Paintings of the sibyls were also collected by individuals. The estate of Lima clergyman Pedro del Castillo in 1640 contained a number of paintings of religious subjects, and twelve canvases representing the sibyls.[15] In eighteenth-century inventories of private collections in Caracas, there are mentions of "*damiselas*" (damsels) that have been interpreted to mean portraits or allegorical figures of young women, a category that would include sibyls.[16] In a number of other Caracas inventories the twelve sibyls are specifically mentioned. Doña María de Castro owned twelve large sibyls (*doce Sibilas grandes*) in 1658, and José García owned eight paintings of sibyls of one *vara* (*ocho cuadros de Sibilas de una vara de largo*) in 1676.[17] Although the early models for South American artists were probably imported paintings, engravings by artists like Jacob van der Heyden and Jacques Granthomme also served as models. A set of sybils in the church of San Pedro González-Telmo in Buenos Aires was likely painted in Cuzco in the eighteenth century after early seventeenth-century engravings by Crispijn van de Passe.[18]

Virgin Martyrs

In 1649 Zurbarán sent to Buenos Aires a shipment of paintings that included fifteen canvases representing virgin martyrs. Zurbarán's autograph paintings of beautiful female saints, such as Saint Margaret of Antioch (London, The National Gallery) and Saint Elizabeth of Portugal (Madrid, Museo Nacional del Prado), are among his most admired works. However, his workshop also created paintings of these full-length figures. Virgin martyrs in a Zurbaranesque style march along the walls of the nave in the church of the Convent of Santa Clara (*Clarisas*) near Seville, leading the congregation toward the altar. They do so likewise in the church of San Agustín in Bogotá (Figs. 2 and 3), and the twenty-four virgin saints Zurbarán painted at the request of the Convent of the Encarnación in Lima were undoubtedly similarly installed as a group. In Lima, artists in the circle of the creole painter Francisco de Escobar (active c. 1660–1700) created a series of virgin saints for the Casa de Ejercicios of the Third Order of the Franciscans. The paintings in Bogotá, as elsewhere in South America, reveal a stylistic as well as iconographical connection to the tenebrism of early seventeenth-century painting in Seville. However, a *Saint Barbara* that was probably painted in Alto Perú (now Bolivia), with its pale palette and bright atmosphere, is evidence of the variety of styles practiced by artists in colonial South America (Fig. 4).

These images of beautiful young women were appealing as well to private patrons and collectors. The Bolivian painting of an unidentified virgin martyr shown in Figure 5 was undoubtedly painted for a private collection. No inscription gives her name, nor is she accompanied by an attribute that would identify her as a particular saint. Note that her skirt is painted quite differently from the Flemish laces and rich brocades that usually adorn the virgin martyrs, for the hem is ringed with the Andean *tocapus* design. The Guarachi family, the Aymara *caciques* of Jesús Machaca (La Paz, Bolivia), had in their home twelve angels marching (*doce ángeles de marcha*.)[19] It would not be surprising if a member of the indigenous nobility owned a series of paintings of virgin martyrs wearing costumes with Andean touches.

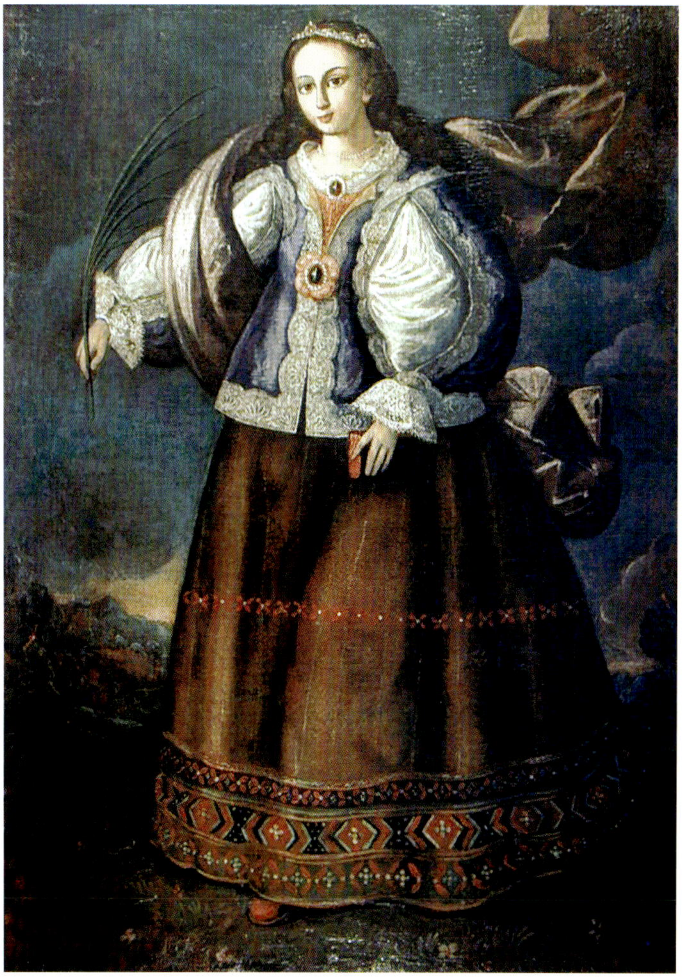

Fig. 5. *A Virgin Martyr*. Bolivia, 18th century. Oil on canvas. 63 x 44 1/8 in. Collection of Richard and Roberta Huber, New York.

The paintings of the Corpus Christi processions produced in Cuzco around 1680 have been interpreted by historians and art historians in various ways.[20] These paintings are also useful indicators of the widespread popularity of certain subjects in painting. In a canvas (Fig. 6) representing the *Altar of the Last Supper*, paintings of virgin saints hang from the buildings along the processional route.

Angels

In both shipments from Spain and decorative programs in South America such as that described by Friar Juan Meléndez at Santo Domingo in Lima, virgin martyrs and angels marched hand in hand. In Spain, Zurbarán and his workshop created series of the archangels for the Capilla de San Miguel in the cathedral of Jaén and for the

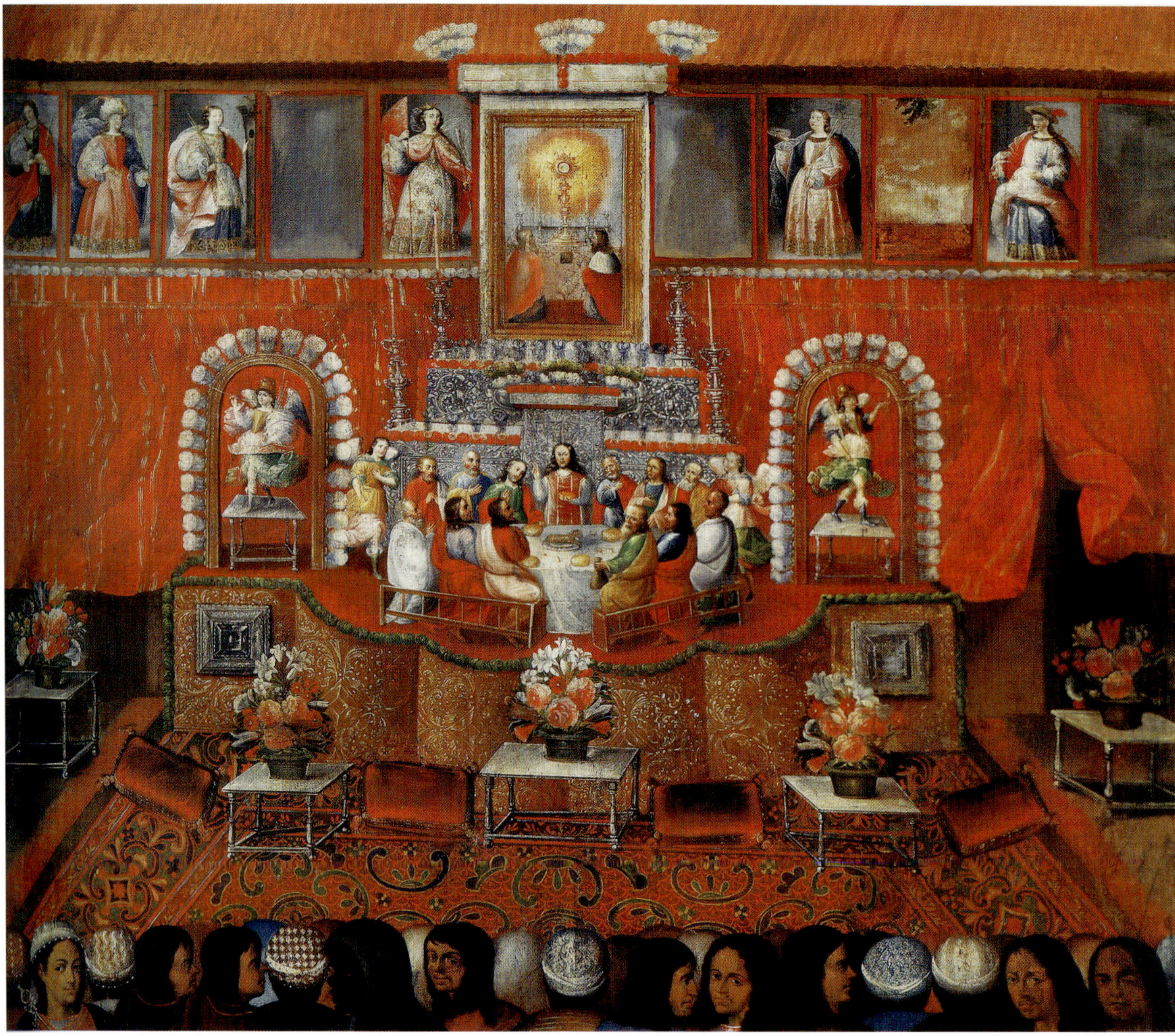

Fig. 6. *Procession of the Altar of the Last Supper*. Archbishop's Palace, Cuzco, Peru, circa 1680. Oil on canvas. Photo: Daniel Giannoni.

Hospital del Pozo Santo in Seville,[21] but also a series for the Convento de la Concepción in Lima. This was a commission, so not strictly apt for our discussion of trade, but there are other shipments of paintings of angels (not necessarily archangels) sent from Seville for the art market. A 1660 shipment from the Sevillian painter Juan de Luzón included eighteen canvases of *vírgenes* and twenty-four of angels.[22] In 1665 the painter Luis Carlos Muñoz agreed to paint 108 canvases, probably for the New World trade. These included, as well as responses to popular devotions such as Our Lady of Solitude and Our Lady of the Rosary, twenty-four angels and two sets of virgin saints (twenty-four in all).[23] The same year, Juan López Carrasco agreed to paint 168 canvases for the market within eight months, including two dozen images of virgin saints and two dozen images of angels.[24] These Spanish paintings were replicated throughout South America; a copy of the *Saint Michael Archangel* that Zurbarán's workshop created for the Encarnación in Lima is in the collection of the Convent of Santa Catalina in Arequipa, and a *Saint Gabriel Archangel* (Fig. 7) in similar style is in the Franciscan monastery in Quito.

However, colonial painters were not bound to Spanish examples, and the artists of Cuzco put a very original stamp on the type (Fig. 8), as well as creating an entirely new genre, representations of angels armed with guns (Fig. 9). The indigenous artist Basilio de Santa Cruz Pumacallao (active 1661–1700) was commissioned by the Franciscans in Cuzco, around 1661, to paint twelve angels and twelve virgin saints for their church,[25] and in the Corpus Christi series, the canvas showing the procession of "Corregidor Pérez" includes paintings of angels festooning the walls along the route (Fig. 10). A further reminder that religious subjects were as apt to have been installed in homes as in religious houses is an engraving from Frézier's memoirs of his travels in South America (Fig. 11), in which the wall of a home in Lima is decorated with paintings of angels.

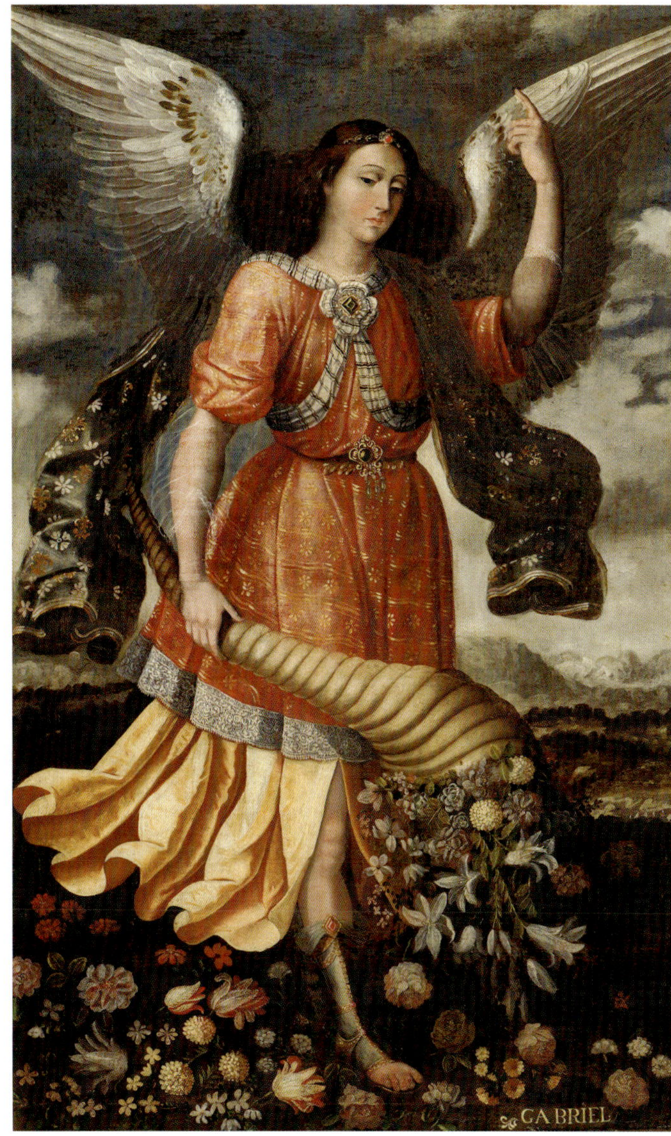

Fig. 7. *The Archangel Gabriel.* 17th century. Oil on canvas, 186 x 110 cm. Museo Fray Pedro Gocial, Monastery of San Francisco, Quito, Ecuador. Photo: Christoph Hirtz.

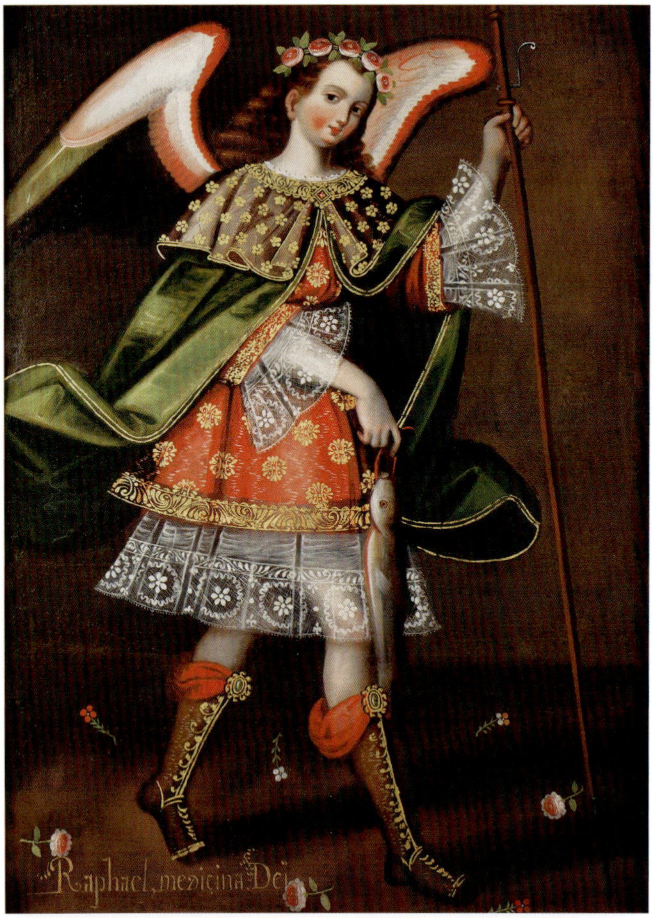

Fig. 8. *Archangel Raphael.* Cuzco, Peru, circa 1720. Oil, gold, canvas. 54 1/2 x 39 1/2 in. Denver Art Museum, Gift of Dr. Belinda Straight; 1985.535.

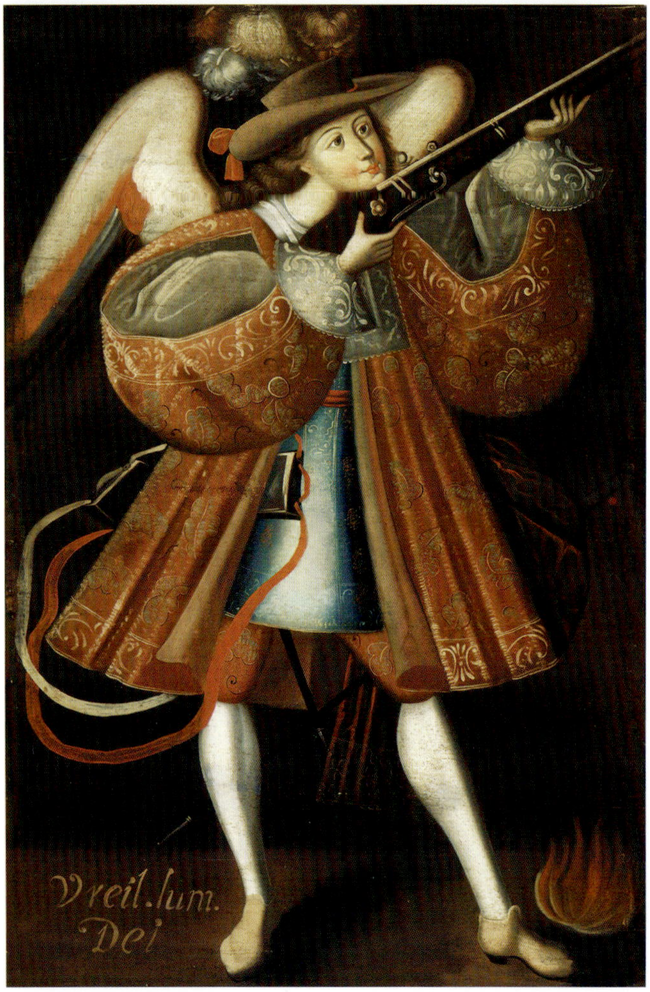

Fig. 9. Circle of Calamarca, *Archangel Uriel.* Bolivia, circa 1725. Oil on canvas. 44 3/4 x 28 3/4 in. Denver Art Museum, Gift of Althea Revere; 1971.463.

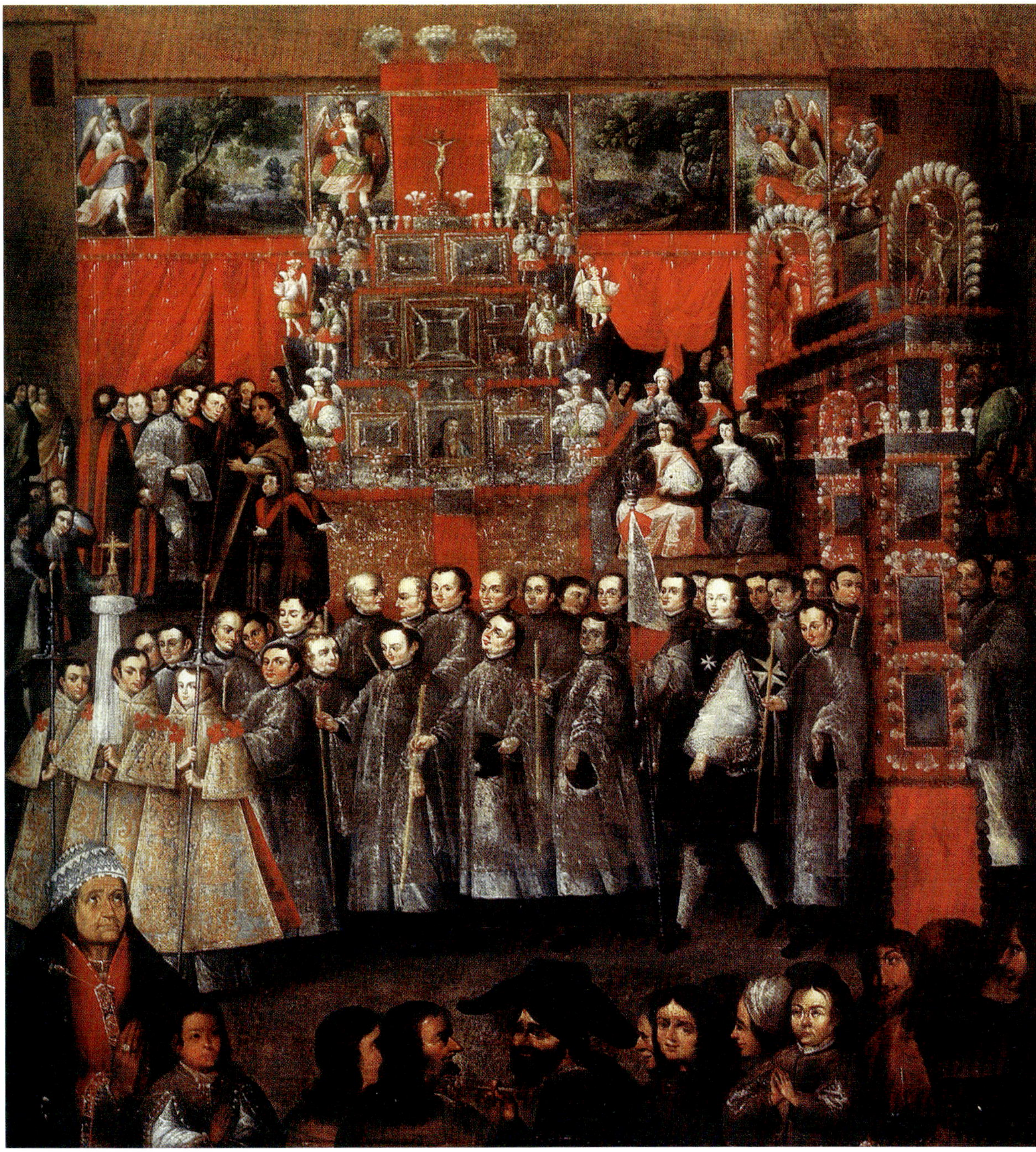

Fig. 10. *Procession of Corregidor Pérez*. Archbishop's Palace, Cuzco, Peru, circa 1680. Oil on canvas. Photo: Daniel Giannoni.

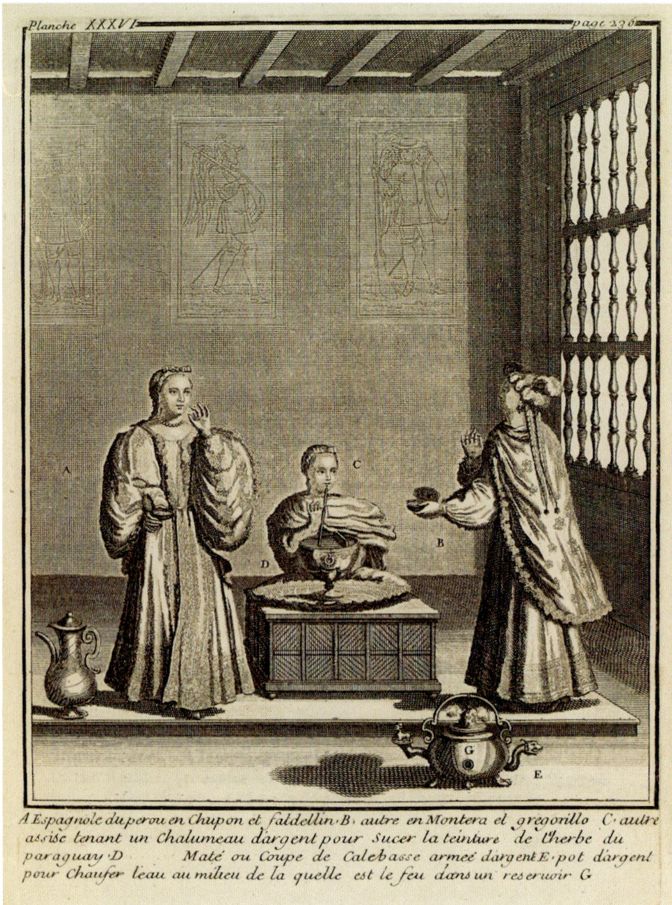

Fig. 11. Amédée François Frézier, *A Voyage to the South-sea . . .* (London: J. Bowyer, 1717), plate 36. Rare Books Division, The New York Public Library, Astor, Lenox and Tilden Foundations.

Patriarchs

In Zurbarán's shipment of 1649 to Buenos Aires were canvases representing twenty-four patriarchs and saints, undoubtedly two series of twelve canvases each. Ten years later, the 1659 shipment from Zurbarán's workshop included another series of twelve patriarchs. The popularity of these series continued through the second half of the century. Among the paintings contracted in 1665 from Carrasco were two dozen images of patriarchs.[26] These two sets represented the twelve sons of Jacob, progenitors of the twelve tribes of Israel. In the Acts of the Apostles they were called "patriarchs," and they came to be interpreted as prefigurations of the twelve apostles of Christ, notably in Saint Isidore of Seville's *Allegoriae Scripturae Sacrae et liber numerorum* (c. 560–636).[27] The patriarchs had special meaning in the Americas. The Dominican missionary Diego Durán argued in his 1585 *Historia de las Indias de Nueva-España* that the similarity between the religious rites of the Indians and those of the Jews of the Old Testament was proof that indigenous Americans descended from the Jews. The Franciscan Diego de Landa, first bishop of the Yucatan, wrote in 1566 that the Mayans believed themselves to have descended from ancestors who crossed the ocean from the east via twelve routes opened by God, and Gregorio García claimed that the Ofir River mentioned in the Bible referred to Peru.[28]

Thirteen paintings representing Jacob and his sons from Zurbarán's workshop are today in Great Britain, distributed between Auckland Castle, in Durham County, and Grimsthorpe Castle, in Bourne, Lincolnshire. The style of the paintings suggests that they were created during the 1640s, the subject matter suggests that they were intended for the New World, and their appearance in England at an early date suggests that they were captured by pirates on the Atlantic, where they were probably en route to the art market in Buenos Aires or Lima. In 1659 Zurbarán left a series of patriarchs with the nuns of San Jerónimo de Buenavista in Seville as security for a debt, another series that was probably intended for export to Spanish America. There are two series of patriarchs in Spanish America attributed to Zurbarán's workshop, one in the collection of the Tercer Orden de San Francisco in Lima and the other in the Museo de la Academia de Bellas Artes in Puebla, Mexico. The series that belongs to the Tercer Orden Franciscana in Lima is undocumented. It might not be by Zurbarán's workshop at all, but rather by the hand of the Lima artist Juana de Valera Escobar, and might even be the very series listed in the inventory of her husband's estate.[29] The height of the canvases mentioned there, two *varas* and a quarter, fits the measurements of the damaged, repainted, and more recently restored paintings in the Franciscan house.[30] If so, then there was another series from Spain in Lima similar to the Durham paintings that she used as a model.

As with other subjects that had roots in European art, South American artists created their own paintings of the patriarchs. On February 4, 1669, the painter Diego Aguilera signed a contract with the Convent of Santa Catalina in Lima for paintings to be placed high on the walls of the *capilla mayor* of the church of the convent: eighteen or more canvases representing in life size the prophets and patriarchs of the Old Testament.[31] And in Quito, an unidentified workshop created a series of twelve paintings of the prophets that still decorate the nave of the Jesuit church there (Fig. 12).

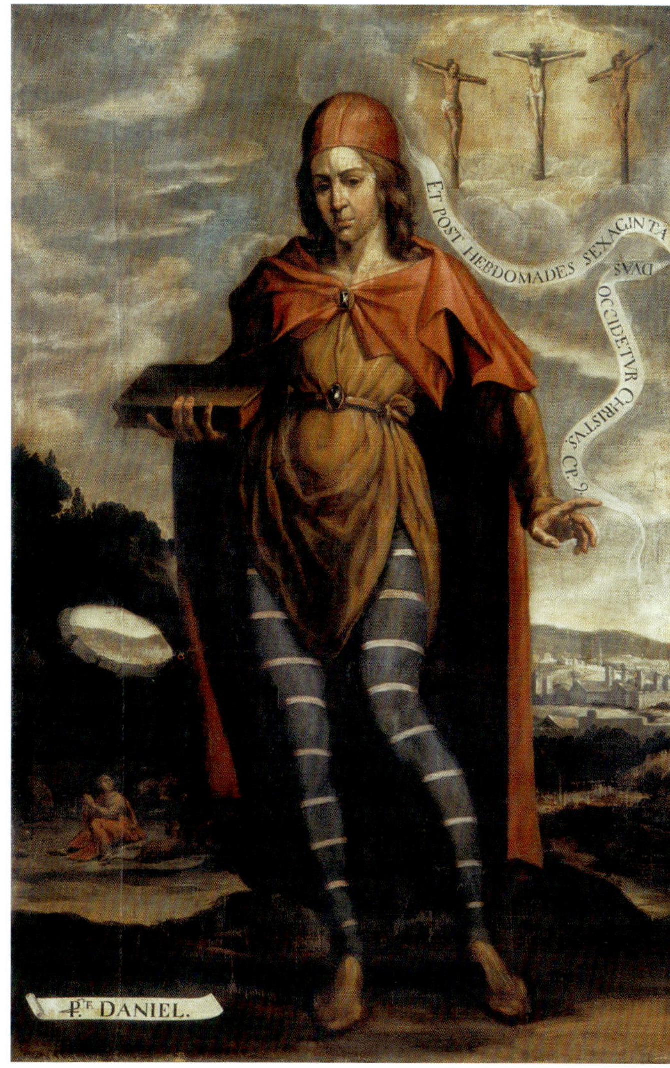

Fig. 12. *The Prophet Daniel*. 17th century. Oil on canvas. 204 x 127 cm. Church of La Compañía, Quito. Photo: Christoph Hirtz.

Apostles

Of all the subjects of religious paintings in Sevillian private collections during the decades from around 1630 to 1670, by far the most popular was the *Apostolado*,[32] representations of the first twelve disciples of Christ famously exemplified in the series by El Greco in the sacristy of the cathedral of Toledo and in another painted by Peter Paul Rubens for the Duke of Lerma in 1603 (Madrid, Museo Nacional del Prado). The 1665 contract with Carrasco included not only the images of virgin saints, angels, and patriarchs mentioned above, but as well two sets of apostles in twenty-four canvases.[33] The contract with his Sevillian colleague Luis Carlos Muñoz signed the same year also included two sets of apostles in twenty-four canvases. There is an *Apostolado* in the monastery

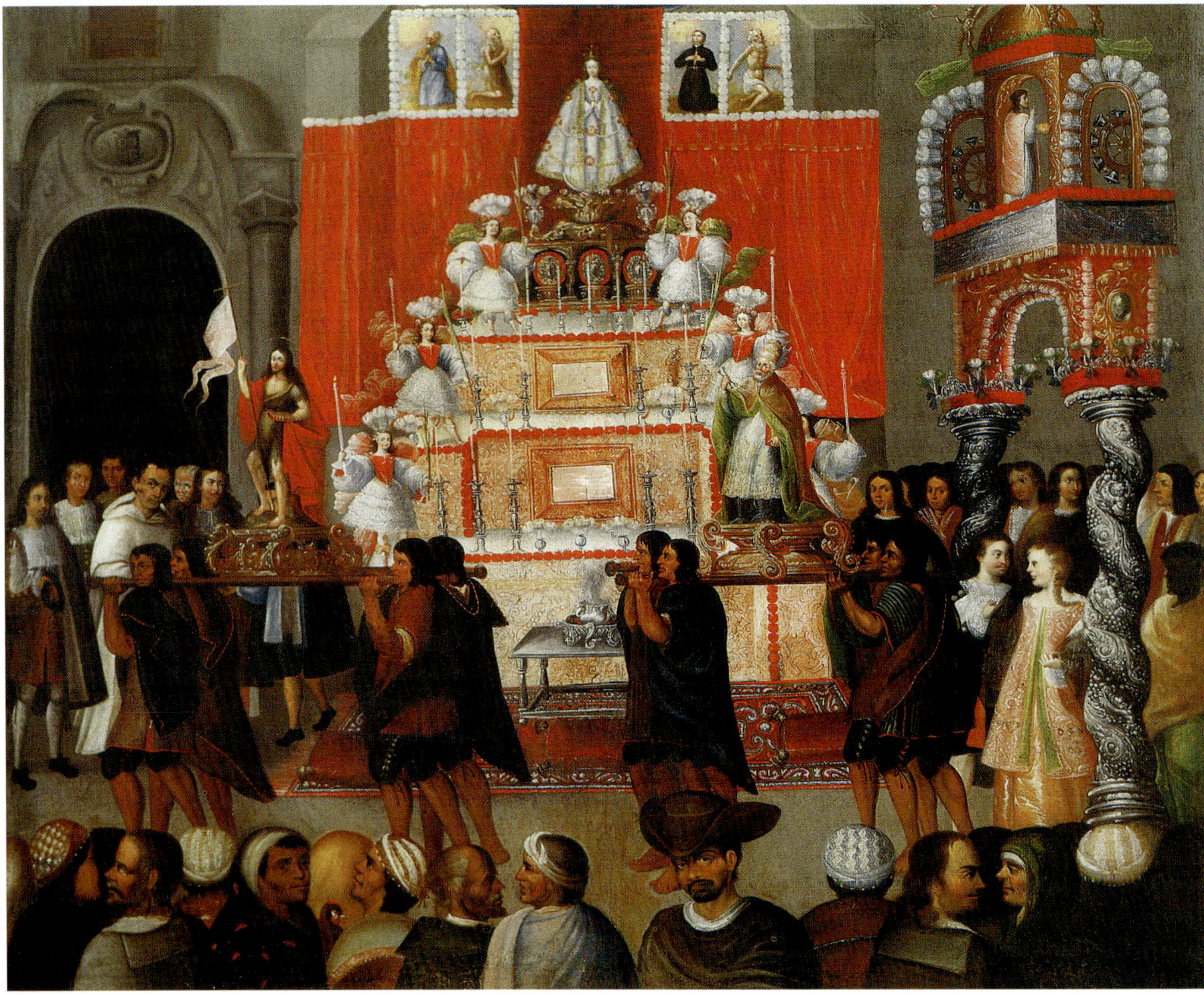

Fig. 13. *Procession of the Confraternities of Saint John the Baptist and Saint Peter*. Archbishop's Palace, Cuzco, Peru, circa 1680. Oil on canvas. Photo: Daniel Giannoni.

of San Francisco of Lima that has long been attributed to the workshop of Zurbarán, though it is not documented. Attributions to "Zurbarán's workshop," so frequently suggested, may deflect us from considering other possibilities. The artists mentioned above, Juan López Carrasco and Luis Carlos Muñoz, whose works are completely unknown, may have closely copied Zurbarán's style in an effort to replicate his success with the South American market. As well, it is possible that paintings attributed to the master's followers in Seville are actually by artists in South America, who proved themselves very adept at adapting their skills to various subjects and styles.

In the Viceroyalty of Peru, many *Apostolados* decorated churches and religious houses. A set of paintings in the sacristy of San Francisco in Popayán, Colombia was attributed by Santiago Sebastián to the "Master of Calibío," whom he thought might have worked in Quito.[34] In Bogotá, there is a seventeenth-century *Apostolado* in the church of San Ignacio,[35] and there are complete series in the churches of Pomata in Peru and Italaque in Bolivia. As in Seville, private individuals collected *Apostolados*. A set was in the collection of the Lima clergyman referred to earlier, and in Caracas, full-length figures of the apostles in large-scale canvases of as much as three *varas* were used to cover the walls of the main rooms and corridors of homes. Indeed, among the subjects of religious paintings in Caracas collections, *Apostolados* ranked third in popularity, only after images of Christ and those of the Virgin Mary.[36]

Hermits

Of course, there were many paintings of favorite saints in Spanish collections besides virgin martyrs. Collections in Seville in the seventeenth century included paintings of hermit saints, variously termed "*hermitaños*" or "*ancoretas*,"[37] such as *Saint Paul the Hermit*, *Saint Jerome in Penitence*, and lesser known figures such as Saint Onophrius, painted by Jusepe de Ribera and his workshop. Some of them, like Saint Jerome, a well-known figure in Catholic iconography, are pictured during a period of penitence; some, like Saint Onophrius or Saint Mary of Egypt, were lifelong hermits, always associated with the lives of privation and prayer to which they dedicated themselves. Nor were they of merely historical interest, for there were some people in the Viceroyalty of Peru who were drawn to the life of a hermit despite the concerns of the established Church.[38]

Very probably, there were many paintings of these subjects identified in collection lists and shipping documents simply as "saints." However, our best evidence for their existence in some numbers in South America may be found in the Corpus Christi series mentioned above. In the canvas representing the *Confraternities of Saint John the Baptist and Saint Peter* (Fig. 13) are paintings representing Saint Francis receiving the stigmata, as well as companion pieces picturing hermit saints. These subjects are rarely specified in colonial inventories. An exception is the mention of two paintings with figures of hermits (*dos lienzos con effigies de ermitaños*) in the collection of the well-to-do Oruro merchant Nicolás Iriarte in an inventory of 1784.[39] Fictive portraits of hermit saints, often in landscape settings, mountainous caves, and deserts, were popularized throughout Europe in print series such as those by Boethius à Bolswert after Abraham Bloemaert and by Johannes Sadeler after Marten de Vos. These are also found in South America and also influenced colonial art.[40]

Kings and Famous Men

Among the paintings of historical subjects that appeared in collections in Seville were kings and emperors, the Nine Worthies (*Los Nueve de la Fama*), and the Princes of Lara (*Infantes de Lara*).[41] In the shipment of paintings from Zurbarán's studio to Buenos Aires in 1649 were fifteen full-length (paintings) of kings and famous men (*quince de cuerpo entero de Reyes y onbres ynsignes*). In 1660 the Sevillian painter Juan de Luzón sent a shipment of ninety-nine canvases for sale in either Cartagena or Portobelo. The shipment included a set of twelve paintings representing famous men.[42] The 1664 contract for paintings by the Sevillian artist Luis Carlos Muñoz specified, among other subjects, twelve canvases representing famous men.[43]

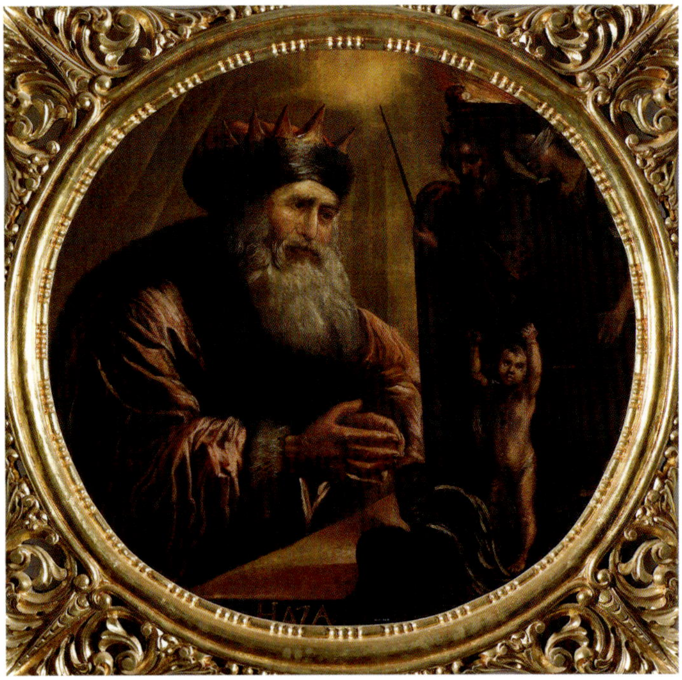

Fig. 14. *King Haza*. Second half of the 17th century, Santo Domingo, Quito. Oil on canvas. 114.5 x 114.5 cm. Photo: Christoph Hirtz.

Though there are a number of documents reflecting series of "kings and famous men," it is difficult to know exactly what they included. Collections in Seville included *Los Nueve de la Fama* (the Nine Worthies). In medieval lore these comprised three ancient figures (Hector of Troy, Alexander the Great, and Julius Caesar); three great men from the Old Testament (Joshua, who conquered Canaan; King David of Israel; and Judas Maccabeus, who led his people in recapturing their temple from the Syrians); and the Christian kings Arthur, Charlemagne, and Godfrey of Bouillon, a leader of the First Crusade.[44] When the Italian painter Mateo Pérez de Alesio died in Lima in 1616, his estate included "portraits" of Romulus, Alexander, and Godfrey of Bouillon, perhaps parts of such a series.[45] Gabriel Murillo, the son of Sevillian painter Bartolomé Esteban Murillo, emigrated to South America, where he served as *corregidor* of Ugaque. When he died in 1700 and an inventory was made of the contents of his house in Bogotá, the list of paintings included twelve still lifes, an *Apostolado*, and twelve images of famous men. To complicate our understanding, there were series perhaps based on the heroic deeds of medieval knights, mentioned in inventories in colonial Caracas.[46]

The "*reyes*" mentioned in these shipments were probably the kings of Israel and Judah, rather than portraits of the Spanish monarchs. In the second half of the seventeenth century, these Old Testament subjects became very popular with artists and their patrons all over South America, where they were often based on engravings after a series of paintings by the French artist Claude Vignon, exemplified here by a representation of King Haza from a series originally numbering fourteen in the Monastery of Santo Domingo in Quito (Fig. 14). There are many series of these found throughout South America from Quito to Mendoza, Argentina.[47] In Cuzco, there is a series of "prophets and kings" in the cathedral, dating from the last third of the seventeenth century,[48] perhaps the models for the paintings reproduced in the Corpus Christi canvas representing the *Procession of the Augustinian Friars* (Fig. 15).

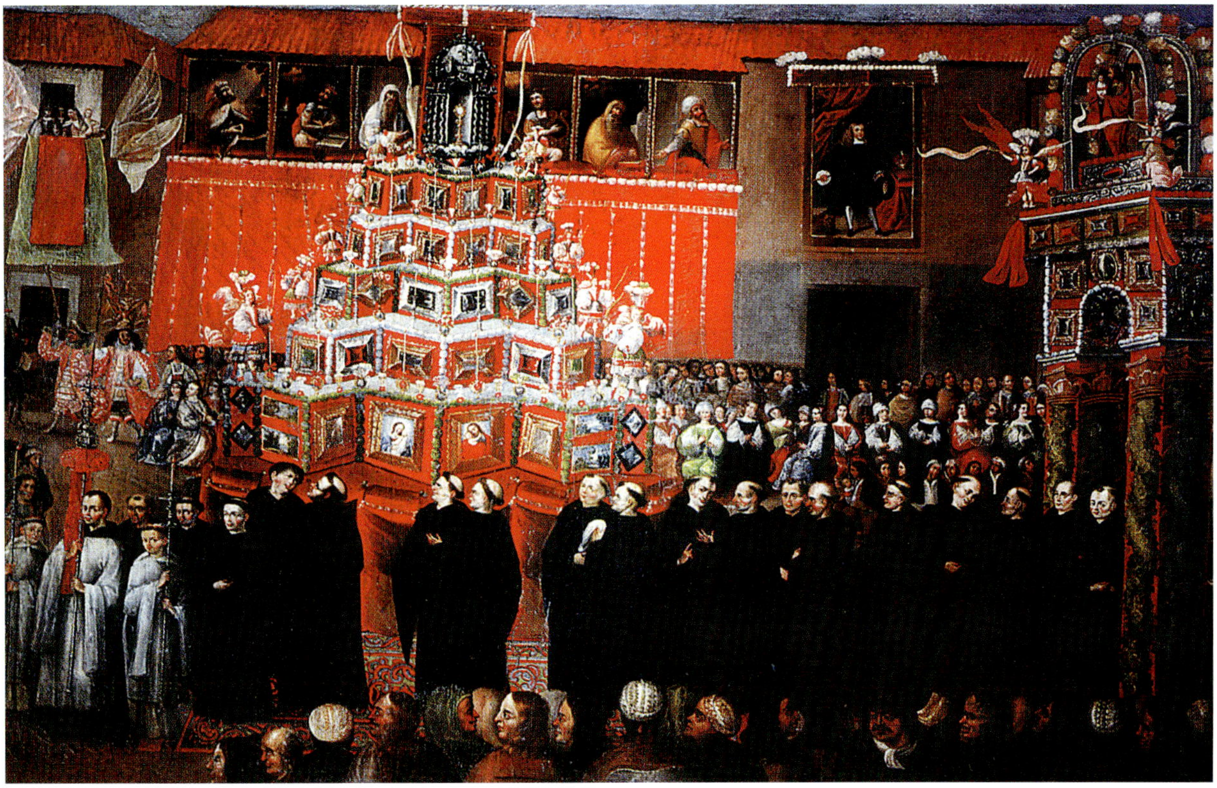

Fig. 15. *Procession of the Augustinian Friars.* Archbishop's Palace, Cuzco, Peru, circa 1680. Oil on canvas. Photo: Daniel Giannoni.

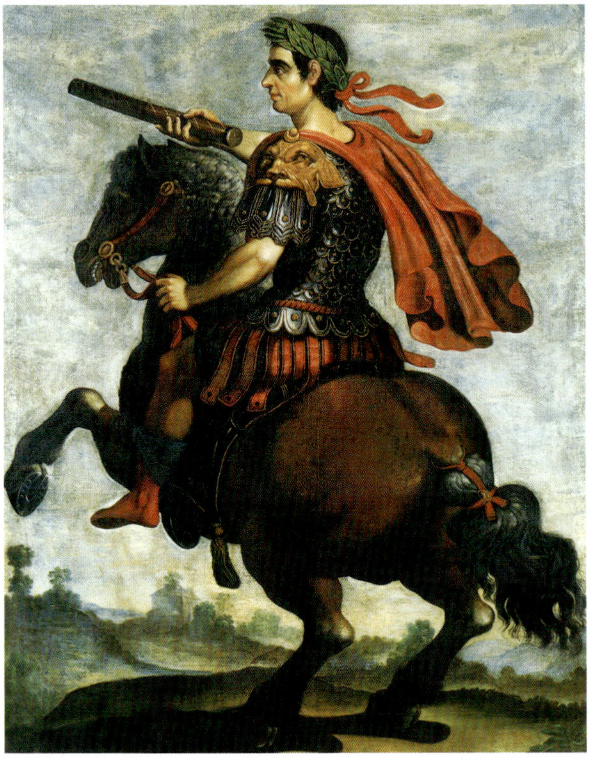

Fig. 16a. Workshop of Francisco de Zurbarán, *Julius Caesar*. Spain, c. 1650. Oil on canvas. Private collection.

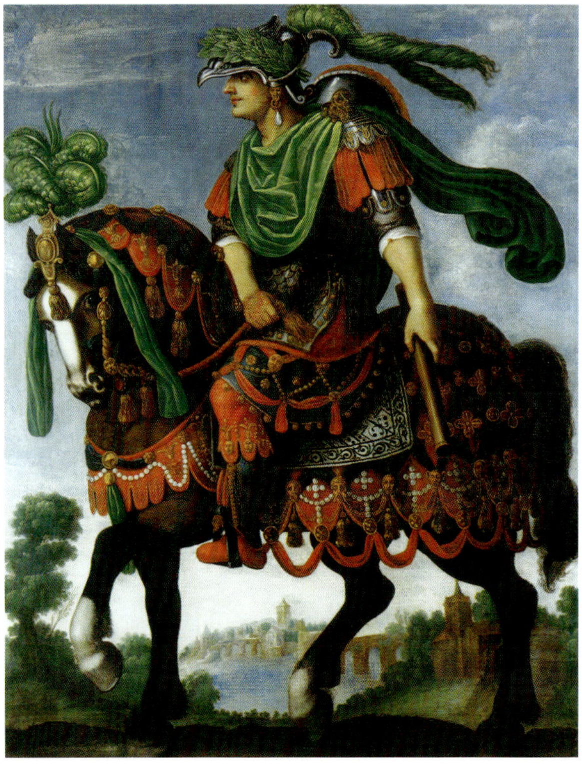

Fig. 16b. Workshop of Francisco de Zurbarán, *Domiciano*. Spain, c. 1650. Oil on canvas. Private collection.

The *Infantes de Lara* (Seven Princes of Lara) is a medieval legend whose roots might have been in a *chanson de geste* such as the *Cantar de mio Cid* or the *Poema de Fernán González.* Its earliest written version is found in the *Estoria de España* compiled in the thirteenth century. It's a bloody tale of family disputes, murder, and vengeance that remained popular in epic romances and in Spanish theater. Various monasteries claim the relics of the assassinated brothers, and series of their fictive portraits were painted for collectors in Spain and the New World. Zurbarán's paintings pictured here, inscribed "P. Bustos de Lara" and "Alvar Velázquez de Lara," belonged to a series representing the *Infantes.* We do not know how many canvases were in this set by Zurbarán, but a series recorded in the Sevillian estate of Francisca de la Fuente in 1690 noted that the story of the Infantes de Lara was told in twelve paintings.[49] In eighteenth-century inventories of the possessions of the well-to-do in Caracas, there are mentions of the seven princes of Lara (*los siete ynfantes de Lara*) and the seven princes of Lara, full-length (*los siete ynfantes de Lara, de cuerpo entero*).[50]

In the 1667 death inventory of Captain Joseph de Mujica, which included paintings by his wife, the painter Juana de Valera, were twelve canvases representing full-length figures of the Infantes de Lara (perhaps a narrative series), twelve of the same size of the tribes of Israel, also full length, and others of the same dimensions representing twelve angels.[51] Although the *Infantes de Lara* do not today figure in our understanding of colonial iconography, Juana de Valera surely would not have painted twelve canvases that she did not expect to be able to sell.[52]

In 1647 Zurbarán entrusted twelve paintings of Roman emperors on horseback (*doce lienços de pintura de doze sesares rromanos* [sic] *a caballo de tres baras menos quarto de alto*) to a ship's captain for sale in Lima. If the captain could not sell them, the agreement stated, then Antonio de Alarcón, a resident of Lima, should try to obtain the best possible price for them.[53] The paintings were probably at least somewhat like paintings from Zurbarán's workshop (private collection) that are based on engravings by Stradanus or Antonio Tempesta after Adrian Collaert (Figs. 16a and b).[54] However, they were not the only paintings representing Roman emperors to have been imported to the Americas, as a series was sent to New Spain as early as 1593.[55] As is the case with the majority of subjects sent by artists for the New World market, this one reflects art collections in Seville, where history paintings, including portraits of kings and emperors, were installed in the homes of the nobility.[56] Emperors on horseback are not among the Spanish themes that became popular in colonial South America, though their history there is long, as witness the panels of a folding screen created in Quito in the late eighteenth century by the workshop of Bernardo Rodríguez (Fig. 17).

The tradition of paintings in sets of twelve became so well established that narrative series that could have been told in any number of canvases became routinely fixed at twelve. For example, the Lima painter Pedro Gerardo contracted in 1643 to create for Captain Don Perafán de Ribera y Mendoza twelve oil paintings narrating the story of Samson.[57] More than a century later a 1754 contract between the painters Mauricio García and Pedro Nolasco and the dealer Gabriel de Rincón specified, among other subjects, twelve canvases representing the life of Saint Rose of Lima, a life of Saint Anthony in twelve paintings, two series of the life of the Virgin in twelve paintings each, and a history of David in twelve canvases.[58]

Flemish Paintings

There was a substantial market for Flemish paintings in Seville, especially landscapes and flower paintings, and the business was increasingly specialized. Salomon Paradis, from Antwerp, established a gallery in Seville in 1610 next to the cathedral. Paintings on copper by Flemish artists were popular with Spanish collectors and were exported to the Americas as well.[59] Several by Willhem Fourchaudt are in the cathedral museum in Sucre, Bolivia. Thousands of paintings were shipped from Antwerp to Seville, with many of them intended for markets in Spanish America, though the latter are difficult to quantify except

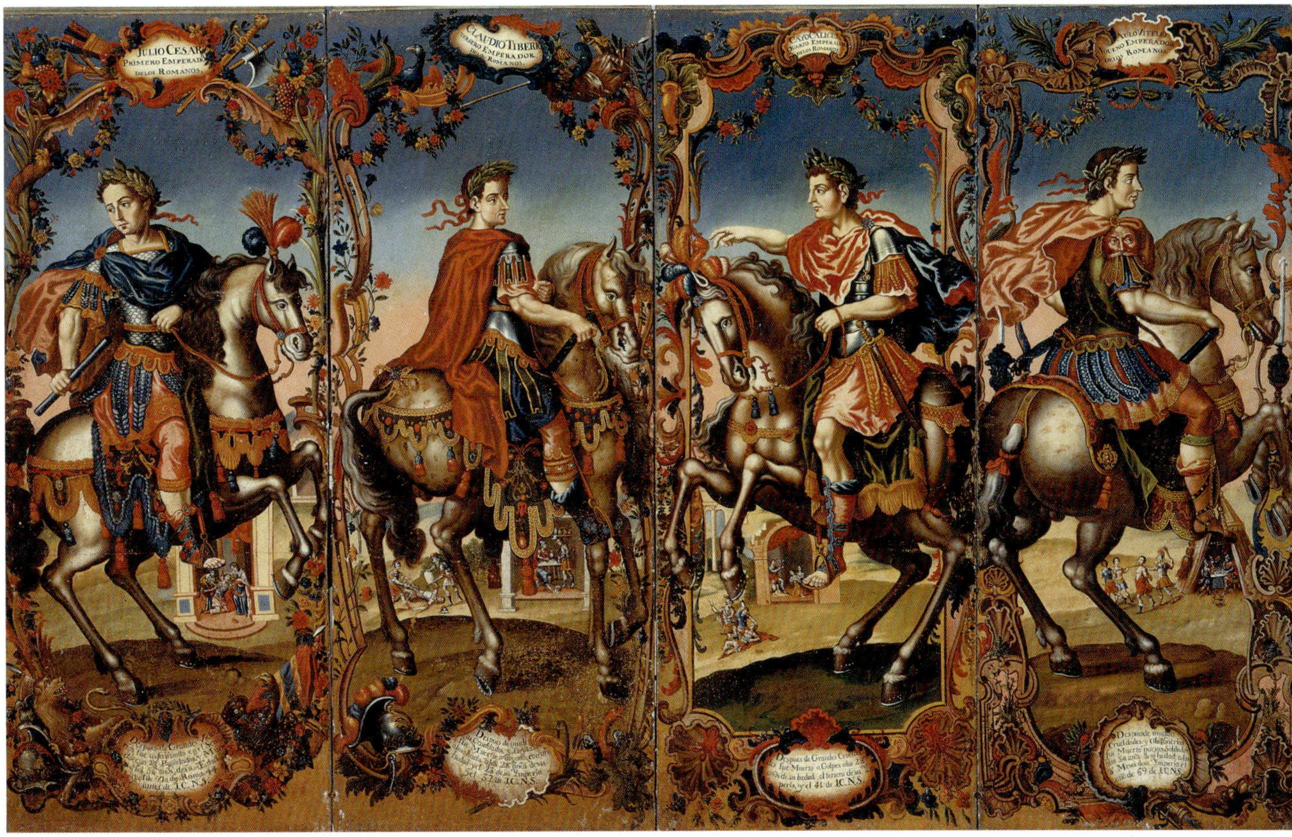

Fig. 17. Workshop of Bernardo Rodríguez, *Four Roman Emperors*. Quito, late 18th century. Oil on canvas. Photo courtesy Museo Soumaya, Mexico City.

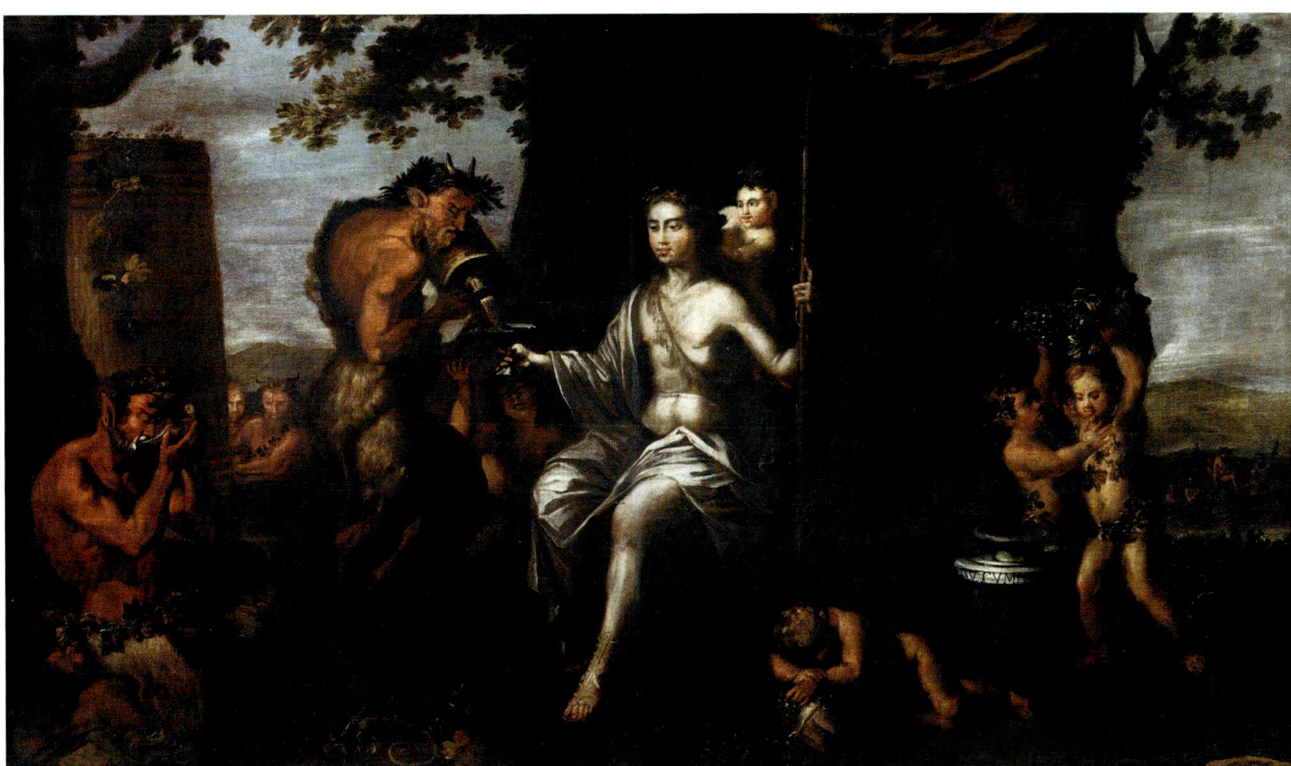

Fig. 18. Miguel de Santiago, *Spring*. Quito, 17th century. Oil on canvas. 126 x 234 cm. Casa de la Cultura Ecuatoriana/Museo de Arte Colonial. Photo: Christoph Hirtz.

for shipments specifically to merchants who purchased exclusively for the New World trade, such as a 1638 shipment of 504 paintings for the Indies (*para yndias*).[60] The market for Flemish paintings was geared toward secular subjects that were less often painted by Spanish artists: "seascapes, landscapes, hunt scenes, battles and sieges, flower pieces, and series: *The Four Elements, The Five Senses*, and *The Times of the Year*."[61] These were surely collected by the wealthier citizens of Peru, in line with the taste of their contemporaries in Seville. In the seventeenth century, the collections of the nobility in Seville had relatively fewer devotional paintings than did the less wealthy members of the merchant and professional classes and, of course, the clergy. Instead, their collections included lots of landscapes, history paintings, still lifes, portraits, and, notably, *láminas de Flandes* (paintings on copper plates from Flanders).[62] However, compared to Spanish paintings imported to South America, Flemish art seems to have had less impact on the practice of making art there, or at least little of it has lasted. An exception is the series representing the four seasons by the seventeenth-century Quito painter Miguel de Santiago, of which three are extant (Fig. 18). These are large canvases perhaps based on much smaller *láminas*. And it is clear in the painting from the Corpus Christi series picturing angels (Fig. 10) that Cuzco painters adapted easily to the compositional and coloristic traditions of Flemish landscape paintings.

South American Workshops

Jorge Cornejo Bouroncle, whose painstaking research in the Archivo Notarial in Cuzco took place in the 1950s, was the first to refer to the painters of Cuzco as a painting industry (*toda una industria pictórica*). The Cuzco workshops produced enormous bodies of work for export to areas with few working artists, or at least a paucity of productive workshops. A Cuzco contract of 1663 specifies a set of twelve "small" canvases a *vara* and a third wide that are to be sold in the provinces (*y que acabados los han de vender en las provincias de arriba*).[63] As a result, there are many examples of Cuzco paintings in present-day Chile and Argentina, such as a series of prophets and kings of Israel and a series of virgin saints in the church of Humahuaca, and other series of angels in the churches of Casabindo and Uquía, all in the province of Jujuy, Argentina.[64]

As we have seen, this way of producing art was not without precedent. The contracts signed in Cuzco in the eighteenth century reflect in a number of details documents regarding shipments of paintings from Seville workshops during the seventeenth century. Muñoz's 1665 contract specified that all 108 paintings were to measure two and one-third *varas* by one and one-third *varas*.[65] Carrasco's 1665 contract specified that the 168 paintings were to be in two sizes: one size for all the religious subjects, but smaller dimensions for the three dozen fruit still lifes.[66] These specifications were designed for ease of shipping the paintings in rolls, a practical means that continued in the art commerce from Spain to the Americas between 1650 and 1700. During that half century 240 rolls of paintings were shipped to the Americas: 171 to Portobelo, 51 to New Spain, and the rest to Honduras, Buenos Aires, and Maracaibo.[67]

In the 1754 Cuzco contract mentioned earlier, of the paintings commissioned 75 were to be two *varas* wide and one and a half high, 150 were to be one and a half *varas* wide and one *vara* high, and 100 were to be one *vara* wide and three quarters high, all priced accordingly.[68] In the same year of 1754 Mauricio García signed a contract with the dealer Miguel Blanco to provide 212 paintings of various topics (*de varias advocaciones*). These subjects were listed in an attached *Memoria* that, alas, we do not have, but the dimensions of the paintings were firmly limited to three specific sizes.[69] Thus the shipments of paintings from Seville to Peru influenced not only subjects and styles, but also the business model of South American artists, who created series of paintings of the same size, easily rolled up and crated together, shipped to a market where they could be sold by the dozen.

Notes

[1] For more about Portobelo see Allyn C. Loosley, "The Puerto Bello Fairs," *The Hispanic American Historical Review,* 13, no. 3 (Aug., 1933): 314–335; John Everaert, "Le commerce colonial de la 'Nation flamande' à Cadix sous Charles II (ca. 1670–1700)," *Anuario de Estudios Americanos* 28 (Seville, 1971): 139–151; and Enriqueta Vila Vilar, "Las ferias de Portobelo: Apariencia y realidad del comercio con Indias," *Anuario de Estudios Americanos* 39 (Seville, 1982): 275–337.

[2] Many prints were created in Flemish centers such as Antwerp for the Spanish and Spanish American markets. See Alfons K. L. Thijs, *Antwerpen Internationaal Uitgeverscentrum van Devotieprenten 17de–18de Eeuw* (Leuven: Peeters, 1993), especially 24–31. The frequent use of engravings by colonial artists has always been noted and continues to receive scholarly attention. See particularly *De Amberes al Cusco: El grabado europeo como fuente del arte virreinal*, edited by Cécile Michaud and José Torres Della Pina (Lima: Centro Cultural Pontificia Universidad Católica del Perú, 2009).

[3] Duncan Kinkead, "Juan de Luzón and the Sevillian Paintings Trade with the New World in the Second Half of the Seventeenth Century," *Art Bulletin* 66, no. 2 (June 1984): 303–310.

[4] Quoted by José de Mesa and Teresa Gisbert, "El pintor Mateo Pérez de Alesio: Roma, Sevilla y Lima," in *El Manierismo en los Andes. Memoria del III Encuentro Internacional Sobre Barroco* (Unión Latina: La Paz, 2005), 28.

[5] Jesús Miguel Palomero Páramo, "Notas sobre el taller de Zurbarán: Un envío de lienzos a Portobelo y Lima en el año 1636," in *Extremadura en la evangelización del nuevo mundo: Actas y estudios: congreso celebrado en Guadalupe durante los días 24 al 29 de octubre de 1988*, edited by Sebastián García (Madrid: Turner/Junta de Extremadura, 1990), 313; Benito Navarrete Prieto, "Zurbarán y su obrador. Pinturas para el Nuevo Mundo," in *Zurbarán y su obrador. Pinturas para el Nuevo Mundo* (Valencia: Museo de Bellas Artes de Valencia, 1998), 23–24. A number of articles about Zurbarán's shipments to the Americas have been published. See references in *Zurburán y su obrador* on pages 241–244.

[6] *Mui buena y la maior parte de ellas eran originales hechos en casa de el dicho Francisco de Surbarán por su mano y de otros oficiales de la arte de la pintura, de los mejores de esta dicha ciudad.*

[7] Palomero Páramo, "Notas sobre el taller de Zurbarán," 316.

[8] Celestino López Martínez, *Notas para la historia del arte: Desde Martínez Montañés hasta Pedro Roldán* (Seville: Tipografía Rodríguez, Giménez y Compañía, 1932), 220.

[9] Juan Miguel Serrera, "Zurburán y América," in *Zurburán* (Madrid: Ministerio de Cultura, 1988): 63–83.

[10] Juan Meléndez, *Tesoros verdaderos de las Yndias en la historia de la gran prouincia de San Ivan Bauvtista del Perv, de el orden de Predicadores . . . Por el maestro F. Ivan Melendez*, 3 vols. (Rome: Tinassio, 1681–1682), 1:55. The paintings were attributed by Meléndez to the Spanish/Italian painter Mateo Pérez de Alesio.

[11] See Paul Guinard, "España, Flandes y Francia en el siglo XVII. Las Sibilas Zurbaranescas y sus fuentes grabadas," *Archivo Español de Arte* no. 170 (1970): 105–122.

[12] Francisco de P. Cuéllar Contreras, "Testamentario y inventario de Francisco Polanco, pintor de imaginería. Año 1651," *Revista de Arte Sevillano*, no. 1 (June 1982): 42.

[13] Noted by Mario Chacón, *Arte virreinal en Potosí* (Seville: Escuela de Estudios Hispanoamericanos, 1963), as mentioned by Carmen Salazar Soler, "Antigüedad desfila en Potosí: Las fiestas de la Villa Imperial (1608, 1624, 1716)," in *La formación de la cultura virreinal II. El siglo XVII*, edited by Karl Kohut and Sonia V. Rose, 421 (Frankfurt: Vervuert/Madrid: Iberoamericana, 2000). The essay, based on descriptions of public festivities described by Arzáns de Orsúa y Vela in his *Historia de la Villa Imperial de Potosí* in the seventeenth century, focuses on the many images drawn from antiquity (and Renaissance sources) that were deployed in temporary decorations in colonial festivities.

[14] José de Mesa and Teresa Gisbert, *Historia de la pintura cusqueña*, 2 vols. (Lima: Fundación Augusto N. Wiese, 1982), 1:294.

[15] Guillermo Lohmann Villena, "Notas inéditas para ilustrar la Historia de Bellas Artes en Lima durante los Siglos XVI y XVII," *Revista Histórica. Órgano del Instituto Histórica del Perú* 13 (1940): 29–30.

[16] Alfredo Boulton, *Historia de la pintura en Venezuela*, 3 vols. (Caracas: Ernesto Armitano, 1964–1972), vol. 1 (1964), 50.

[17] Carlos F. Duarte, "La Provincia de Venezuela durante el siglo XVII en relación a la obra de Francisco de Zurbarán," in *Zurbarán y los conventos de América* (Caracas: Museo de Bellas Artes/Banco Mercantil, 1988), 48.

[18] The paintings were recently restored. Their history is outlined in www.unsam.edu.ar/escuelas/humanidades/centro/c_ceircab/sibilas.pdf. For a study of their iconography, see Hugo Francisco Bauzá, *La tradición sibilina y las sibilas de San Telmo* (Buenos Aires: Fondo Nacional de las Artes, 1999).

[19] Teresa Gisbert, "Del Cusco a Potosí. La religiosidad del sur andino," in *El barroco peruano*, edited by Ramón Mujica Pinilla (Lima: Banco de Crédito, 2002), 73.

[20] For fundamental studies of these paintings, see Luis Eduardo Wuffarden, "La serie del Corpus. Historia, pintura y ficción en el Cuzco del Siglo XVII," in *La procession del Corpus en el Cuzco* (Sevilla: Litografía Sáenz, 1996); and Carolyn Dean, *Inka Bodies and the Body of Christ. Corpus Christi in Colonial Peru* (Durham and London: Duke University Press, 1999).

[21] Enrique Valdivieso, *Pintura barroca sevillana* (Seville: Guadalquivir Ediciones, 2003), 47–48.

[22] Kinkead, "Juan de Luzón and the Sevillian Paintings Trade," 303.

[23] Kinkead, "Juan de Luzón and the Sevillian Paintings Trade," 305.

[24] Ibid.

[25] Luis Eduardo Wuffarden, "'Mirar sin envidia.' Emulación, diferencia y exaltación en la pintura del virreinato del Perú," in *Pintura de los reinos. Identidades compartidas. Territorios del mundo hispánico, siglos XVI–XVII*, 4 vols. (Mexico City: Grupo Financiero Banamex 2008), 2: 665.

[26] Kinkead, "Juan de Luzón and the Sevillian Paintings Trade," 305.

[27] Gabriele Finaldi, "Las doce tribus de Israel: Reencuentro familiar en el Museo del Prado," in *Zurbarán: Las doce tribus de Israel* (Madrid: Museo del Prado, 1995), 9–11.

[28] Ibid., 18–19.

[29] Lohmann Villena, "Notas inéditas," 28.

[30] Benito Navarrete Prieto, "Génesis y descendencia de 'Las Doce Tribus de Israel' y otras series zurbaranescas," in *Zurbarán. Las doce tribus de Israel. Jacob y sus hijos* (Madrid:

Museo del Prado, 1995), 54–55.
[31] Ibid., 9. ". . . all dressed in their traditional garments with corresponding attributes; each measuring two and one quarter *varas* tall so that all attain a perfect stature." (*todos vestidos con sus trajes e insignias correspondientes; midiendo dos varas y cuarta de alto para que puedan quedar de estatura perfecta.)*
[32] Francisco Manuel Martín Morales, "Aproximación al estudio del mercado de cuadros en la Sevilla barroca 1600–1670," *Archivo Hispalense*, ser. 2, vol. 69, no. 210 (1986): 154–160.
[33] Kinkead, "Juan de Luzón and the Sevillian Paintings Trade," 305.
[34] For a discussion of the popularity of the *Apostolados*, see Santiago Sebastián, *El barroco iberoamericano. Mensaje iconográfico* (Madrid: Ediciones Encuentro, 1990), 190–193.
[35] These paintings have been tentatively attributed to a Portuguese Jesuit, Domingo de Vasconcelos (c. 1605–c. 1670). Carlos Arbeláez Camacho and E. Gil Tovar, *El arte colonial en Colombia* (Bogotá: Ediciones Sol y Luna, 1968), 161.
[36] Boulton, *Historia de la pintura en Venezuela*, 122.
[37] See Martín Morales, "Aproximación al estudio del mercado de cuadros," 154–160.
[38] See Antonio Linage Conde, *El monacato en España e Hispanomérica* (Salamanca: Universidad Pontificia, 1977), 643–648.
[39] Fernando Cajias de la Vega, "Colecciones particulares de obras de arte en Oruro en el siglo XVIII," in *Manierismo y transición al barroco. Memoria del III Encuentro Internacional Sobre Barroco* (La Paz: Unión Latina, 2005), 129.
[40] Reflections of the engravings of anchorites may be found at www.colonialart.org, Galleries. Gallery 8. The Blessed Anchorites of Cuzco.
[41] Martín Morales, "Aproximación al estudio del mercado de cuadros," 154–160, and María Jesús Sanz and María Jesús Dabrio, "Inventarios artísticos sevillanos del siglo XVIII. Relación de obras artísticas," *Archivo Hispalense*, second series, vol. 57 (1974): 110.
[42] Kinkead, "Juan de Luzón and the Sevillian Paintings Trade," 303.
[43] Kinkead, "Juan de Luzón and the Sevillian Paintings Trade," 305.
[44] Martín Morales, "Aproximación al estudio del mercado de cuadros," 154–160.
[45] Mesa and Gisbert, "El pintor Mateo Pérez de Alesio," 42.
[46] Duarte, "La Provincia de Venezuela," 48.
[47] Agustina Rodríguez, "De Paris a Cuzco: Los caminos del grabado francés en los siglos XVII y XVIII," *Goya* no. 327 (April–June 2009): 112–131.
[48] Mesa and Gisbert, *Historia de la pintura cusqueña*, 1:169. The authors' suggestion that these images were intended to promote allegiance to the kings of Spain is speculative.
[49] Navarette Prieto, "Zurbarán y su obrador," 76.
[50] Duarte 1964, 50.
[51] Lohmann Villena, "Notas inéditas," 28.
[52] Although I do not know of a single representation of these medieval princes in South America, I am informed that there are a couple of Mexican versions in the Museo Franz Mayer in Mexico City.
[53] The document was published by Celestino López Martínez, *Notas para la historia del arte: Desde Martínez Montañés hasta Pedro Roldan* (Seville: Tipografía Rodríguez, Giménez y Compañía, 1932), 224–225. See also César Pemán, *Zurbarán y otros estudios sobre pintura del XVII español* (Madrid: Editorial Elpuerto, S.A., 1989), 259.
[54] For illustrations, see Navarrete Prieto 1999, 188–191.
[55] Pemán, *Zurbarán y otros estudios,* 259. See also María Luisa Caturla, "Otros dos Césares a caballo zurbaranescos," *Archivo Español de Arte* 38, nos. 151–152 (1965): 197–203.
[56] Martín Morales, "Aproximación al estudio del mercado de cuadros," 152 and 154–160.
[57] Lohmann Villena, "Notas inéditas," 12.
[58] Jorge Cornejo Bouroncle, "Arte cuzqueño," *Revista del Archivo Histórico del Cuzco* 1 (1951): 286.
[59] See Clara Bargellini's essay on paintings on copper in New Spain and Francisco Stastny's on Peru in *Copper as Canvas: Two Centuries of Masterpiece Painting on Copper, 1575–1775*, exh. cat., Phoenix Art Museum, Phoenix, AR (New York: Oxford University Press, 1999). In inventories of some private collections in Seville around 1700, one finds works of art described as *láminas de cobre, láminas de tabla, láminas en papel,* and even *láminas en lienzo*. The word *estampa* is used rarely, *grabado* not at all. It is therefore likely that many *láminas* listed in shipping documents and death inventories were in fact engraved prints. See Sanz and Dabrio, "Inventarios artísticos sevillanos," 89–148.
[60] See Neil De Marchi and Hans J. Van Miegroet, "Exploring Markets for Netherlandish Paintings in Spain and Nueva España," in *Kunst voor de Markt/Art for the Market 1500–1700, Nederlands Kunsthistorisch Jaarboek 1999, Deel 50/Netherlands Yearbook for History of Art 1999* (volume 50), edited by Reindert Falkenburg, Jan de Jong, Dulcia Meijers, Bart Ramakers, and Mariet Westermann (Zwolle: Waanders Uitgevers, 2000), 87. The title of this extremely useful article is a bit confusing, as the authors use "New Spain" to mean all of Spanish America, not just Mexico.
[61] Ibid., 88.
[62] Martín Morales, "Aproximación al estudio del mercado de cuadros," 152.
[63] Jorge Cornejo Bouroncle, "Arte cuzqueño," *Revista del Archivo Histórico del Cuzco* 2 (1952): 94.
[64] See, for example, Liliana Madrid de Zito Fontán, *El camino de los ángeles andinos: Argentina, Bolivia, Perú* (Salta, Argentina: Gotica, 2001), 12.
[65] Kinkead, "Juan de Luzón and the Sevillian Paintings Trade," 305.
[66] Ibid.
[67] Lutgardo García Fuentes, *El comercio español con América, 1650–1700* (Seville: Escuela de Estudios Hispano-Americanos, Consejo de Investigaciones Científicas, 1980), 324 and 505–506.
[68] Cornejo Bouroncle, "Arte cuzqueño," part 1, 286.
[69] Ibid., 289–291.

Royal Funerary Rites in Seventeenth-Century Lima

The Catafalque of Margaret of Austria

Jaime Mariazza F.

The exportation of works of art from Spain to the Viceroyalty of Peru, items that from the sixteenth century were registered as merchandise on shipboard, constituted one of the many factors contributing to transculturation. Major changes in the lives and ideas of native Americans were produced by the apparent replacement of traditional customs and ancestral beliefs by the recent arrivals. The export of these art objects signified more than merely their physical transfer from Spain to the New World. They embodied a novel repertory of images for official, public, and private use in tandem with the concepts and beliefs that underlay their plastic forms and their symbolic significance. The dissemination of these concepts formed an integral part of the catechizing duties of the missionary fathers throughout the viceroyalty. In their sermons the missionaries encouraged devotion to the imported images that illustrated the virtues and life events of the Holy Family and the saints. Similarly, the indigenous population gradually became accustomed to ceremonies in which both Catholicism and the Spanish monarchy were celebrated. As state and Church were identified as a single entity, a metaphoric vocabulary could be developed and put into practice during feast days, enabling both institutions to reinforce the fealty of the common people.

The religious and secular festivals of the viceregal calendar provided ample occasions for public celebrations. Among the latter, the most important ones were related to the king and his family, such as the birth of an heir or of other princes and princesses, enthronement, marriages, and funerals, forming a cycle repeated with every new monarch.[1] The viceroy was entitled to similar treatment, which was extended to his immediate family and to the clergy. The arrival of a new viceroy or his death would be marked by celebratory acts of enormous magnitude in which all social classes participated in a spectacle of both allegory and eulogy.[2] These fiestas were accompanied by ephemeral structures especially designed to display the signs and symbols that would encourage consideration of the merits of religion and government. For example, the death of a king was construed as a political event that emphasized the continuation of the dynasty, whose eternity was symbolized in funerary decorations by the phoenix, the sun, the moon, or the eagle. Royal funerary rites celebrated in Lima were designed to equate the eternity of the monarchy with the eternity of the Catholic faith. Kings were associated with mythical heroes and queens with female saints.[3] The funerary ceremony had three basic components: the catafalque, the public rites with their carefully structured protocols, and a narration published in book form in which all of the details of the ceremony were meticulously recorded.

The Catafalque

The catafalque was the monument around which all of the funerary rites revolved. In planning its construction, the viceregal government conducted a competition to choose the best design and decoration that the local builders and artisans could offer.[4] It was a simple architectural structure, atop a tall wooden stepped base, built of longitudinal and transverse beams and veneered with perishable materials such as plaster, fabric, and wood. Guided by the architectural vocabulary in fashion at the time, the artisans and professional decorators created columns, capitals, entablatures, and friezes. After it was painted, the structure was decorated with hanging draperies, sculptures, paintings, cartouches with literary quotations, and other writings in verse and prose. Paintings usually represented emblems or hieroglyphs.[5] The decoration replicated the scene inside the church where the tomb was placed, in order to conform to the tradition of *apparatus funebris*, which specified that the altars of the church be covered with cloths

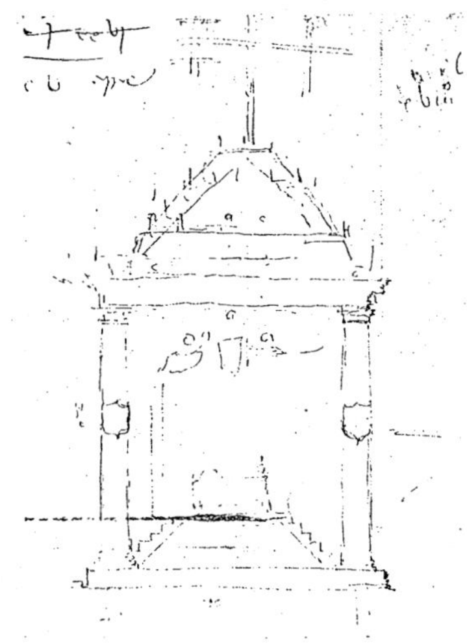

Fig. 1. Pedro Machuca, *Catafalque of María of Portugal.* 1549. Photo: J. Mariazza. Source: Antonio Bonet Correa.

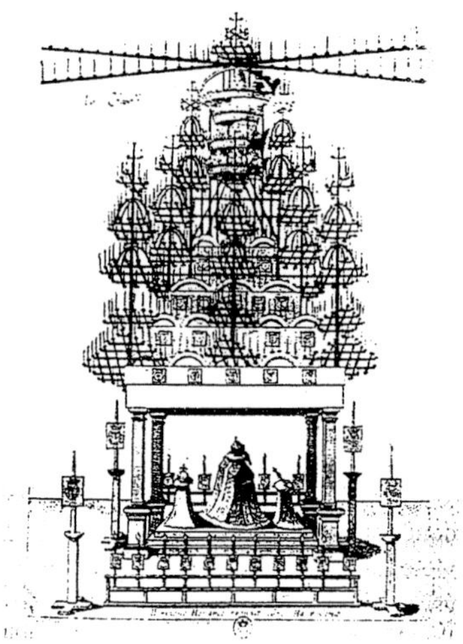

Fig. 2. *Catafalque of Charles I of Spain.* Brussels, 1559. Photo: J. Mariazza.

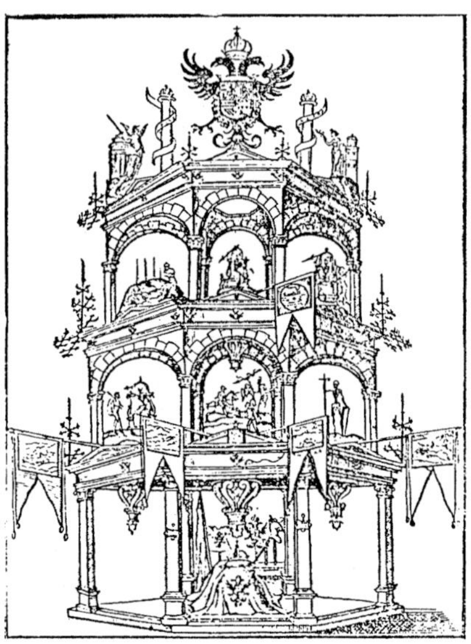

Fig. 3. *Catafalque of Charles I of Spain.* Valladolid, 1559. Photo: J. Mariazza. Source: Antonio Bonet Correa.

of black velvet. The windows were also covered, leaving the many wax torches on the catafalque itself as its only illumination during the mourning ceremonies. The themes expressed in the paintings and sculptures were often metaphors for the royal virtues praised in the eulogies.

The catafalque, commonly called *túmulo* in Spanish,[6] evolved from a funerary structure used in the Middle Ages, called *capelardente* by Spanish academics, an arrangement in which a symbolic coffin was placed atop a high, stepped wooden base and surrounded by candles.[7] In the mid-sixteenth century it was conceived as a small temple, as illustrated in a design by Pedro Machuca for the funeral of María of Portugal in 1549 (Fig. 1). With the death of Charles V in 1558, these funerary structures reached the apogee of their development and decorative complexity (Figs. 2, 3). It was this elaborate model that was exported to Peru, where it continued in use until the nineteenth century.

Protocol and Society: Death as Spectacle

Towards the end of the seventeenth century, the painters' workshops in the Viceroyalty of Peru created an iconographic model called the *Defense of the Eucharist* (Figs. 4, 5). It depicts a tabernacle containing the Host placed in a monstrance that is being menaced by infidels dressed in the manner of Muslims. They attempt to topple it with cords, while the holy object is defended by saints such as Thomas Aquinas, by archangels such as Michael, and by the king of Spain, sword in hand. This subject, which enjoyed multiple variations and great popularity in the decorative programs of the eighteenth century, expressed through the images the traditional role assigned to Spanish monarchs ever since Philip II structured his political agenda around the defense of the Catholic faith. Several generations of historians and researchers have agreed that Philip II, called "the prudent king," was a fervent Catholic who, in contrast to the emphasis on dynastic continuity in the politics of his father Charles I of Spain (Charles V of the Holy Roman Empire), conceived of his role as liberating the universe from heresy. Philip's zealous defense

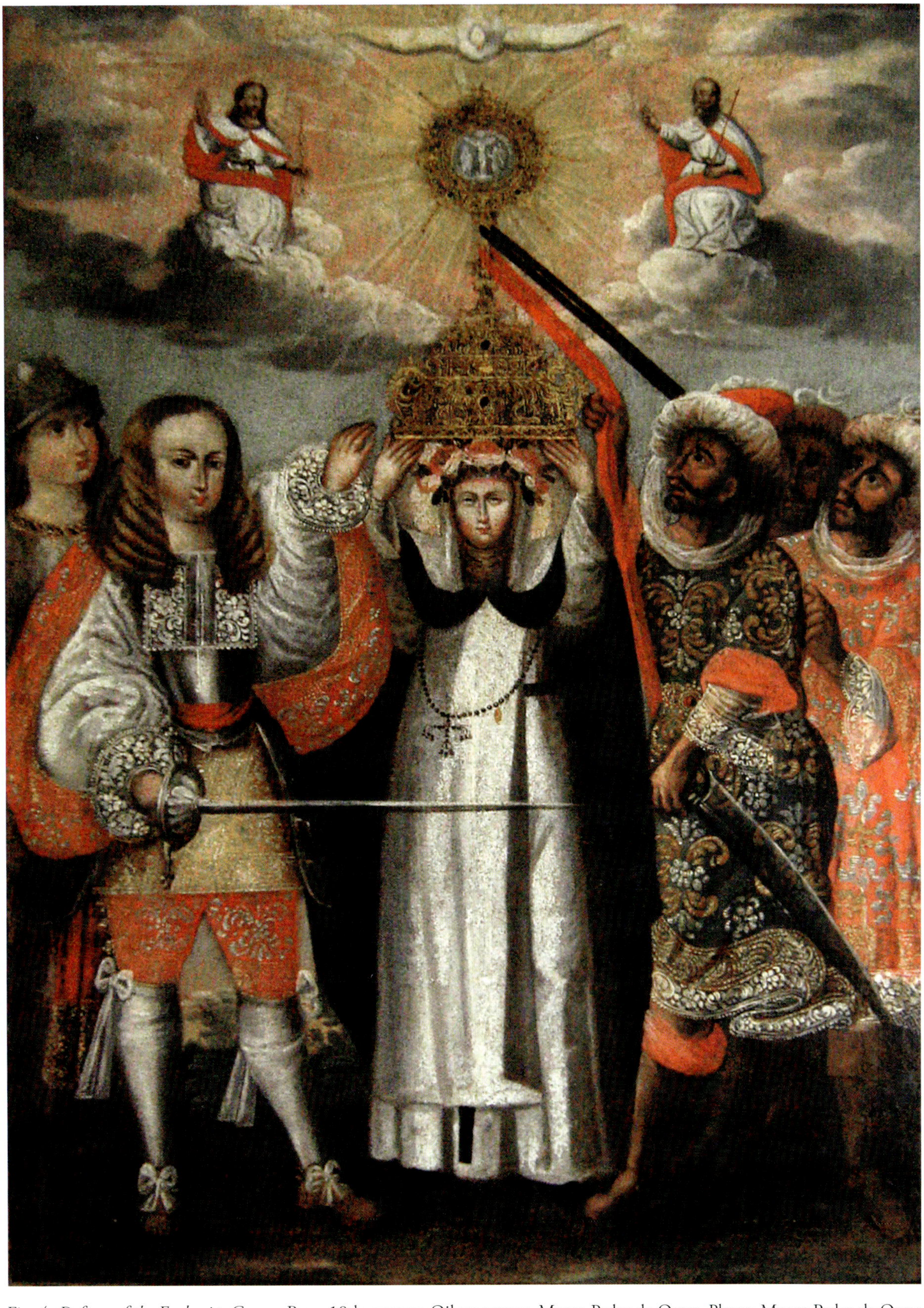

Fig. 4. *Defense of the Eucharist*. Cuzco, Peru, 18th century. Oil on canvas. Museo Pedro de Osma. Photo: Museo Pedro de Osma.

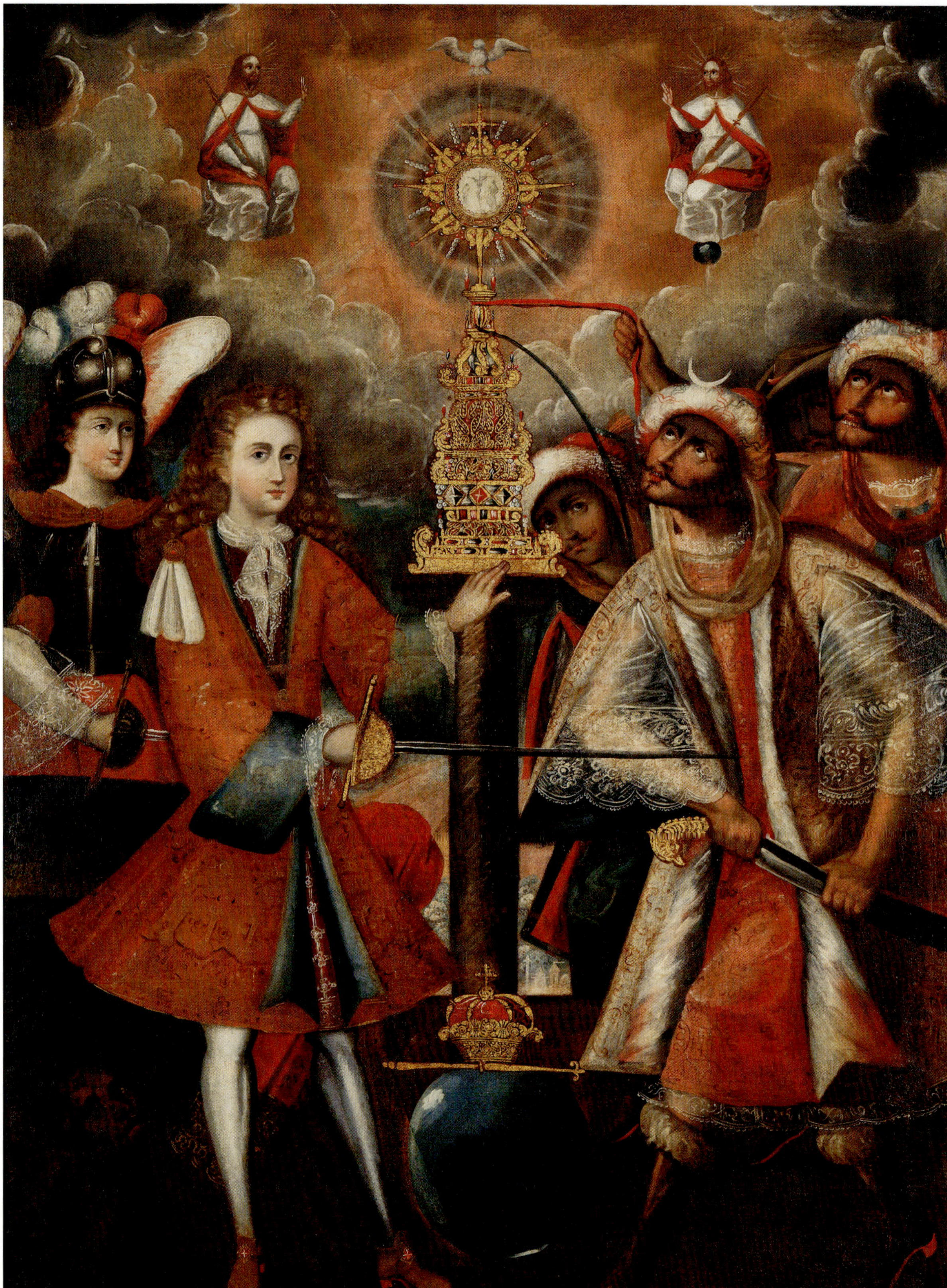

Fig. 5. *Defense of the Eucharist*. La Paz, Bolivia, 18th century. Oil on canvas. Denver Art Museum, Gift of Frank Barrows Freyer II for the Frank Barrows Freyer Collection; 1969.348.

of the faith, converted into a guiding principle of state politics, became a legacy that successive Spanish Habsburg kings regarded as a sacred duty to which they dedicated all available resources.[8] The Defense of the Eucharist theme clearly presents the king as the principal protagonist, and funeral narratives lauded the kings as heroes, comparing them to figures from antiquity such as Hercules, Achilles, and the Roman emperors. So, in their final public appearance, the monarchs merited the same recognition as was granted to mythical and ancient heroes, whose funerary observances were intended not only to honor them, but also to preserve in the collective memory the virtues demonstrated during their lives. The merits attributed to Spanish kings formed the basis of a tradition that expanded in richness and complexity the formal etiquette and decorative symbolism accompanying royal funerals. This process commenced with the funerary ceremonies of Emperor Charles V in 1558, and reached its most elaborate expression with the death of Philip IV in 1665. During these years, the funerary protocol established at the court in Madrid was repeated step by step in Spanish America. In the Viceroyalty of Peru, the complex rituals were enhanced by the melodramatic aspect of the ceremonies, which moved the attendees through both piety and curiosity. The funeral observances included a strong component of theatricality and street spectacle, whose sole pivot was reverence for the king's person.

The public festival in honor of the dead king consisted of processions in the streets in which the officials of state institutions marched on the day of mourning, to be followed by funerary rites in the cathedral of Lima, where the members of the viceregal government, both civil and military, took places assigned by the archbishop and the viceroy.

At the funeral of Mariana of Austria in 1697, a variant in the protocol was introduced. Since the viceroy was regarded as the member of Lima society most closely related to the king and his family, it was established that he would receive the condolences from local authorities as the first act of the ceremony.[9] Then the festival would continue in the interior of the cathedral, where the richly adorned catafalque contained a framed chart of the praise and eulogies for the deceased for the use of the attendees. In the days that followed, and for six months thereafter, daily masses in the presence of the public and lesser officials were offered in honor of the deceased. The symbolic coffin and monument remained in place for several days after the funeral rites and were later dismantled. Throughout the seventeenth and eighteenth centuries, until the last viceregal funeral was celebrated in Lima in honor of Archbishop La Reguera in 1805, all the ceremonies maintained similar protocol.[10]

The Book of Narration

The custom of writing a description of the funeral ceremony and its decorations originated in the Middle Ages. It was used in prominent political and religious circles to honor their most illustrious members in the form of a pamphlet containing poems and comments praising the deceased. In the modern era, the narration evolved into a book composed of several sections: royal approvals, anagrams, epigrams, and stanzas in honor of the deceased emphasizing his piety, as well as extolling the author of the narrative. Later, what may be called the heart of the book was added, that is, a meticulous narration of the funerary ceremonies and a detailed description of the rites prescribed for the period of mourning. Often, a description of the catafalque was included, which became increasingly complex in accordance with the size and form of the structure. An engraving of the catafalque was inserted into the book as a necessary visual aid for the text.

Such narrative texts were first used in Spain to mark the death of Charles V, and their use became widespread thereafter. By the beginning of the seventeenth century, funeral books had become increasingly complex in both composition and vocabulary. These rhetorical devices would reach their most elaborate development in the mid-1600s and would be repeated in all the books until the second half of the following century.

The first publication of this type in the Viceroyalty of Peru was printed in 1613 during the celebration of the funerary rites of Queen

Margaret of Austria, wife of Philip III.[11] Allegorical figures commonly appeared on the covers of these books, along with the approval of the viceregal council, historical information, and references to the receipt of the royal dispatch confirming the death. Another section might recount the schedule of the rites and detail the construction of the tomb and decorative emblems. There was great variety among the poems and prose selected to celebrate the virtues of the deceased. One striking difference between the books produced in Spain and those in Peru is that some Spanish writers would dwell upon the king's illness and subsequent embalmment, a topic not discussed by the writers in Lima, even in the case of local dignitaries. The official record of the events pertaining to the rites of mourning involved the viceregal academic world, and became a select space for cultivated expression. Lima's intellectuals regarded this task as an opportunity to enhance their personal prestige through a display of their erudition. Thus, they frequently alluded to pagan mythology and to classical authors such as Virgil, Homer, and Herodotus, as well as to historical heroes like Alexander the Great and to certain Roman emperors. They often explained the meaning of the iconographic attributes, or justified their use in the eulogistic context of the composition. Allusions to figures mentioned in the Bible, stories from the Old Testament, and references to faith and justice became recurrent themes.

The city of Lima has preserved nearly all of the descriptions of state funerals occurring during the viceroyalty. They constitute a fundamental source of information for the study of viceregal funerary customs. Many of the books included engraved illustrations of diverse subjects: allegorical figures, coats-of-arms, heraldic elements, portraits, vignettes, and, of course, an image of the catafalque, but not always realized with the rich ornamentation mentioned in the text. Sometimes, the names of the architect who designed the tomb and the engraver who preserved it with his burin were given. A final section in some books was dedicated to lamentations and poems in memory of the deceased, in which the most distinguished writers of the moment competed.

In some cases, the book's author would seek technical advice in order to describe the funerary monument with precise terminology. In others, the descriptions of the catafalques are less rigorous, emphasizing instead the pomp and pageantry of the rites. From the quality of the writing, it is not difficult to distinguish writers who had actually attended the ceremony and seen the *apparatus funebris* from those who merely cobbled together experiences from past ceremonies.

Because of the high cost of printing illustrated books, typically only one or two copies would contain the engraving of the tomb. The larger size of the illustration required extra labor to attach it to the book, thereby increasing the price. The illustrated books would be given to the king and viceroy, whereas the highest court functionaries would receive the text only. This explains why some copies of the book narrating the funeral rites of Queen Margaret of Austria lack the engraving of the catafalque, while the copy in the library of the Congress of Deputies in Madrid, originally held in the Royal Library there, does include it. Four narrative books pertaining to the funerary rites of kings Charles II and Philip V, two for each, do contain the engravings. Of the illustrated books for Charles II, one copy is in the National Library of Peru, and a similar one is in Spain. Of those in honor of Philip V, one is kept in the Library of the Pontificia Universidad Católica del Perú, and the other held at Yale University. The other books that have survived intact and are held in libraries in Lima, Cuzco, and Arequipa surely came from the highest circles of viceregal authorities.

The Tomb of Queen Margaret of Austria-Styria in Lima

The death of Margaret of Austria, wife of Philip III, took place on October 3, 1611 in San Lorenzo of the Escorial. Her memory was honored in a variety of ceremonies in Spanish and American cities. In Madrid, Cuenca, Mexico City, Quito, and Lima, the funerary rites of the queen were performed in strict accordance with the tradition established in the fifteenth century. In the case of Lima the official notice confirming the death of the queen was contained in the royal dispatch of October 1612, though travelers arriving from Buenos Aires and Mexico City brought the news earlier. Of particular interest was the news from Mexico, where impressive ceremonies for the queen had already taken place, owing to the fact that the official confirmation of her death arrived earlier there than in Lima. Upon hearing the rumors, the viceroy, Don Juan de Mendoza, Marquis de Montesclaros, acted quickly and ordered the city's master builders to go forward with the design and construction of the tomb. By the time the official communication from Philip III arrived, the construction of the funerary architecture, created by Juan Martínez de Arrona, was well advanced; it was completed by November 15. Public notices spread the news around the city while other preparations were being made, such as the selection of the Augustinian priest fray Martín de León for the reading of the funeral service, which took place on 23 and 24 November 1612.[12]

The cover of the book of narration bears an engraving by Francisco Bejarano, which probably was designed by him (Fig. 6). It consists of two horizontal plaques placed above mannerist ornamentation and containing inscriptions. The title of the book appears in the top portion, while the dedication to the viceroy by the author of the narration occupies the lower portion. To the extreme left is found the name of Francisco Bejarano as the engraver, and on the opposite side "Lima 1612." A coat-of-arms occupies the central part. It rests upon a scroll-like ornament with a royal crown at the crest and corresponds to the arms of Viceroy de Montesclaros as they appeared in a publication of 1609 celebrating his arrival in Lima.[13] A double cord hangs from the upper plaque suspending a circular medallion on each side. The left side shows the sun with a human face; the right, a heart pierced by two arrows and a Latin inscription.

This book differs slightly from the one found in Madrid. Though the text is identical, the covers are not. In the Madrid version (Fig. 7), a small medallion formed by laurel leaves appears above the shield with the human-faced sun, along with

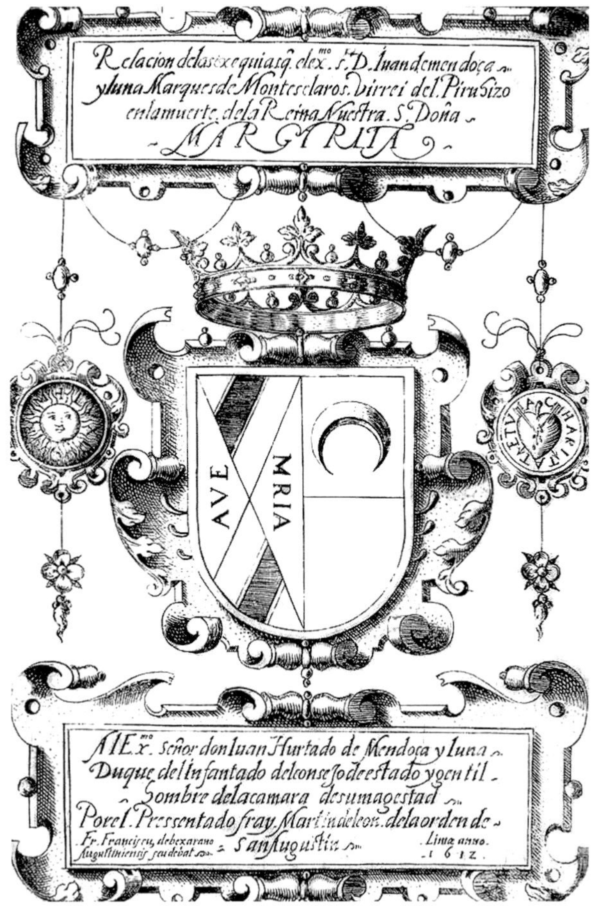

Fig. 6. (front page) *Funerary book of Margaret of Austria*. Lima, 1613. Biblioteca Nacional del Perú. Photo: Biblioteca Nacional del Perú.

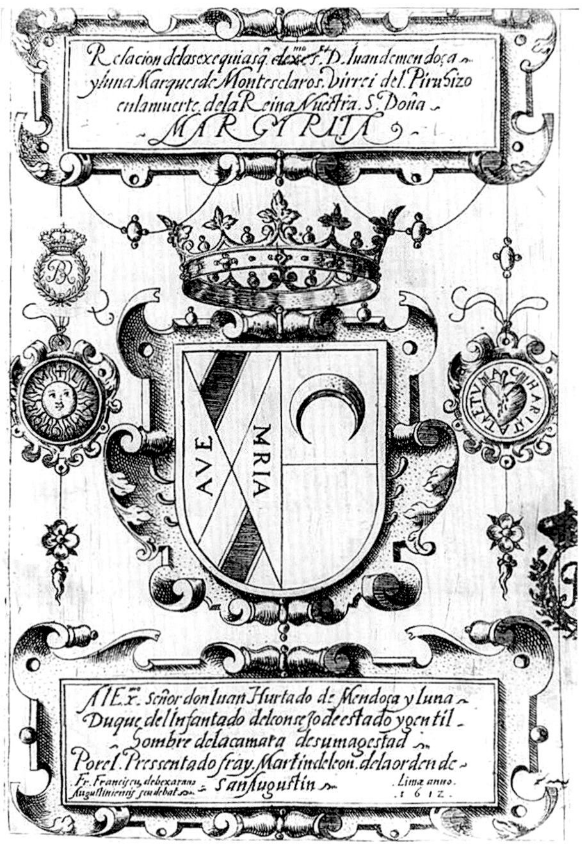

Fig. 7. (front page) *Funerary book of Margaret of Austria*. Lima, 1613. Library of Congress of Deputies, Madrid. Photo: Rafael Ramos S.

an imperial crown with the initials BR inside. This ornamental detail does not appear on the cover of the book in Lima. It is a small engraving glued over the original paper in order to indicate its location and to whom it belonged. On the Madrid copy, the initials reveal that the book had been held originally in the Royal Library (Biblioteca Real). Its cover also bears a seal with similar characteristics on the opposite side.[14]

The cover of the book of Margaret's funeral rites, being the first of its kind printed in the Viceroyalty of Peru, must have made a very favorable impression upon the writers and printers of the time. In the same year, 1613, The *Registry of Indians Living in Lima* was also published. Produced by Miguel de Contreras, the royal notary, the cover of the book is an exact copy of the funerary book cover (Fig. 8), except for the inscriptions in the upper and lower cartouches and in the side medallions.[15]

From an analysis of its structure, one can conclude that several authors were involved in the composition of a book of funerary honors. Their contributions, as in other small literary works, served to enrich the central theme and to reinforce its laudatory character, which was directed not only to the deceased, but also to the authorities and the named author. The responsibility of the latter was to relate meticulously the events surrounding the arrival of the news in Lima, the death of the royal personage, the funerary arrangements, the ceremony itself, and the tomb, with mention of each bit of ornamentation and the writing enclosed within. Included also was a section dedicated to the hieroglyphs placed in the tomb, which were selected by a contest held among the local priests; the book classified and exhibited their contributions in strict order of merit.

The ceremonies that accompanied the funerary rites of the queen were the first to be attended by representatives of nearly all organs of the viceregal administration. Father Martín de León mentioned in his account the participation of the archbishopric, including students from the school of Saint Toribio, priests from the parishes of Lima, royal chaplains, chorus masters from the cathedral, clergymen, and finally, the archbishop and his servants. Lastly, the retinue of the viceroy marched in the procession along with other dignitaries, political, administrative, and academic. All of these groups, wearing elegant garments and carrying banners, processed through the streets in silence en route to the cathedral, where services would be held.

The catafalque of Margaret of Austria was of the temple/tower type, as were all of the others constructed in Lima during the first half of the seventeenth century (Fig. 9). It consisted of two sections, one in the form of a small temple, ending in a cupola with a lantern, on top of which a crowned skull was placed. The lower portion had a square ground plan, measuring about 7.5 m. per side (the flanking sections are not included) and 17.5 m. in height. The wall surfaces were decorated with plastered wood panels painted to look like dark-colored marble, which, because of the projecting wall panels, produced a quilted look. Rectangular panels covered the lower portion of the wall and square ones the top section. A beveled molding separated the two zones. This same decoration was repeated in the side portions. According to Father Martín de León, there were four columns on the front side that formed angles over which rested round arches. On the upper part twelve Doric columns were distributed in groups of three on top of the pillars: one in each angle and flanked by the other two. This program was repeated on each of the four sides.

The engraving shows the front of the structure looking towards the main door of the temple. There were four Doric columns, two on each side of the central vault surmounted by an entablature. The book of narration states that these columns bore inscriptions that alluded to the queen's virtues. The entablature was formed by an architrave, a frieze decorated with Latin inscriptions, and a cornice with the letters DOMS. The structures on either side of the lower section were of the same height and nearly 12 m. long each. They consisted of two quadrangular pillars that formed four archways. The outer two had round arches and the inner ones had lintels on both sides of the central

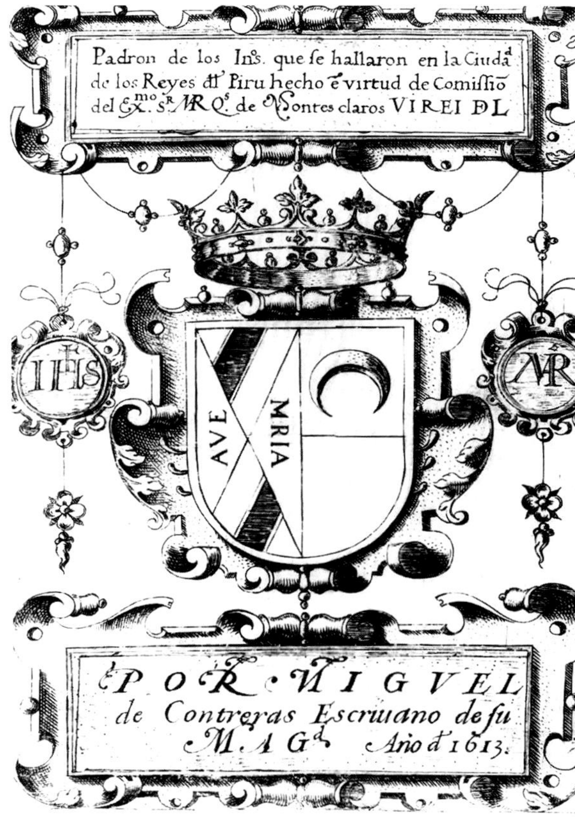

Fig. 8. (front page) *Registry of Indians Living in Lima.* 1613. Photo: Rafael Ramos S.

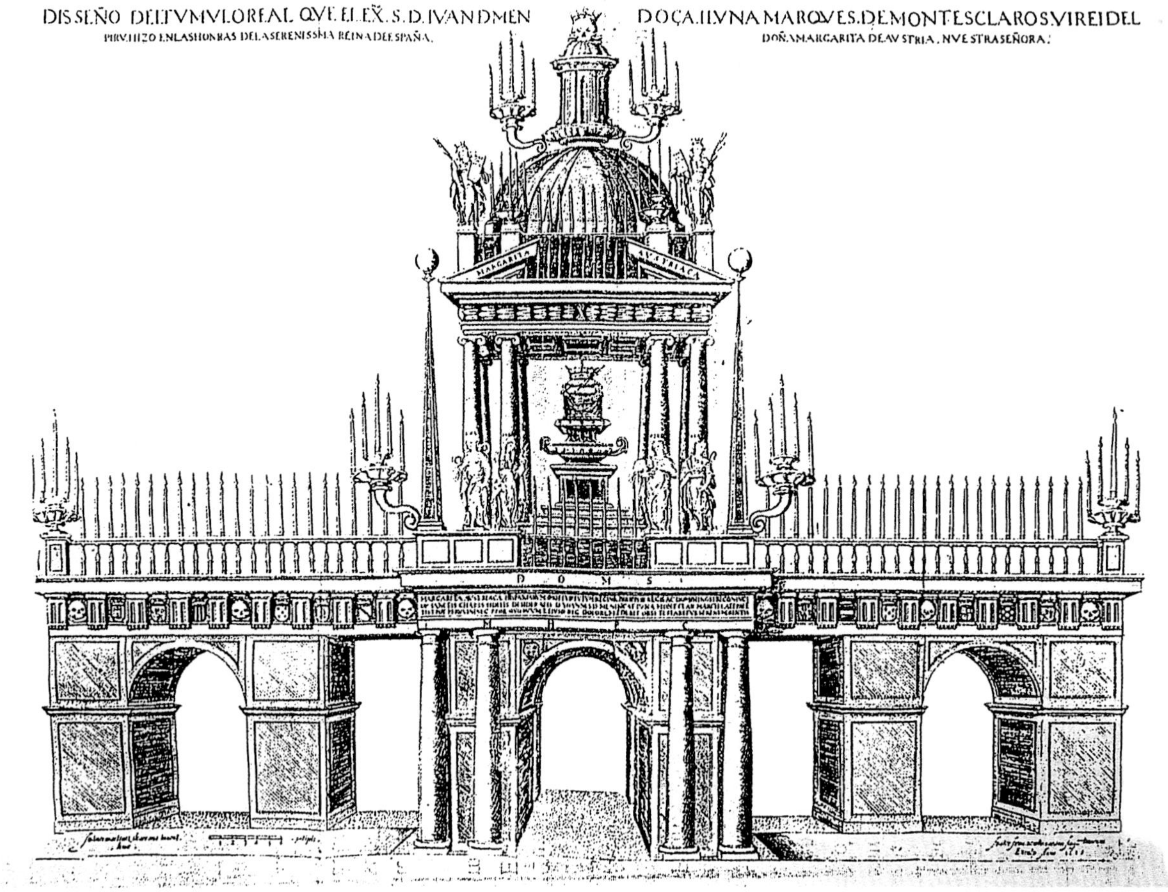

Fig. 9. *Catafalque of Margaret of Austria*. Lima, 1612. Library of Congress of Deputies, Madrid. Photo: J. Mariazza.

Fig. 10. Detail of Fig. 9.

space, thus forming a façade of five open spaces with interspersed arches and lintels. The side sections and the lower central structure were equal in height so that their entablatures met to form one continuous entablature band with the only difference occurring in the frieze where the triglyphs appeared together with the skulls, and the shields of the cities of the Spanish empire replaced the metopes (Fig. 10). So triglyphs, metopes, and skulls alternate in logical fashion, and a candelabrum was placed at each end. To complete these structures, a balustrade of wax torches and a candelabrum of five lights were placed on each end.

The top structure was also in the form of a temple, though of smaller dimensions than the lower portion (Fig. 9). It rose from a base divided into two segments whose front part, open and decorated with three insets on each side, led to a small balustrade with eight lighted torches. In each angle, and independent of the base, were four pinnacles ending in spheres that coincided with the angular columns of the lower structure, giving to both portions a stylistically homogenous appearance as a compact tower form. The structure was supported by twelve Ionic columns arranged in groups of three, one of which was located in the angle, accompanied on each side by the other two. The entablature was decorated with a running frieze of laurel leaves and a triangular broken pediment bearing the inscription, *MARGARITA AUSTRIACA*, one word in each portion of the cornice atop the pediment. The royal cenotaph was placed in the center of the structure. As in the case of the lower structure, cartouches bearing inscriptions testifying to the virtues of the queen were placed over each column of the upper portion. Next to the columns were sixteen sculptures of the strong women of the Old Testament, four on each side, whose virtues were identified with those of the queen. A balustrade topped this portion, and, on high pedestals, were sculpted figures representing the four Saint Margarets, with torches on top and two candelabra of five lights on each side. A cupola and a lantern surmounted the entire structure, with two candelabra of five lights at the base. A crowned skull was placed over the lantern.

The catafalque of Queen Margaret of Austria in Lima shares many characteristics with the tomb in honor of Philip II in the cathedral of Seville in 1598[16] (Fig. 11). The continuation of this plan in other tombs in Lima during the first half of the seventeenth century, such as the one dedicated to Philip III in 1622 (Fig. 12), invites a reflection on the symbolism of the structure, which differs in many respects from catafalques constructed after 1645. Tombs like Queen Margaret's were designed around two linear axes, one horizontal and the other vertical, which refer metaphorically to the human body and mind respectively. These concepts are related to ancient astrological theories, applied to architecture and to the study of natural phenomena by Greek theorists such as Ctesibios (285–222 B.C.), and to the philosophical analyses of Roman thinkers, followers of oriental eclecticism, such as Marcus Terentius Varro (116–27 B.C.). These sources were revisited by Vitruvius (80/70–15 B.C.) in his commentaries on geometrical forms, symmetrical arrangement, and dimensions, in particular, his observations of the universe and planets in the ninth book of his *De architectura libri decem*, known during the Middle Ages and continually republished after 1486. The horizontal section is associated with the earth through the symbolism of the square form, upon which the ground plan of the small temple below the tomb itself was based. It connects with the side structures, whose elaborate decoration, as will be described later, emphasizes skulls and skeletons. This type of ornamentation reinforced the idea of death as related to the human being/earth body. The vertical section of the tomb pertains to the mind and soul because both aspire to reach God, the first through knowledge and the second through the desire to unite with him to form a single entity, according to medieval texts that deal with the stages of the mystical life. Accordingly, the virtues are the most significant symbolic element in this sector, occupying a major role in the ornamentation of the second and third levels of the monument. The low, medium, and high registers identify with the notions of medieval philosophy regarding the body, mind, and soul

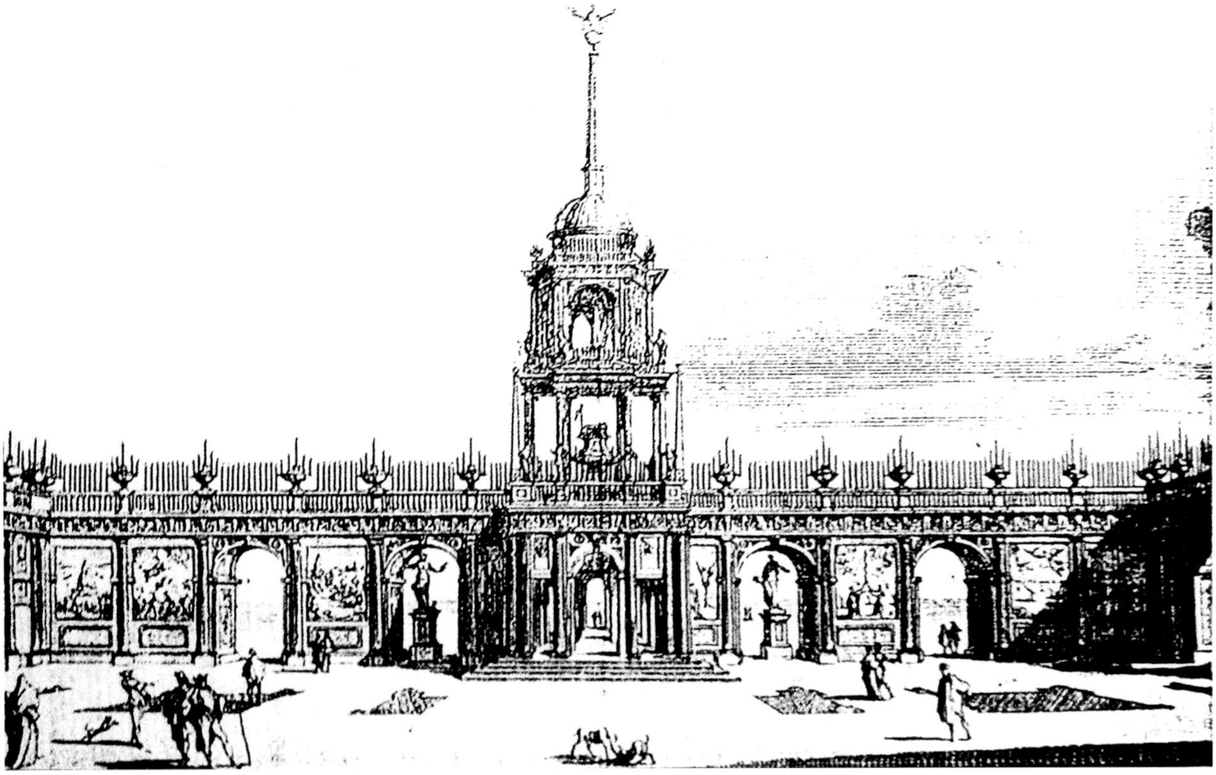

Fig. 11. *Catafalque of Phillip II*. Seville, 1598. Photo: http://elninofrito.blogspot.com/2010_06_01_archive.html.

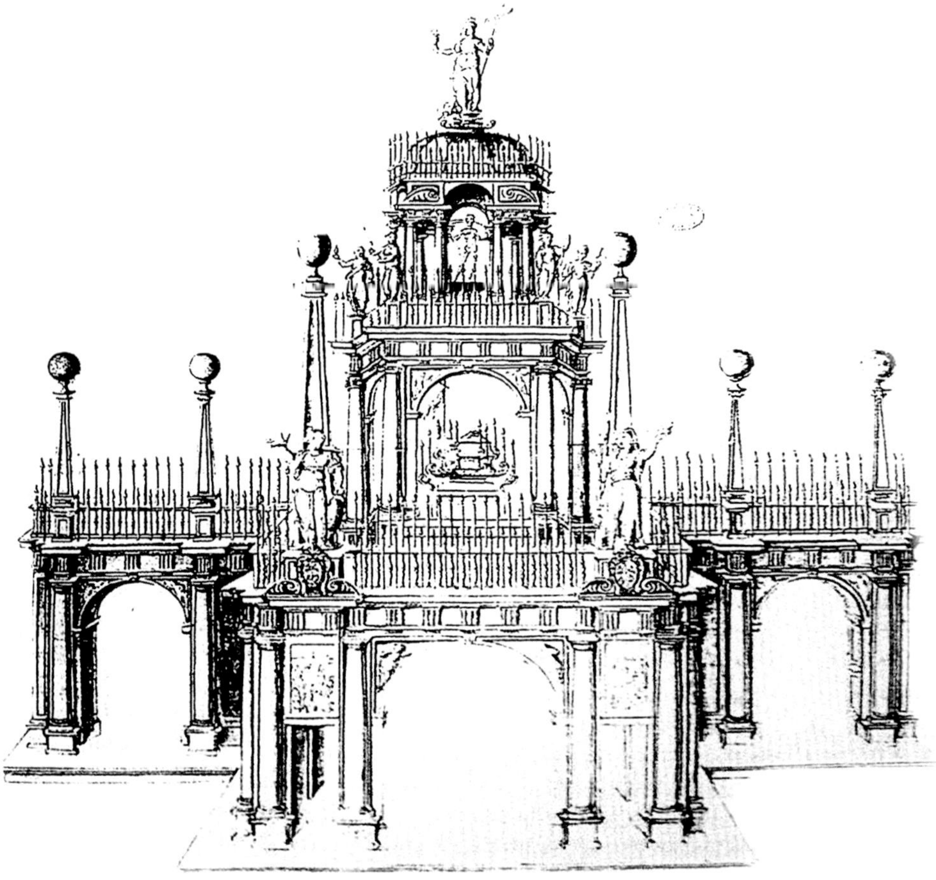

Fig. 12. *Catafalque of Phillip III*. Lima, 1622. Photo: Enrique Marco Dorta, *Fuentes para la historia del arte hispanoamericano. Estudios y Documentos*. Sevilla, 1951.

respectively. The guiding principle of the design is embodied in the intersection of the two axes. The distribution of the columns of the second level, where the royal cenotaph was placed, indicates a symbolic concept of space. However, if the columns at the angles are united in one's imagination, a square is obtained. Likewise, if we unite the two columns that accompany the first in each of the four angles, an octagon is formed. The square and octagon appear as an allegory of the universe, polarized between earth and heaven, the first synonymous with life and the second a metaphor for the resurrection of the spirit.[17]

The triumph of death was expressed by several plastic formulas, the most common of which was the crowned skull. In the catafalque of Queen Margaret it surmounts the entire funerary structure. Other concepts, such as the triumph over death popularized by the allegorical repertories of the Renaissance, alluded to here in the figures of the virtues and holy women, were replaced by an emphasis on the merits of royalty. Over time, this tradition coalesced into the idealization of monarchical values.

According to the writings of Fr. Martín de León, the side sections of the catafalque of Margaret of Austria-Styria were decorated with eight paintings, four to a side. Occupying the space of metopes, the paintings symbolized death in the form of skulls, each bearing its epithets and Latin verses, which Martín de León translated. Death is described as *certain, uncertain, impartial, unfair, rapid, unexpected, overly hasty* and *unforeseen*. These adjectives emphasize the commonality of death and the fact that, even when death is expected, no one knows when it will come. These musings on death alternate in the program with heraldic elements, such as coats of arms and other symbols of political power, painted and accompanied by Latin verse.

On the other side, personifications of the four continents in female form appear next to the figure of death, who receives a pearl from each of them. This scene alludes to the name of the queen and her journey from the land of the living to the dwelling of the dead. Her virtues are expressed through the images of the strong women of the Bible. Paintings of plants and trees are also included, accompanied by Latin inscriptions whose symbolic significance is found in the writings of Hesiod and Ovid, the Old Testament, the Gospels, and the book of Revelation. Martín de León cites the palm as related to eternal life and associates the laurel with triumph. He attributes to the cypress a funerary significance based upon myths narrated by Ovid. The poplar symbolizes the passion of Christ. The pine is related to immortality. In a passage in the book of Isaiah God promises him the multiplication of his descendants, comparing them with willows. The olive is a symbol of peace. The grapevine acquires a Eucharistic significance when interpreted as a symbol of Christ's blood, but it is also considered a metaphor for conjugal harmony and friendship, qualities attributed to Queen Margaret as wife, friend, and a woman of deep faith.[18]

Celebrated in this manner, the death of the king or of a high-ranking dignitary of Church or state in both Spain and America was not only an aesthetic and intellectual practice, but also an ideological exercise of great importance, repeated cyclically. The funerary rites provided a valuable opportunity to present an iconographic discourse that subliminally established a mindset and a standard of social behavior in accordance with the dictates of political and religious power. If, in other aspects of viceregal culture, there existed signs of resistance to the requirements of authority, this celebration, like all official acts, promoted a policy of homogeneity in compliance with both ritual exigencies and the content of their symbolic messages.

Notes

[1] Alejandra Osorio, "El Rey en Lima. El simulacro real y el ejercicio del poder en la Lima del diecisiete," *Documento de Trabajo, 140. Serie Historia, 27* (Lima: Instituto de Estudios Peruanos, 2004), 8–12.

[2] José (1640–1686) and Francisco (1686–1697) Mugaburu, *Chronicle of Colonial Lima*, translated and edited by Robert Ryal Miller (Norman: University of Oklahoma Press, 1975), 43–233.

[3] Víctor Minguez, *Los reyes solares: Iconografía astral de la monarquía hispánica* (Valencia: Publicaciones de la Universidad Jaime I, 2001), 12–34.

[4] Fr. Martín de León y Cárdenas, *Relación de las exequias q. el ex.mo Sr. D. Juan de Mendoça y Luna Marques de Montesclaros…izo en la muerte de la Reina Nuestra S. Doña Margarita…* (Lima: Pedro de Merchán y Calderón, 1613), 5–54.

[5] Lorene Pouncey, "Túmulos of Colonial Peru," *The Art Bulletin of the College of Art of America* 67, no. 1 (1985). Olga Berendsen, "The Italian Sixteenth and Seventeenth Century Catafalques" (Ph.D. diss., New York University, 1961).

[6] Berendsen, "The Italian Sixteenth and Seventeenth Century Catafalques."

[7] Antonio Bonet Correa, "Túmulos del Emperador Carlos V," *Archivo Español de Arte* 33 (1960); Victoria Soto Caba, *Los catafalcos reales del barroco español. Un estudio de arquitectura efímera* (Madrid: U.N.E.D., 1992), 14–22.

[8] Rafael Altamira, *Manual de historia de España* (Buenos Aires: Editorial Sudamericana, 1946), 77–120.

[9] Rafael Ramos Sosa, *Arte festivo en Lima virreinal siglos XVI y XVII* (Sevilla: Junta de Andalucía y Consejería de Cultura y Medio Ambiente, 1992), 22–54.

[10] The last colonial catafalque was built in Arequipa. See Cristina Esteras and Ramón Gutiérrez, "Un túmulo funerario neoclásico en Arequipa (Perú)," *Anales de Historia del Arte* 9 (1999): 237–244.

[11] Fr. Martín de León y Cárdenas, *Relación de las exequias,* 1613.

[12] José Simón Díaz, *Bibliografía de la literatura hispánica,* vol. 13, nos. 1326, 1327, and 1328 (Madrid: CSIC-Instituto Miguel de Cervantes de filologia hispanica, 1984). For a more extensive biography see Juan José Vallejo Penedo, *Fray Martín de León y Cárdenas, OSA, obispo de Pozzuoli y arzobispo de Palermo, 1584–1655* (Madrid: Editorial Revista Agustiniana, 2001).

[13] Pedro de Oña, *Temblor de Lima Año de 1609….* (Lima: Imprenta de Francisco del Canto, 1609).

[14] A kind suggestion by Dr. Rafael Ramos S.

[15] Photo courtesy of Dr. Rafael Ramos S.

[16] Adelaida Allo Manero, "Aportación al estudio de las exequias reales en Hispanoamérica. La influencia sevillana en algunos túmulos limeños y mejicanos," *Anuario del Departamento de Historia y Teoría del Arte* 1 (1989): 121–137.

[17] Platón, *Diálogos: Timeo o de la naturaleza,* vol. 2 (México, D.F.: Editorial Porrúa, 2007), 333–384.

[18] Hesiodo, *Teogonía* (Madrid: Alianza Editorial, 2008); Ovidio, *Metamorfosis*, vol. 10 (Madrid: Cátedra Letras Universales, 2009); Cayo Plinio Segundo, el Viejo, *Historia Natural* 14, no. 10, and 35, no. 13 (Madrid: Visor Libros, 1998); Guy de Tervarent, *Atributos y símbolos en el arte profano. Diccionario de un lenguaje perdido* (Barcelona: Ediciones del Serbal, 2002), 28–32.

Molded and Modeled
Sculptural Replication in the Early Modern Transatlantic World

Sara Ryu

Although still relatively unknown outside of Spain and Mexico, the Christ of Telde has attracted the interest of scholars throughout the second half of the twentieth century since Pedro Hernández Benítez's 1940 publication, *El santo Cristo del altar mayor de la parroquia de San Juan Bautista de Telde*. The 2002 study of the sculpture by Pablo Amador, *Traza española, ropaje indiano. El Cristo de Telde y la imaginería en caña de maíz*, has invigorated renewed interest in the cult statue. The following essay would not have been possible without Amador's groundbreaking research. Amador not only restored the Christ of Telde but also, more recently, has questioned the long-standing assumption that the technique used to create such sculptures was of indigenous origins. What is more, in a 2009 publication he proposed that the technique was developed in Europe, drawing an historical connection between the use of mold-made sculpture in Granada and in New Spain. Amador's dissertation and forthcoming book promise further major contributions to the study of this corpus. Building upon these earlier discoveries, in the following article I examine the Christ of Telde in light of three concepts—replication, dissimulation, and reuse—as a means to consider how the facture of art informs its interpretive analysis.

While the histories of many cult images are enlivened with famous legends attesting to the miraculous nature of an object's creation and peregrinations, the narrative of the Christ of Telde's arrival in the Canary Islands is, simply put, a matter of conquest and commerce (Figs. 1 and 2).[1] The only record of the sculpture's arrival on the island of Gran Canaria is provided by the seventeenth-century Spanish medical doctor Tomás Arias Marín de Cubas. In the 1694 redaction of his *Historia de las siete islas de Canaria* the author sets aside the central themes of his study on pre-Hispanic Canarian life and European conquest of the archipelago to expound at length upon the cult image venerated in his hometown. Although this statue is located in one of the oldest Christian sanctuaries on the island, the church of San Juan Bautista in Telde, it was not, according to Marín de Cubas, locally made:

> Above the tabernacle on the central wall of the high altar there is a Crucified Christ of life size, its face divinely beautiful, very holy and of many miracles; its fabrication was in the West Indies by Spanish hands and, thanks to the first fruits of wine and sugar on this island [Gran Canaria], it was brought to Telde by the first settlers of the Indies: its material is spongy, like a soft paper [*fungosa, papírea, ó bombicínea*], made of the heart of stalks of corn similar to the heart of the branch of the fig tree, of reed or fennel: and yet our true pursuit brings us to the other Crucified Christ, a wonder with no equal in Nature because it is completely Divine.[2]

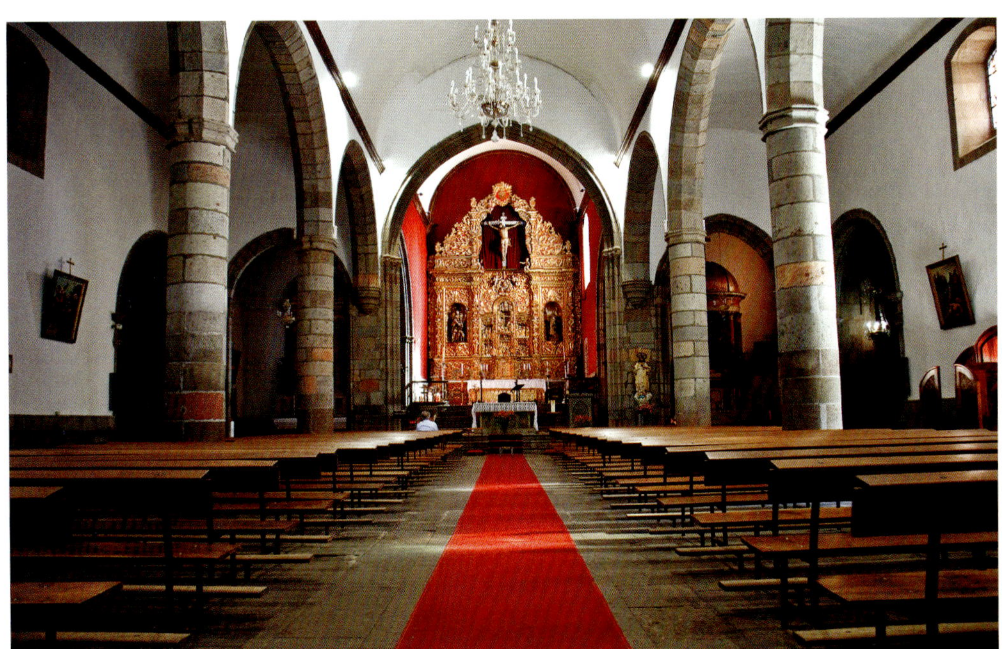

Fig. 1. Central nave, Church of San Juan Bautista. Telde, Gran Canaria, Spain. Photo: author.

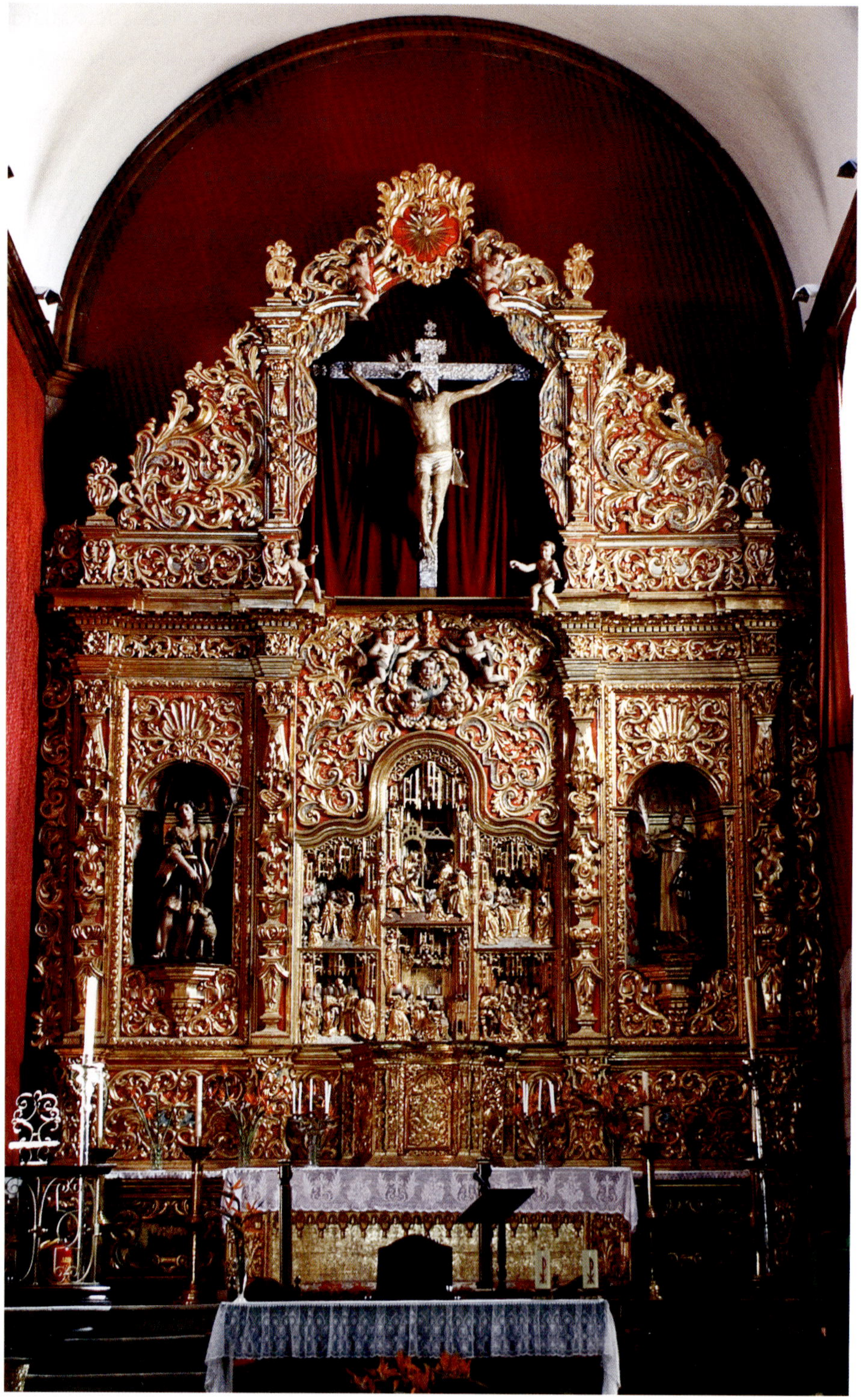

Fig. 2. High altar, Church of San Juan Bautista. Telde, Gran Canaria, Spain. Photo: author.

Sugar and wine, the first two principal crops cultivated on the Canary Islands after the archipelago was conquered by the Crown of Castile in 1496, were mono-cultivations produced for the sole purpose of global export. The isolated islands depended on an economy of exportation in order to bring in everything else: people to settle the land, manufactured products such as tools to work the land, foodstuffs and other bare necessities, and, as we see here, works of art. From the Valley of Mexico to Gran Canaria, the Christ of Telde was borne aloft the trade winds that united the Atlantic world, leaving one site of Spanish conquest only to be destined for another. In an era of European overseas expansion, art found itself inextricably involved in matters of conquest and commerce. The Atlantic Ocean separated the creation of the image from its reception, but that was of little consequence for Marín de Cubas. He never traveled to the New World; the New World traveled to him.

The varied histories of New World objects in transit across the globe have recently become a subject of renewed scholarly interest.[3] Studies across disciplines converge on the shared task of tracing the social biography of things, treating the lives of objects as entrances into the larger project of understanding the interconnectedness of the early modern world.[4] But to simply state that an object moved along pathways of empire and trade is, of late, an insufficient claim. Scholars are now seeking to reconstruct the aftermath of such transatlantic journeys, when an object's value shifted and its status transformed, becoming a wondrous object in the princely *Wunderkammer*, a commodity on the wealthy dinner table, or a sacred image on the Christian altar.[5] Recent discussions, in particular, have focused on the visibility—and, by extension, the connotation—of the New World in the Old.[6] Could a distinct quality of American Otherness mark an artifact, and, if so, could such Otherness be visibly deduced? Marín de Cubas considers the Christ of Telde to be different on account of its provenance and its material, that is, its origins in the West Indies and its incorporation of maize, the essential sustenance of Mesoamerica. Such alterity, however, was and remains invisible on the surface of the object. The appearance of the Christ of Telde fails to disclose information about either its etiology or its materiality. Our seventeenth-century source, in effect, performs an exercise in describing the unseen; the words "*fungosa, papírea, ó bombicínea*" capture not the contours of the sculpted artifact, but rather the qualities of what is hidden inside it.

The central focus of this essay is an image of the Crucifixion that draws exceptional attention to neither its subject matter nor its style (Fig. 3). The Christ of Telde is a conventional work of art, indexing not difference but sameness. In fact, it is this very quality of sameness that makes it a successful cult image. As a sacred portrait the cult image employs likeness to make present that which is absent, the sacred personage, and thereby motivates the viewer in acts of remembrance and prayer.[7] For Marín de Cubas, the Christ of Telde fulfilled precisely this function: the remainder of this chapter in the *Historia* consists of an exegetical, experiential account of the author's devotion to Christ as inspired by this particular image. But in order to achieve a state of empathic engagement with the divine prototype, Marín de Cubas must disregard the hidden alterity of the image. The author alludes to this cognitive switch when he turns from the earthly to the divine nature of Christ in the last line of the passage quoted above.

Further on in his visual description of the sculpture, the author is reminded of another, much better-known cult statue, the Christ of Burgos.[8] Evidently, his expectations of what the Crucifixion should look like are largely based on a general impression drawn from a mutually reinforcing network of images. Similitude, then, operates not only in relation to the divine prototype, but also in relation to other images. In the late Middle Ages and well into the early modern period, images acquired authority and legitimacy through "legibility," that is, by looking like one another.[9] Although the Christ of Telde is made, among other things, of maize, and the Christ of Burgos is fashioned from materials including leather and human hair, both point to a shared prototype and could, in effect, stand in for one another.[10] Images were able to substitute for one another across a range of artistic media.[11] In terms of the image's devotional efficacy, it is irrelevant that the Christ of Telde is from the New World and made of New World materials. In fact, it is better for such difference to remain unseen.

If the definition of the Christ of Telde as a cult object tells us *how* it is to be seen, that is, as a sacred work of art with a particular ritual function, the location of the sculpture in the Canary Islands tells us *where* it is to be seen, namely, in a land whose colonization provided an immediate context for the discovery and conquest of the New World. This essay further explores ways in which we may see this artifact, and examines what the Christ of Telde makes visible about the historical conditions in which it was made and used. As art historians, we intuitively presume and indeed depend upon art objects as seen entities. The visibility of art is a precondition of our discourse. The Christ of Telde, however, undercuts such assumptions in complex ways. I thus also seek to examine how this artifact persistently renders visibility—of its provenance, its materiality—opaque and even invisible. In so doing, I look behind the premise of cultic function and global trade networks to the paradox of what, and how, the image absconds.[12]

While it is appropriate, even expected, that the Christ of Telde should look like other cult statues, there remains the striking fact that such conventionality in subject and style is achieved through an act of persuasion on the level of medium. It tries to convince its viewer it is something it is not: carved and polychromed wood. This is a function not merely of materiality, but of how material is worked during the process of creation. Scholars have recently discovered the extent to which this image is the result of a mixed-media technique, incorporating much more than just maize and largely dependent on the use of molds. That is, one of the essential stages in fashioning the Christ of Telde was a pseudo-mechanized process of replication. The Christ of Telde is the outcome of a recasting between media that attempts to conceal the very medial transposition out of which it is born. This act of substitution is imperceptible on the surface of the image; it leaves no visible trace.

One aim of this essay is to realign the art historical approach to the early modern artifact by attending to its facture. I build upon the idea proposed by Joseph Koerner that facture, defined as the "process and product" of making, is not only a quality inherent in the art object, but also an essential vantage point from which to view it.[13] What is more, I have chosen to write a history of the Christ of Telde from the point of view of its fabrication that looks beyond the immediate moment of its making to the ways in which that very artistic process maps onto broader epochal shifts. The early modern period encouraged experimentation in and between media. A crucial trajectory of such experimentation pursued the path of replication, most notably the print. Mechanical reproduction ushered in a new era of the image, when pictures became characterized by multiplicity and mobility. Print technology, however, was not the only form of serial production that affected the way in which images could be reproduced and disseminated. The Christ of Telde attests to an historical moment when replication technologies advanced alongside overseas expansion, extending the image's reach to far corners of the world.

Borderlands

> When borders gain a paradoxical centrality, margins, edges, and lines of communication emerge as complex maps and histories.
> —James Clifford[14]

A term coined by the anthropologist James Clifford, "borderlands" are zones of passage characterized by their liminal existence between places of origin and destination. Their importance lies in understanding "routes rather than roots" as essential threads of human connectivity.[15] A chain of islands centrally located in the Atlantic Ocean and yet, at the same time, peripherally suspended between the Old World and the New, the Canary Islands constituted an early modern borderland. They were a space through which people and things moved. In the mid-sixteenth century, then,

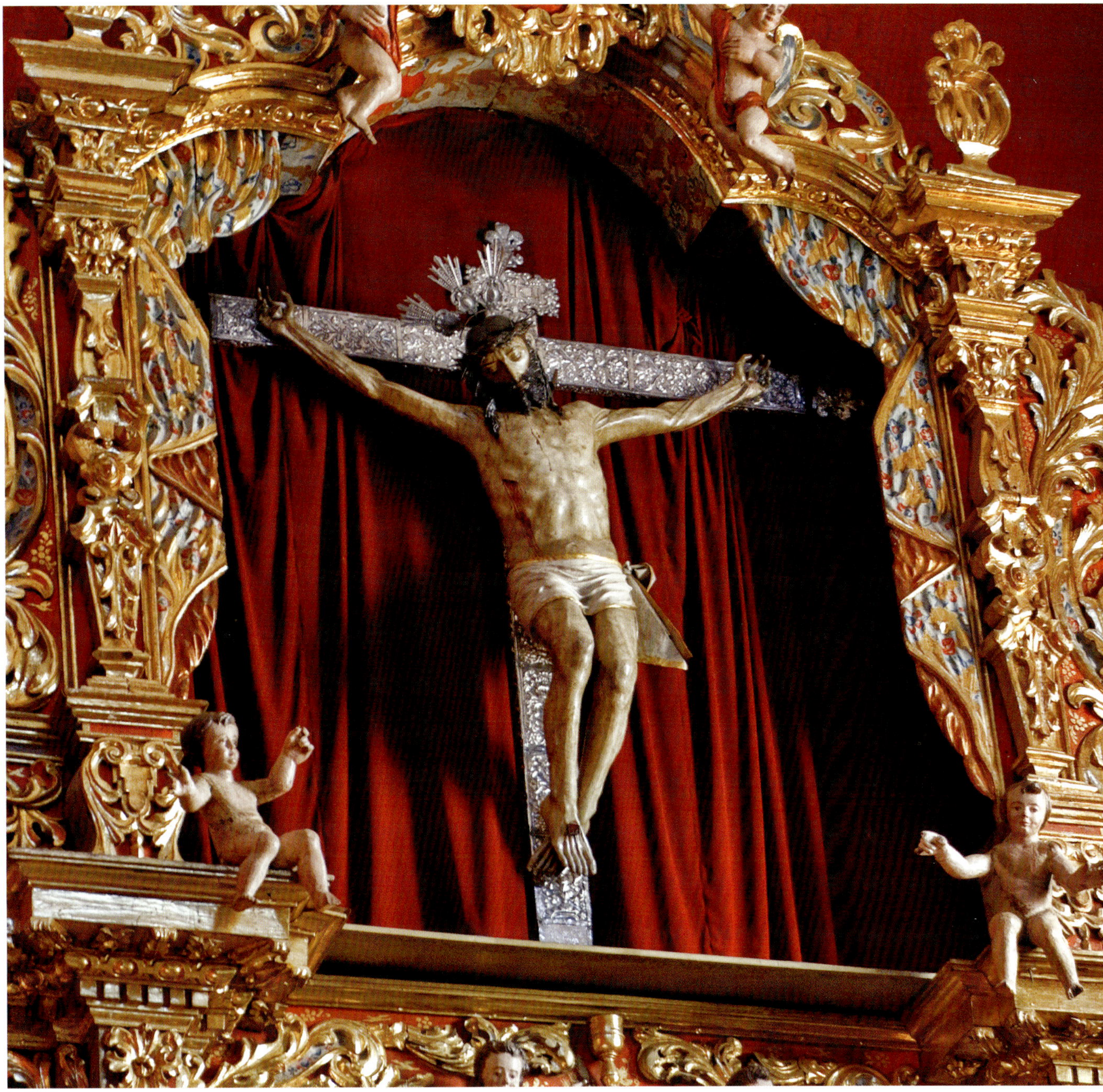

Fig. 3. *Crucifix*. Mexico, circa 1550. Paper, cornstalk paste, wood, and polychrome. 180 x 170 cm. Church of San Juan Bautista. Telde, Gran Canaria, Spain. Photo: author.

a Mexican statue of the Crucified Christ arrived at a particularly circumscribed corner of the world, a place that had recently acquired a "paradoxical centrality" in the transatlantic world.

The Canary Islands had been since antiquity the westernmost point of the known world.[16] Although they did not possess the wealth, history, and allure of the East, they nonetheless partook of a certain aura that only the shores of distant islands can command. Located between ninety and three hundred miles off the coast of Morocco, the archipelago was used by Ptolemy as the prime meridian for calculating longitude. Pliny provides the fullest ancient description of the islands, which he designated the Fortunate Isles. They also assumed other equally tantalizing identities, including the island of Geryon, where Hercules performed his tenth labor, the Elysium of Homer, and the islands of heroes mentioned by Hesiod. Despite being known and named, the chain of seven islands remained through the Middle Ages an unseen but imagined space suspended at the end of the world, an inviting screen for the projection of myth.

The islands were unvisited by continental Europeans until the fourteenth century, when navigators began to penetrate beyond the Mediterranean into the Atlantic.[17] These early explorers were driven less by conquest and colonization than by the prospect of trade, largely in slaves and gold from Africa. Exploration of the Canary Islands was under way by the 1330s, but it was only at the turn of the fifteenth century that "rediscovery" resolved into a more pointed interest in long-term settlement.[18] A series of attempted conquests unfolded over the course of a century, each supported by different political allegiances and with different enterprising conquistadors at the helm, before the seventh and final island, Tenerife, was finally conquered in 1496. The conquest of Gran Canaria, in particular, had been notoriously drawn out. The indigenous inhabitants, although few in number and without navigation or metallurgy, resisted Spanish incursions for six years, relying on their knowledge of the terrain and their fierce, guerrilla-style tactics. The year of the first military campaigns on the island, 1478, also marked the beginning of royal involvement in the archipelago.[19]

Castile's involvement in the conquest of the Canary Islands coincided, of course, with other, more well-known campaigns: the Reconquest of Granada and Columbus's first two voyages.[20] In one sense, the conquest of the Canary Islands was justified as an "extension" of the Reconquest; the campaigns of both Gran Canaria and Granada were funded by papal indulgences, and both territories were declared "kingdoms" upon their incorporation into the Crown of Castile.[21] Yet Granada provided only a partial grid through which Castile could view the Canary Islands. The wars in Al-Andalus culminated in 1492 with a *re*-conquest, taking back highly coveted land on the Iberian Peninsula from Muslims who were, strictly speaking, infidels in the eyes of "Christian" Spain. The Canary Islands, on the other hand, were distant, isolated, and populated by tribes who, upon arriving from North Africa sometime around 200 B.C.E., settled into a lifestyle viewed by the Christian world as distinctly pagan.

The concept of the pagan would soon be applied to indigenous groups discovered on the other side of the Atlantic. After his first encounter with the inhabitants of the Caribbean Islands, Columbus made the comparison with the people of the Canary Islands not only explicit, but logical: "None of them is black, rather the color of the Canary islanders, which is to be expected since this island lies E-W with the island of Ferro [Fuerteventura] in the Canaries on the same latitude."[22] Regardless of the fact that Columbus went in search of a route to the East Indies and ventured instead to "the ultimate Western land," he applies his sense of geography towards an explanation of this first encounter.[23] Shared geographical latitude becomes a means to establish racial congruence, compelling him to create a new middle ground on the spectrum of human skin color, the category of the Canarian, who is neither white like a European nor black like an African, but something in between.[24]

While it is tempting to view the Canary Islands as a "testing ground" for what would

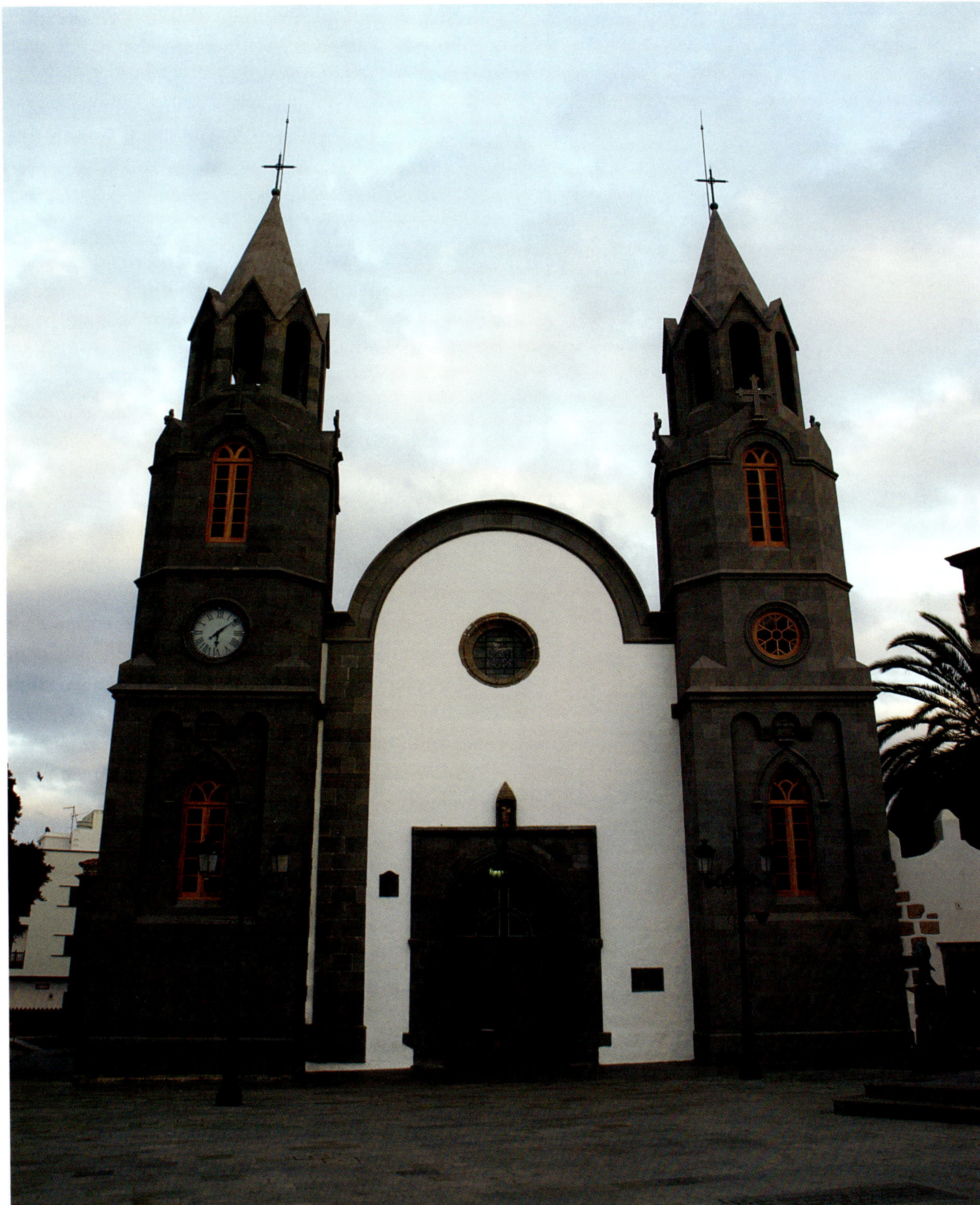

Fig. 4. West façade, Church of San Juan Bautista. Telde, Gran Canaria, Spain, completed 1539. Photo: author.

unfold in the Americas, historians have emphasized that such a claim is only partially true.[25] One essential difference was the indigenous presence in these lands both before and after their respective conquests. There were fewer Canary Islanders; after almost a century of battle, they had been largely decimated or enlisted into slavery. This would proceed to leave an indelible mark in the post-conquest years, for it necessarily entailed massive European settlement in almost every echelon of society.[26]

Columbus's words are nonetheless prescient, for they underscore the liminal, a quality of being caught between worlds, which would continue to characterize the history of the Canary Islands throughout the early modern period. While not the only Atlantic archipelago of interest to Mediterranean navigators—the other major examples being Madeira and the Azores—the Canary Islands would turn out to play an exceedingly important role in the history of European expansion. Columbus had, after all, set sail in 1492 from Gomera, a western island of the archipelago. In fact, every ship that left the Iberian Peninsula for the New World stopped in the Canary Islands before heading out on the thirty-day journey across the Atlantic; it was a key point on the commercial network that, guided by the winds, flowed from Andalusia to America.

If this small chain of islands had begun as a mythical edge of the ancient world and then a frontier in early Atlantic exploration, it proceeded to become a pivotal borderland in Spain's transatlantic economy. The archipelago was largely settled by Castilians, but further played host to an impressive population of foreigners, most notably Portuguese, who constituted the core of skilled laborers, and Genoese, the major capital investors.[27] Merchants from all over Europe, Flanders in particular, flocked to the islands, as they offered a viable alternative to more distant American ports while nevertheless tapping into the riches of Castile's overseas empire.[28] Many scholars have been inclined to focus on the transatlantic dimension of the archipelago's trade network, but Felipe Fernández-Armesto has argued that commercial relations with the European continent were of equal if not greater import, as the Old World remained the central consumer of the crops cultivated on the islands.[29] Fernández-Armesto further emphasizes the importance of attending to the "more complex relationships—the inner and outer circles—which joined the shores of the Atlantic and gave it commercial unity."[30] Galleons headed to the Indies were stocked with victuals for the long ocean journey, and ships headed back to markets on the European continent were loaded with sugar and wine. And yet, despite such intense commercial traffic, the population of the islands stagnated after the first phase of settlement ended in the first quarter of the sixteenth century. That is, while people came and went, very few stayed.[31]

Absent Makers

Perhaps the sixteenth-century Canary Islands are most noteworthy for precisely what they lacked: artists. The archipelago did not become a center of artistic production in its own right until the mid to late seventeenth century, when artists began immigrating to the islands, establishing workshops in major cities.[32] Up until that point, all art was imported art. This circumstance provides a crucial context for understanding the Christ of Telde.

During the years of settlement and subsequent economic development, the Canary Islands witnessed the foundation of their earliest Christian sanctuaries.[33] Churches, monasteries, and hermitages were quickly filled with paintings, sculptures, liturgical items, and other sacred gifts that expressed the devotion of their donors, many of whom had participated in the conquest. The church of San Juan Bautista in Telde, for example, was begun by the conquistador Hernán García del Castillo at the turn of the sixteenth century and completed by his son, Cristóbal García del Castillo, by 1539 (Fig. 4).[34] Sometime before 1515, even as construction of the edifice was still under way, Cristóbal donated to the church a carved and polychromed altarpiece, which, he writes, "was brought to me from Flanders."[35] This altarpiece, which depicts six scenes of the life of the Virgin and the Christ Child, still graces the high altar of

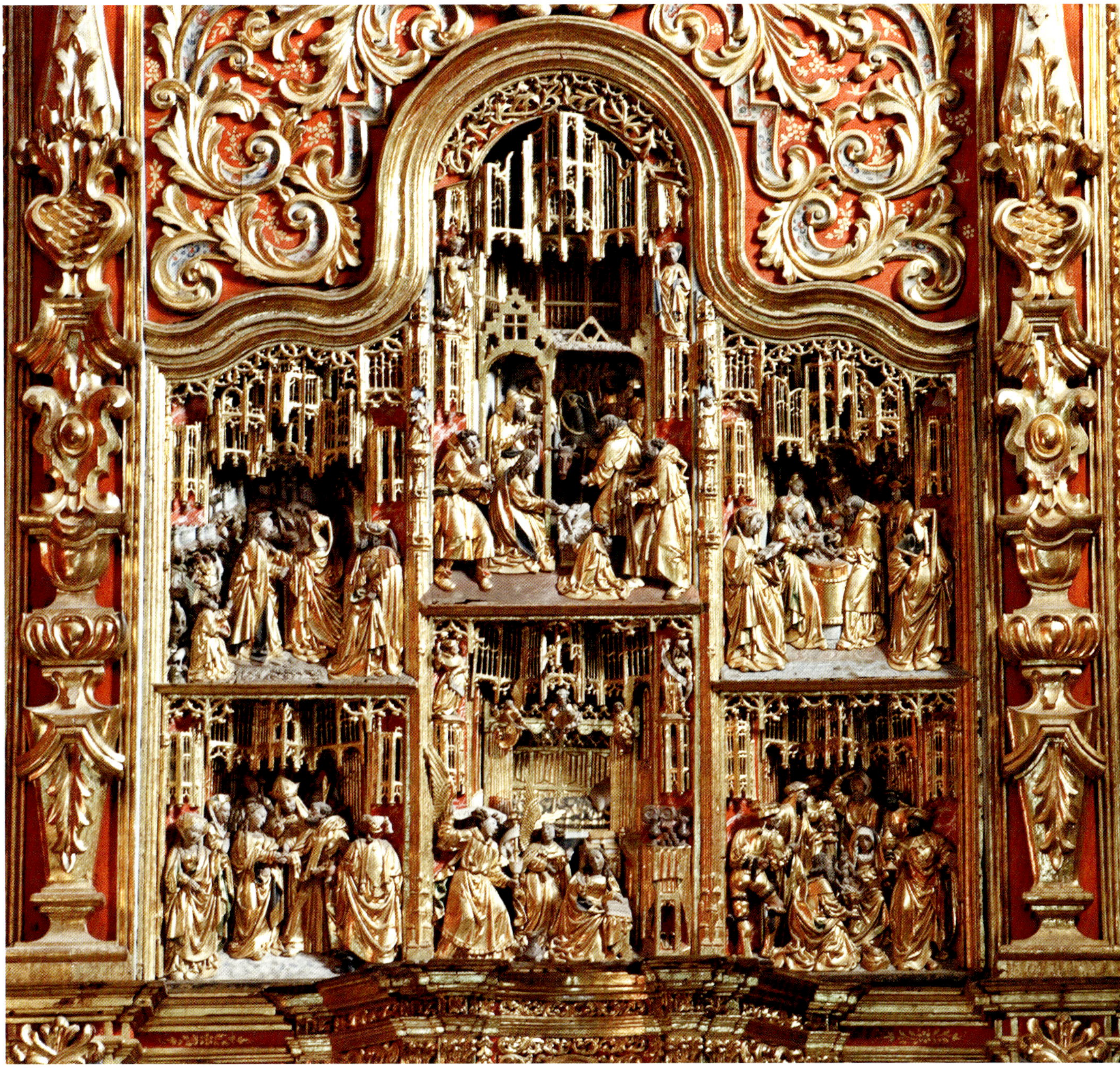

Fig. 5. *Life of the Virgin and Christ Child*. Flanders, circa 1515. Carved and polychromed wood. 290 x 240 cm. Church of San Juan Bautista. Telde, Gran Canaria, Spain. Photo: author.

the church for which it was originally destined—just below the Christ of Telde (Fig. 5).[36]

The altarpiece in Telde was thus shipped from Flanders at the bequest of a prominent member of the city. Cristóbal García del Castillo was not only the son of a conquistador, but also a wealthy entrepreneur who owned a large sugar mill on the island of Gran Canaria.[37] With an established circle of Flemish traders on the islands, some owners of sugar mills and others dealers transporting sugar back to Europe, it is likely the altarpiece traveled on a merchant ship from a commercial center in the Low Countries.[38] Certain features of the work support the claim that it was produced for export. Analysis of the back of the altarpiece reveals that it had been shipped in two pieces, which were assembled upon arrival at its overseas destination.[39] Stamps on the altarpiece register the work to a particular locale, the city of Antwerp.[40] The stamping of carved Netherlandish altarpieces began in the middle of the fifteenth century as a means to ensure quality control; it appeared for the first time in the guild regulations of Antwerp in 1470 and took the form of two symbols: a hand in reference to the wood and a castle for the polychromy.[41] A kind of registered trademark, the stamp indexes the value of the work of art in terms of quality of material and execution.

The stamping of carved altarpieces reveals a commercial system of art-making. As Filip Vermeylen has argued, a pivotal development in sixteenth-century Antwerp was the sudden drive to create works of art on speculation for the open market.[42] Relatively fewer works were made on commission, and instead merchants and dealers would come to the famed weekly Friday markets and biannual art fairs in search of ready-made works to purchase, especially for export.[43] Lynn F. Jacobs's research into the mass marketing of early Netherlandish carved altarpieces has elucidated this moment in the commodification of art.[44] In an attempt to create highly standardized altarpieces for quick consumption, workshops began to incorporate pseudo-industrial methods of production, such as the division of labor, the repetition of standard iconography, and the incorporation of prefabricated parts. The development of techniques of mass production capitalized on an ever-growing demand that was often international. Cristóbal García del Castillo typifies this market. He wanted to donate an altarpiece to the church he was building in the Canary Islands, but if he had commissioned a work, he would have had to wait up to two years—the average time to complete a carved altarpiece—before the finished work could make the journey back to Gran Canaria.[45]

The Telde altarpiece makes explicit certain changes occurring in the creation and reception of art in early modern Europe, namely, the rise in the mass production and dissemination of standardized works of art. Innovative strategies of reproduction and commercial advancements introduced new separations between artist, artifact, and beholder.[46] The stamps are indicative of this situation. Cristóbal was not in Antwerp himself to verify that the artwork met guild standards. Instead, the stamp interjected itself as a guarantee of quality that negotiated among the maker, the distant customer, and his surrogate, the merchant. It is as a commodity at the moment of sale that such a trademark is valuable. In other words, the stamp, intended for the buyer—not the viewer—of the artwork, signifies differently than an artist's signature. To author a work of art is to labor over it, to physically work the body in the manipulation of certain materials, and the signature is a proclamation of that singular artistic process. While the altarpiece in Telde is an authored work of art in the sense that it was carved and painted by hand, its authorship is plural. And the trademarks it bears point us not to a named artist, but rather to market standards of mass production.

The Spanish market for art of the Low Countries was well established by the time this work arrived on Gran Canaria. Backed by the prestige of royal patrons, especially Queen Isabella, the Flemish style spread rapidly throughout Castile. Stylistic influence became so entrenched at the turn of the sixteenth century that scholars have coined the term "Hispano-Flemish" to refer to this moment of artistic production in Spain.[47] Artists emigrated from the Low Countries to meet growing demand on the peninsula, and their style was quickly copied.[48] With no community of Flemish artists on the Canary Islands, the archipelago is nonetheless a veritable museum of imported Flemish art.

Of course, not all art imported to the archipelago came from the Low Countries. A number of cult images arrived from the Iberian Peninsula itself, Seville in particular.[49] Objects also traveled from Spain's overseas empire in the form of donations by Canary Islanders who immigrated to the Americas, maintained commercial relations with the *ultramar*, or had family members abroad. According to a recent inventory of New World artifacts on the island of Gran Canaria, silverwork was the most frequently donated sacred gift, followed by sculpted artifacts, then printed images, and lastly paintings.[50] But the greatest flowering of American art on the Canary Islands did not occur until two centuries after the arrival of the Christ of Telde, in the eighteenth century.[51] During the years immediately following the conquest, the artistic milieu of the Canary Islands was constituted by "inner and outer circles," to borrow the evocative phrase of Fernández-Armesto, that linked the transatlantic world. The artistic link with the Americas was only one within a larger network.[52] The Telde altarpiece has been chosen from among the archipelago's treasures of imported art for its exemplarity. It establishes a framework for understanding early modern techniques of mass production. That is, this work is distinctly proximate to the Christ of Telde, not only in terms of its shared space on the altar, but also in light of the fact that it was serially produced in a manner alternative to print technology.

The Technique

The Christ of Telde typifies a specific kind of cult image often referred to as *Cristos de caña*, or three-dimensional sculptures of the Crucifixion fashioned in Mexico out of *caña de maíz* and *pasta de caña de maíz*, or cornstalk and cornstalk paste.[53] As the name suggests, *Cristos de caña* are defined not only by their subject, Christ, but also by the material out of which they are made, maize. In the pre-Hispanic world, maize was not only a sacred, life-giving substance, but also an artistic medium. There is evidence that ephemeral images of gods were made out of dough and organic pastes, including "corn meal," which were edible and even ritually consumed.[54] If, in pre-Hispanic traditions, the act of fashioning objects out of maize possessed ritual and ideological significance, in the colonial period this material acquired, as it were, a new face: it was transformed into a medium of the Christian god.[55] Cult statues such as the Christ of Telde are thus normally valued for their inclusion of the famed plant native to the Americas, but the disproportionate attention granted to this material by modern scholars tends to cast an aura of New World otherness onto these artifacts without accounting for the complexity of their manufacture.

The Christ of Telde measures 180 centimeters high and 170 centimeters wide, and yet weighs a mere 6.5 kilograms, or approximately 14 pounds.[56] To achieve such a lightweight quality, *Cristos de caña* were made using a method of construction that depended largely on molds. The process began with the creation of the hollow chest cavity. Layers of paper together with an agglutinant were added to the outside of two molds, one forming the rudimentary shape of the chest, the other the shape of the back. When the paper dried, the molds were removed and replaced with armatures of dried and bundled cornstalks, tubes of rolled paper, or, as with the Christ of Telde, pieces of lightweight wood to support and reinforce the outer thoracic frame. The chest and back of the figure were then joined together to create the torso. After a similar inner framework was constructed for each individual arm and leg, the limbs were appended to the central thoracic structure through the use of a lightweight wood; these wooden joints further strengthened the sculpture at load-bearing points.

Molds were also used to fashion the head, but in this case a negative impression was cast. Into a mold of the head was placed finely ground *pasta de caña de maíz* that had been mixed with a binder made of animal glue. This primary layer of cornstalk paste was reinforced with alternating layers of paper and *pasta de caña de maíz*. While the mold provided general contour, additional features such

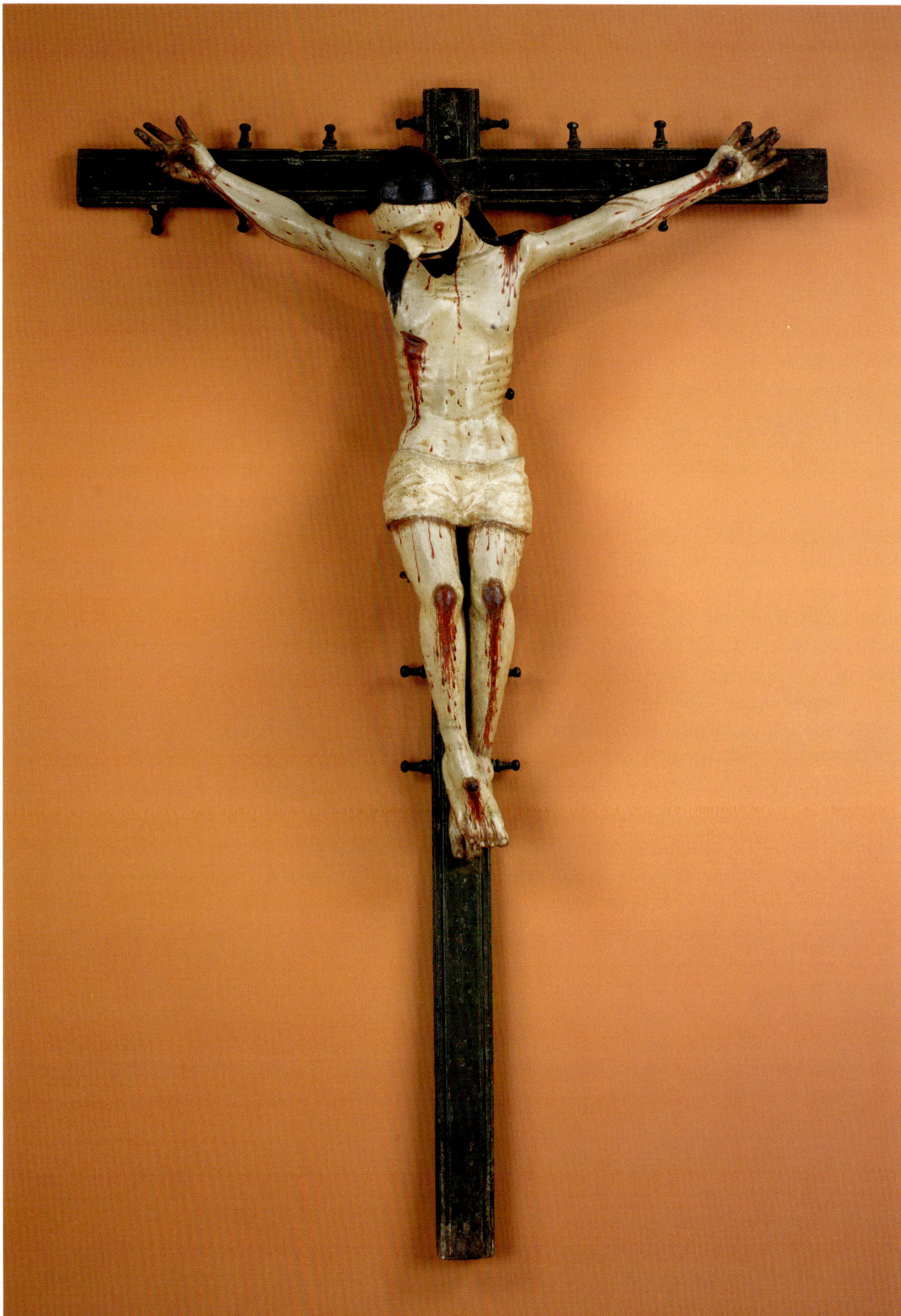

as Christ's beard were formed out of cornstalk paste or wood and added to the piece. Wooden pegs were then employed to attach the head to the body of the sculpture. The entire sculpture was then covered with large sheets of paper, upon which was applied a layer of gesso and glue, creating a durable stucco or *papier mâché*. When still wet, this final layer of paper was worked by hand to give the figure its ultimate anatomical form. Lastly, the entire sculpture received a layer of polychrome.

As this brief technical synopsis reveals, *Cristos de caña* are a diverse group of objects perhaps best described as multimedia works of art (Fig. 6). The process of fabrication is inherently flexible, accommodating the use of various materials throughout many stages of construction. Thanks to the intervention of modern restoration, major advances are being made towards better understanding this artistic technique.[57] In particular, the restorer and art historian Pablo Amador has made a number of invaluable contributions. In addition to restoring the Christ of Telde, Amador has arduously sought out, analyzed, and cataloged *Cristos de caña* throughout New Spain and Spain.[58] Many *Cristos* once believed to have been made of *caña de maíz* are not made of this material at all, but rather of *papelón*, a technique that incorporates paper as well as *serrín de madera*, or wood paste, and linen cloth.[59] All of these objects, however, do have one quality in common: they are lightweight. Many scholars thus prefer to place sculptures made from the artistic technique of *caña de maíz* within a different, broader typological category, *escultura ligera*, or lightweight sculpture.[60]

Ever since the early colonial period, *Cristos ligeros* have been celebrated for this very defining feature. In his *Historia de los indios de la Nueva España* from 1541, the Franciscan friar Toribio de Benavente, known more commonly as Motolinía, commented, "even if the crucifix was as large as a man, a child could lift it with one hand."[61] Later in the century, in his *Historia eclésiastica indiana*, fray Jéronimo Mendieta, another Franciscan, wrote, "they also took [to Spain] hollow Crucifixions made of *caña* which, being the size of a large man, weighed so little that a young boy could carry

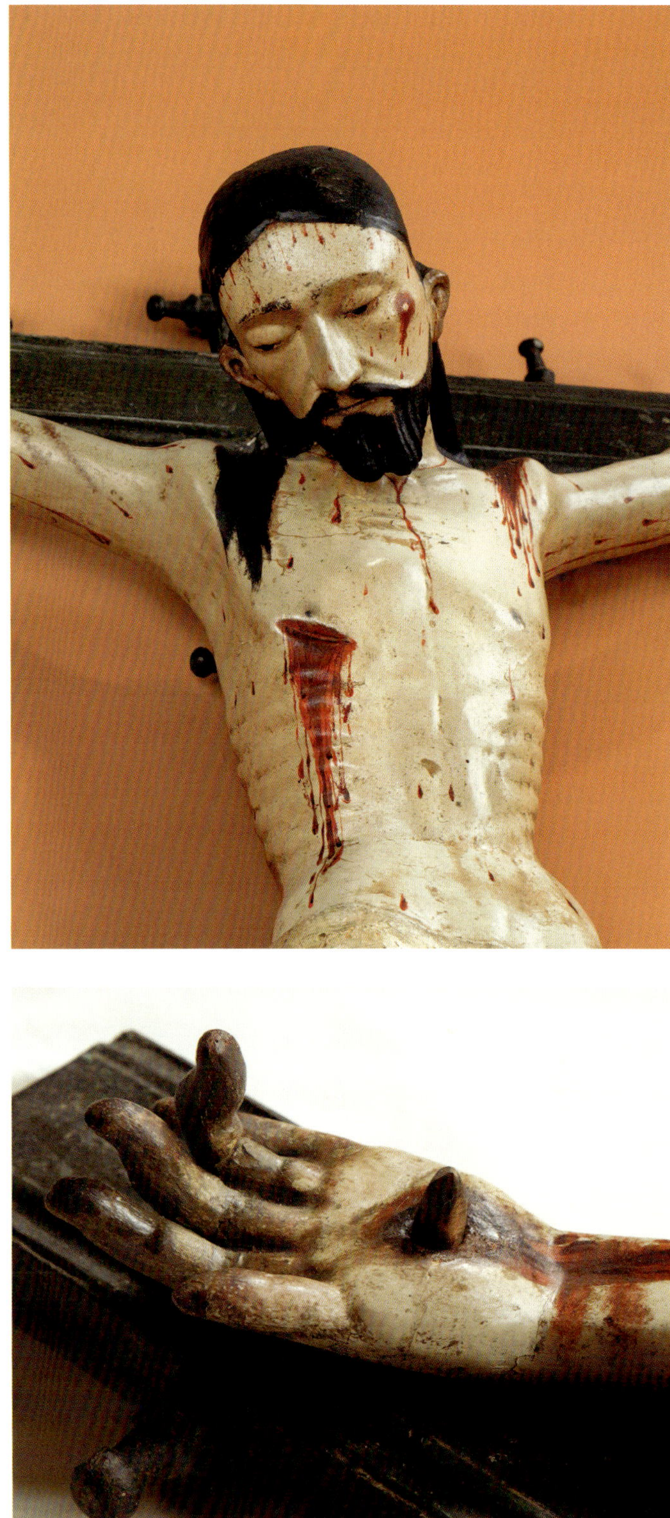

Fig. 6. (opposite, above) *Crucifix*. Mexico, 1600s. *Caña de maíz* technique (*celerín* wood [*tzompantle*], corn paste, gesso, fabric, oil paint). 119.4 x 101.6 cm. Denver Art Museum, Museum exchange; 1968.192.

them."[62] Both passages reiterate that these objects were processional sculptures carried through city streets, for example during Holy Week. Their lightweight quality thus met the demands of a particular ritual function.[63]

Beyond a handful of mendicant sources, which tend to be both sparse and vague, few colonial texts mention the artistic technique of working with *caña de maíz*. The processes and materials used to fashion these lightweight sculptures never appeared in the guild ordinances for sculptors practicing in New Spain. Such ordinances were directed at only three sculptural media—wood, bone, and stone—and were issued three times, in 1568, 1589, and 1703 respectively.[64] This has led María del Consuelo Maquívar to suppose that the technique of *caña de maíz*, at least during the sixteenth century, remained largely limited to the artistic workshops established in the orbit of the mendicant orders. In these famed locales of indoctrination native artists, scribes, and craftsmen were trained in European techniques of art-making while also encouraged to pursue preconquest traditions such as feather painting and manuscript production in the service of the Christian faith. By the mid-sixteenth century, for example, the technique of *caña de maíz* was being practiced at the Franciscan school of San José de los Naturales in Mexico City.[65]

These *Cristos* were thus, like many colonial artifacts, the product of an interaction between Spanish and indigenous artists. As Amador has shown, while maize as an artistic medium was surely pre-Columbian, it now seems that a European technique of casting lightweight processional sculptures from pastes of wood and paper was imported to New Spain soon after the conquest and adapted to the new environment through the appropriation of a material indigenous to Mexico.[66] The development of this technique in Europe is important to our understanding of its application in New Spain.

Before the advent of the woodcut in the second half of the fifteenth century, hollow, freestanding devotional statues were serially produced using molds. The major centers of production were clustered in the Rhineland and the Netherlands, where *pijpaarden beeldjes*, Dutch for pipe-clay images, of the Virgin, the Christ Child, and saints were cast from two-sided molds of the same material.[67] Utrecht, in particular, became an artistic center from which sculptures formed from molds were exported throughout Europe, including the Iberian Peninsula.[68]

While both the process and product of mold-made sculptures differ from printed images, it is important to note the parallel development of these two replication technologies. Both testify to the rise of the "multiple image," that is, the work of art replicated with greater facility, rendered more available and mobile, disseminated across greater distances, and tasked with a broad range of communicative functions.[69] These reproductive techniques relate to the standardized production of wood altarpieces in the Low Countries, including the example in Telde discussed above. The wood matrix, the clay mold, and the assembly line—each is concretely motivated, striving to mass produce serial images for an open market. Compared to the mode of serial production in an Antwerp woodworking workshop, however, the printed image and the molded sculpture were born of a crucial moment of experimentation with media and replication that flowered in the middle of the fifteenth century.

Objects ranging from small household altars to pilgrim badges began to be made in alternative, often cheaper and ephemeral materials, including terracotta, plaster, metals such as lead and tin, wax, paper, *papier mâché*, and even dough.[70] As a part of this "germinal phase" of experimentation, when, according to Peter Schmidt, "the possibilities of mechanical replication of image and text were being tested," artists serially produced devotional statues out of materials that were lighter in weight than baked clay and therefore more portable, such as leather and macerated paper.[71] One advantage of the mold-making technique was its inherent adaptability, given that it could incorporate a variety of materials into the act of mechanical replication.

What is the historical relationship that established a typological congruence between baked clay Madonnas made in the fifteenth-century Netherlands and multimedia *Cristos* made in post-Conquest Mexico? The Spanish monarchy, with its distinct penchant for the art of the Low Countries and its task of spreading empire across the Atlantic, provides a link recently discussed by Felipe Pereda.[72] During the years following the Reconquest of Granada from the Muslims, the surge in mass baptisms produced a desperate need for images to decorate the new parishes full of recent converts. In the year 1500, Queen Isabella personally commissioned one master and his workshop to create images and other liturgical items quickly and en masse.[73] This *entallador*, or sculptor, went by the name of Huberto Alemán—Hubert the German. A document in the National Historical Archive of Spain recounts Huberto's personal encounter with the Queen and his pride in having introduced to the city of Granada the technique of casting sculptures from molds.[74] The artist emphasizes how, with this technique, he could not only produce sculptures in large quantities, but also create lightweight statues easily transportable to difficult-to-reach places; and he proclaims his commercial desire to apply this technique to the far corners of the monarchy.

Information surrounding the life of the artist is scant, but it can be gleaned from his name that Huberto Alemán originated in Northern Europe.[75] Pereda has further established that the imagery destined for new Morisco parishes consisted of statues of saints and, most prevalently, the Virgin.[76] Although none of the commissioned images is known to survive, a series of devotional statues of the Virgin and Child clustered in Andalusia that date to the turn of the sixteenth century are of the same iconography and size as those stipulated in Isabella's commission. The Virgin of the Remedies in Villarrasa, Spain, for example, is a mold-made sculpture consisting of a paste made from paper and pieces of cloth reinforced with glue size (Fig. 7); these materials are suspended beneath a layer of polychromed gesso and built up around a wooden beam running along the center of the object.[77] A nearly identical version resides in the city of Lucena del Puerto, and a third example can be found in Antequera.[78] These sculptures bear an uncanny resemblance to *pijpaarden beeldjes* made in the Netherlands.

Pereda contends that Huberto Alemán effectively adapted the technique of fashioning *pijpaarden beeldjes* to the demand for images after the Reconquest. The tremendous popularity of Marian devotion and the concomitant demand for imagery of the Virgin and Child coincided with the development of serialized techniques of production in both Northern Europe and the Iberian Peninsula. In the words of Pereda, "the mechanism was pseudo-industrial much more than artisanal."[79] The Crucifixion also underwent this transformation: in the sixteenth and seventeenth centuries, certain workshops in Seville specialized in the production of processional sculptures made of molded paper and *pasta de madera,*[80] a compelling cognate to the emergence of *Cristos ligeros* in New Spain. The latter, I contend, should be viewed as part of this broader phenomenon of mold-made sculpture. Whether or not Huberto succeeded in his dream to amass wealth by spreading this technology of evangelization throughout the Iberian Peninsula, it surely made its way across the Atlantic—where, again, it was put in the service of a spiritual conquest.[81]

Objects of Dissimulation

It has long been acknowledged that the technology of mechanical reproduction was a catalyst for global change in the early modern period.[82] Printmaking and the expanded system of communication it engendered brought Europe—its chivalric romances, images, Christian doctrine, and the Latin and Castilian languages—to the New World. Illustrated printed books, woodcuts, and engravings served as models for works of art created in colonial Mexico. The replication of the Old World in the New was an essential aspect of acculturation, and the medium of the print played a pivotal role in the dissemination of knowledge and the formation of transatlantic colonies. The Dominican missionary and historian Bartolomé de Las Casas wrote,

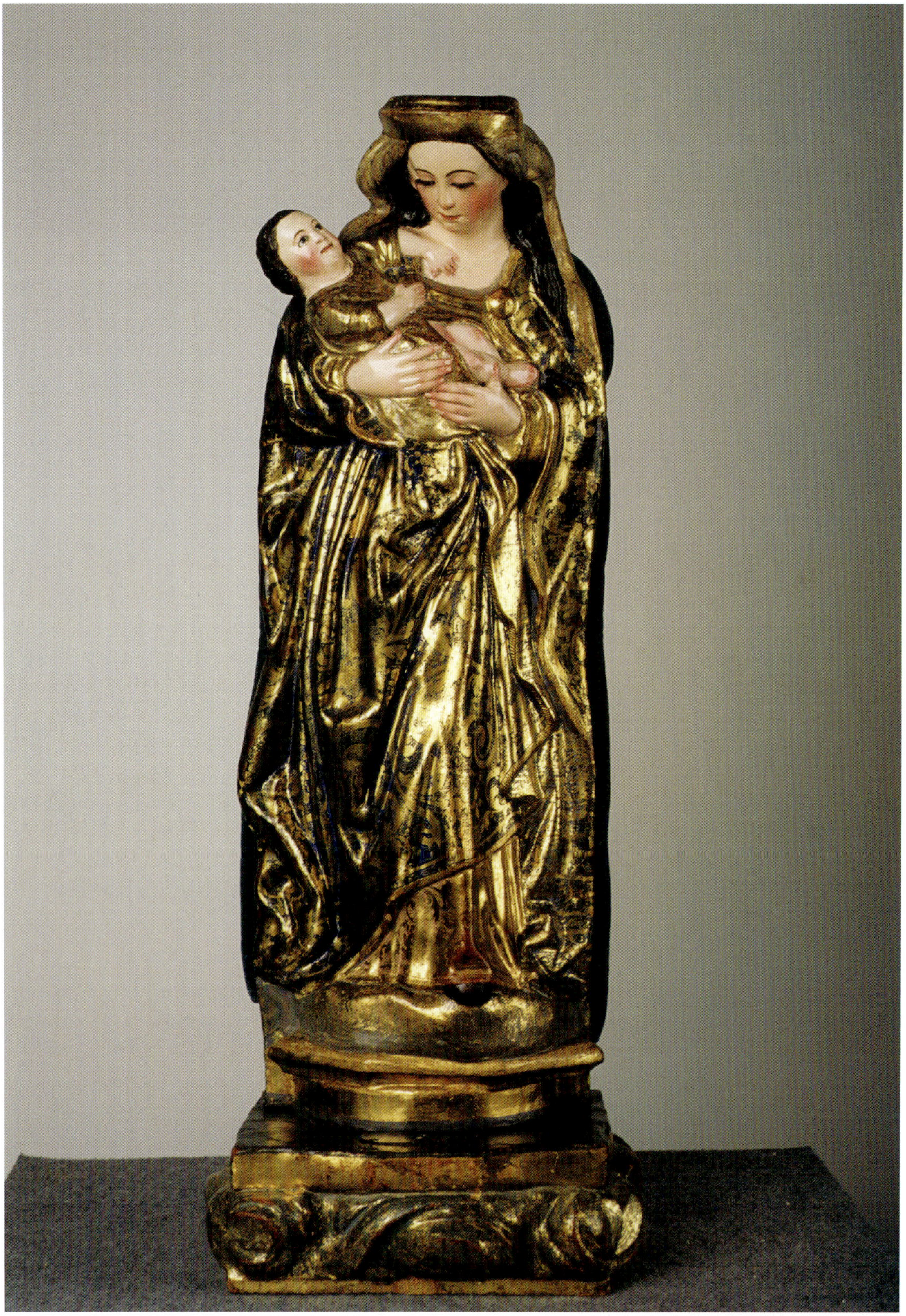

Fig. 7. *Virgin and Christ Child*. Spain, circa 1500. Cloth reinforced with glue size, paper paste, wood, and polychrome. 88 cm. Chapel of los Remedios, Villarrasa, Huelva, Spain. Photo: José Manuel Santos Madrid, courtesy of Instituto Andaluz del Patrimonio Histórico.

> I have in my possession a letter that was sent to me by the Indians of New Spain, myself being at the Court, and I brought it to the Council of the Indies to show, and the people of the Council being so endowed with knowledge and prudence, they spent much time looking and speculating letter for letter if it was printed or by hand [*de molde o de mano*]; and, finally, it was determined by some of the men saying yes, others no, when in truth it had been made by hand by an Indian of New Spain.[83]

As this passage reveals, colonial society not only was founded upon the imitation of European forms, but also entailed the imitation of European technologies. The handwritten letter and the printed missive verge on inscrutable elision. "*De molde o de mano*": the handmade and the mechanically made become mutually refracting lenses. In the early modern period, to hold a handmade artifact in one's hands was to beg the question of how it was like or unlike its machine-made counterpart.

This brings me to a central paradox of *Cristos ligeros*. From the outside, they look like carved and polychromed wood. Process cannot be determined from product. While it is not uncommon for art to obfuscate its making, the interpretive resistance of such a work positions itself at a crucial nexus. The artifact renders its own facture invisible and, in effect, belies its true origins. The artifact, I propose, is an object of dissimulation at the nexus between the handmade and the mechanically made.

During his restoration of the Christ of Telde, Amador noted the faint presence of "huellas dactilares," fingerprints, on the outer surface of the sculpture.[84] That is, once the sculpture was cast from its various molds, the artist proceeded to model the surface of the outer layer of gessoed paper. The final work of art is both molded and modeled, cast and wrought, mechanically made and handmade. Mexican *Cristos* embody an early modern moment when people, their cultures, media, and technologies were coming into contact with one another. This was a moment when the mechanically reproduced was still dependent on the handmade—printed books were still bound by hand, printed type was still imitating the appearance and conventions of handwritten script, and printed images were still positioning themselves as interlocutors with paintings, recalling their form, content, and style. A similar phenomenon is at play with these *Cristos*, objects that strive to look like their purely handmade counterparts and even incorporate the handmade into their own pseudo-mechanized construction.

Let us consider how paper—a manufactured product in itself—was heavily worked throughout the creation of the Christ of Telde: it was rolled up into tubes, slathered with pastes and glues, layered one sheet over another, suspended onto molds. Take, for example, the purity cloth that covers Christ's loin. From a point resting on the figure's left hip, bunched and gathered paper forms a dense knot from which cascades of pleats emerge. Within the inner surfaces of these folds one discovers not blank sheets of paper but documents. When the purity cloth was removed from the sculpture during restoration, it revealed a tribute list, that is, a colonial tax record listing payments collected from an indigenous community in the Valley of Mexico. More documents were found throughout the hollow cavity of the figure, including tax records in a different hand lining the interior of the figure's head. The Christ of Telde is not the only example of *escultura ligera* made in New Spain in which documents are granted a second life. During a 1946 earthquake in Mexico City, the Christ of Mexicaltzingo fell from its altar and broke open to reveal a cache of reused documents.[85] Since then, several sculptures of the Crucifixion made in Mexico soon after the conquest have been found to contain recycled paper.[86]

Most scholars take the inclusion of these recycled documents to be meaningless, the act of reuse interpreted as an act of mere necessity. But if something has been repurposed, has it been relegated to the abject? The reuse of paper in these *Cristos*, I believe, is an ecological act.[87] This ecology is a matter of how art-making relates to its environment, both natural and historical. Despite its ubiquitous presence in modern society, paper was a highly valued commodity in the early modern world, especially in New Spain.[88] Already in 1533, fray Juan de Zumárraga, the first bishop of Mexico, wrote a letter to the Council of the Indies expressing the need for a printing press and a paper mill.[89] A few years later, he wrote yet another letter, this time to Charles V, reiterating that "printing can advance very little for the shortage of paper."[90] While the first printing press in the New World was formally established in Mexico City in 1539, an official paper mill was never approved by the Crown.[91] The press consistently faced shortages of paper and, in fact, linen paper would remain the one material of the printmaker's trade hardest to come by throughout the colonial period.[92] An alternative was *amate*, indigenous paper made by hand from the inner bark of the fig tree, which has been produced from the pre-Columbian period through today.[93] Both kinds of paper were used in the construction of these sculptures.

All of this is to say, paper was precious. With such a small amount in circulation, it was repurposed. To destroy one artifact was to create another. But why tribute lists? Within the framework of an ecology of art-making, tribute lists provided an endless supply of recycled paper. Once tribute had been paid, the documentary testament was no longer needed; what is more, reforms in the tribute system during the sixteenth century (disallowing payment in kind other than maize and money)[94] may have rendered earlier tribute records obsolete.[95]

The history of paper and the history of the tribute system point us toward a logical explanation for the inclusion of these recycled documents, but such concrete histories fail to interpret the poetics of their presence. What are we to make of absconded art, hidden from view, never actually meant to be seen? A piece of paper on which words were inscribed was made, used, discarded—and yet, its material existence was extended. Upon shedding its former life as a document, it was reinscribed into the lifeworld of a work of art. These recycled documents challenge us to consider not only the making of art, but its remaking; to consider not only the use of artifacts, but their reuse. These documents are not repurposed in the mode of palimpsests, with their surfaces scraped clean to serve again as receptacles for writing. Yet neither are they instances of spoliation, war booty stripped from the vanquished and inserted into artful frames wrought by the victor like trophies on display. Covered with gesso and folded into origami-like shapes, these pieces of paper abandon their function as flat, two-dimensional surfaces for writing and participate in the embodied, three-dimensional presence of God. Art, by way of its very material nature, figures a complex interface between human and divine, between the bodies of indigenous individuals and the body of Christ.

I have called the Christ of Telde an object of dissimulation. It looks like solid wood, but is actually a strange amalgam of paper, paste, and cornstalk. It claims to be handmade while it also partakes in the mechanically reproduced. One could say this is the artwork's lie of origin. Analogously, the artwork performs another lie of stability. It claims to be a stable cult statue, unproblematically venerated as a likeness and presence of the Christian godhead, when, in fact, it conceals a troubled nexus of the forces of colonialism. The artwork is, literally, a matter of tribute. The problems of colonialism and the problems of conversion are the very reason for this work of art having come into being. And yet it does not just exemplify these problems. It reconfigures them. Tribute is the primary motivation of the sculpture, but like its own materiality, this motivation is bound up and concealed in the process of its facture. The Christ of Telde, I argue, figures the colonial enterprise; the extension of Christian cult and the extraction of commodities for profit—the artifact embodies these tasks of the conquest of the *ultramar* while it also absconds them from view.

Notes

[1] The material presented here derives from a chapter of my doctoral dissertation, which is being supervised by Christopher Wood and Mary Miller. I am indebted to them for their support and insightful comments. I would also like to thank the following individuals for their generous and invaluable help at various stages of my research: Pablo Amador, Claudia Brittenham, Derek Burdette, William Christian Jr., Nathaniel Jones, Jennifer Josten, Barbara Mundy, and Alessandra Russo. I owe special thanks to Donna Pierce for inviting me to participate in the Mayer Center Symposium. Unless otherwise noted all translations are my own.

[2] Tomás Arias Marín de Cubas, *Historia de las siete islas de Canarias* (Canarias: Reedición Canarias Clásicas, 1993), 339. "Tiene en el testero la capilla mayor sobre el Sagrario un Crucifijo de cuerpo grande, el rostro divinamente hermoso, muy devoto y de muchos Milagros; su fábrica fue en las Indias Occidentales de mano de españoles, que allá se hubo de los primeros frutos de vino y azúcar de esta Isla, y lugar de Telde en las primeras poblaciones de Indias: su materia es fungosa, papírea, ó bombicínea, del corazón de piñas de maíz semejante al blanco del corazón del ramo de la higuera, del junco ó hinojo: más nuestro asunto nos lleva á otro Crucifijo, prodigio no igual en la naturaleza pues ella toda es Divina." This passage was first published in relation to the Christ of Telde in Pedro Hernández Benítez, *El santo Cristo del altar mayor de la parroquia de San Juan Bautista de Telde* (n.p.: Imprenta España, 1940), 11.

[3] Byron Ellsworth Hamann, "The Mirrors of *Las Meninas*: Cochineal, Silver, and Clay," *Art Bulletin* 92 (2010): 6–35.

[4] For an important contribution to this approach, see Igor Kopytoff, "The Cultural Biography of Things: Commoditization as Process," in *The Social Life of Things: Commodities in Cultural Perspective*, edited by Arjun Appadurai (Cambridge: Cambridge University Press, 1986), 64–94. See also, more recently, the special issue of the *Journal of the History of Collections*, "Captured Objects: Inventories of Early Modern Collections," edited by Jessica Keating and Lia Markey (2011).

[5] On collecting, see Adriana Turpin, "The New World Collections of Duke Cosimo I de'Medici and Their Role in the Creation of a *Kunst-* and *Wunderkammer* in the Palazzo Vecchio," in *Curiosity and Wonder from the Renaissance to the Enlightenment*, edited by Robert John Weston Evans and Alexander Marr (Aldershot, England; Burlington, VT: Ashgate, 2006), 63–86. On foodstuffs, see Marcy Norton, *Sacred Gifts, Profane Pleasures: A History of Tobacco and Chocolate in the Atlantic World* (Ithaca: Cornell University Press, 2008). On cult images, see Patricia Barea Azcón, "Localización de pinturas novohispanas en España," *Revista Complutense de Historia de América* 32 (2006): 251–268.

[6] James S. Amelang, "The New World in the Old? The Absence of Empire in Early Modern Madrid," *Cuadernos de Historia de España* 82 (2008): 147–164. See also the responses to Hamann's "The Mirrors of *Las Meninas*," which formed the Interventions essay series in a recent issue of the *Art Bulletin*, in particular Felipe Pereda, "The Invisible? New World," *Art Bulletin* 92 (2010): 47–52. For the canonical study on the question of the impact and (in)visibility of the New World in the Old, see John Huxtable Elliott, *The Old World and the New 1492–1650* (Cambridge: Cambridge University Press, 1970).

[7] On the cult image in the later Middle Ages and early modern period, see, in particular, Hans Belting, *Likeness and Presence: A History of the Image before the Era of Art*, translated by Edmund Jephcott (Chicago: University of Chicago Press, 1994); see also his earlier *The Image and Its Public in the Middle Ages: Form and Function of Early Paintings of the Passion*, translated by Mark Bartusis and Raymond Meyer (New Rochelle, NY: Aristide D. Caratzas, 1990).

[8] Marín de Cubas, *Historia*, 341: "parecióme a modo del Santo Cristo de Burgos."

[9] Amy Powell, "A Point 'Ceaselessly Pushed Back': The Origin of Early Netherlandish Painting," *Art Bulletin* 88 (2006): 707–728.

[10] On the Christ of Burgos, see María José Martínez Martínez, "El Santo Cristo de Burgos. Contribución al estudio de los Crucifijos articulados españoles," *Boletín del Seminario de Estudios de Arte y Arqueología* 69–70 (2003–2004): 207–246.

[11] Alexander Nagel and Christopher S. Wood, *Anachronic Renaissance* (New York: Zone Books, 2010), especially chapter 3 entitled, "What is Substitution?", 29–34. According to the substitutional theory proposed by Nagel and Wood, the Christ of Telde possessed a double historicity, that is, Marín de Cubas took the image to be both a travel souvenir, pointing to a particular moment of creation in the New World, and a holy image, pointing to the now absent life of Christ.

[12] For an excellent and wide-ranging collection of essays on the phenomenon of absconding art, see *RES: Anthropology and Aesthetics* 55/56 (Spring/Autumn 2009).

[13] Joseph Leo Koerner, "Factura," *RES: Anthropology and Aesthetics* 36 (Autumn 1999), 10. See also chapter 1, "Facture," in David Summers, *Real Spaces: World Art History and the Rise of Western Modernism* (New York: Phaidon, 2003), 61–116.

[14] James Clifford, *Routes: Travel and Translation in the Late Twentieth Century* (Cambridge, MA: Harvard University Press, 1997), 7.

[15] Ibid., 8. Although Clifford's study examines the relations between twentieth-century travel and ethnography, his concepts of borderlands and routes aptly characterize the premodern world as well. See, for example, Finbarr B. Flood, *Objects of Translation: Material Culture and Medieval "Hindu-Muslim" Encounter* (Princeton: Princeton University Press, 2009).

[16] On the Canary Islands as a mythical space in ancient Mediterranean thought, upon which the following summary is based, see Peter Hulme, "Tales of Distinction: European Ethnography and the Caribbean," in *Implicit Understandings: Observing, Reporting, and Reflecting on the Encounters between Europeans and Other Peoples in the Early Modern Era*, edited by Stuart B. Schwartz (Cambridge: Cambridge University Press, 1994), especially 174–176.

[17] The Genoese were the first, but were soon followed by, among others, Portuguese and Castilians. On this early phase of Atlantic exploration, see Felipe Fernández-Armesto, *Before Columbus: Exploration and Colonization from the Mediterranean to the Atlantic, 1279–1492* (Philadelphia: University of Pennsylvania Press, 1987).

[18] Eduardo Aznar Vallejo, "The Conquests of the Canary Islands," in *Implicit Understandings*, 134.

[19] John Huxtable Elliott, *Empires of the Atlantic World: Britain and Spain in America, 1492–1830* (New Haven: Yale University Press, 2006), 18. Castile's decision to intervene was largely in response to the more immediate concern of the rising presence, both political and economic, of the Portuguese overseas.
[20] Fernández-Armesto, *Before Columbus*, 212.
[21] Ibid., 213.
[22] Christopher Columbus, *Journal of the First Voyage*, edited and translated by B. W. Ife (Warminster: Aris & Phillips, 1990), 31. The passage quoted here is from the entry dated October 3, 1492.
[23] Francesco Pellizzi, "North by Northwest: Time Lapses and Monumental Vertigo," *RES: Anthropology and Aesthetics* 42 (Autumn 2002), 259.
[24] Hulme, "Tales of Distinction," 164.
[25] Miguel Angel Ladero Quesada, "Spain, circa 1492: Social Values and Structures," in *Implicit Understandings*, 99.
[26] Felipe Fernández-Armesto, *The Canary Islands after the Conquest: The Making of a Colonial Society in the Early Sixteenth Century* (Oxford: Clarendon Press; New York: Oxford University Press, 1982), 12. This history resonates with the initial moments of colonization in the Caribbean, but contrasts sharply with the reality of major metropolitan centers in the New World.
[27] On settlement of the islands, see Manuel Lobo Cabrera, *Grupos humanos en la sociedad canaria del siglo XVI* (Las Palmas de Gran Canaria: La Mancomunidad de Cabildos, Plan Cultural, y Museo Canario, 1979); Fernández-Armesto, *The Canary Islands after the Conquest*, especially chapters 1 and 2, 13–47.
[28] For a summary on merchant presence on the islands, see Manuel Lobo Cabrera, "Las colonias mercantiles europeas en Canarias en el reinado de Felipe II," in *XIII Coloquio de Historia Canario-Americana*, edited by Antonio Bethencourt Massieu (Las Palmas de Gran Canaria: Ediciones del Cabildo de Gran Canaria, 2000), 159–177.
[29] Fernández-Armesto, *The Canary Islands after the Conquest*, 174. On trade between the Canary Islands and the Americas, see Francisco Morales Padrón, *El comercio canario-americano (siglos XVI, XVII, y XVIII)* (Sevilla: Escuela de Estudios Hispano-Americanos, 1955); José Peraza de Ayala, *El régimen comercial de Canarias con las Indias en los siglos XVI, XVII, y XVIII* (Sevilla: Servicio de Publicaciones de la Universidad, 1977); Manuel Lobo Cabrera, "Estado actual de la investigación sobre el comercio canarioamericano," in *X Coloquio de Historia Canario-Americana (1992), Tomo I*, edited by Francisco Morales Padrón (Las Palmas de Gran Canaria: Ediciones del Cabildo de Gran Canaria, 1994), 143–159.
[30] Fernández-Armesto, *The Canary Islands after the Conquest*, 175.
[31] Ibid., 146–147. In addition to trade, a key factor in human mobility was emigration from the Canary Islands to the Americas, especially once the islands' population reached saturation in the second half of the seventeenth century (Elliott, *Empires of the Atlantic World*, 260). See also Antonio M. Macías Hernández, "La emigración canaria á América. Estado de la cuestión," in *X Coloquio de Historia Canario-Americana (1992), Tomo I*, 405–443.
[32] Carlos Rodríguez Morales, "Escultura en Canarias del Gótico a la Ilustración," in *Arte en Canarias, siglos XV–XIX: Una mirada retrospectiva*, edited by María de los Reyes Hernández Socorro, 2 vols. (Santa Cruz de Tenerife; Las Palamas de Gran Canaria: Viceconsejería de Cultura y Deportes, 2001), 1:125.
[33] On the history of the earliest building campaigns after the conquest, see Graziano Gasparini, *La arquitectura de las Islas Canarias: 1420–1788* (Caracas: Armitano, 1995).
[34] On the history of Telde and the church of San Juan Bautista, see Pedro Hernández Benítez, *Telde: Sus valores arqueológicos, históricos, artísticos y religiosos* (Las Palmas de Gran Canaria: Imprenta Telde, 1958), especially 65 ff.; Gasparini, *La arquitectura de las Islas Canarias*, 85–87; *Guía del Patrimonio Arquitectónico de Gran Canaria* (Las Palmas de Gran Canaria: Cabildo de Gran Canaria, 2005), 427 ff.
[35] Cristóbal García del Castillo, quoted in Hernández Benítez, *Telde*, 86. The written testament by Cristóbal García del Castillo, dated 1539, states, "Item, declaro que un retablo el qual está en la dicha iglesia del Señor San Juan, el qual me truxeron de Flandes, que al presente está en al Altar Mayor, que yo lo hice traer en vida de mi primera mujer Marina Rodríguez [d. 1515]..." (85–86). The altarpiece today is framed by an eighteenth-century *retablo*.
[36] The six scenes include the Annunciation, the Betrothal of the Virgin, the Birth of Christ, the Circumcision, the Presentation in the Temple, and the Adoration of the Kings. On the iconography of the scenes, see Pedro Hernández Benítez, *El retablo del altar mayor de la parroquia de San Juan de Telde* (Las Palmas de Gran Canaria: Editorial Canaria, 1938). For further bibliography on the altarpiece, see Francisco José Galante Gómez, ed., *Lumen canariense: El Cristo de la Laguna y su tiempo*, 3 vols. (San Cristobal de La Laguna: Ayuntamiento, D.L., 2003), 2:116; Constanza Negrín Delgado et al., *Intervención en cinco imagenes flamencas: Las esculturas de Era de Mota* (Las Palmas de Gran Canaria: Cabildo de Gran Canaria, 2005), 20, footnote 15.
[37] Luis Pérez Aguado, *La caña de azúcar en el desarrollo de la cuidad de Telde (siglo XVI)* (Telde: La Comisión de Cultura de M.I. Ayuntamiento de Telde, 1982), 4.
[38] Eddy Stols and Werner Thomas, "Flanders and the Canary Islands in the First Widening of the World. 1450–1550," in Galante Gomez, ed., *Lumen Canariense*, 3:36.
[39] Hernández Benítez, *Telde*, 86.
[40] Negrín Delgado, *Intervención*, 15.
[41] Lynn F. Jacobs, "The Marketing and Standardization of South Netherlandish Carved Altarpieces: Limits on the Role of the Patron," *Art Bulletin* 71 (1989): 213. See also Hans Nieuwdorp, "De oorspronkelijke betekenis en interpretatie van de keurmerken op Brabantse retabels en beeldsnijwerk," *Archivum artis Lovaniensis: Bijdragen tot de geschiedenis van de kunst der Nederlanden, opgedragen aan prof. em. Dr. J.K. Steppe*, edited by M. Smeyers (Leuven: Peeters, 1981): 85–98. For information on stamping see Myriam Serck-Dewaide, "Support and Polychromy of Altarpieces from Brussels, Mechlin, and Antwerp: Study, Comparison, and Restoration," in *Painted Wood: History and Conservation*, edited by Valerie Dorge and F. Carey Howlett (Los Angeles: Getty Conservation Institute, 1998), 82–99.
[42] Filip Vermeylen, "Exporting Art across the Globe: The Antwerp Art Market in the Sixteenth Century," *Nederlands Kunsthistorisch Jaarboek* 50 (1999): 13–25. For a bibliographic review up to 1990, see John Michael Montias, "Socio-Economic Aspects of Netherlandish Art from the Fifteenth to the Seventeenth Century: A Survey," *Art Bulletin* 72 (1990): 358–369. See also Lorne Campbell, "The Art Market in the

Southern Netherlands in the Fifteenth Century," *Burlington Magazine* 118 (1976): 188–198; Elizabeth Alice Honig, *Painting and the Market in Early Modern Antwerp* (New Haven: Yale University Press, 1998).

[43] On the sale of art at the weekly markets, or *panden*, see Dan Ewing, "Marketing Art in Antwerp, 1460–1560: Our Lady's Pand," *Art Bulletin* 72 (1990): 558–584.

[44] Lynn F. Jacobs, *Early Netherlandish Carved Altarpieces, 1380–1550: Medieval Tastes and Mass Marketing* (Cambridge: Cambridge University Press, 1998); Jacobs, "Marketing and Standardization."

[45] Jacobs, *Early Netherlandish Carved Altarpieces*, 199. Jacobs calculates that approximately 75 percent of all Netherlandish carved altarpieces were produced on speculation (ibid., 9).

[46] For a thought-provoking discussion on these new conditions of art-making through the lens of Albrecht Dürer and his work, see Joseph Leo Koerner, *The Moment of Self-Portraiture in German Renaissance Art* (Chicago: University of Chicago Press, 1993), especially chapter 10, "The Law of Authorship," 203–223, as well as the author's later formulations on this theme in his "Albrecht Dürer: A Sixteenth-Century Influenza," in *Albrecht Dürer and His Legacy: The Graphic Work of a Renaissance Artist*, edited by Giulia Bartrum (Princeton: Princeton University Press, 2002),18–38.

[47] On the concept of a Hispano-Flemish style, see Robert Didier, "L'Art Hispano-Flamand. Reflexions critiques. Considerations concernant des sculptures espagnoles et brabançonnes," in *Actas del Congreso internacional sobre Gil Siloe y la escultura de su época* (Burgos: Institución Fernán González, Academia Burgense de Historia y Bellas Artes, 2001), 113–144; Clementina Julia Ara Gil, "Flemish Roots in Late Gothic Sculpture in Spain," in Galante Gomez, ed., *Lumen canariense*, 3:83–100; and, also by Gil, "El problema de la delimitación entre lo flamenco y lo hispánico en la escultura castellana del siglo XV," in *El arte en la corte de los Reyes Católicos*, edited by Fernando Checa and Bernardo J. García García (Madrid: Fundación Carlos Amberes, 2005), 223–246.

[48] For a discussion on the emigration of artists from Northern Europe to the Iberian Peninsula, see Dorothee Heim, "Die Suche nach Geld, Freiheit und Ansehen: Künstlermigration nach Kastilien im 15. Jahrhundert," in *"Das kommt mir spanisch vor." Eigenes und Fremdes in den deutsch-spanischen Beziehungen des späten Mittelalters*, edited by Klaus Herbers and Nikolas Jaspert (Munster: Lit Verlag, 2004), 315–338.

[49] Rodríguez Morales, "Escultura en Canarias," 139–140.

[50] María de los Reyes Hernández Socorro, ed., *Arte hispanoamericano en las Canarias Orientales: Siglos XVI–XIX* (Las Palmas de Gran Canaria: Cabildo de Gran Canaria, 2000), 40. See also Jesús Pérez Morera and Carlos Rodríguez Morales, *Arte en Canarias: Del Gótico al Manierismo* (Santa Cruz de Tenerife; Las Palmas de Gran Canaria: Viceconsejería de Cultura y Deportes, 2008). On the importation of silver from the Americas to the Canaries, see Jesús Pérez Morera, *Arte, devoción y fortuna. Platería Americana en las Canarias Occidentales* (San Cristobal de La Laguna: Gobierno de Canarias, 2010).

[51] Hernández Socorro, *Arte hispanoamericano en las Canarias Orientales*, 35.

[52] For a discussion of the place of the Americas within the network of cultural influence in early modern Spain, Madrid in particular, see Amelang, "The New World in the Old?" especially 156–158.

[53] The Spanish term "*Cristo*" was commonly used in the early modern period to refer to large, three-dimensional sculptures of Christ. For the earliest technical analysis of a *Cristo de caña*, see Abelardo Carrillo y Gariel, *El Cristo de Mexicaltzingo, técnica de las esculturas en caña* (México: Dirección de Monumentos Coloniales, 1949). From among the numerous publications that have emerged since Carrillo y Gariel's pioneering work, see most notably and for further bibliography, Rolando Araujo Suárez, Alejandro Huerta Carrillo, and Sergio Guerrero Bolan, *Esculturas de papel amate y caña de maíz* (Mexico City: Fideicomiso Cultural Franz Mayer, 1989); Antonio García-Abásolo, Gabriela García-Lascuráin, and Joaquín Sánchez Ruiz, eds., *Imaginería indígena mexicana. Una catequesis en caña de maíz* (Córdoba: Publicaciones de la Obra Social y Cultural Cajasur, 2001); Pablo F. Amador Marrero, *Traza española, ropaje indiano. El Cristo de Telde y la imaginería en caña de maíz* (Telde: Ayuntamiento de Telde, 2002); and, also by Amador Marrero, his more recent "Imaginería ligera en Oaxaca. El taller de los grandes Cristos," *Boletín de Monumentos Históricos* 15 (2009): 45–60. The description of the technique that follows is largely based upon Araujo Suárez, Carrillo, and Bolan, *Esculturas*, and Amador Marrero, *Traza española*, especially 61–79.

[54] Esther Pasztory, *Aztec Art* (New York: H.N. Abrams, 1983), 78.

[55] These *Cristos* thus correspond to the conception of colonial art as a "hybrid" art. On the discourse of hybridity in colonial Latin American art history, see Carolyn Dean and Dana Leibsohn, "Hybridity and Its Discontents: Considering Visual Culture in Colonial Spanish America," *Colonial Latin American Review* 12 (2003): 5–35.

[56] Amador Marrero, *Traza española*, 82.

[57] See, for example, the conservation report from Mexico's *Escuela Nacional de Conservación, Restauración y Museografía "Manuel del Castillo Negrete"*: Seminario Taller de Restauración de Escultura Policromada, *Informe de los trabajos realizados de dos esculturas policromadas de la colección del museo de arte religioso del Exconvento de Santa Monica de Puebla, Tomo 1: Cristo Liguero con Cruz* (Mexico City: Instituto Nacional de Antropología e Historia, Sept. 2003–Feb. 2004).

[58] He has located ninety-seven examples in Spain (personal correspondence with Pablo Amador Marrero, April 29, 2011).

[59] Most recently the Christ of Garachico, imported to the Canary Islands from New Spain, was discovered to be made of *papelón* and not, as it was long believed, *caña de maíz*: Pablo Francisco Amador Marrero, "El Santo Cristo *Reliquia Muy Milagrosa*. Análisis interdisciplinario de una imagen novohispana de papelón," in *Garachico y sus fiestas del Cristo. Apuntes históricos y crónicas de prensa*, edited by Cirilo Velázques Ramos (Garachico: Ayuntamiento de la Villa y Puerto de Garachico, 2010), 29–53. Very little has been published on the history of *papelón*, but the related tradition of *cartapesta*, another kind of *papier mâché* from early modern Italy, has begun to receive scholarly attention: Francesca Baldry Becattini, *Crocifisso Di Pietro Tacca a Settignano: Restauro Di Un'inedita Cartapesta Policroma* (Florence: Madragora, 2001); Maria Grazia Vaccari Massimo Bonelli, *Iacopo Sansovino: la Madonna in cartapesta del Bargello: Restauro e indagini* (Rome: Instituto Centrale per il Restauro: Gangemi, 2006); Raffaele Casciaro, ed., *La scultura in cartapesta: Sansovino, Bernini e i maestri leccisi tra tecnica e artificio* (Cinisello Balsamo: Silvana, 2008).

[60] For a sculpture belonging to the expanded category of *escultura ligera* that is made solely of gessoed and polychromed wood rather than *caña de maíz*, see Fanny Unikel Santoncini and Mercedes Murguía Meca, eds., *Informe de los trabajos realizados de seis esculturas policromadas provenientes de San Miguel Cerezo, Hidalgo, Tomo 1: Cristos* (Mexico City: Instituto Nacional de Antropología e Historia, Sept. 2002–Feb. 2003), especially 7–8.

[61] Toribio de Motolinía, *Historia de los indios de la Nueva España* (Barcelona: Linkgua ediciones S.L., 2009), 137: "aunque el crucifijo sea tamaño como un hombre, le levantara un niño del suelo con una mano."

[62] Géronimo de Mendieta, *Historia eclesiástica indiana* (Barcelona: Linkgua ediciones S.L., 2007), 417: "Como llevan también [a España] los crucifijos huecos de caña, que siendo de la corpulencia de un hombre muy grande, pesan tan poco, que los puede llevar un niño."

[63] For a history of processional sculpture in early modern Spain, see Susan Verdi Webster, *Art and Ritual in Golden-Age Spain: Sevillian Confraternities and the Processional Sculpture of Holy Week* (Princeton: Princeton University Press, 1998). In the year 2000, the Christ of Telde was processed to Las Palmas de Gran Canaria, the first time the statue had left Telde since its arrival in the sixteenth century. In the Cathedral of Las Palmas it was united with the Virgin of the Pine Tree, venerated in Teror, Gran Canaria, in celebration of the new millennium. On the procession of the Christ of Telde, see Francisco González González, *Historia de un viaje jubilar* (Telde: M.I. Ayuntamiento de Telde, 2004).

[64] María del Consuelo Maquívar, "Reseña de 'Traza española, ropaje indiano. El Cristo de Telde y la imaginería en caña de maíz' de Pablo F. Amador Marrero," *Anales del Instituto de Investigaciones Estéticas* 26, no. 084 (2004): 214. See also her earlier work on New Spanish sculpture and the guild system, *El imaginero novohispano y su obra: Las esculturas de Tepotzotlán* (Mexico City: Instituto Nacional de Antropología e Historia, 1995); as well as her *La escultura religiosa en la Nueva España* (Mexico City: Consejo Nacional para la Cultura y las Artes, 2001).

[65] Danièle Dehoeve, "Le Christ et le plumassier en Nouvelle-Espagne au XVIe siècle," in *Des Indes occidentales à l'Amérique Latine, à Jean-Pierre Berthe*, edited by Alain Musset and Thomas Calvo (Paris: ENS Editions, 1997), 2:8.

[66] Pablo Amador was the first to question the indigenous origins of the technique used in the creation of these sculptures, and to propose an alternative theory of the origins of the technique from Europe, in particular by drawing the historical connection between the use of mold-made sculpture in Granada and in New Spain discussed below. See his "Imaginería ligera en Oaxaca," 47; see also his "El Santo Cristo Reliquia Muy Milagrosa," 34–35. Scholarship has traditionally focused on the use of *caña de maíz* in Michoacán, with particular attention paid to the role of Vasco de Quiroga, the first bishop of Michoacán, and the artistic practices of the Tarascans or Purépecha, the indigenous inhabitants of the area. It is important to note, however, that this method based in Michoacán differs in certain essential respects from the technique more prevalent in Mexico City and its immediate environs, where the grinding of cornstalk into an agglutinative paste was more common than the insertion of dried bundles of this material; it is the development of the latter tradition that is the focus of the present study. Historical and technical research on this issue remains ongoing. The following publications were formative in establishing the historiographic tradition on *caña de maíz* in Michoacán: Julian Bonavit, "Esculturas tarascas de caña de maíz y orquídeas fabricadas bajo la dirección del Ilmo. Sr. D. Vasco de Quiroga," *Anales del Museo Michoacano* 3 (Sept. 1944); Enrique Luft, "Las imágenes de caña de maíz de Michoacán," *Artes de México* 153 (1972): 15–26 and 85–89. See also, more recently and for further bibliography, Sofía Irene Velarde Cruz, *Imaginería michoacana en caña de maíz*, 2nd ed. (Morelia: Centro de Documentación e Investigación de las Artes, 2009); Elizabeth Ávila Figueroa, *Técnicas y materiales de la escultura ligera novohispana con caña de maíz: Una aproximación historiográfica* (M.A. Thesis, Universidad Nacional Autónoma de México, 2011).

[67] On *pijpaarden beeldjes*, see Sebastiaan Ostkamp, "Productie en gebruik van pijpaarden en terracotta devotionalia in de Nederlanden (ca. 1350–ca. 1550)," in *Judocus Vredis. Kunst uit de stilte—een kloosterwerkplaats uit de tijd van Dürer*, edited by Antonius Böing and Günther Inhester (Munster: Westfälisches Landesmuseum für Kunst und Kulturgeschichte, 2001), 188–256. See also Powell, "A Point 'Ceaselessly Pushed Back,'" 709–711 and 725 for further bibliography.

[68] Jaap Leeuwenberg, "Die Ausstrahlung Utrechter Tonplastik," in *Studien zur Geschichte der europäischen Plastik: Festschrift Theodor Müller, zum 19. April 1965*, edited by Kurt Martin et al. (Munich: Hirmer Verlag, 1965), 151–166; Ostkamp, "Productie," 213. See, for example, the Virgin and Child that was housed in the church of Prádanos de Bureba, province of Burgos, Spain, but whose whereabouts are currently unknown; Leeuwenberg includes a photographic reproduction of the work (156, Fig. 8). See also Ostkamp, 209–210 on the probability that Utrecht molds, not just the sculptures themselves, were traded outside of the Netherlands.

[69] Peter Schmidt, "The Multiple Image: The Beginning of Printmaking, between Old Theories and New Approaches," in *Origins of European Printmaking: Fifteenth-Century Woodcuts and Their Public*, edited by Peter Parshall and Rainer Schoch (Washington, DC: National Gallery of Art, in association with Yale University Press, 2005), 37–56. Important recent contributions to the early modern multiple image have focused largely, although not exclusively, on the early woodcut. In addition to this catalogue from the exhibition mounted by the National Gallery of Art in Washington, DC, and the Germanisches Nationalmuseum in Nuremberg, see Peter Parshall, ed., *The Woodcut in Fifteenth-Century Europe* (Washington, DC: National Gallery of Art, in association with Yale University Press, 2009); David S. Areford, *The Viewer and the Printed Image in Late Medieval Europe* (Aldershot, England; Burlington, VT.: Ashgate, 2010).

[70] See, for example, the pilgrim badge made of colored *papier mâché* pressed from a mold and currently housed in the Germanisches Nationalmuseum, Nuremberg, Pl.O. 2472 (Parshall and Schoch, *Origins of European Printmaking*, 60–61, cat. 1d). Molds for pilgrim badges were often made of slate or soapstone, as well as baked clay, tin, or limestone; according to Rainer Schoch, these molds could yield hundreds of thousands of badges (ibid., 60). On pilgrim badges, see the research of Kurt Köster, for example his contributions to the exhibition catalogue, *Rhein und Maas, Kunst und Kultur, 800–1400. Eine Ausstellung des Schnütgen-Museums der Stadt Köln und der belgischen Ministerien für französische and niederländische Kultur*, 2 vols. (Cologne:

Schnütgen Museum, 1972), 1:142–160.
[71] Schmidt, "The Multiple Image," 46. On devotional statues made of leather, see Wolfgang Krönig, "Rheinische Vesperbilder aus Leder und ihr Umkreis," *Wallraf-Richartz-Jahrbuch*, 24 (1962): 97–192. On devotional statues made of macerated paper, see the examples mentioned in Hubert Wilm, *Gotische Tonplastik in Deutschland* (Augsburg: Benno Filser Verlag, 1929), 81; Leeuwenberg, "Die Ausstrahlung," 160–161.
[72] Felipe Pereda, *Las imágenes de la discordia: Política y poética de la imagen sagrada en la España del cuatrocientos* (Madrid: Marcial Pons, 2007), especially the third section, entitled "La industria de las imágenes," 249–402.
[73] For Pereda's discussion of Isabella's commission, upon which this summary is based, see ibid., 292 ff.
[74] AHN, Diversos, Colección, n. 288 (Colección diplomática, 82 and 83) as cited in Pereda, *Las imágenes de la Discordia,* 309. Pereda provides a transcription of the complete text in the appendix (382–383).
[75] On the identity of the artist, see Pereda, *Las imágenes de la discordia*, 314 ff. The term "Alemán" was often conflated with other Northern European nationalities; Pereda proposes that the artist may have been originally from Utrecht.
[76] There are, however, records of other commissions in which Huberto Alemán was called upon to produce life-size sculptures of the Crucifixion. Pereda (ibid., 305) proposes that Christological iconographies were in greater demand in monastic communities, in which the images were used for both pastoral and meditative practices. Regarding the unique role of Marian devotion in the religious practice of the Moriscos, see 339 ff. Printed images also played an important role in conversion in Granada.
[77] Eva Villanueva Romero and Gracia Montero Saucedo, "Investigación y tratamiento de la Virgen de los Remedios de Villarrasa (Huelva)," *Boletín del Instituto Andaluz del Patrimonio Histórico* 29 (1999): 99–109.
[78] Ibid., 101, Figs. 4 and 5. On this series of statues, see also Pereda, *Las imágenes de la discordia*, 327–339.
[79] Pereda, *Las imágenes de la discordia*, 312: "El mecanismo era pseudo-industrial mucho más que artisanal."
[80] Webster, *Art and Ritual*, 105–107. See also Celestino López Martínez, "La Hermanded de Nuestra Señora de la Esperanza, de San Gil y el escultor Pedro Nieto," *Calvario* (1950): n.p.; and, by the same author, "Materiales constructivos en imágines en talleres sevillanos del siglo dieciséis," *Calvario* (1951): n.p.
[81] Vasco de Quiroga was in Granada during Isabella's image campaign; see Francisco Miranda, "Antecedentes granadinos de don Vasco de Quiroga," *Ábside* 35 (1971): 146–165.
[82] Scholarship on the effects of the printing press is vast. See, for example, William M. Ivins, *Prints and Visual Communication* (Cambridge, MA.: Harvard University Press, 1953); Marshall McLuhan, *The Gutenberg Galaxy: The Making of Typographic Man* (Toronto: University of Toronto Press, 1962); Elizabeth L. Eisenstein, *The Printing Press as an Agent of Change: Communications and Cultural Transformations in Early-Modern Europe* (Cambridge: Cambridge University Press, 1979); Mario Carpo, *Architecture in the Age of Printing: Orality, Writing, Typography, and Printed Images in the History of Architectural Theory*, translated by Sarah Benson (Cambridge, MA: MIT Press, 2001); Christopher S. Wood, *Forgery Replica Fiction: Temporalities of German Renaissance Art* (Chicago: University of Chicago Press, 2008).
[83] Bartolomé de las Casas, *Apologética historia sumaria*, edited by Edmundo O'Gorman (Mexico City: Universidad Nacional Autónoma de México, Instituto de Investigaciones Históricas, 1967), 327: "Yo tengo en mi poder una carta que me enviaron de la Nueva España los indios estando yo en la Corte, y la metí en el Consejo do las Indias para mostralla, y siendo las personas del Consejo de tanta sabiduría y prudencia dotadas, estuvieron mucho espacio de tiempo mirando y especulando letra por letra si era de molde o de mano; y finalmente, del todo se determinaron unos de aquellos señores diciendo sí, otros que no, como en la verdad fuese ya hecha de mano de indio de la Nueva España."
[84] Amador Marrero, *Traza española*, 72.
[85] Carrillo y Gariel, *El Cristo de Mexicaltzingo*. The documents are now housed in the Biblioteca Nacional de México, Mexico City. On the *Códices del Cristo de Mexicaltzingo*, see John B. Glass, *Catálogo de la colección de codices [del Museo Nacional de Antropología]* (Mexico City: Museo Nacional de Antroplogía,
[86] The Christ of Bornos, one of the more recent of these discoveries, resides in the church of Santo Domingo de Guzmán in Bornos, Cádiz. A document from this parish in southern Spain states that members of the Hieronymite monastery obtained a sculpture of the Crucifixion that had been brought from the Indies (personal correspondence with Pablo Amador Marrero, September 27, 2010). The fact that a group of religious brothers purchased the artwork in the public square of a neighboring city in the year 1553 testifies to the early trade of New Spanish art for a market of on-spec buyers. Evidently, the technology of *escultura ligera* made its way to New Spain quite soon after the conquest and was quickly put to use.
[87] On reuse as an ecological act, see Nagel and Wood, *Anachronic Renaissance*, 180.
[88] The work of Hans Lenz, first published in 1950 and subsequently reissued, remains the touchstone for this understudied topic: Hans Lenz, *Historia del papel en México y cosas relacionadas, 1525–1950* (Mexico City: M.A. Porrúa, 1990). See also María Cristina Sánchez de Bonfil, *El papel del papel en la Nueva España 1740–1812* (Mexico City: Instituto Nacional de Antropología e Historia, 1993); María del Carmen Hidalgo Brinquis, "La fabricación del papel en España e Hispanoamérica en el siglo XVII," in *V Jornadas Científicas Sobre Documentación de Castilla e Indias en el siglo XVII*, edited by Susana Cabezas Fontanilla and María del Mar Royo Martínez (Madrid: Departamento de Ciencias y Técnicas Historiográficas, Universidad de Madrid, 2006), 207–224.
[89] Lenz, *Historia del papel*, 38.
[90] Juan de Zumárraga, quoted in Lenz, *Historia del papel*, 39: "Poco se puede adelantar en lo de la imprenta por la carestía de papel."
[91] Lenz, *Historia del papel*, 89.
[92] Kelly Donahue-Wallace, *Prints and Printmakers in Viceregal Mexico City, 1600–1800* (Ph.D. diss., University of New Mexico, 2000), 14. For a history of printmaking in New Spain see also the excellent work of Marina Garone Gravier, in particular her *Historia de la tipografía para lenguas indígenas* (Ph.D. diss., Universidad Nacional Autónoma de México, 2009).
[93] On *amate*, then and now, see Hans Lenz, *El papel indígena mexicano: Historia y supervivencia* (Mexico City: Editorial Cultura, 1948); Alan R. Sandstrom and Pamela Effrein Sandstrom, *Traditional Papermaking and Paper Cult Figures of Mexico* (Norman: University of Oklahoma Press, 1986);

Jonathan D. Amith, ed., *La Tradición del amate: Innovación y protesta en el arte mexicano / The Amate Tradition: Innovation and Dissent in Mexican Art* (Chicago: Mexican Fine Arts Center Museum; Mexico City: La Casa de las Imágenes), 1995; Philip P. Arnold, "Paper Rituals and the Mexican Landscape," in *Representing Aztec Ritual: Performance, Text, and Image in the Work of Sahagún*, edited by Eloise Quiñones Keber (Boulder: University Press of Colorado, 2002), 227–250.

[94] According to Charles Gibson, up to midcentury, each member of an indigenous community could be expected to pay a specified amount of maize, another product such as a turkey, firewood, or textiles, and additionally, a certain quantity of *reales* or, for fractions of *reales*, cacao beans. Around the year 1550, however, strict reforms were put into place, and tribute paid in the form of commodities was eliminated. Henceforth all payments were, at least in theory, to be made only in the form of maize and money. On these mid-century tax reforms, see Charles Gibson, *The Aztecs Under Spanish Rule: A History of the Indians of the Valley of Mexico, 1519–1810* (Stanford: Stanford University Press, 1964), 198. On the history of tribute in New Spain, see also José Miranda, *El tributo indígena en la Nueva España durante el siglo XVI* (Mexico City: El Colegio de México, 2005 [1952]); and, more recently, the following collection of essays: Victor Bulmer-Thomas, John H. Coatsworth, and Roberto Cortés Conde, eds., *Cambridge Economic History of Latin America*, 2 vols. (Cambridge: Cambridge University Press, 2008).

[95] Also of interest is the question of exemptions granted artists and artisans. A compelling source for this issue is the so-called *Anales de Juan Bautista*, recently translated into Spanish from the original Nahuatl: Luis Reyes García, ed. and trans., *¿Cómo te confundes? ¿Acaso no somos conquistados? Anales de Juan Bautista* (Mexico City: Centro de Investigaciones y Estudios Superiores en Antropología Social, Biblioteca Lorenzo Boturini Insigne y Nacional Basilica de Guadalupe, 2001).

Casta Paintings and Self-Fashioning Artists in New Spain

James M. Córdova and Claire Farago

Scholars do not usually consider the production of *casta* paintings in light of the rising status of the artist and his art.[1] In fact, most of the literature suggests just the opposite, by focusing on this viceregal genre's inclusion in scientific collections and curiosity cabinets, not the grand painting and sculpture galleries of wealthy European patrons of art. Extending the arguments and research of María Concepción García Sáiz, Elena Estrada de Gerlero, Ilona Katzew, Magali Carrera, and others, Susan Deans-Smith has recently located records showing that *casta* paintings were usually not expensive items to acquire and that individuals from different socioeconomic strata in New Spain possessed them.[2] Yet the literature has also noted that the artists who produced the earliest sets of *casta* paintings were associated with the formation of the art academy in Mexico City. Katzew emphasizes that the development of an academy is crucial to understanding how the *castas* genre evolved over the course of the eighteenth century.[3] To explain these connections, she and others have argued that *casta* paintings, with their depictions of racial mixing in harmonious family settings, may be a Creole expression of pride in the homeland.[4]

The extensive scholarship on *casta* paintings considers them as if they were transparent windows directly reflecting real or imagined social conditions. Was the relationship between artistic representation and social conditions really so straightforward? Complicating this view, Deans-Smith has located documents that highlight the relation between many of the artists who made *casta* paintings and their advocacy for an academy that would restrict admission to Spaniards and some members of the indigenous nobility.[5] Efforts to establish an art academy where painting would be taught as a liberal art were directly linked to efforts to *exclude* indigenous and *casta* (racially mixed) artisans from the profession along with unlicensed and untrained craftsmen and vendors. And far from identifying with the miscegenated underclass they depicted so sympathetically, many locally born artists who painted *casta* sets claimed pure blood (*limpieza de sangre*) status for themselves.

What are we to make of the apparent contradiction between these artists' depictions of a harmonious social order and their documented efforts to distinguish themselves from the underclass? The following analysis of the different agencies involved in the invention, production, and circulation of *casta* paintings argues that the agency of the artist in the social and economic network has been undertheorized. The evidence internal to *casta* paintings, together with other forms of documentation, suggests that an elite corps of artists in New Spain developed the genre as part of their bid to elevate painting to the status of a scientifically based liberal art. Revisiting the invention of the genre from the perspective of viceregal artists such as Juan Rodríguez Juárez (1675–1728), José de Ibarra (1685–1756), and Miguel Cabrera (1695–1768), we argue here that *casta* paintings offered an unprecedented opportunity to display inventiveness in composing narrative scenes, in virtuoso handling of paint, and in meeting the highest European standards of academic artistic practice. Yet, in generating depictions of the Americas that were considered exotic cultural geographies by those who collected them, the artists ultimately reinforced their own colonial subordination: in the very act of trying to emulate their Academic counterparts in Europe, the leading artists of New Spain reinscribed their subordinate position in their choice of genre and subject matter, as the documented history of collecting practices attests.

Despite this retrogradation, much can be learned from the manner in which *casta* paintings were associated with the ambition of artists to be treated as members of the highest social echelon by virtue of their mastery of painting

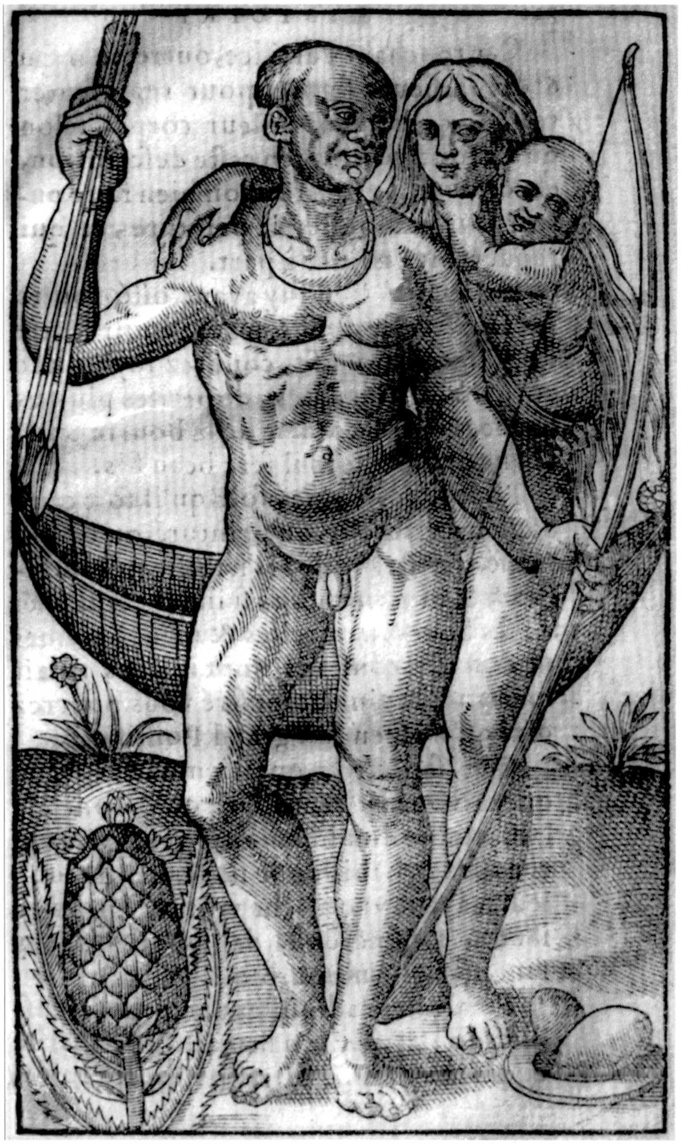

Fig. 1. Jean de Léry, *Tupi Family*. From *D'un Voyage Fait en la Terre du Bresil, Autrement dite Amerique*, 1578.

defined as a liberal art. A cross-cultural approach to reconstructing the intellectual environment in which *casta* paintings circulated in both New Spain and Europe shows that similar tensions between artistic license and the religious decorum of images were at stake in both places, despite clear differences in local conditions. In their American venue, arguments for the status of painting based on its scientific underpinnings were adapted to the discourse on sacred images. The visual and textual evidence in turn enables us to consider, on a more nuanced historical and conceptual foundation, the significance of arguments for the intellectual status of the artist and his artistic license that had been taking place in Europe since the mid-sixteenth century.

Viceregal Agencies and the Rise of *Casta* Paintings

As a type of viceregal genre painting, *casta* paintings are most closely related to ethnographic representation, which first developed in sixteenth-century illustrated cultural geographies produced in Europe. These illustrated books and broadsheets represent not individuals but cultural types based largely on costume and physiognomy. As the genre developed and diversified, ethnographic illustrations came to include typical plants, animals, landscapes, and activities associated with various peoples and places in the world. As entertainment and as scientific information popular with various European audiences for several hundred years, ethnographic illustrations appeared in a wide variety of forms (Fig. 1 and Figs. 2a and b).

The *castas* genre is a new variant of the ethnographic illustration that first appeared in the early eighteenth century, painted by locally trained artists (Fig. 3). *Casta* paintings are so innovative in appearance, in fact, that their indebtedness to an existing European genre of visual ethnography came as a surprising discovery to modern scholars interested in their historical origins.[6] Until now, however, the historical relationships between European and viceregal variants of the genre have not been explored beyond the location of sources and the cataloguing of examples. The present work

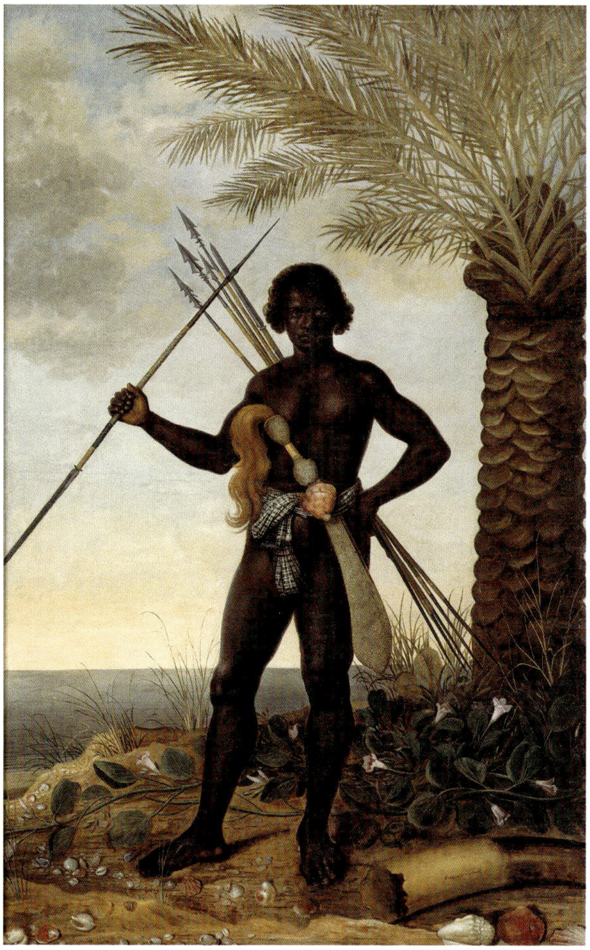

Fig. 2a. Albert Eckhout, *African Man.* 1641. Oil on canvas. National Museum of Denmark, Copenhagen. Photo: National Museum of Denmark.

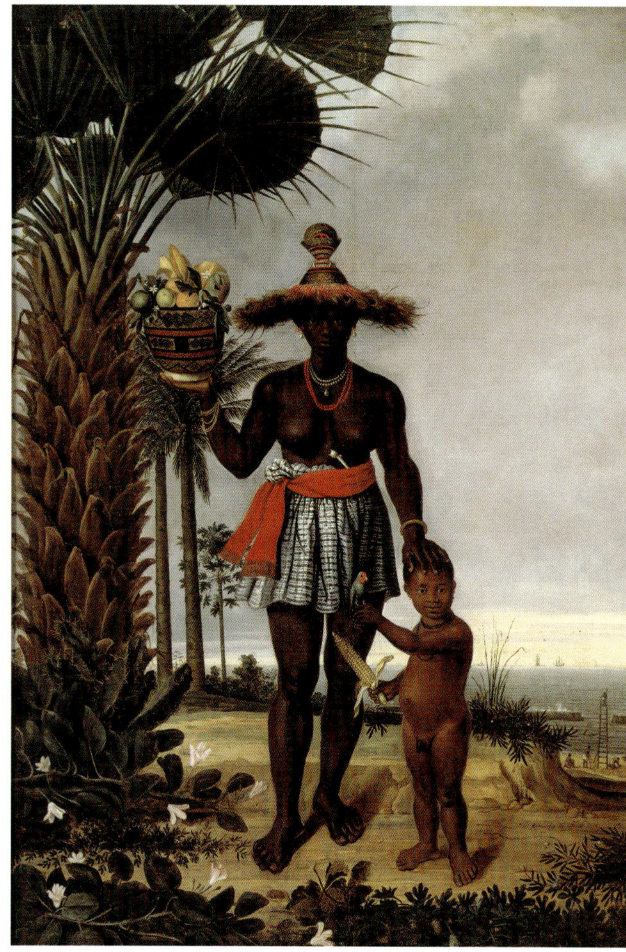

Fig. 2b. Albert Eckhout, *African Woman and Child.* 1641. Oil on canvas. National Museum of Denmark, Copenhagen. Photo: National Museum of Denmark.

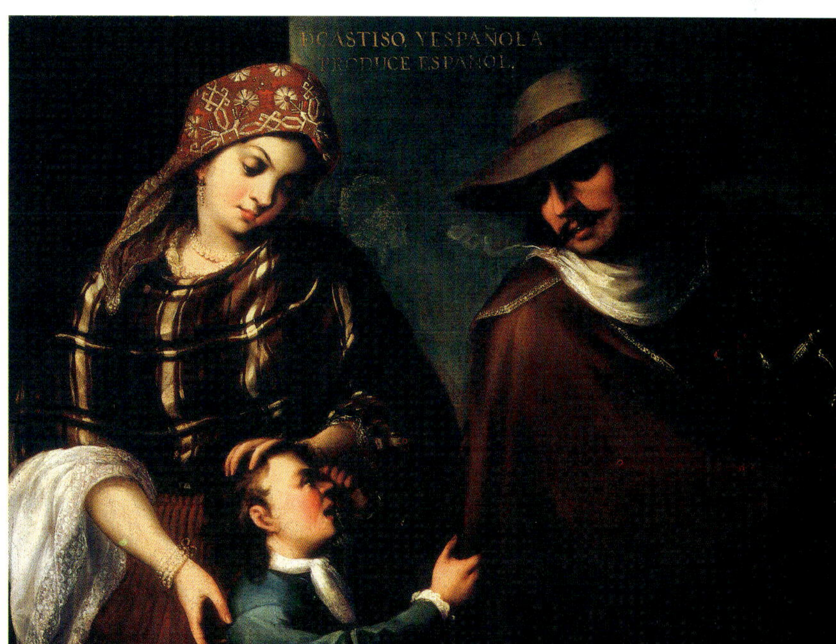

Fig. 3. Juan Rodríguez Juárez, *De castizo y española, produce español* (*Castizo and a Spaniard Produce a Spaniard*). Mexico, c. 1715. Oil on canvas. 31¼ x 41½ in. Braemore House, England.

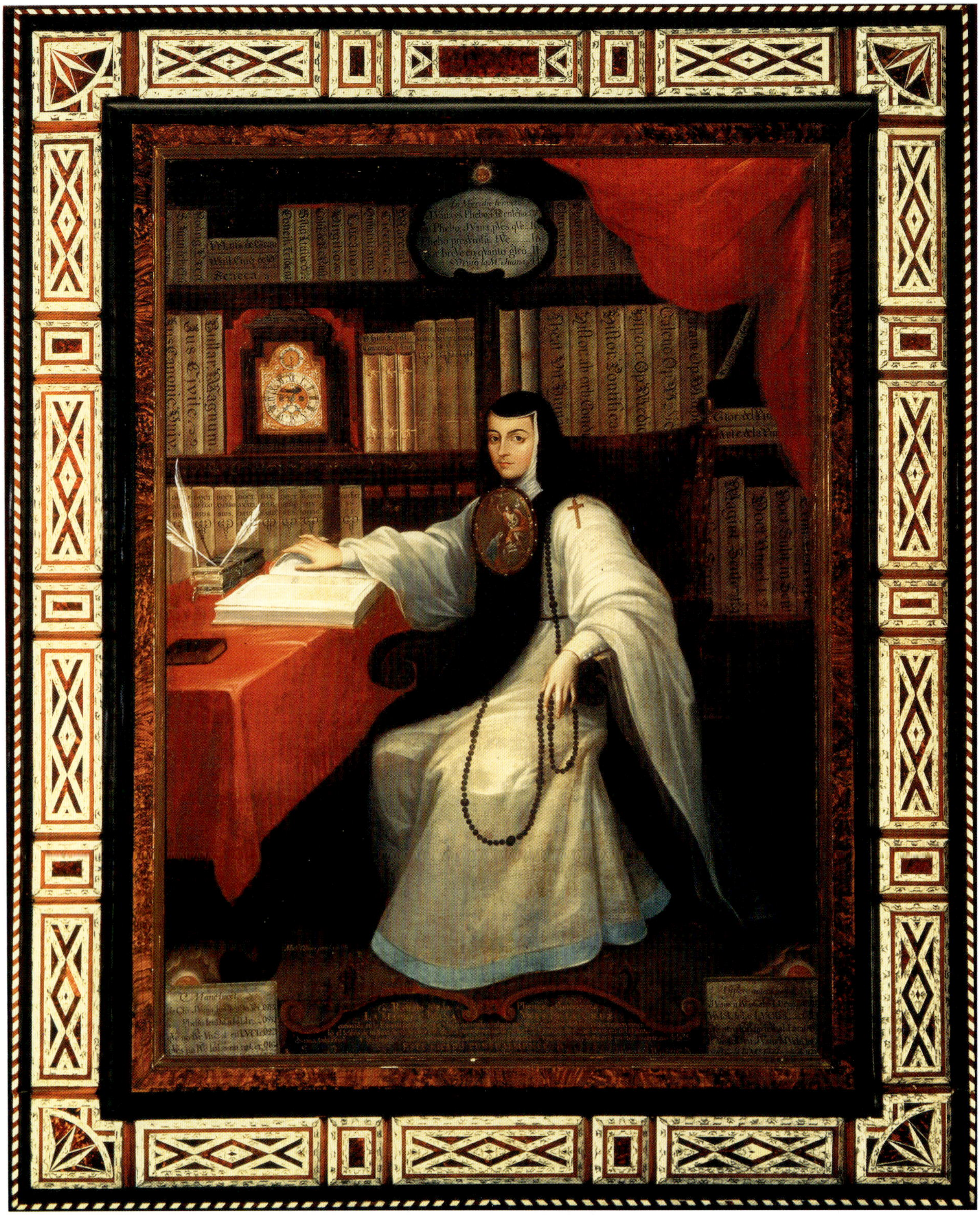

Fig. 4. Miguel Cabrera, *Portrait of Sor Juana Inés de la Cruz*. Mexico, c. 1750. Oil on canvas, 81½ x 58¼ in. Museo Nacional de Historia, Mexico City. Photo: Art Resource.

expands beyond these perimeters by examining the related sociopolitical and professional agendas of the New Spanish artist in inventing and developing the *castas* genre along a particular artistic trajectory.

Significantly, the earliest *casta* paintings—viceregal interpretations of well-established visual ethnography popular with European audiences—were executed not by artists working for missionaries or scientific expeditions, but by some of New Spain's leading artists. It is instructive to compare the newly invented genre with portraiture, because both demanded the skillful rendering of natural appearances. The canons accepted for official and courtly portraits on the Iberian peninsula were introduced to the viceroyalties of New Spain and Peru without any significant modifications, according to Rogelio Ruiz Gomar:[7] the pose is almost always the same standing three-quarter view, the sitter gazing directly at the viewer to establish contact (albeit with an opaque expression), with the same elements of setting constantly repeated: drapery, table with objects underlining the uniqueness of the sitter, a status-conferring coat of arms, an inscription describing the person's place of origin, dates of birth and death, lineage, and marriage in the case of women. An inkwell with pens describes the sitter as an official or a distinguished writer, a stack of books signifies erudition, a watch or a flower refers to the nature of worldly vanities and the unstoppable passage of time arrested in the portrait.[8] In the largely masculine world of colonial portraiture before the late eighteenth century, Miguel Cabrera's painting of Sor Juana Inés de la Cruz, executed c. 1750 (Fig. 4), follows a conventional portrait formula to depict exceptional, erudite men, who are also pictured as authors and seated at their writing desks in a library. The same general formula is followed in the portrait of José Pérez de Lanciego y Eguilaz, Archbishop of Mexico, painted c. 1715 by Juan Rodríguez Juárez (Fig. 5).

The new *castas* genre demanded imaginative powers of invention and encouraged painterly handling of the surface largely missing from the established formulaic portraits. The sumptuous

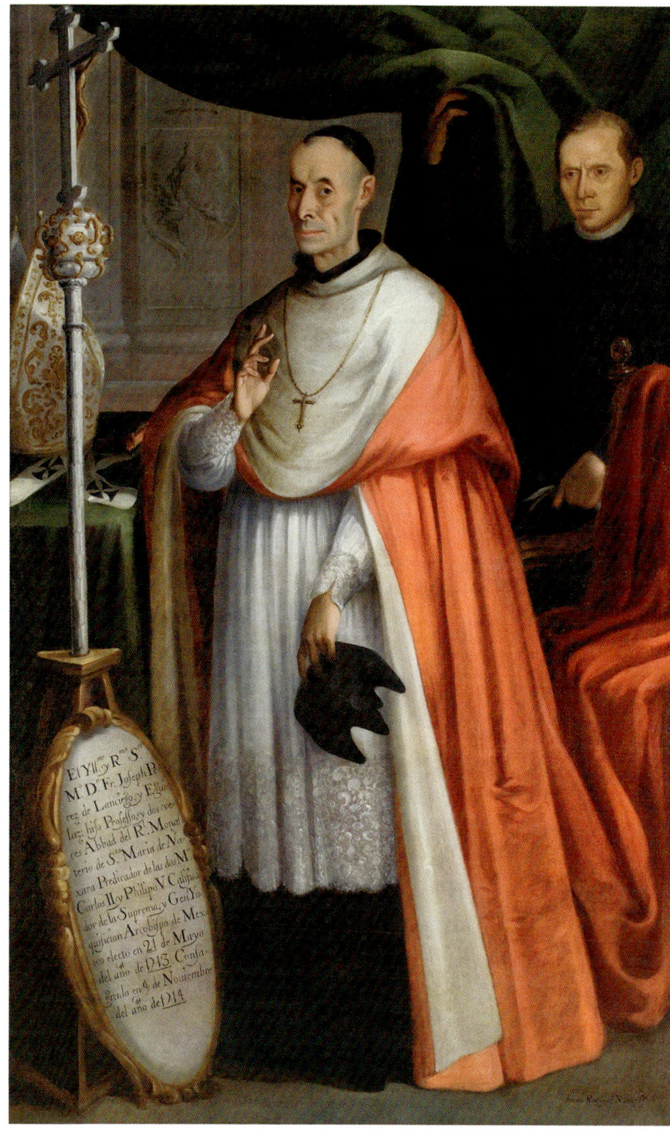

Fig. 5. Juan Rodríguez Juárez, *Portrait of Archbishop José Pérez de Lanciego y Eguilaz*. Mexico, c. 1715. Oil on canvas. 81½ x 48¾ in. Denver Art Museum, Collection of Frederick and Jan Mayer; M2003.001.

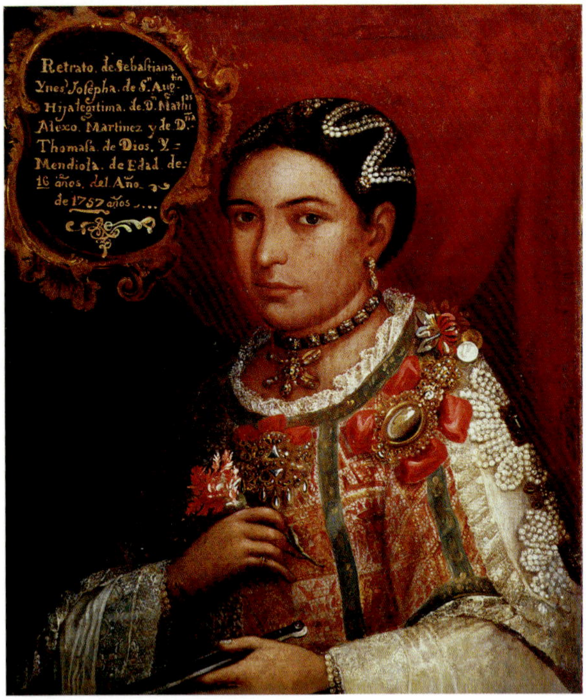

Fig. 6. *Portrait of Sebastiana Inés Josefa de San Agustín.* Mexico, 1757. Oil on canvas. 26 3/8 x 22 in. Museo Franz Mayer, Mexico City.

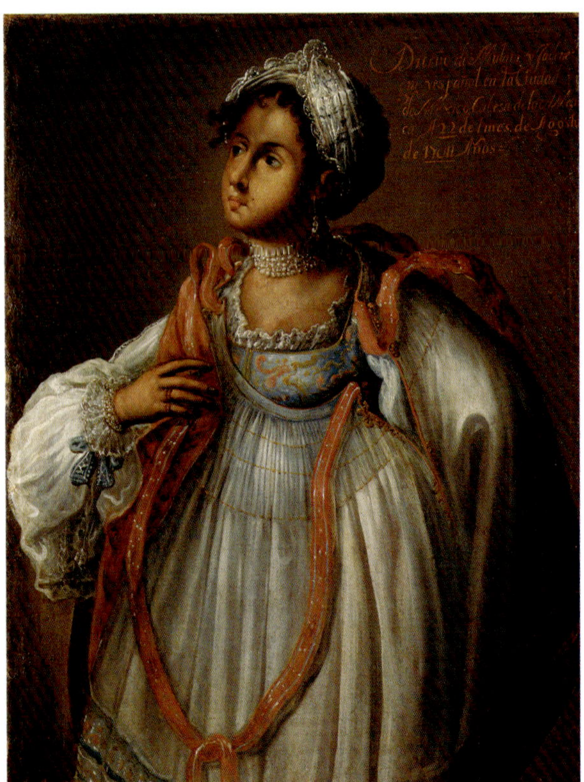

Fig. 7. Arellano, *Diceño de mulata (Design of a Mulatto Woman).* Mexico, 1711. Oil on canvas. 40 x 29¼ in. Denver Art Museum, Collection of Frederick and Jan Mayer; TL-24502.

brushwork so evident in many *casta* paintings, beginning with the earliest sets executed, has not drawn comment from contemporary scholars. How, we ask, did the painterly artifice of these paintings matter to their original audiences? What can the material presence of *casta* paintings tell us now?

First, it is important to consider that the figures in *casta* paintings are not portraits of actual individuals, but depictions of imaginary types. In their virtuoso display of brushwork, the dramatic exaggeration of chiaroscuro (light/dark contrast), complexity of the figural invention, and imaginative details that symbolize the racial mixtures depicted, *casta* paintings represent their non-Spanish subjects quite differently from portraits even in the case of non-Spanish individuals, such as the indigenous noblewoman Sebastiana Inés Josefa de San Agustín, portrayed in 1757 when she was sixteen years old and on the eve of entering the convent of Corpus Christi in Mexico City (Fig. 6). Portraits of well-to-do indigenous subjects like this one testify to the indigenous nobility's assimilation of a Spanish lifestyle (on its own terms) through dress, pose, identifying inscription, and the occasion for commissioning the portrait—choices that mimic and inflect conventions for portraying Euro-American (Creole) and peninsular subjects. Such works meticulously emphasize the textures of the materials portrayed and not the inventive brushwork of the artist. In making the facture invisible, the artist absented himself from the portraits while, by contrast, the bold facture of many *casta* paintings was a constant reminder of his presence. Since some artists worked simultaneously in both genres, these striking differences in execution cannot be explained as individual stylistic traits. The manner of execution must have been a conscious choice. The question is why—on what basis were these choices made and what did the differences signal to their intended audiences?

The new genre of ethnographic representations is different from any of its precedents in other respects as well. Even in the earliest known examples, signed by Arellano in 1711—which, unlike subsequent examples of the genre, contain only one adult figure per panel—the subject portrayed is a type. In one case, Arellano identifies his subject in the painting's inscription as "Design of a mulatto woman, daughter of a black woman and a Spanish man in Mexico City, capital of America on 22 August 1711" (Fig. 7).[9] In another example (Figs. 8a and b), and utilizing the same phraseology, he provides a "Design of a Chichimec man" and "Chichimec woman" on a pair of canvases. ("Chichimec" generally refers to nomadic native groups of northern Mexico that popularly symbolized savagery in pre-Hispanic and viceregal times.[10]) Arellano's deliberate use of the term "design" (*diseño*) in both works suggests his knowledge of the early modern European identification of painting as a Liberal Art—a crucial topic discussed in greater detail below. As the genre developed, artists like Juan Rodríguez Juárez and José de Ibarra continued to exploit exotic types and the sensuous qualities of the painted surface through dramatic brushstroke, composition, and color, while replacing Arellano's single-figure compositions with interracial couples and their offspring depicted together on a single panel (Fig. 9). Increasing details of costume and setting were added, including symbolic and allegorical elements that also signal the novelty of these paintings as luxury items.[11]

The *casta* sets created by Miguel Cabrera (Fig. 10) conform to the basic compositional formula established by Rodríguez Juárez, but they emphasize costume and setting, including flora and fauna indigenous to the Americas, and the interaction of family figures in them stresses cooperation and productivity. Cabrera's *casta* paintings include the inscription "Painted by Miguel Cabrera, Mexico," a sign that they catered to an export market.[12] In fact, most *casta* painting sets survive in European collections, confirming their function as desirable objects made for export, a novel, high-end variation of the ethnographic type, for which there was a large existing market in Europe. Provenance patterns and a small body of documentary evidence indicate that a portion of this audience consisted of high-ranking Spanish bureaucrats and prelates returning to Europe once their tenure in the

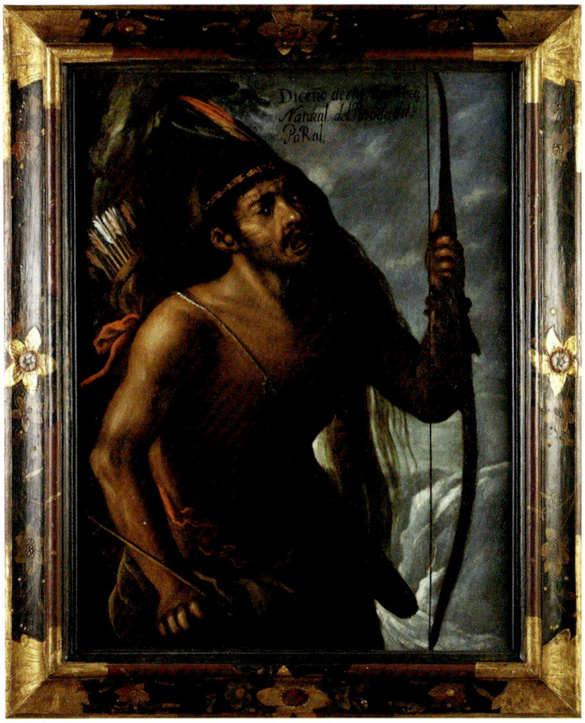

Fig. 8a. Arellano, *Diceño de chichimeco (Design of a Chichimec Man)*. Mexico, 1711. Oil on canvas. 40.7 x 30.9 in. Museo de América, Madrid. Photo: Museo de América.

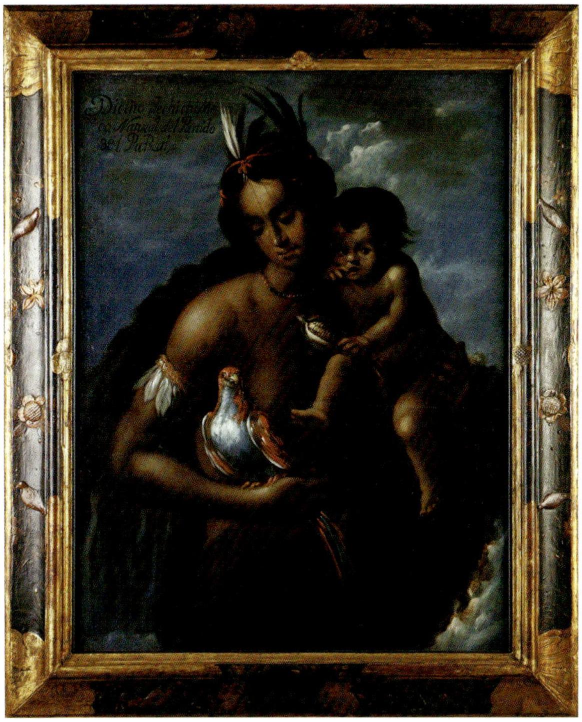

Fig. 8b. Arellano, *Diceño de chichimeca (Design of a Chichimec Woman)*. Mexico, 1711. Oil on canvas. 40.7 x 30.9 in. Museo de América, Madrid. Photo: Museo de América.

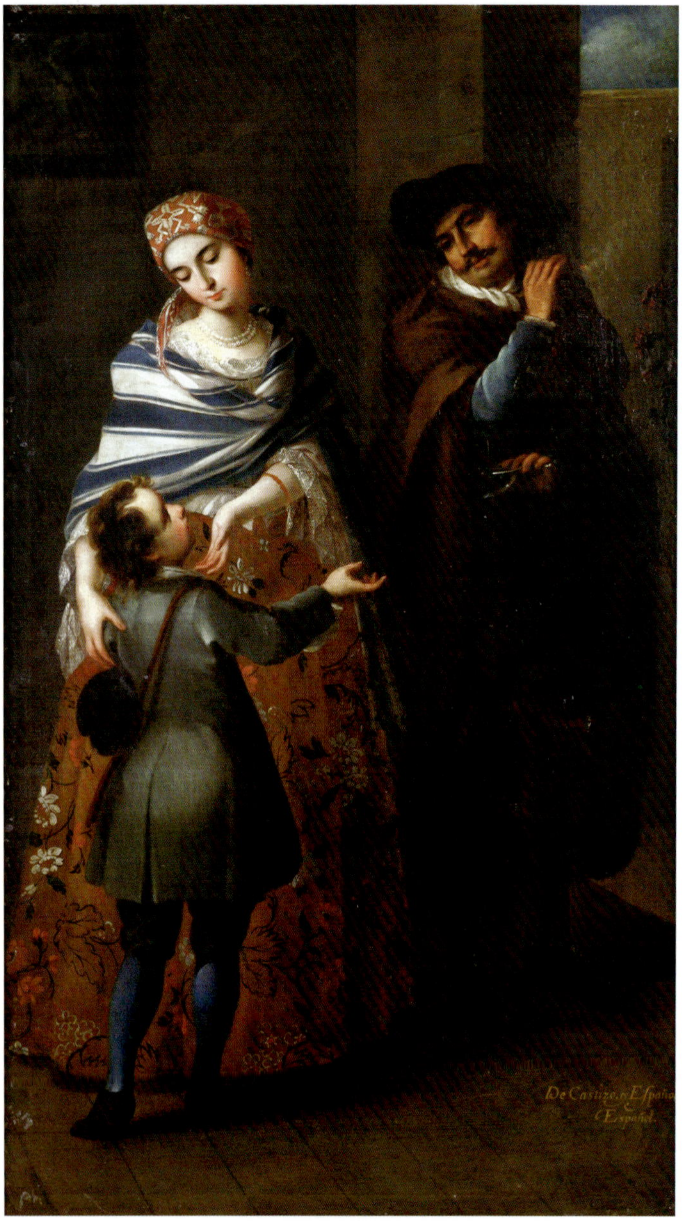

Fig. 9. Attributed to José de Ibarra, *De castizo y española, español (From Castizo and Spaniard, Spaniard)*. Mexico, c. 1725. Oil on canvas. 64.6 x 35.8 in. Museo de América, Madrid. Photo: Museo de América.

Americas expired.[13] As an export item, *casta* paintings were often paired with natural specimens and American exotica intended for curiosity cabinets.[14] The most prestigious curiosity cabinet, of course, was the Spanish king's Real Gabinete de Historia Natural in Madrid, which held "all types of Nature's curious productions indigenous to the lands and towns" that were a part of the king's empire.[15] In fact, we know that at least two *casta* painting sets were commissioned by the New Spanish and Peruvian viceroys specifically for the king. One set (see Fig. 3), perhaps the first one of its kind, was commissioned by New Spain's Viceroy Fernando de Alencastre Noroña y Silva, Duke of Linares (p. 173, Fig. 31) between 1711 and 1716. It was very probably inspired by a cultural geography published by Athanasius Kircher to which Linares had access.[16] However, lower-ranking elites in New Spain also had access to these works. It is clear that by the late eighteenth century, *casta* paintings were available to, and desired by, a range of individuals from high-ranking Spanish bureaucrats and prelates to well-to-do merchants.[17]

Current scholarship regards this new genre as direct evidence of intense interest in racial mixing, one manifestation of a "new Creole identity."[18] Katzew and others have argued that the positive light that *casta* paintings shine on viceregal society echoes the Bourbon reform emphasis on productivity and industry, promoted in New Spain to alleviate and prevent social problems.[19]

But in order to understand *casta* paintings as manifestations of Creole identity, one has to know what "Creole identity" was in the actual social fabric. Although today we refer to Creoles in Spanish America as those who were of Spanish stock but born in the Americas, in viceregal times the term had different connotations among different groups.[20] While the Spanish-American understanding of the term Creole was favorable, Europeans associated it with *mestizos* who carried the stigma of illegitimate birth—a phenomenon that began in the sixteenth century, when the first *mestizos* were often the product of extramarital relations between Spanish men and native women. For this and other reasons, Spaniards regarded

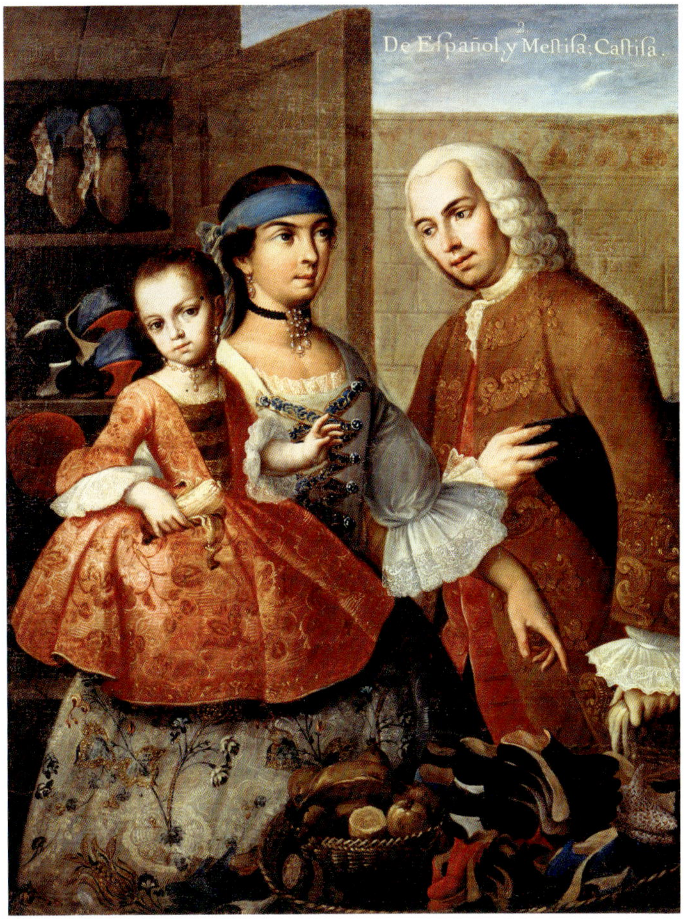

Fig. 10. Miguel Cabrera, *De español y mestiza, castiza (From Spaniard and Mestiza, Castiza)*. Mexico, 1763. Oil on canvas. 52 x 39.8 in. Museo de América, Madrid. Photo: Art Resource.

Creoles as their inferiors and prohibited their access to high political and ecclesiastical offices.[21] In a more positive, local perspective, Creoles positioned themselves as the rightful heirs of the mighty Spanish conquistadors as well as the great Aztec past.[22] But *casta* paintings do not project this more positive picture; rather, they focus on the devolution of miscegenation, as can be readily seen in many examples, including a composite version on a single panel reproduced here, in which increasingly dark-complexioned couples produce increasingly darker-complexioned progeny of lower economic as well as social status (Fig. 11). As we show below, even individual paintings in which the cross-racial household seems harmonious may contain clues to more complicated attitudes.

Moreover, there was not a singular "Creole response" to these works. In fact, there seems to have been a kind of double vision in play. An unfavorable view is clearly expressed in a 1746 letter penned by José Arce y Miranda to Juan José Eguiara y Eguren, in which he complains that *casta* paintings picture "that which damages us, from which we will not benefit, that which dishonors us, not that which ennobles us as would the mixture of Gachupín (peninsular) blood with Indian or Creole blood."[23] The implication here is that miscegenation, especially with those of lower social echelons, endangers the dignity that Creoles claimed. Perhaps this explains, in part, why the majority of *casta* paintings picture Spaniards paired with upper-class natives, while lower-class natives are paired with racially mixed plebeians.

For a European audience, these idealized and largely imaginary images might have relieved anxieties about dire social realities in New Spain.[24] As R. Douglas Cope has argued, New Spain's social structure was theoretically based on the internal stability of separate Spanish and Amerindian identities, but in practice, the ideal segregation was considerably threatened by miscegenation.[25] In the constant flux of colonial society, vertical social mobility was difficult to prevent, since typing by skin color was a highly imprecise art and simply changing one's costume and demeanor could enable entry to a

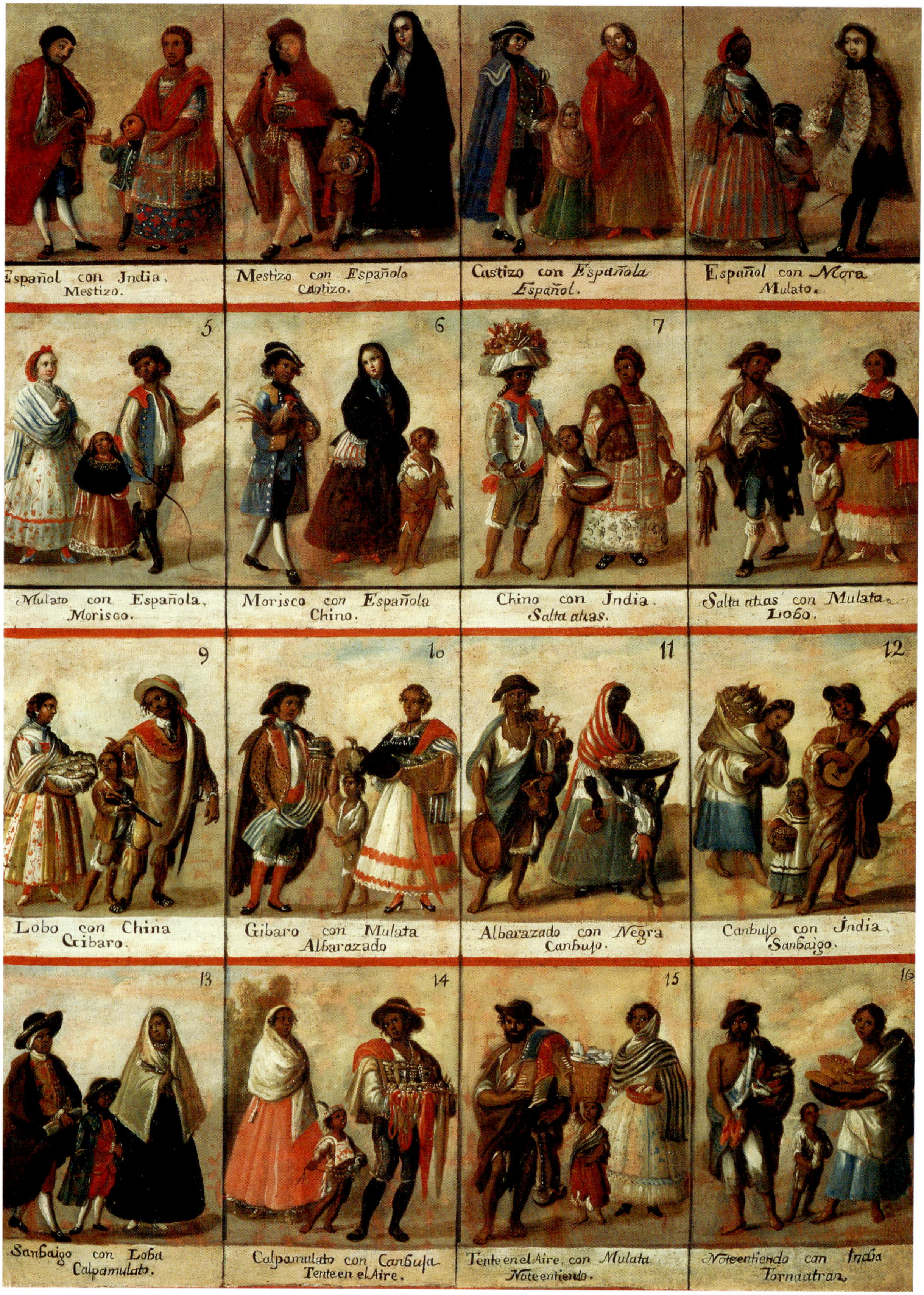

Fig. 11. *Castas* categories. Mexico, 18th century. Oil on canvas. 40.94 x 58.26 in. Museo Nacional del Virreinato, Tepotzotlán, Mexico. Photo: Art Resource.

higher social status.[26] As Katzew has noted, *casta* paintings must have eased Spanish anxieties about New Spain's socio-racial complexity by creating the illusion of a harmonious society that was rigidly ordered according to the *sistema de castas*, which placed Europeans at the top of the socio-racial system and everyone else on its lower rungs.[27]

While the elite commissioned individuated representations of themselves in the form of portraits, the underclasses were represented by others, for others, in richly elaborated, beautifully crafted typologies that focused on the particular but not on individual identity. The contrast between formal portraiture and *casta* paintings is a significant symptom of evolving class-based differences in seventeenth- and eighteenth-century New Spain. Yet New Spain's complex and tense social circumstances do not fully explain why the social realities depicted in *casta* paintings were usually painted as sympathetically as they were, and in an overtly painterly style, by the best artists, rather than by scientific illustrators. Simplistic categories of positive and negative portrayals do not do justice to the complex interplay between artistic representation and the social conditions involved.

Colonial Art Academies and the Status of Painters

To address these questions, it is essential to examine the institutional structure in which artists functioned. Beginning in the late seventeenth century, the leading artists of Mexico City tried to reform the dysfunctional guild system by stressing the importance of *calidad*, a racializing category that fused race, class, honor, and skill, to the practice of painting.[28] It is unclear whether the guild was to be supplemented or replaced by a new institution, the art academy.[29] In any case, in a colonial context where one's station in life depended on socio-racial classification and occupation, an academy would have amplified its members' social status and presumed their own unsullied European bloodline.[30] Many of the same artists were involved in both movements, as Katzew, Deans-Smith, and others have emphasized. Rodríguez Juárez, responsible for some of the earliest *castas* sets, and for some of the paintings of highest artistic quality, tried to found an art academy in Mexico City in 1722 or even earlier, that is, within a decade of his first *casta* paintings. Guillermo Tovar de Teresa has proposed that this earliest attempt to establish an academy imitated the drawing academy founded by Bartolomé Esteban Murillo and Francisco Herrera the Younger in Seville in 1660, with the express purpose of elevating the status of painting as one of the liberal arts of the viceroyalty, endorsed by the king himself.[31] The academy in Seville (like its predecessors in Paris, Rome, and Florence) had been established to demonstrate that painting was an intellectual pursuit and not simply a manual craft.[32] In support of these institutional similarities, New Spanish painters involved in their own academy movement designed ephemeral architectural constructions requiring collaboration with other artists as well as poets and writers for public celebrations, signed their works in ways that indicate the intellectual foundations of their profession, and referred to themselves as "Spaniards" and "professors."[33]

Throughout the eighteenth century New Spanish painters continued to petition for an officially sanctioned art academy in Mexico City.[34] In 1753 José de Ibarra and Miguel Cabrera, like Rodríguez Juárez central to *castas* painting production, founded a second Academy of Painting, a direct continuation of the Rodríguez Juárez brothers' academy, but also a response to the Royal Academy of Art of San Fernando, founded in Madrid in 1752. This second academy also failed to secure royal protection; success came only in 1783 with the founding of the Royal Academy of San Carlos under the surrogate patronage of Viceroy don Matías de Gálvez y Gallardo.[35]

Two works capture the very differing interests of those who wished to found an art academy in New Spain. Around 1790 an artist, possibly Andrés López of Mexico City, painted a posthumous portrait of the Royal Academy's patron Gálvez y Gallardo (Fig. 12). When we compare this portrait with Juan Rodríguez Juárez's earlier self-portrait of c. 1715 (Fig. 13), one key element clearly stands out: a notable difference in paint handling or

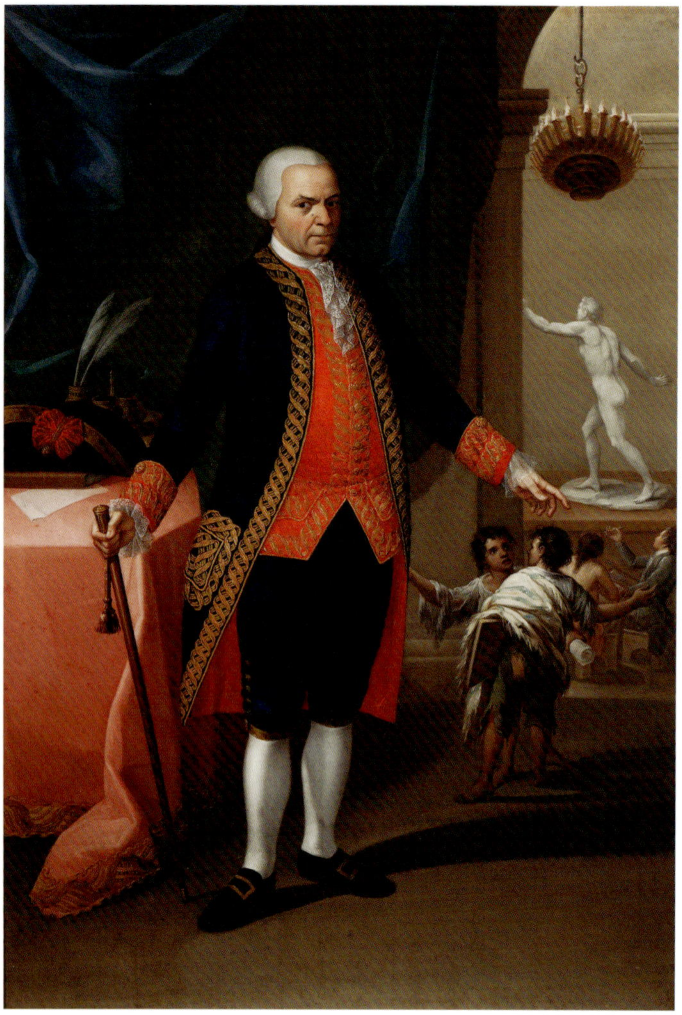

Fig. 12. Attributed to Andrés López, *Portrait of Don Matías de Gálvez y Gallardo as Viceprotector of the Academia de San Carlos*. Mexico, 1790–1791. Oil on canvas. 89 x 61 in. Museo Nacional del Virreinato, Tepotzotlán, Mexico. Photo: Javier Hinojosa, Museo Nacional del Virreinato.

facture. The official portrait conforms to contemporary preferences for a mirror-like surface that effaces all evidence of its craftsmanship, while the self-portrait—one of the earliest by a New Spanish artist—is intimate and painterly. In the first portrait, the viceroy, standing in the foreground, gestures with an air of authority toward two dark-skinned children dressed in tattered clothing, one of whom holds a roll of drawing paper and a drawing board.[36] Meanwhile, in the background, two art students draw and sight a plaster statue in a room lit by candlelight that emphasizes the relief structure through heightened juxtapositions of light and dark. This official portrait illustrates academic training on European terms while also emphasizing that the new academy was to provide educational and employment opportunities for the poor and disadvantaged, thus averting a dangerous social situation. The position embodied in this portrait is clearly that of the Creole elite and peninsular officials advocating Bourbon reforms.[37]

Rodríguez Juárez's self-portrait (Fig. 13), executed about 75 years earlier, portrays him as a gentleman and a sensitive, even pensive, highly poeticized intellectual. He deliberately calls attention to the art of painting with apparently spontaneous, painterly brushstrokes that are especially daring in the rendering of his scarf and delicately articulated hand, in which he clutches a brush or drawing instrument. The pose, made famous in Spain by Diego Velázquez in *Las Meninas* (1656) and quoted by many artists subsequently, is a self-conscious declaration of the intellectual quality of painting that distinguishes it from the mechanical arts.[38] While the sitter is a study in quiet self-observation, the painterly surface demonstrates assured judgment and skill of hand established by European period standards.[39] Rodríguez Juárez's intense gaze, pronounced forehead, and angular face, cast in a dramatic juxtaposition of deep shadows and highlights, strategically underscore this self-aware image of the artist claiming an intellectual status.[40]

Considered together, the Gálvez and Rodríguez Juárez portraits identify a complex intersection of agencies. At the invitation of a top ranking peninsular state official, Mexico City's most important (self-identified) "Spanish" artists sought to elevate the status of their craft to the level of an intellectual calling.[41] In doing so, they catered to an elite Creole and peninsular Spanish audience by producing works—among which *casta* paintings feature prominently—that demonstrated a new freedom from the mere imitation of nature associated with formal portraiture.

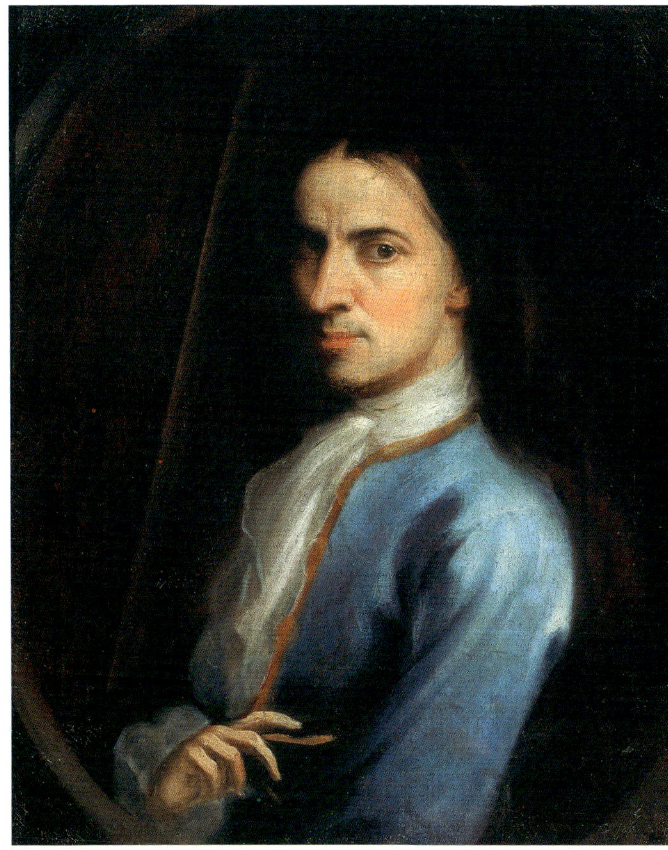

Fig. 13. Juan Rodríguez Juárez, *Self-portrait*. Mexico, c. 1719. Oil on canvas. 26 x 21¼ in. Museo Nacional de Arte, Mexico City.

The Ontological Status of Painting in Europe and New Spain

Both colonial artists' agency and their attitude toward agency are suggested by the longstanding debates on the authenticity of the sacred portrait of the Virgin of Guadalupe, considered to have been made without human intervention—a sacred image produced in the manner of a contact relic like the Shroud of Turin.[42] The disputes and discussion regarding the nature of this sacred image, not surprisingly, also involved the status of copies made by artists. An edict of 1637, for example, condemned inaccurate copies of the original Guadalupe image on view in the basilica dedicated to her in Mexico City. It is not surprising, then, that in 1656, when José Juárez (1617–1660) made a painting preserved in the Convent of the Conceptionists in Agreda, Spain (Fig. 14), he labeled its central panel a "true portrait and exact copy" (*retrato verdadero y copia punctual*) of the original image.

Examination of the original painting by artists placed on a commission to do so was first recorded in 1666, and they declared the image miraculous and perfect on the basis of their assessment of materials and artistic technique. Another inspection took place in 1751, and in 1756, Miguel Cabrera (a leading innovator of *casta* paintings and the author of at least three copies of Guadalupe made in 1752 directly from the original) published a volume describing the sacred image in detail, which included six colleagues' opinions on the divine origins of the painting. Cabrera's publication is an academic performance in the Ciceronian genre utilized by early humanists since the fourteenth century, in which debating a question from all sides (employing rhetorical methods for inventing arguments) enables the participants to demonstrate their expertise. Leonardo da Vinci adapted this classical rhetorical model, partly by way of medieval sources, to defend painting against poetry, sculpture, music, and the mechanical arts; and similar arguments were disseminated by the mid-sixteenth century, partly because they were included in Baldassare Castiglione's widely read *Il Libro del Cortegiano,* first published in 1528.[43]

Entitled *Maravilla americana* (Fig. 15), and published together with the "rules of the art of painting," Cabrera's text of 1756 documents the difficulty of negotiating between an intellectual liberation associated with the European art academy and the artistic responsibility of producing accurate copies of a sacred model, where originality consists in signaling the artist's humble fidelity to the divinely made original. What is at stake is an ontological issue. In the case of a miraculous image produced without human intervention, the truth of the sacred representation is incontestable: it is ensured by direct contact with the divine. But—given human fallibility—what secures the truth of a sacred portrait made by human hands? The concept of innovation, from a Christian ontological standpoint, is dangerous in granting the artist an active, independent role—in this case, the artist is no longer simply a passive recipient of God's "offspring" by which God communicates his likeness in "multiplication of itself"[44] (to invoke the Scholastic terminology grounded in the scientific language of formal optics). The medieval concept of human artifice is indebted not only to the Augustinian idea that God alone creates *ex nihilo*, but also to later Scholastic definitions of nobility and perfection. According to Saint Thomas Aquinas, material substances receive likenesses (similitudes) of the intelligible by way of the sensory powers.[45] Writing in similar terms, Saint Bonaventure claimed that an artistic product

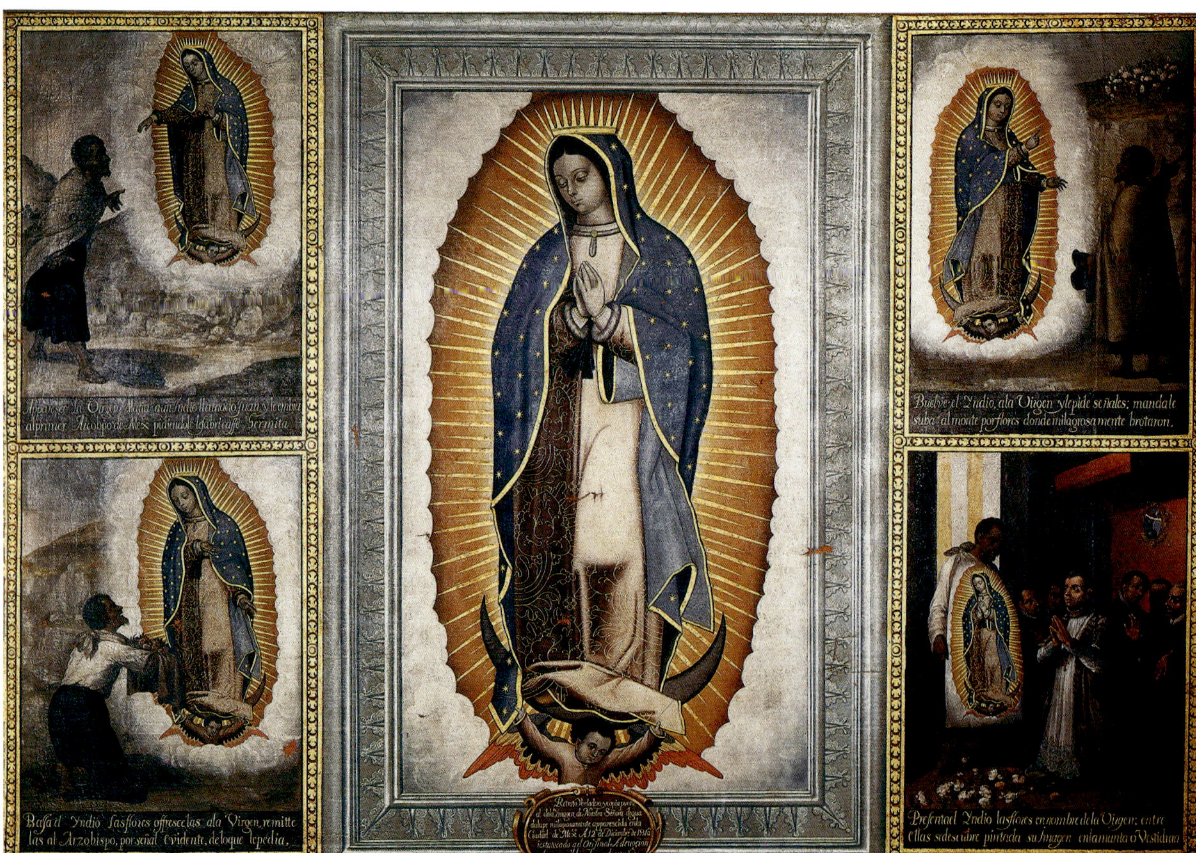

Fig. 14. José Juárez, *Virgin of Guadalupe with Apparitions*. Mexico, 1656. Oil on canvas. 82¾ x 116¼ in. Convent of the Conceptionists, Agreda, Soria, Spain.

proceeds from a similitude existing in the artist's mind in the same way that God produces "creatures" bearing his vestige.[46]

There is evidence that these Scholastic ideas were still relevant four centuries later, when the artist's license to invent was well established in the literature on art. The artist's autonomy and freedom to invent are central to modern, secular notions of art.[47] Yet in sacred paintings, artifice was valued as the indexical sign of God's presence, that is, as the impression of a material substance with God's likeness. The inscription on José Juárez's painting in Agreda (Fig. 14) and other examples that have been recently published by Clara Bargellini are, as Bargellini emphasizes, evidence of the artists' need to negotiate not only their autonomy and right to invent things out of their imaginations, but also their direct contact with the divine to ensure the truth of their artistic representations.[48] About a century later, Cabrera carried out a similar negotiation in *The Virgin of Guadalupe's Patronage of the Franciscan Order*, which he painted for the Colegio de Propaganda Fide in Zacatecas (Fig. 16). An exact copy of the Virgin of Guadalupe, which Cabrera renders with precision in the same flat, uninflected style of the original miraculous image, appears prominently in the work's center, where it contrasts starkly with his handling of the rest of the composition, a tour-de-force exercise in volumetric modeling and expressive brushstroke. Such a deliberate contrast in painting styles within a single work demonstrates the inventive abilities of the artist in a two-fold manner: he was simultaneously capable of expressing his own animated style and of rendering a miraculously produced acheiropoietic image, where it was appropriate to efface the painter's hand or *maniera*. Two orders of imitation are involved here: the sacred vision, painted by the artist in imitation of natural forms and appearances, includes his painting of a sacred image produced without human intervention.

Within the matrix of the Christian belief system, the perennial challenge was to establish the ontological status of the artistic representation in relation to divine truth. Catholic Reformation

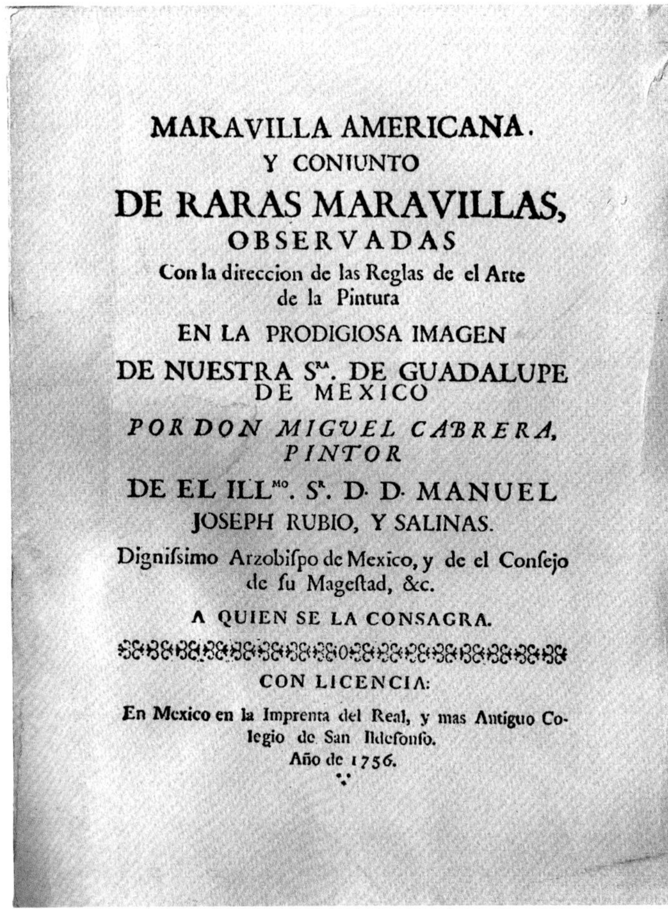

MARAVILLA AMERICANA.
Y CONIUNTO
DE RARAS MARAVILLAS,
OBSERVADAS
Con la direccion de las Reglas de el Arte
de la Pintura
EN LA PRODIGIOSA IMAGEN
DE NUESTRA S^RA. DE GUADALUPE
DE MEXICO
POR DON MIGUEL CABRERA,
PINTOR
DE EL ILL^MO. S^R. D. D. MANUEL
JOSEPH RUBIO, Y SALINAS.
Dignifsimo Arzobifpo de Mexico, y de el Confejo
de fu Mageftad, &c.
A QUIEN SE LA CONSAGRA.
CON LICENCIA:
En Mexico en la Imprenta del Real, y mas Antiguo Colegio de San Ildefonfo.
Año de 1756.

Fig. 15. Title page, *Maravilla americana*. Mexico, 1756.

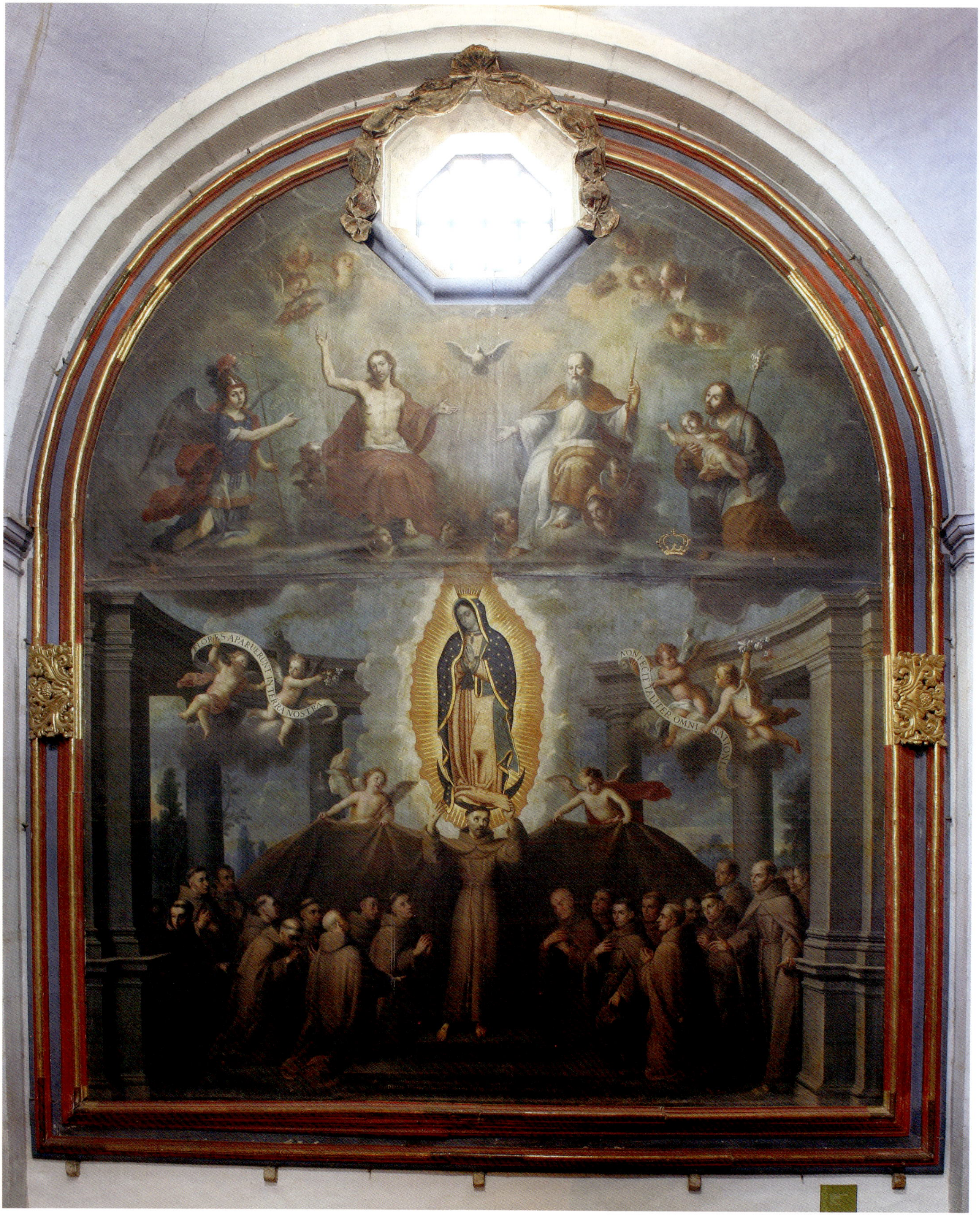

Fig. 16. Miguel Cabrera, *The Virgin of Guadalupe's Patronage of the Franciscan Order*. Mexico, c. 1770. Oil on canvas. Museo Regional de Guadalupe, Zacatecas, Mexico. Photo: Museo Regional de Guadalupe.

writer Archbishop Gabriele Paleotti (1522–1597), whose 1582 treatise on correcting the abuses of painters and sculptors was widely read, understood the truth of sacred images in just these ontological terms. He considered that the abstract and incorporeal images used by theologians, like the *fantasmi* and *concetti* conceived by painters, are a "gift of God and a sign of the loftiness of human nature."[49]

The painter/theorist Federico Zuccaro (1540/41–1609), founder of the Accademia di San Luca in Rome and closely associated with its precedent in Florence, navigated cautiously through ontologically dangerous territory after the Tridentine Decree on Images of 1563 placed strict limits on artistic license in order to preserve the religious decorum of sacred subject matter.[50] Zuccaro identified human *disegno* with an "agent intellect" that "makes all things," found in the human soul, which derives its intellectual light from God himself, the soul's creator. Thus the fallible, particular intellect of the human individual is enlightened and sustained by the mind of God.[51] Painting distinguished by coloring, shading, lighting, and so on gives figures such spirit and vividness that they seem "living and true," appealing intuitively and universally to all beholders.[52] Imitative painting, wrote Paleotti in similar optical terms less than two decades earlier, speaks a universal language: it is immediately recognized by everyone because such artistic images represent the similitudes of things just as things themselves appear to the sense of sight.[53]

Seventeenth- and eighteenth-century Spanish artists and theorists endorsed these ideas about the truth of artistic representation to promote the nobility of painting and to negotiate the ontologically slippery terrain between independent artistic invention and the truthfulness of sacred images. And they continued to assign a leading role to the science of optics, which enabled artistic invention to conform to the truth of natural appearances. Nature, in other words, regulates the decorum observed by artists. For example, in *Diálogos de la pintura* (1633), Vincente Carducho (1576–1638) defines *disegno* (or *dibujo*) as a method of understanding and revealing what is real and true in nature.[54] Francisco Pacheco (1564–1654) confirms this notion in his *Arte de la pintura* (1638) and takes it a step further by stating that invention is inseparable from decorum, from which "all of the good parts of drawing are derived."[55] Carducho and Pacheco also infuse their definitions of *disegno* with a scientific grounding in symmetry, proportion, anatomy, and perspective, which they identify as *disegno's* constituent elements.[56]

Arellano's use of this same term ("diseño") in his portraits of a mulatto woman (Fig. 7) and Chichimec couple (Figs. 8a and b) not only suggests the presence of these concepts in at least one of New Spain's artist circles, it also indicates that these works are ontologically truthful representations of their subjects because Arellano has masterfully grounded them in the scientific principles of the art of painting as delineated by Carducho and Pacheco. Years later, New Spanish painters involved in the academy movement wrote petitions that demonstrate their familiarity with these authors. In *Maravilla americana* (1756), Miguel Cabrera and his colleagues qualify the excellence of the Guadalupe image in strikingly similar terms. For them, the perfect utilization of these scientific principles makes the invisible present and visible to humankind and is proof of divine authorship.[57] In making this argument, they deliberately call attention to the specialized knowledge that allowed them to carry out their important and erudite examination of the Guadalupe. Although studies regarding the potential impact that early modern Spanish painting treatises had on viceregal artists remain to be carried out, the conceptual basis that informs *Maravilla americana* bears a striking resemblance to that promoted in those texts. The hypothesis that Cabrera and his circle had access to these Spanish sources is also supported by the inclusion of Pacheco's *Arte de la pintura* and *Gloria del pintor* in Cabrera's portrait of Sor Juana Inés de la Cruz (Fig. 4).[58]

This theoretical background may also explain why the 1783 Royal Academy of San Carlos made drawing the foundation of professional training for artists practicing all media in New Spain—as it had been in Spanish and other European academies founded on the model of the Florentine and Roman academies, both of which Zuccaro had helped to found.[59] A late eighteenth-century *casta* painting painted around this time exhibits the centrality of *disegno* to the status of the artist. One of a pair within a larger set, it imagines a visual and professional parity between the artist's studio and the physician's examination room (Figs. 17a and 17b). Each panel portrays its professional as a skilled Spanish gentleman whose clients also enjoy elevated social rank. In the artist's studio a Spanish gentleman, dressed in French high fashion, sits before his subject, an *albino* woman (offspring of a Spaniard and a *morisco*), while painting her portrait. Demonstrating the nobility of his profession and the specialized knowledge and judgment that it demands of its practitioners, the painter bases his portrait both on direct observation of his sitter and on a drawing, held up by his racially mixed assistant, that is apparently copied from one of the classical busts arranged on a shelf just above an apprentice dressed in rags. *Disegno* combines knowledge of design with the practice of drawing from nature, a concept familiar in Europe since the latter part of the sixteenth century. The boy's drawing pad on the floor next to his chair shows scribbled markings that may associate his inexperience with his lowly racial designation as *torna atrás* (literally, "turn backward").

Casta Paintings as Academic Art

Let us now return fully to the case of *casta* paintings, a secular form of artistic production remarkably free of any religious reference.[60] In *Diálogos de la pintura,* Carducho stresses that painters had the special ability to render visible the otherwise invisible nature of their subjects through science.[61] A portrait is a matter of copying nature accurately, *ritrarre* in the Italian, while a *casta* painting is a matter of idealized invention, corresponding to the higher calling of *imitare*.[62] Both had their place in New Spain. From the New Spanish artist's point of view, *casta* painting provided an opportunity to invent a new composition painted in a modern, painterly, naturalistic style complete with inventive embellishments that underscore the central message of the subject matter. The Denver Art Museum's painting by José de Alcíbar (c. 1735–1803) of a Spanish man and a black woman producing a mulatto (c. 1760) provides an excellent case in point (Fig. 18). Its academic features include painterly brushwork, heightened juxtapositions of light and dark, clear organization into overlapping optical planes based on these same juxtapositions of value, and painterly imitation of textile patterns in both Asian fabrics and local cloth worn by African women. Also notable are the intimate gestures shared by father and son, respectively stoking and holding a brazier to light the father's cigarette. And the bravura handling of the brush is an important ingredient in this coloristic visual display.

Casta painting allowed New Spanish artists to exhibit their grasp of current notions of science, including scientific knowledge of human expression as well as the optical principles of painting from nature—two important ingredients of both academic artistic training and the arguments used to elevate the status of painting.[63] Thus, in late-eighteenth-century *casta* paintings physiognomy, expression, and gesture (that is, the outward expression of the subjects' inner nature) relate their appearance and behavior to their racial classification.[64] This is especially evident in the work of José Joaquín Magón (active c. 1754–1770), who pictorially emphasizes the human temperaments and assigns them to the figures' racial designations in the paintings' inscriptions. In the first painting from a set of sixteen, Magón portrays a Spanish man, his native wife, and their *mestizo* child in a domestic study (Fig. 19a). The framed inscription in the upper-center portion of the composition reads, "In the Americas people of different colors, customs, temperaments, and languages are born." Just below that, another inscription identifies the figures: "Born of the Spaniard and Indian woman is the *mestizo*, who is generally humble, tranquil, and straightforward."[65]

Pictured between his smartly dressed Spanish father, who is fingering a copy of *Don Quixote*, and his native mother, who is bejeweled and dressed in an elaborate lace-bordered *huipil* (a traditional

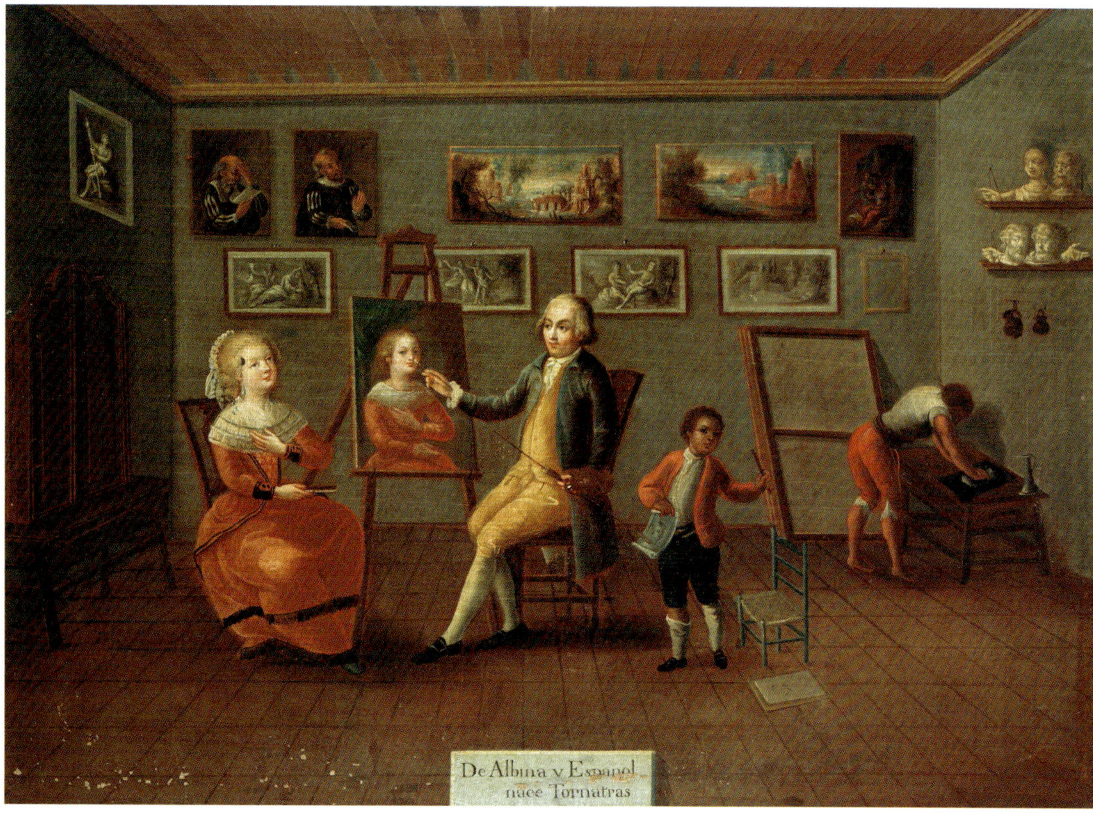

Fig. 17a. *De albina y español, nace torna atrás (From an Albino and a Spaniard, a Turn-Backward is Born)*. Mexico, c. 1785–1790. Oil on canvas. 24.6 x 32.8 in. Private collection on loan to Fomento Cultural Banamex A.C., photograph by Rafael Doniz.

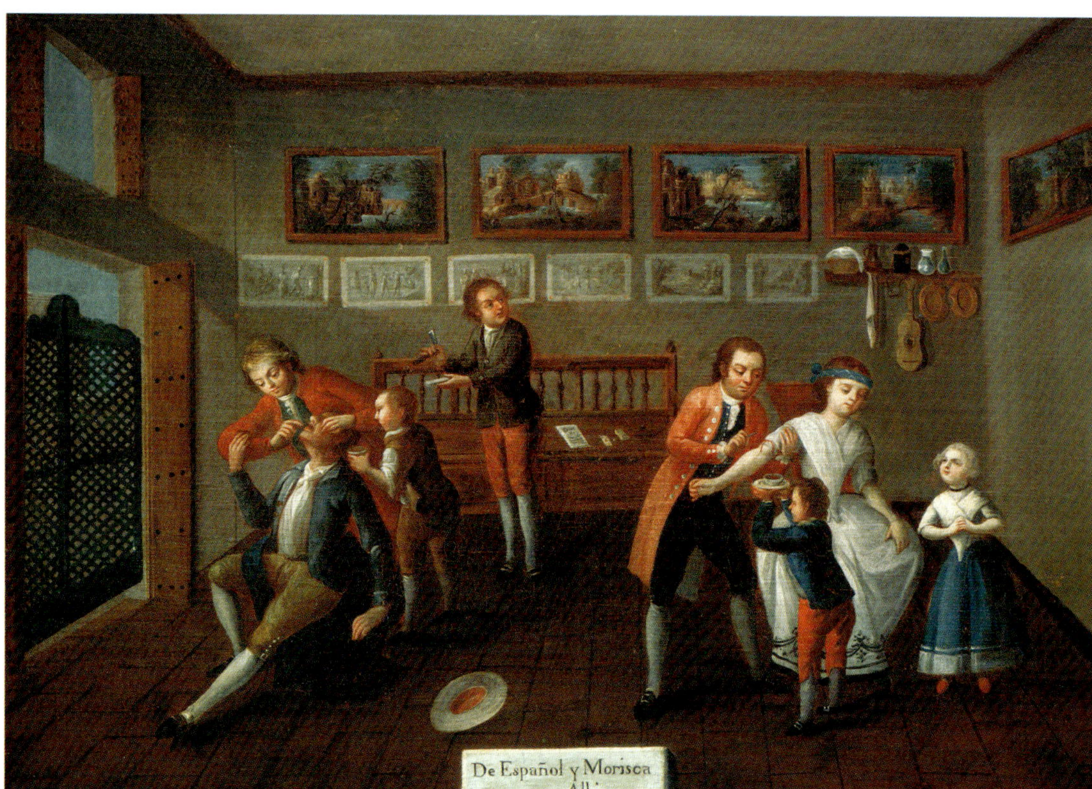

Fig. 17b. *De español y morisca, nace albina (From a Spaniard and Morisca, Albino is Born)*. Mexico, c. 1785–1790. Oil on canvas. 24.6 x 32.8 in. Private collection on loan to Fomento Cultural Banamex A.C., photograph by Rafael Doniz.

blouse for native women), the *mestizo* child holds up a sheet of paper to his father as if to show him (and the painting's viewers) his writing exercise. The term *PARCO* written on the boy's page reinforces *mestizos'* supposed qualities: *parco* signifies someone who is laconic or uncommunicative. In viceregal times, literacy was a quality ascribed by Europeans as natural to themselves, but not to indigenous people.[66] For example, in his 1552 biography of Hernán Córtes, historian López de Gómara emphasizes the importance of teaching the natives how to read and write alphabetic text: it is through "letters that they are truly men."[67] The boy's mother holds an inscribed sheet of paper to which she points, revealing an undecipherable grouping of letters repeated in list format—she is an illiterate native. Meanwhile, the Spanish father/husband looks upon his intellectually (less) compromised *mestizo* son with affectionate approval because he has mastered a few decipherable letters. Perched on the backrest of the Spaniard's chair is a scarlet macaw, a native American bird that, like the more traditionally depicted European parrot, imitates human speech without understanding what it means.

Compromising racialized distinctions are even more evident in other panels in Magón's series. Contrasting with the familial harmony that Magón depicts at the top of the social hierarchy is the conflictive grouping in the eleventh panel in the same series, entitled *Lovo, é Yndia, Cambujo, es de ordinario pesado, y perezoso de ingenio tardo* ("From a *Lobo* man and an Indian woman, the *Cambujo* is usually slow, lazy, and cumbersome") (Fig. 19b).[68] Here a *Lobo* (literally "wolf"—the offspring of African and Amerindian parents) father

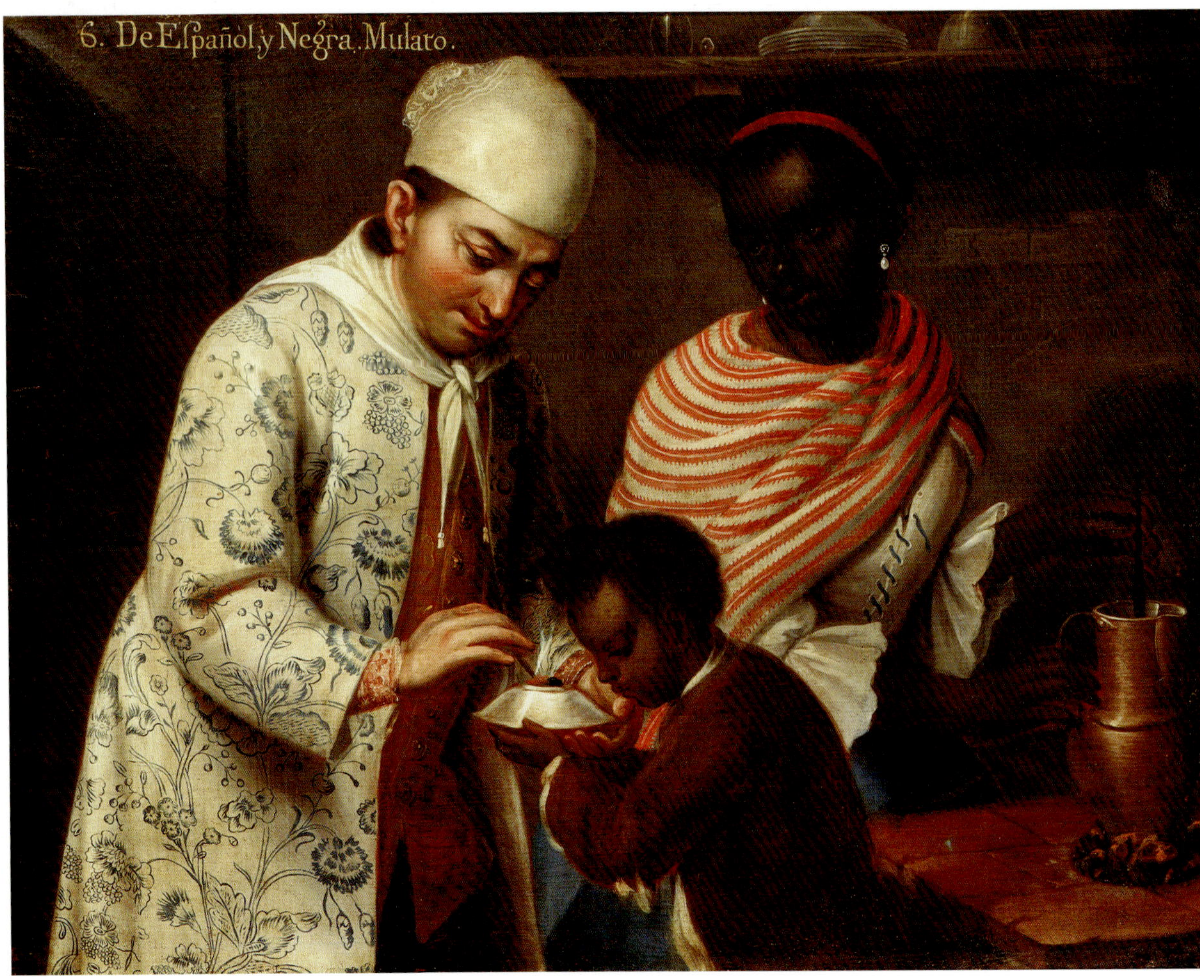

Fig. 18. José de Alcíbar, *De Español y Negra, Mulato* (*From Spaniard and Black, Mulatto*). Mexico, c. 1760. Oil on canvas. 31 x 38¼ in. Denver Art Museum, Collection of Frederick and Jan Mayer; TL-17535.

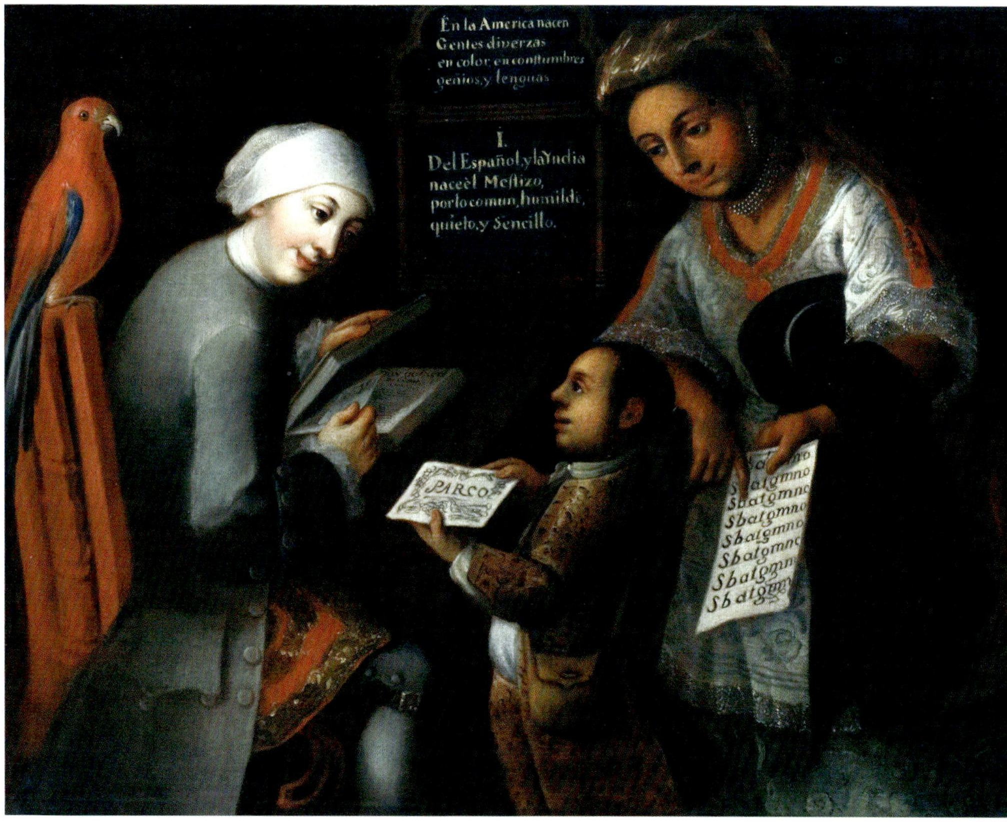

Fig. 19a. José Joaquín Magón, *I. Del Español y la Yndia, nace el Mestizo, por lo común, humilde, quieto, y sencillo (I. Born of the Spaniard and Indian is the Mestizo, who is generally humble, tranquil, and straightforward)*. Mexico, c. 1770. Oil on canvas. 40.2 x 49.6 in. Private collection.

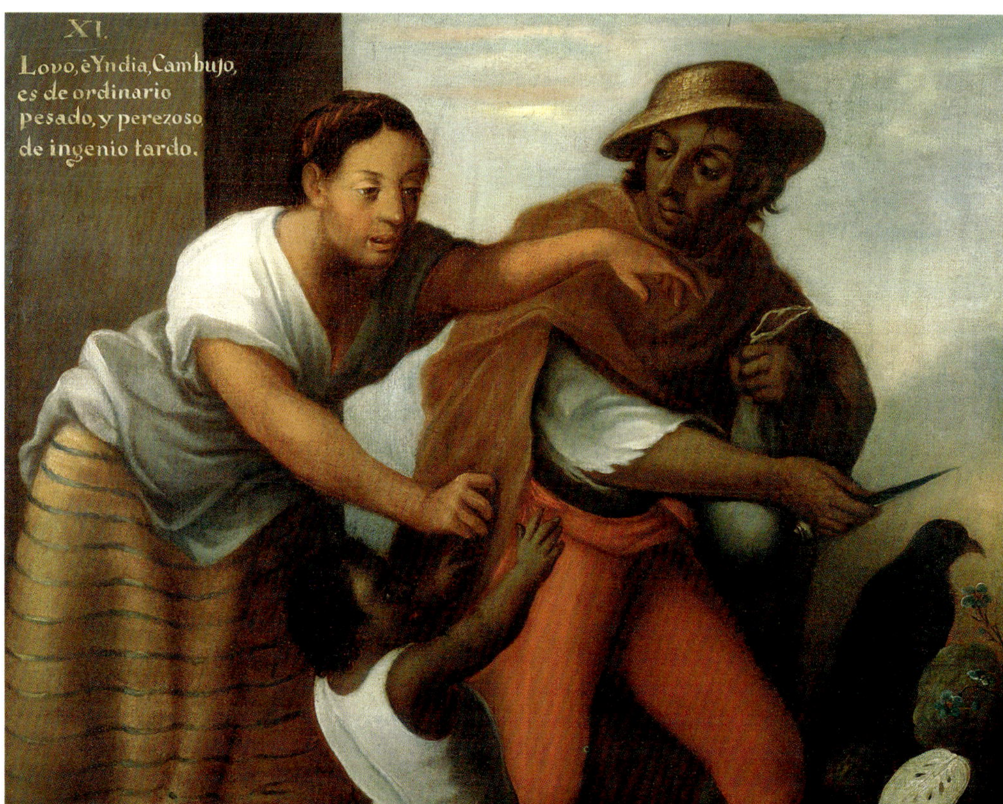

Fig. 19b. José Joaquín Magón. *XI. Lovo, e India, Cambujo, es de ordinario peaado, y perezoso de ingenio tardo (XI. From Lobo and Indian, the Cambujo is usually slow, lazy, and cumbersome)*. Mexico, c. 1770. Oil on canvas. 40.2 x 49.6 in. Private collection.

turns his back to his Amerindian wife and *cambujo* child, who are reaching for a bag with undetermined contents that he protectively holds behind a dagger. In the bottom-right corner of the composition a blackbird or raven (either one symbolizing sin and corruption in Christian art) is perched next to an opened fruit.[69] Resonating with this traditional symbol of evil, the father's retreating gesture, concealed goods, and dagger compose the image of a criminal.[70] The father's tattered clothing and the child's simple, sleeveless shirt convey this family's low socioeconomic standing in comparison to other families in this series that claim more European heritage.

At the same time that Magón embedded racializing content in his paintings he exhibited his elevated standing as an artist familiar with academic values. Magón's series of *casta* representations demonstrates the artist's ability to make visible the mental state of actors in a historical narrative. Mastery of this ability had been central to discussions of artistic invention at least since Alberti's treatise on painting of 1435, and it was consistent with the post-Tridentine redirection of artistic license to represent the similitudes of things convincingly to the sense of sight. It seems reasonable, then, to suggest that from the perspective of leading New Spanish painters, moralizing genre scenes established their parity with European painters, who already enjoyed an elevated status as practitioners of a liberal art grounded in scientific principles and taught in prestigious academies.

Yet if we imagine the efficacy of the same paintings from a European vantage point, the deluxe ethnographic subjects were *still* objectifying, exoticizing representations that situated New Spanish society and its most talented artists in a subordinate position in a transcultural, transatlantic social and artistic hierarchy. Ethnographic illustrations, even lusciously painted ones imaginatively composed and filled with what were appreciated as both fascinating exotica and informative scientific information, were destined for scientific collections and curiosity cabinets, not collections of painting and sculpture.

What the visual and documentary evidence suggests to us is that *casta* paintings are not just direct reflections of Creole patriotism or interest in racial mixing. Like the miraculous image of Guadalupe and artistic copies made of it, *casta* paintings function as the site of conflicting agencies in a heterogeneous society where different subgroups sought their own autonomous ends. "Managing the interstices with a measure of creativity"—as Nestor García Canclini puts it—artists operated in conditions that gave rise to modern, culturally bifurcated ideas of art and to the modern status of the artist, both of which are indebted to Christian theories of sacred images embedded in the modern, secular notion of art.[71] These interconnections and similarities between discourses taking place on both sides of the Atlantic can be glimpsed only by repeatedly redirecting our gaze between Europe and its overseas colonies, not settling in either place but trading back and forth like the objects under discussion themselves.

Notes

This essay originated as individual conference papers on *casta* paintings developed and presented separately by the authors. In 2009 Claire Farago presented "The Face of the Other: The Particular versus the Individual" at the Renaissance Society of America. In 2009 James M. Córdova presented "Materiality and Order in *Casta* Paintings and *Monjas Coronadas* Portraits from New Spain" at the Latin American Studies Association, and again in revised form at the Denver Art Museum the same year. The present work grew out of the authors' subsequent collaboration. Claire Farago thanks Michael Brown, Mayer Center Fellow, Denver Art Museum, for his bibliographical assistance and intellectual generosity in enabling her research on unfamiliar ground. Both authors also thank Clara Bargellini for generously reading and commenting on an earlier version of this paper. Finally, thanks to the authors' conference audiences for their helpful comments and discussion.

[1] *Casta* painting—a category that developed at the beginning of the eighteenth century—consists of series of individual canvases representing racially mixed families local to New Spain. Notable publications on *casta* paintings include María Concepción García Sáiz, *Las castas mexicanas: Un género pictórico americano* (Milan: Olivetti, 1989); Ilona Katzew, *New World Orders: Casta Painting and Colonial Latin America*, edited by John A. Farmer and Ilona Katzew (New York: The Americas Society, 1996); Elena Estrada de Gerlero, "Las pinturas de castas, imágenes de una sociedad variopinta," in *México en el mundo de las colecciones de arte*, María Luisa Sabau García, general director (Mexico City: Universidad Nacional Autónoma de México, 1994), 79–113; Elena Estrada de Gerlero, "La reforma borbónica y las pinturas de castas

novohispanas," in *El arte y la vida cotidiana. XVI Coloquio Internacional de Historia del Arte*, edited by Elena Estrada de Gerlero (Mexico City: Instituto de Investigaciones Estéticas, 1995), 217–252; Magali Carrera, *Imagining Identity in New Spain: Race, Lineage, and the Colonial Body in Portraiture and Casta Paintings* (Austin: University of Texas Press, 2003); Ilona Katzew, *Casta Painting: Images of Race in Eighteenth-Century Mexico* (New Haven: Yale University Press, 2004); Susan Deans-Smith, "The Colonial Subject: *Casta* Paintings, Collectors, and Critics in Eighteenth-Century Mexico and Spain," *Colonial Latin American Review* 14, no. 2 (December 2005): 164–204; Deans-Smith, "'Dishonor in the Hands of Indians, Spaniards, and Blacks': The (Racial) Politics of Painting in Eighteenth-Century Mexico," in *Race and Classification: The Case of Mexican America*, edited by Ilona Katzew and Susan Deans-Smith (Stanford: Stanford University Press, 2009), 43–72.

[2] Deans-Smith, "The Colonial Subject." On the patronage and function of scientific illustrations in the Americas, see Victor Peralta Ruiz and Charles F. Walker, "Viajeros naturalistas, científicos y dibujantes: De la ilustración al costumbrismo e las artes (siglos XVIII y XIX)," in *Vision y Simbolos: Del virreinato criollo a la República peruana*, edited by David A. Brading, Ramón Pinilla, and Scarlett O'Phelan Godoy (Lima: Banco de Crédito, 2006); and Londa Schiebinger and Claudia Swan, eds., *Colonial Botany: Science, Commerce, and Politics in the Early Modern World* (Philadelphia: University of Pennsylvania Press, 2005), both with extensive bibliographies.

[3] Katzew, *Casta Painting*, 9.

[4] Katzew, *Casta Painting*, chapter 3, especially p. 63; *New World Orders*, 9–29. This is discussed further below.

[5] Deans-Smith, "The (Racial) Politics of Painting."

[6] This historical context was first argued by Estrada de Gerlero, "La reforma borbónica," and developed further by Katzew, *Casta Painting*, and others since.

[7] Rogelio Ruiz Gomar, "La pintura de retrato en la Nueva España/Portrait Painting in New Spain," *El retrato novohispano en el siglo XVIII*, exh. cat. (Puebla: Museo Poblano de Arte Virreinal, 1999), 9–22, 135–144.

[8] For an expanded discussion of floral imagery in New Spanish portraiture and religious painting see James M. Córdova, "Clad in Flowers: Indigenous Arts and Knowledge in Colonial Mexican Convents," *The Art Bulletin* 93, no. 4 (December 2011): 449–467; and Córdova, *Colonial Professions: Religious Women and Monastic Arts in Bourbon Mexico* (Austin: University of Texas Press, forthcoming).

[9] *Diceño de mulata yja de negra y español el la Ciudad de Mexico, Cabesa de la America A 22 del mes de Agosto de 1711 Años* (Design of a *mulata*, daughter of a black woman and a Spaniard, in Mexico City, Head of America. [Painted] on August 22, 1711). Donna Pierce, "Rendering of a Mulatto," in *The Arts of Latin America, 1492–1820* (Philadelphia, PA: Philadelphia Museum of Art, 2006) 399, notes that this work and related ones by Arellano may have been made to welcome the new Spanish Bourbon viceroy to New Spain, Fernando de Alencastre Noroña y Silva, the Duke of Linares (1711–1716), and to educate him and the Spanish king about their New Spanish subjects.

[10] In Nahuatl (an indigenous Central Mexican language spoken by the Aztecs, among others collectively referred to as Nahuas), *Chichimec* literally signifies "lineage of the dog," and generally refers to northern-Mexican nomadic groups, who, according to the Nahuas, lived in caves rather than cities, hunted with bows and arrows, wore animal skins, and were ignorant of agriculture. In this sense, they were considered barbaric and uncivilized. However, the Nahuas of the late Postclassic and early modern periods professed partial *Chichimec* lineage, along with noble Toltec lineage. While they claimed the right to political rule by virtue of their Toltec heritage, they also took pride in their Chichimec roots, despite some of the term's more negative connotations. Thus, *Chichimec* seems to have been a malleable term depending on its usage. For an overview of its multifaceted significations, see the *Handbook of Middle American Indians*, Robert Wauchope, general editor, v. 11, pt. 2 (Austin: University of Texas Press, 1964–1976), 461–465.

[11] See Carrera, *Imagining Identity*, for the colonial implications of the expanding pictorial field in late eighteenth-century *casta* paintings.

[12] For example, Deans-Smith, "The Racial Politics of Painting," 56, cites Miguel Cabrera's *casta* painting of 1763, "*De español y de India, mestiza*," which is signed "painted by Miguel Cabrera, Mexico."

[13] For an extensive study of *casta* painting collectors and the reasons for collecting these works see Deans-Smith, "Creating the Colonial Subject," 181–183. Also see García Sáiz, *Las castas mexicanas*, 49; Elena Estrada de Gerlero, "La reforma borbónica," 221; Katzew, *Casta Painting*, 203.

[14] García Sáiz, *Las castas mexicanas*, 44.

[15] Ilona Katzew, *Una visión del México del Siglo de las Luces. La codificación de Joaquín Antonio Basarás* (Mexico City: Landucci, 2006), 15.

[16] This account is corroborated by the theologian Andrés Arce y Miranda, writing in 1746 that Viceroy Linares had conceived the idea of presenting images of different racial mixtures to the king of Spain and his court through a series of paintings, which Arce y Miranda thought would perpetuate Mexico's colonial status by promoting an image of an industrious society; the racial dimension of Arce y Miranda's criticism is discussed below. Katzew suggests that Linares conceived the idea specifically from Kircher's *China Monumentis*, 1667, which had been bequeathed by Sigüenza y Góngora to the Jesuit College of San Pedro y San Pablo in Mexico City (the book figures on the shelves in a portrait of Sigüenza y Góngora's friend Sor Juana Inés de la Cruz; see Fig. 4).

[17] Deans-Smith, "Creating the Colonial Subject," 181.

[18] Katzew, *Casta Painting*, 63.

[19] See especially Katzew, *Casta Painting*, and Estrada de Gerlero, "La reforma borbónica."

[20] Walter Mignolo, *The Idea of Latin America*, 61–65, drawing upon the Ecuadorian-born philosopher Bolivar Echeverría, distinguishes between white Creole elites and Afro-creoles and Indians. By the late seventeenth century, the Creole elite became internal colonizers who devoted themselves to emulating European intellectuals and hiding colonialism. Our study of viceregal artists corroborates and extends Mignolo's findings. Mignolo identifies the idea of "Latin America" that emerged in the second half of the nineteenth century with these Creole elites, who had detached themselves from the Spanish and Portuguese past, and turned their backs on Indians and blacks to embrace the ideology of the French Revolution.

[21] Anthony Pagden, "Identity Formation in Spanish America," in *Colonial Identity in the Atlantic World, 1500–1800*, edited by Nicholas Canny and Anthony Pagden (Princeton: Princ-

eton University Press, 1987), 51–93; D. A. Brading, *First America: The Spanish Monarchy, Creole Patriots, and the Liberal State, 1492–1867* (New York: Cambridge University Press, 1991); D. A. Brading, *Origins of Mexican Nationalism* (Cambridge, UK: Centre of Latin American Studies, Cambridge University, 1985). Ruth Hill, *Hierarchy, Commerce, and Fraud in Bourbon Spanish America: A Postal Inspector's Exposé* (Nashville, Tennessee: Vanderbilt University Press, 2005); *Imperial Subjects: Race and Identity in Colonial Latin America*, edited by Andrew B. Fisher and Matthew D. O'Hara (Durham: Duke University Press, 2009); Matthew O'Hara, *A Flock Divided: Race, Religion, and Politics in Mexico, 1749–1857* (Durham: Duke University Press, 2010).

[22] For example, see John Leddy Phelan, "Neo-Aztecism in the Eighteenth Century and the Genesis of Mexican Nationalism," in *Culture in History: Essays in Honor of Paul Radin*, edited by Stanley Diamond (New York: Published for Brandeis University by Columbia University Press, 1960), 760–777; Jacques Lafaye, *Quetzalcoatl and Guadalupe: The Formation of Mexican National Consciousness*, translated by Benjamin Keen (Chicago: Chicago University Press, 1976); Anthony Pagden, "Identity Formation," 51–93; James M. Córdova, "Aztec Vestal Virgins and the Brides of Christ: The Mixed Heritage of New Spain's *Monjas Coronadas*," *Colonial Latin American Review* 18, no. 2 (August 2009): 189–218.

[23] Translated in Deans-Smith, "Creating the Colonial Subject," 191. Cited originally in Efraín Castro Morales, "Los cuadros de castas de la Nueva España," *Jahrbuch für Geschichte von Statt, Wirtschaft, Gesellschaft Lateinamerikas* 20 (1983): 672–690. Also cited in Katzew, *Casta Painting*, 13, and Carrera, *Imagining Identity*, 49–50.

[24] Some *casta* paintings, however, picture discords among their figures. The implication of these works is that the union of particular ethnic types is inauspicious. For example, see Katzew, *Casta Painting*, and Carrera, *Imagining Identity*.

[25] R. Douglas Cope, *The Limits of Racial Domination: Plebeian Society in Colonial Mexico City, 1660–1720* (Madison: University of Wisconsin Press, 1994), 15.

[26] See Cope, *Limits*, for documented cases of "passing," that is, disguising oneself as a member of another socioracial group to acquire the benefits that members of that group supposedly enjoyed.

[27] Katzew, "Casta Painting, Identity and Social Stratification in Colonial Mexico," in *New World Orders*, 8–29.

[28] The initial restructuring of the painters' guild in Mexico City took place in 1686. See Deans-Smith, "The (Racial) Politics of Painting"; Katzew, *Casta Painting*, especially chapter 1. For a thorough examination of *calidad* in viceregal society, see Carrera, *Imagining Identity*, xvi, 6, and 14.

[29] According to Andrés Ubeda do los Cabos, *Pensamiento artístico español del siglo XVIII. De Antonio Palomino a Francisco de Goya* (Madrid: Aldeasa, 2001).

[30] This seems to have been the case also in Spain; see Peter Cherry, "Murillo's Drawing Academy," in *Bartolomé Esteban Murillo (1617–1682): Paintings from American Collections*, edited by Suzanne L. Stratton-Pruitt (New York: Harry N. Abrams, Inc., 2002), 49.

[31] Guillermo Tovar de Teresa, *Miguel Cabrera: Pintor de Cámara de la Reina Celestial* (Mexico City: InverMéxico Grupo Financiero, 1995), 44; discussed by Katzew, *Casta Painting*, 16–17. Both build on the study of Pacheco's Academy by Jonathan Brown, *Images and Ideas in Seventeenth-Century Spanish Painting* (Princeton: Princeton University Press, 1978). On the historical and theoretical context for these arguments in Seville, see further Javier Navarro de Zuvillage, "The *Trattato* in Seventeenth- and Eighteenth-Century Spanish Perspective and Art Theory," in *Re-Reading Leonardo: The Treatise on Painting across Europe 1550–1900*, edited by Claire Farago (Aldershot: Ashgate, 2009), 327–347.

[32] One of the earliest surviving documents from New Spain to argue that painting should be recognized as one of the liberal arts, by Puebla painter Pedro Benavides, dates from 1655, that is, within a few years of the founding of the Académie Royale de Peinture e de Sculpture in Paris (1648) and the first printed editions of Leonardo da Vinci's *Treatise on Painting* (French and Italian printed editions were published in Paris, 1651, and the text had been circulating in manuscript since the 1580s), which fueled these discussions of the status of painting and was instrumental to the Academic training of artists. On Benavides, see Juan Manuel Serrera, "La defensa novohispana de la ingenuidad de la pintura," *Boletín de la Real Academia de Bellas Artes de San Fernando* 81 (1995), 275–288, cited by Katzew, *Casta Painting*, 208, n. 40.

[33] By the end of the seventeenth century, Cristóbal de Villapando signed his works as having "invented" them. Historian Deans-Smith, "The (Racial) Politics of Painting," has collected extensive citations concerning artists' efforts to gain higher status. One of the most telling documents she has found is a notarized deposition by a group of painters to grant power of attorney to an otherwise anonymous person named Luis Bertucat in 1768, in which they refer to themselves as "professors of the Very Noble Arts of Painting and Sculpture." At one point in this document, the word "master" is crossed out and replaced by "professor." Deans-Smith, 49, citing Archivo de Notarias de la Ciudad de México, Antonio José Olaondo, #472, 1768, fol. 41v.

[34] Deans-Smith, "The (Racial) Politics of Painting." Several generations of the Juárez and Echave families provided the driving force behind these reform efforts to establish new institutions. On the intellectual foundations for associating painting with other liberal arts such as perspective and poetry, and disassociating it from the mechanical arts, identified with the guilds, see Paula Mues Orts, "Merezca ser hidalgo y libre el que pinto lo santo y respetado: La defensa novohispana del arte de la pintura," in *El Divino Pintor: La creación de María de Guadalupe en el taller Celestial*, exh. cat. (Mexico City: Museo de la Basilica de Guadalupe, 2001), 29–59; Mues Orts, *La libertad del pincel: Los discursos sobre la nobleza de la pintura en Nueva España* (Mexico City: Universidad Iberoamericana, 2008); and Clara Bargellini, "Originality and Invention in the Painting of New Spain," in *Painting a New World*, 79–91.

[35] Perhaps not surprisingly, the academy that finally received support from the king was founded by a Spaniard, Jerónimo Antonio Gil. See Michael Brown and Thomas E. Chávez, "Portrait of Don Matías de Gálvez y Gallardo as Viceprotector of the Academia de San Carlos," cat. N. 40, in *Painting a New World*, 247–250. Carlos III sent his master engraver Gil to supervise the Royal Mint; by 1781 Gil and mint director José Mangino petitioned the viceroy to expand the scope of the mint's training facilities from techniques for the production of coins to include the disciplines of painting, architecture, and sculpture. Viceroy Mayorga did this on his own, without even consulting Mangino.

[36] According to the viceregal statutes of the Academy of San

Carlos, "four full-blooded Indians of New Spain desirous to dedicate themselves to any one of the Arts taught in this Institution, all having the union of poverty with ability" were eligible for pensions. See Jean Charlot, *Mexican Art and the Academy of San Carlos, 1785–1915* (Austin: University of Texas Press, 1962), 54.

[37] In 1766–1772, Gálvez's brother José initiated the political restructuring of colonial government known as the Bourbon Reforms; his brother Matías and son Bernardo worked, surreptitiously before and overtly after Spain declared war on Great Britain in 1776, to help the American cause.

[38] Jonathan Brown, "On the Meaning of *Las Meninas*," in *Images and Ideas in Seventeenth-Century Spanish Painting*, 109.

[39] The painterly style developed by Diego de Velázquez at his father-in-law Pacheco's academy follows on longstanding collecting practices of the Spanish monarchs, beginning with Philip II's love of Titian. See Rosemary Mulcahy, *Philip II of Spain: Patron of the Arts* (Dublin: Four Courts Press, 2006).

[40] Brown, "On the Meaning," 102, further notes that in Spain, the elevation of painting as a liberal art would free painters from paying the *alcabala*, a state tax that applied to the manual trades such as shoes, clothing, and—to many artists' dismay—painting. In New Spain the painters José de Ibarra and Pedro de Benavides, separately and on different occasions, petitioned viceregal officials to exempt painters from paying this tax. See Mina Ramírez Montes, "En defensa de la pintura. Ciudad de México, 1753," *Anales del Instituto de Investigaciones Estéticas* 78 (2001): 119 and Serrera, "La defensa novohispana de la ingenuidad de la pintura," 275–288. Status seeking and pressing economic factors had been interconnected since the formation of the earliest art academies in Italy; see Peter M. Lukehart, "Delineating the Genoese Studio: *Giovanni accartati* or *sotto padre*?" in *The Artist's Workshop*, edited by Peter M. Lukehart (Washington: National Gallery of Art distributed by Hanover-London: University Press of New England, 1993), 37–59, for an excellent introduction to the scholarship; and Robert Willliams, "The Artist as Worker in Sixteenth-Century Italy," in Julian Brooks et al., *Taddeo and Federico Zuccaro: Artist-Brothers in Renaissance Rome,* exh. cat. (Los Angeles: J. Paul Getty Museum, 2007), 95–104.

[41] For a survey of the racial backgrounds of many of New Spain's painters and the racial qualifications established to restrict non-Spanish entry into New Spain's guilds and art academies, see Deans-Smith, "Dishonor."

[42] Also see Pedro Angeles Jiménez, "Apeles y *tlacuilos*: Marcos Griego y la pintura cristiano indígena del siglo XVI en la Nueva España," in *De arquitectura, pintura y otras artes. Homenaje a Elisa Vargaslugo* (Mexico City: UNAM, 2004), 115–33; Rodrigo Vera, "La Guadalupana: Tres imágenes en una," *Proceso* 34 (26 May 2002): 51–53, cited in Bargellini, "Originality and Invention," 85. The painting of Guadalupe is attributed to the native painter Marcos Cipac today. See Jeanette Peterson, "Creating the Virgin of Guadalupe," *The Americas* 61, no. 4 (April 2005): 571.

[43] This form of publication—collected opinions on a central artistic issue—recalls Benedetto Varchi's famous questionnaire of 1546 (published along with two lectures he delivered to the Accademia Fiorentina in March 1547) directed to leading Florentine artists on the relative merits of painting versus sculpture: *Due Lezzioni di M. Benedetto Varchi nella prima delle quale si dichiara un sonetto di M. Michelangelo Buonarroti. Nella seconda si disputa quale sia piu nobile arte la scultori, sopra la quistione sopradetta* (Florence: Lorenzo Torrentino, 1549). See Leatrice Mendelsohn, *Paragoni: Benedetto Varchi's Due Lezzioni and Cinquecento Art Theory* (Ann Arbor: UMI Research Press, 1982); François Quiviger, "Benedetto Varchi and the Visual Arts," *Journal of the Warburg and Courtauld Institutes* 50 (1987): 219–224. Charlene Villaseñor Black has studied the popularity of classicizing comparisons of painting and poetry in Spanish literature in relation to Leonardo's writings; see "Pacheco, Velázquez, and the Legacy of Leonardo in Spain," in *Re-Reading Leonardo,* 349–372.

[44] See Farago, *Leonardo da Vinci's 'Paragone,'* 305–306.

[45] St. Thomas Aquinas, *Comm. Metaphysics*, XII.L8: C2543.

[46] "Omnes res . . . in artifice creato dicentur vivere," St. Bonaventure, *I. Sent.* d. 36, a. 2, q. 1, ad. 4; see further, J. M. Bissen, *L'exemplarisme divin selon Saint Bonaventure,* Paris, *1929*, 29 ff.; Panofksy, *Idea*, 40, on Thomas Aquinas's characterization of the artist's "quasi-idea" as analogous to the working of the divine mind; and further discussion in Farago, *Leonardo da Vinci's 'Paragone,'* 139.

[47] For a useful introduction to the issues and historical texts, see Rudolf Wittkower, "Genius: Individualism in Art and Artists," *Dictionary of the History of Ideas: Studies of Selected Pivotal Ideas*, edited by Philip P. Weiner, 5 vols. (New York: Charles Scribner's Sons, 1973), 3:297–312. For a recent contribution that remains wedded to an explanation based on classical sources, see Patricia A. Emison, *Creating the "Divine" Artist from Dante to Michelangelo* (Leiden-London: Brill, 2004).

[48] Bargellini, "Originality and Invention," 79–81, discusses the break with this tradition due to the privileging of originality understood as a "progressive sequence of individual achievements as an index of the quality and worth of works of art in general," beginning with José Bernardo Couto (*Diálogo sobre la istoria de la pintura en México*, 1872), a prominent Conservative lawyer and former president of the board of directors of the Academia Nacional de San Carlos in Mexico City.

[49] Gabriele Paleotti, *Discorso alle imagini sacre e profane* (Bologna, 1582), cited from *Trattati d'arte del cinquecento fra manierismo e controriforma*, edited by Paola Barocchi (Bari, 1960), 3:117–509, citing 132–142. Paleotti cites Augustine, *De doctrina Christiana* II.1. David Summers, *The Judgment of Sense: Optical Naturalism and the Rise of Aesthetics* (Cambridge, 1987), 146–150, discusses Paleotti's text in connection with ancient and medieval sources of the topos about the resemblance between father and son.

[50] Federico Zuccaro, *L'idea de' Pittori, Scultori e Architetti* (Turin: A. Disserolio, 1607); facsimile edition in Detlef Heikamp, ed., *Scritti d'arte di Federico Zuccaro* (Florence: Leo S. Olschki, 1961).

[51] Although we are only a "small copy of the excellence of divine art," Zuccaro wrote, the human intellective soul by its nature (that is, through sense experience) can know "spiritual forms representing all things of this world" that come from God; by virtue of this ability, man may be "almost a second God." Similar statements were made by Leonardo da Vinci a century earlier when he claimed that "painting is born of nature; but to be more correct,…[painting is] the grandchild of nature because all perceptible things are born from nature, and painting is born from the nature of those things." Leonardo is referring to nature as eternal and claiming nobility for the artist by virtue of his proximity to the intelligible acts of

God and his knowledge of the geometric science of optics, concerned with explaining the action of light.

[52] Zuccaro, *L'idea,* in Heikamp, ed., *Scritti d'arte,* 158–185, 225–232. Zuccaro cites Thomas Aquinas, *Summa theologiae,* I.15.1, I.75.2, and I.79.4. The resemblance of Zuccaro's language and ideas to Leonardo da Vinci's treatise, a copy of which Zuccaro owned, has been noted by David Summers, whose discussion of Zuccaro we follow; see *Judgment of Sense,* 282–308. Zuccaro's understanding of scientific naturalistic painting, as Summers notes (these continuities are in fact at the core of his argument), are in line with discussions of painted *relievo* since Cennini (c. 1390) and Leon Battista Alberti (1435), two touchstones in the modern understanding of painting as imitating the world we see directly through the sense of sight. Summers himself is indebted to Panofsky's reading of Zuccaro in *Idea: A Concept in Art Theory* (Columbia: University of South Carolina Press, 1968); Panofsky associates the artist's theory with "Mannerism." On Zuccaro, see also Robert Williams, *Art, Theory and Culture in Sixteenth-Century Italy: From Techne to Metatechne* (Cambridge: Cambridge University Press, 1997), 135–150. Missing from the modern scholarship is recognition that Zuccaro's (and Paleotti's) arguments conform with longstanding Christian theories of images that ground the truth of artistic representations in their contact with the divine.

[53] Paleotti, *Discorso alle imagini,* 132–142. On the Christian logic of indexicality in relationship to modern secular notions of art, see further Donald Preziosi and Claire Farago, *Art Is Not What You Think It Is* (Oxford-Malden: Wiley-Blackwell, forthcoming).

[54] Carducho, *Diálogos de la pintura,* 172–173.

[55] Pacheco, *Arte de la pintura,* 2:284.

[56] Pacheco, 364; Carducho, 174.

[57] Deans-Smith, "Dishonor," 65, states, "It is surely no coincidence that a major push to establish a Mexican academy occurred within the context of the inspection of the Virgin of Guadalupe in 1751, the creation of the Royal Academy of San Fernando of Madrid in 1753, and the publication of Cabrera's *Maravilla Americana* in 1756."

[58] For a more extensive synopsis of the various possible ways in which New Spain's artists had access to, and participated in, the contemporaneous discourse on painting, see Deans-Smith, "Dishonor," 53–56.

[59] Regarding the importance of *disegno* in the context of Academic principles and instruction associated with Catholic Reformation ideals, is worth noting that Zuccaro was instrumentally associated with the foundational moments of academies in Florence, Rome, and Seville. Zuccaro was founder and first director of the Roman Accademia di San Luca, established by artists in 1577 and authorized by Pope Sixtus V in 1588. It was realized in 1593 under the protection of Clement VIII. In the 1560s and 1570s, Zuccaro had been a member of the Florentine Academy, the first such bureaucratic organization, founded by Giorgio Vasari under the protection of Cosimo I de' Medici in 1563. In a letter dating between 1575 and 1578, Zuccaro called for educational reforms at the Florentine Accademia del Disegno that formed the basis of instruction at his academy in Rome. See Nikolas Pevsner, *Academies of Art Past and Present* (1940; reprint, New York: Da Capo Press, 1973), 51–52; and further, *The Accademia Seminars: The Accademia di San Luca in Rome, c. 1590–1635,* ed. Peter M. Lukehart (Washington, DC: National Gallery of Art, 2009). In terms of the transmission of ideas about the education of the artist, it is worth noting that, from January 1586 until the end of 1588, Zuccaro worked at the new Escorial Palace for Philip II of Spain. Brown, *Images and Ideas in Seventeenth-Century Spanish Painting,* 31, 93, discusses Zuccaro's connections with Seville, particularly via Pablo de Céspedes, an artist and writer, academician, and friend of Pacheco, who worked in Rome with the writer/artist Giovanni Baglione. These connections merit further investigation. On the history of the early European academies, see further, Karen-edis Barzman, *The Florentine Academy and the Early Modern State: The Discipline of Disegno* (Cambridge: Cambridge University Press, 2000). On Zuccaro, see Cristina Acidini Luchinat, *Taddeo e Federico Zuccari: Fratelli pittori del Cinquecento,* 2 vols. (Milan: Jandi Sapi, 1998).

[60] Luis de Mena's composite *casta* painting canvas is the only known example that includes a religious subject. In it the Virgin of Guadalupe appears above compartmentalized scenes that contain the usual racial admixtures seen in this genre.

[61] Carducho, 123. Both Carducho and Pacheco are indebted to Leonardo's text; see Villaseñor Black and Navarro de Zuvillaga, both in *Re-Reading Leonardo.*

[62] See discussion of this fundamental distinction in David Summers, *Michelangelo and the Language of Art* (Princeton: Princeton University Press, 1982), 279–282, citing Vincenzo Danti, *Il primo libro del trattato delle perette roporzion di tutte le cosec che imitare e ritrarre si possano con l'arte del disegno* (Florence, 1567).

[63] An extensive selection of texts and academic institutional contexts are discussed in *Re-Reading Leonardo.*

[64] A point well made by Carrera, *Imagining Identity,* 42.

[65] Translation in García Sáiz, *Las castas mexicanas,* 103.

[66] Walter Mignolo, "When Speaking Was Not Good Enough: Illiterates, Barbarians, Savages and Cannibals," in *Amerindian Images and the Legacy of Columbus,* edited by René Jara and Nicholas Spadaccini (Minneapolis: University of Minnesota Press, 1992), 335.

[67] Francisco López de Gómara, *Cortés: The Life of the Conqueror by His Secretary,* translated and edited by Lesley Byrd Simpson (Berkeley: University of California Press, [1552] 1964), 367.

[68] Translation in García Sáiz, 108.

[69] For example, while at prayer, Saint Benedict was confronted by the Devil, who took the form of a blackbird. George Ferguson, *Signs and Symbols in Christian Art* (New York: Oxford University Press, 1961), 24. Images of Saint Paul the Hermit and Saint Anthony Abbot, however, imbue the raven with a more positive meaning. According to this story, a raven brought saints Anthony and Paul a loaf of bread each day that they spent together in the desert. Ferguson, *Signs and Symbols,* 13.

[70] In fact, the previous painting in this series, which features a *lobo* child as the offspring of a black father and Amerindian woman, describes him as a thief and pickpocket. See García Sáiz, *Las castas mexicanas,* 108.

[71] Néstor García Canclini, *Hybrid Cultures: Strategies for Entering and Leaving Modernity,* translated by C. Chiappari and S. López (Minneapolis: University of Minnesota Press, 1995), 204. Using a term coined by Michel Foucault, García Canclini analyzed contemporary South American art and material culture as a "heterotopic" capitalist network maintained by/as a fictive (in reality, "codependent") division between "tradition" and "modernity."

"At the Ends of the Earth"
Asian Trade Goods in Colonial New Mexico, 1598–1821

Donna Pierce

Evidence of the globalization of culture and international trade can be detected in the art of New Spain and Spain during the early modern era. For example, in the Mexican *Still Life* from 1765 by Antonio Pérez de Aguilar, a porcelain plate imported from China is visible on the lower shelf (Fig. 1). Still life paintings from Spain at times show objects clearly Mexican in origin, such as the *jícara* (lacquered gourd) cup seen in a painting by Antonio de Pereda from 1652 (Fig. 2, top right of chest). Even religious paintings occasionally reflect aspects of international trade, such as the painting of the statue of the Christ of Chalma with Chinese porcelain jars flanking the sculpture (see p. 33, Fig. 11). Portraits and *casta* (caste) paintings depict imported European clothing styles as well as European and Asian decorative arts in the Americas (Fig. 3). Implicit in the paintings, particularly portraits, is the association between "foreign" objects and status.

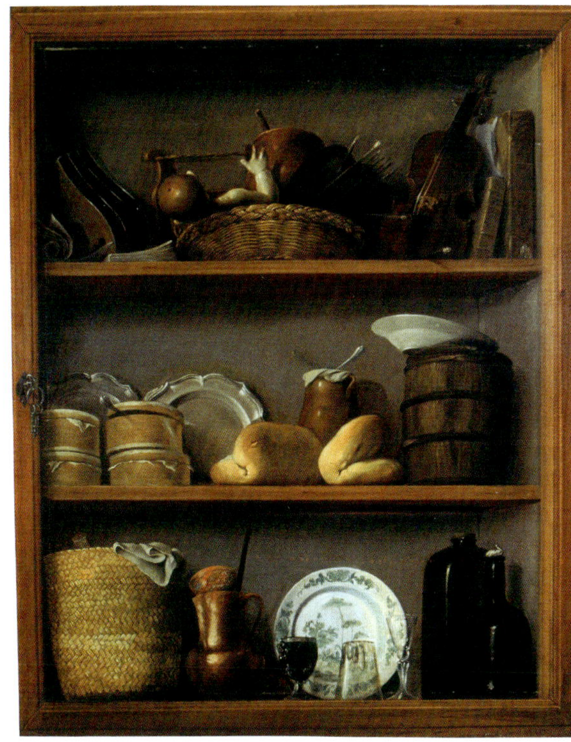

Fig. 1. Antonio Pérez de Aguilar, *The Painter's Cabinet*. Mexico, 1765. Museo Nacional de Arte, Mexico City. Note the Chinese porcelain plate and copper chocolate pot on lower shelf.

The geographical extent of globalization during the early modern era has been much debated, with some scholars claiming that it was pervasive while others argue that it was restricted to urban and political centers.[1] As a case study of the extent of early modern globalization, this paper focuses on the northernmost frontier of New Spain, the province of New Mexico, now part of the southwestern United States (see map, p. 9).[2] Geographically, New Mexico was over a thousand miles from Mexico City and was described by its governor Diego de Vargas in 1692 as "at the ends of the earth and remote beyond compare."[3] Yet archeological and documentary evidence indicates that New Mexico participated in the international trade market and the globalization of culture from the earliest days of settlement. Although Asian trade goods are documented in churches and missions in New Mexico, I focus exclusively here on the presence of Asian trade goods in colonial New Mexican domestic settings.[4]

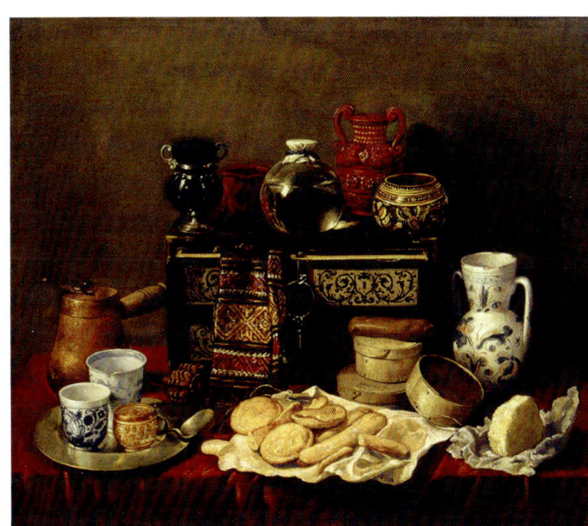

Fig. 2. Antonio de Pereda, *Still Life with Ebony Chest*. Spain, 1652. Oil on canvas. The State Hermitage Museum, St. Petersburg (GE-327). Photograph © The State Hermitage Museum / photo by Vladimir Terebenin, Leonard Kheifets, Yuri Molodkovets. Note the Mexican gourd cup on upper right of chest. The utensils and products surrounding the chest are associated with the preparation and consumption of hot chocolate.

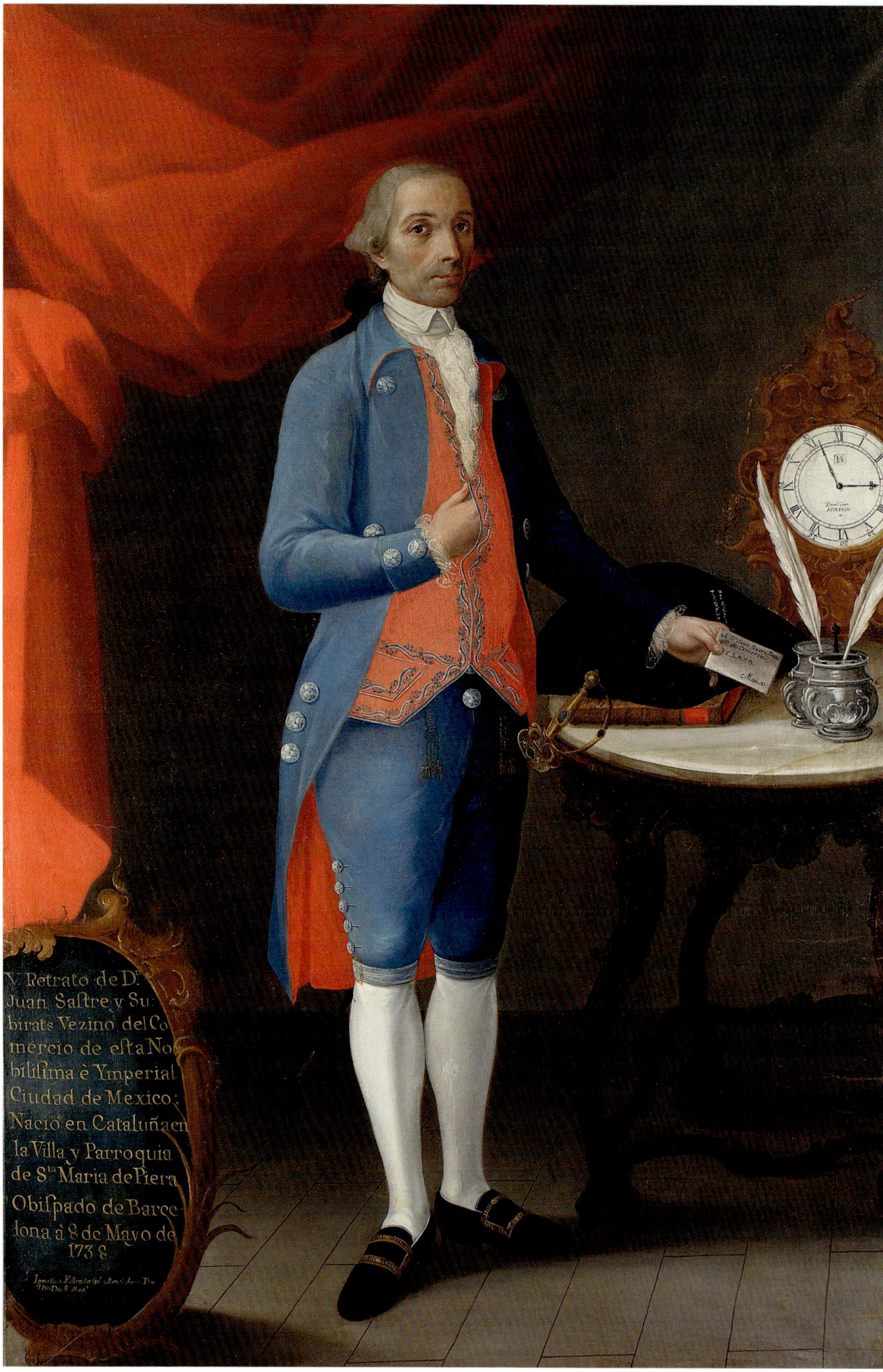

Fig. 3. Anonymous, *Portrait of Don Juan Sastre y Subirates*. Mexico, 1738. Denver Art Museum, Collection of Frederick and Jan Mayer; M1996.044. The English clock on the table is from London.

An examination of the material culture of New Mexico during the 223 years it was part of the Viceroyalty of New Spain (1598–1821) reflects not only interdependency between Spanish settlers and local Pueblo Indian peoples, but also the introduction of objects produced by various Plains Indian tribes from surrounding areas as well as objects imported from central Mexico, Europe, and Asia. Combined with the archeological record, documentary information indicates that domestic settings in New Mexico were microcosms of cultural exchange and reflected the international trade of the era, even in one of the most geographically distant areas of the Spanish viceroyalties. Since few intact artifacts survive from the early period of New Mexico settlement, in the illustrations here I have matched archeological fragments or written descriptions with similar extant objects or with details in paintings from central Mexico.

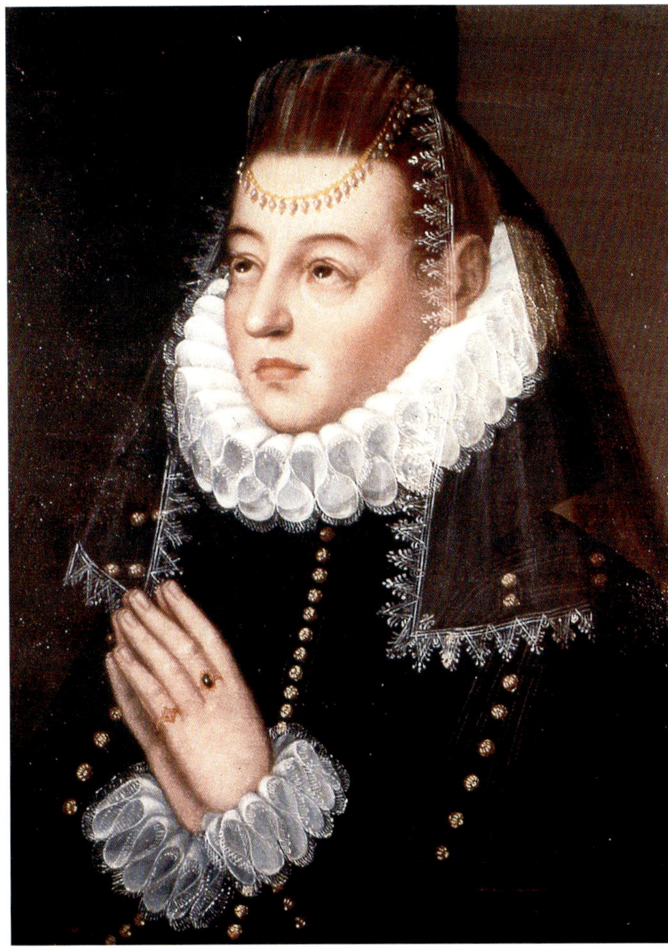

Fig. 4. Báltazar de Echave Ibía, *Portrait of a Lady*. Mexico, c. 1615–1620. Museo Nacional de Arte, Mexico City.

First Spanish Settlement (1598–1610) San Gabriel del Yunque

When the first Spanish settlers led by Juan de Oñate arrived in New Mexico in 1598, they settled next to one of the local Pueblo Indian villages.[5] In the 1960s portions of this first Spanish settlement, known as San Gabriel del Yunque, were excavated.[6] It is clear from the artifacts recovered as well as written records that daily life from the beginnings of the viceregal period in New Mexico evidenced cultural exchange and global trade.

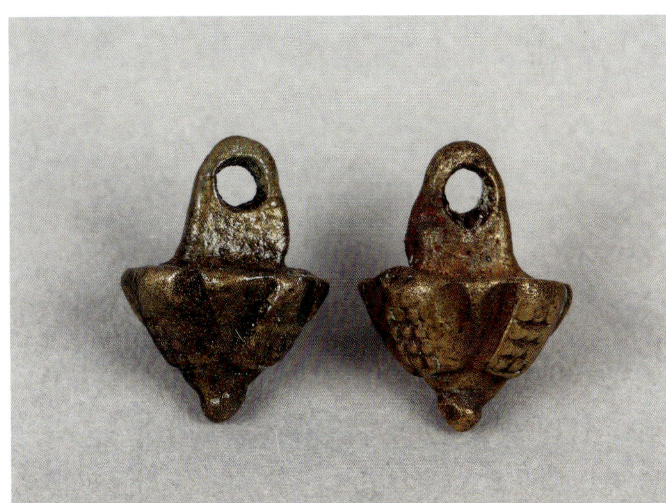

Fig. 5. Gilt brass buttons. Spain or Mexico, c. 1590–1600. Excavated at San Gabriel del Yunque site, San Juan Pueblo, New Mexico. Courtesy of the Maxwell Museum of Anthropology, University of New Mexico. Photography by Bernie Barnard, 68.43.69a–b.

This is reflected in the belongings of one of the Spanish couples who immigrated to San Gabriel from Mexico in December 1600, Doña Francisca Galindo and her husband, Captain Antonio Conde de Herrera.[7] According to the expedition inventory, Doña Francisca's wardrobe included nine dresses of velvet, satin, and silk taffeta, trimmed with lace cuffs and starched ruffs, and fastened with gold clasps and buttons, likely similar to those in a portrait of a woman from Mexico City (Fig. 4). In fact, several gilt brass buttons, like those in the portrait, were recovered from the excavations at San Gabriel (Fig. 5). Like the woman in the painting, Francisca Galindo owned a headdress of pearls. Unlike the woman in

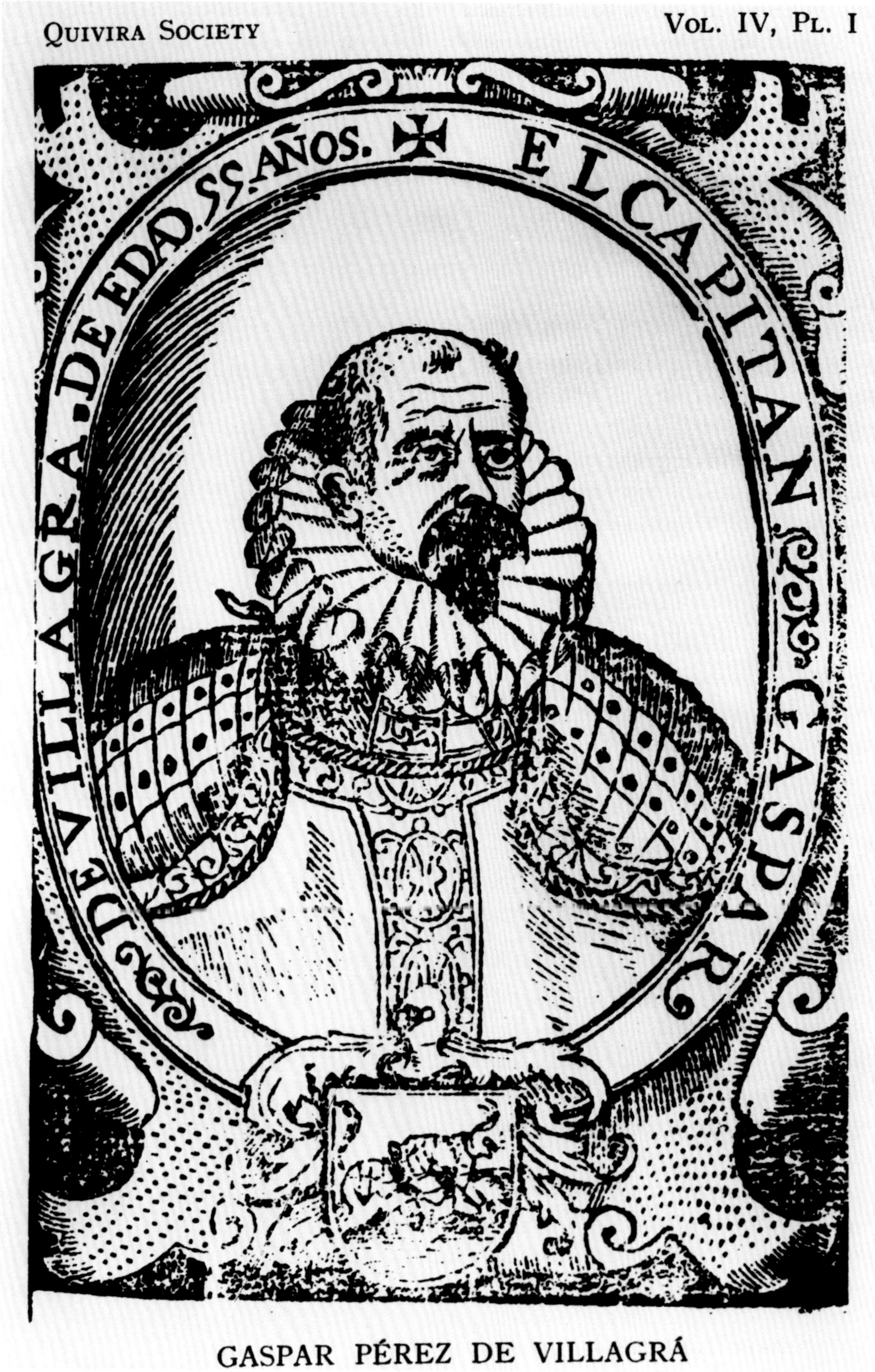

Fig. 6. *Portrait of Gaspar Pérez de Villagrá*. 1610. Engraved book frontispiece from Gaspar Pérez de Villagrá's *Historia de Nuevo México*, Alcalá, Spain, 1610. Courtesy Palace of the Governors Photo Archives (NMHM/DCA), #152680.

the painting, she preferred brightly colored fabrics, including red, green, and yellow silks. Her husband brought seven suits of wool, silk, and silk taffeta with lace-trimmed cuffs and collar ruffs, similar to those shown in the engraving depicting Captain Gaspar Pérez de Villagrá, the only surviving portrait of a member of the original settlement expedition (Fig. 6).[8]

Among other items, the couple's household goods included eight chairs, a wash tub, silver tableware, a bed with a crimson taffeta bedspread trimmed in lace, eight bed sheets, and bolsters and pillows embroidered in multicolored silk. Although only one skirt and none of the decorative arts listed in this early inventory are specifically described as Asian, it is probably safe to assume that at least some of the silks among the wardrobes and household furnishings were Asian in origin. The inventory provides an introductory glimpse of the quantity and quality of household goods and personal effects brought by some of the settlers to the northern frontier.

When the site of the adobe settlement of San Gabriel was excavated nearly four centuries later, several sherds of Chinese porcelain were recovered (Fig. 7). These fragments are particularly interesting since they were brought to New Mexico by 1598–1600, quite a short time after the opening of trade with Asia. Decorated in blue underglaze and red overglaze enamels, one of the fragments has been dated between 1522 and 1566 during the Jiajing dynasty (Fig. 7, upper right) and can be compared to a bowl in the Idemitsu Museum of Arts (Fig. 8). The other sherds date from the reign of Wanli (1573–1619).[9] They are the earliest examples of Chinese porcelain known to have been brought to New Mexico, and their use dates between 1598 and 1617, when San Gabriel was abandoned. The only other specifically Asian objects excavated at San Gabriel were ivory beads that could have been made in Asia or in Mexico from Asian bulk ivory.

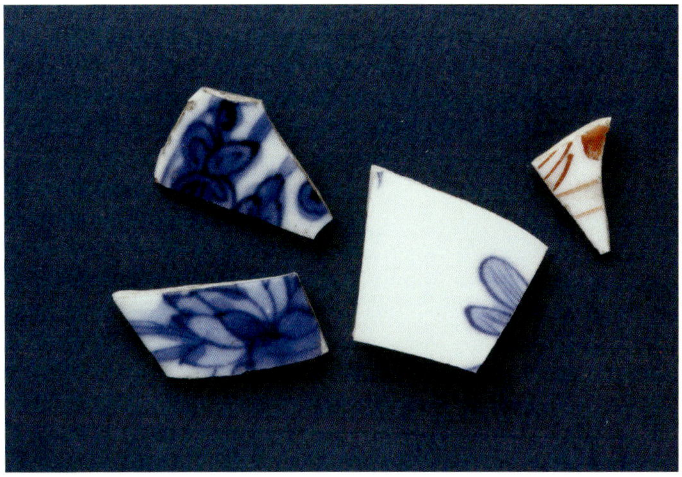

Fig. 7. Porcelain sherds. China, 1522–1617. Excavated at San Gabriel site, San Juan Pueblo, New Mexico. Courtesy of the Maxwell Museum of Anthropology, University of New Mexico.

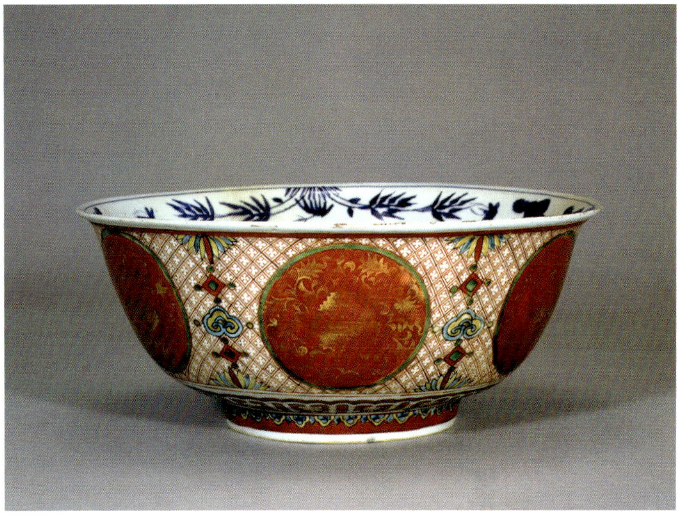

Fig. 8. Bowl. China, 1522–1566. Ming Dynasty, Jiajing Period. Idemitsu Museum of Arts.

Santa Fe (1610–1680)

In the winter of 1609–1610, the new governor, Pedro de Peralta, moved the capital of New Mexico from San Gabriel to the site of present-day

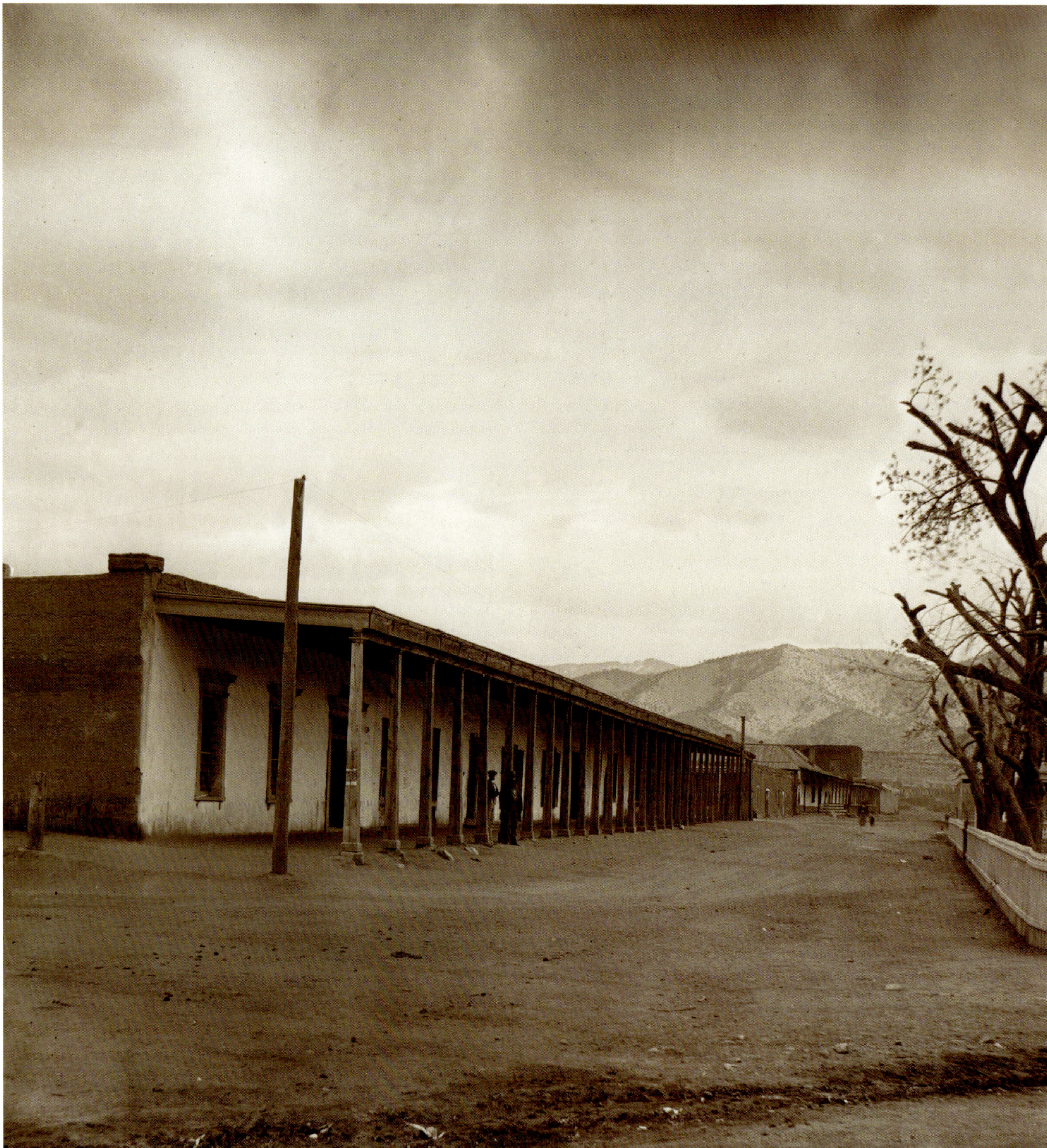

Fig. 9. Palace of the Governors. Santa Fe, New Mexico, begun 1610. Photo: Nicolas Brown, 1868. Courtesy Palace of the Governors Photo Archives (NMHM/DCA), #045819.

Santa Fe. Built around a plaza with a parish church on one side, the *casas reales* (royal buildings) originally occupied the three other sides.[10] The only section of those adobe buildings remaining today is a small portion of the north side now known as the Palace of the Governors (Fig. 9). In addition to serving as administrative offices of government, the royal buildings were home to the governor of New Mexico, his family, and his servants, as well as to other government officials and their respective families and servants.

Twentieth-century archeological excavations in the Palace of the Governors yielded items that represent domestic life and decorative arts in New Mexico from 1610 to 1680 and document participation in international trade.[11] As at San Gabriel, Chinese porcelain sherds were recovered from excavations in the Palace of the Governors (Fig. 10). All date before 1680; several pieces have been dated to the late sixteenth or early seventeenth century (before the end of the Ming dynasty in 1644).[12] Two sherds with green and red enamel on one side and blue underglaze on the reverse have been dated between 1522 and 1566 (Fig. 11). Four sherds from a cup or small bowl with C-scroll or comma designs (Fig. 12a), two sherds with plant motifs (Fig. 12b), and two sherds from a cup or small bowl decorated with gold leaf designs on a solid cobalt-blue background (Fig. 13a) were made before 1644. The latter can be compared to an intact bowl in the Metropolitan Museum of Art (Fig. 13b).

The remainder of the Chinese porcelain sherds date before 1680, including a fluted rim from a small cup or bowl, likely used for drinking chocolate (Figs. 14a and b). Spaniards had adopted the custom of drinking chocolate, a product native to the Americas, from the indigenous peoples of central Mexico in the early colonial period (see Figs. 1–2). In a document from 1660 a Pueblo Indian servant working in the Palace of the Governors described serving chocolate to the

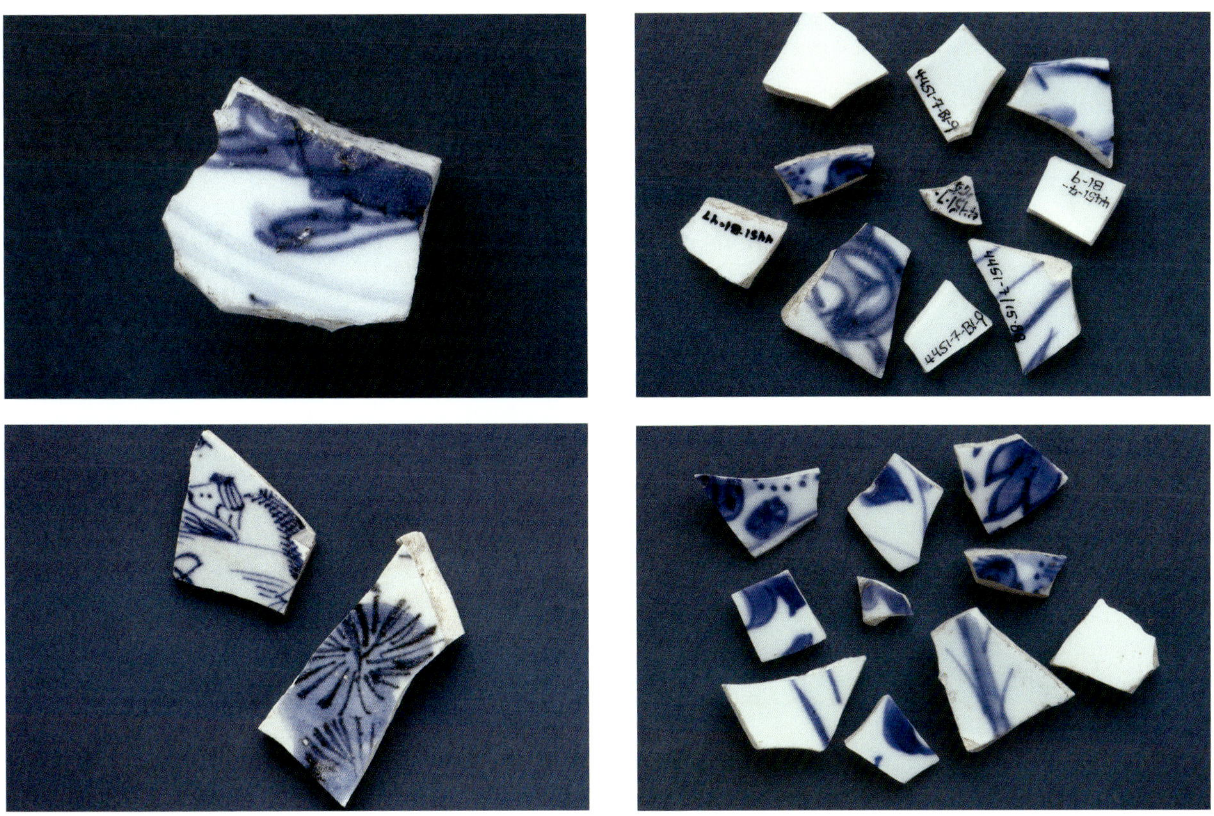

Fig. 10. Porcelain sherds. China, before 1680. Excavated from the Palace of the Governors, Santa Fe. Laboratory of Anthropology, Museum of New Mexico. Photography by Blair Clark.

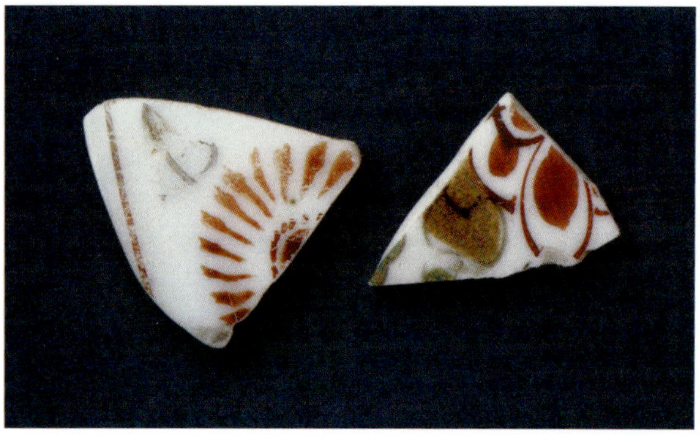

Fig. 11a. Porcelain sherds. China, 1522–1566. Excavated from the Palace of the Governors, Santa Fe. Laboratory of Anthropology, Museum of New Mexico. Photography by Blair Clark.

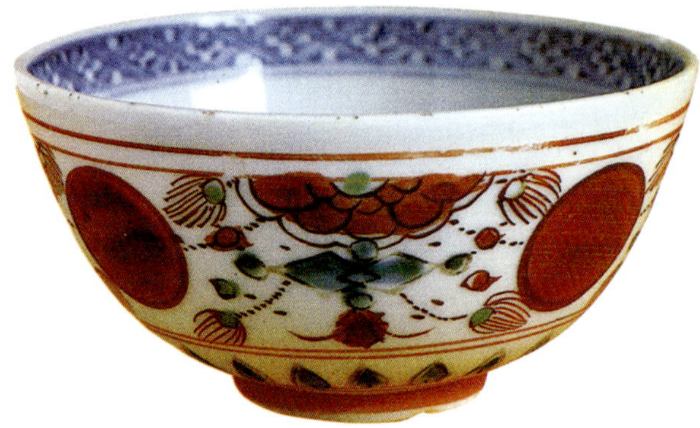

Fig. 11b. Bowl. China, c. 1580–1600. Princessehof Museum.

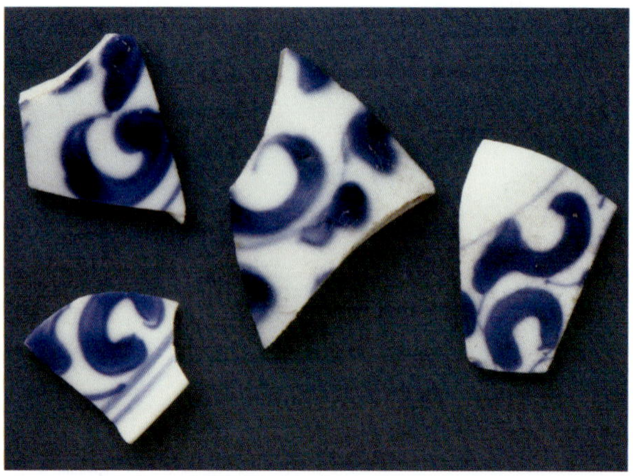

Fig. 12a. Porcelain sherds. China, before 1644. Excavated from the Palace of the Governors, Santa Fe. Laboratory of Anthropology, Museum of New Mexico. Photography by Blair Clark.

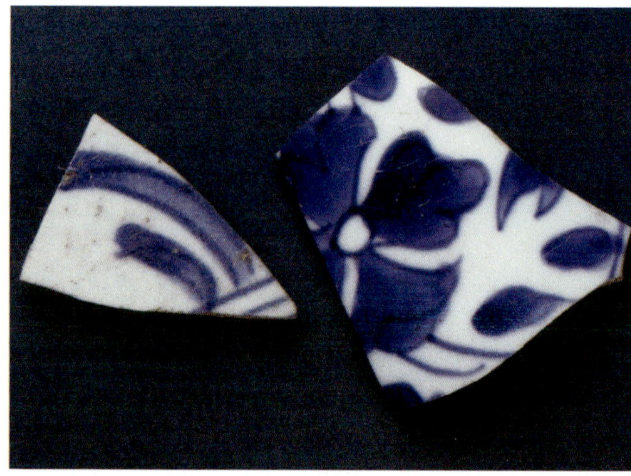

Fig. 12b. Porcelain sherds. China, before 1644. Excavated from the Palace of the Governors, Santa Fe. Laboratory of Anthropology, Museum of New Mexico. Photography by Blair Clark.

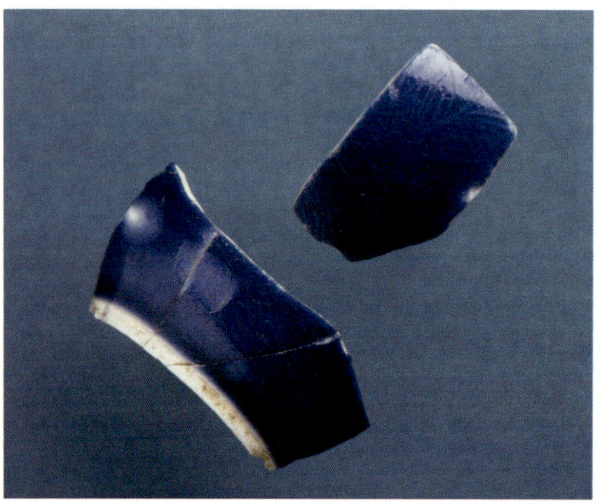

Fig. 13a. Porcelain sherds. China, before 1644. Excavated from the Palace of the Governors, Santa Fe. Laboratory of Anthropology, Museum of New Mexico. Photography by Blair Clark.

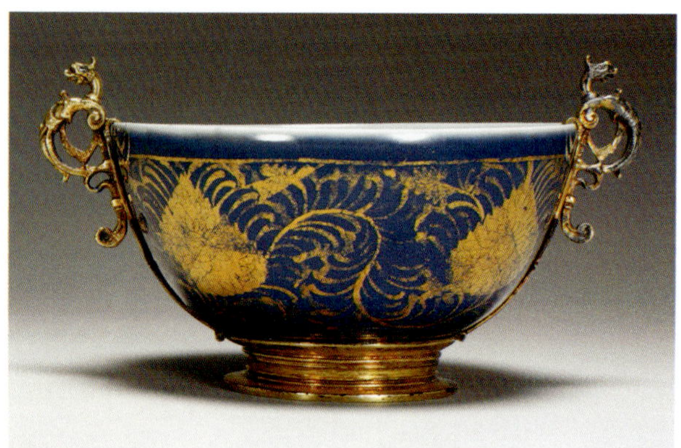

Fig. 13b. Bowl with silver-gilt mounts. China. Ming dynasty (1368-1644), Jiajing period (1522-66), mid-16th century. Porcelain painted in underglaze blue, with blue glaze and gold decoration. Metropolitan Museum of Art, New York, NY, U.S.A.. Image copyright © The Metropolitan Museum of Art. Image source: Art Resource, NY.

governor of New Mexico and his wife every day at three o'clock in the afternoon.[13] Unfortunately, the servant did not describe what the chocolate was served in, but handle-less Chinese porcelain cups, Mexican majolica (glazed earthenware) cups, coconut cups mounted in silver, and Aztec-style lacquered gourd cups (*jícaras*) were all used for drinking chocolate in central Mexico and in New Mexico as well.

Imported ivory objects discovered in the Palace excavations include turned finials that may be pieces of a miniature chess set or a piece of furniture (Fig. 15). In addition, a turned ivory handle from a cane and an ivory comb were found. Like the ivory beads from San Gabriel, these may have been imported from Asia ready-made, or made in Mexico from Asian bulk ivory. Excavated metal straight pins, needles, silver-thread buttons, and remnants of gold and silver galloon indicate that clothing was made or repaired on the premises from imported materials, probably including Asian silk fabrics.

Although the impact of Asian goods on the local arts of New Mexico is beyond the scope of this paper, I would like to cite one case. In an example of international and cross-cultural artistic

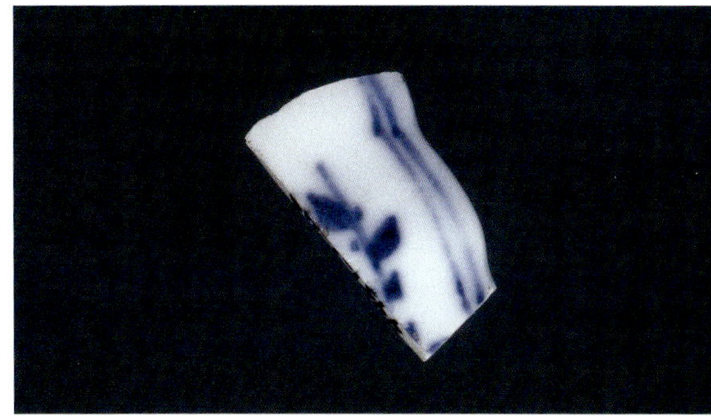

Fig. 14a. Porcelain sherd from a cup. China, before 1680. Excavated from the Palace of the Governors, Santa Fe. Laboratory of Anthropology, Museum of New Mexico. Photography by Blair Clark.

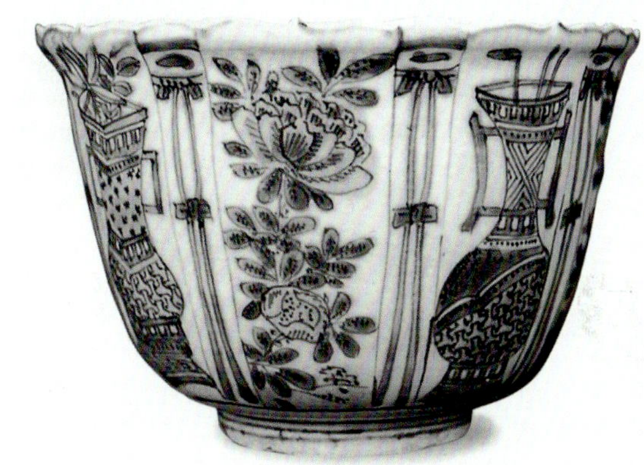

Fig. 14b. Porcelain cup. China, Wanli Period (1573–1619), 1590–1600. Museo de José Luis Bello y González, Puebla, Mexico.

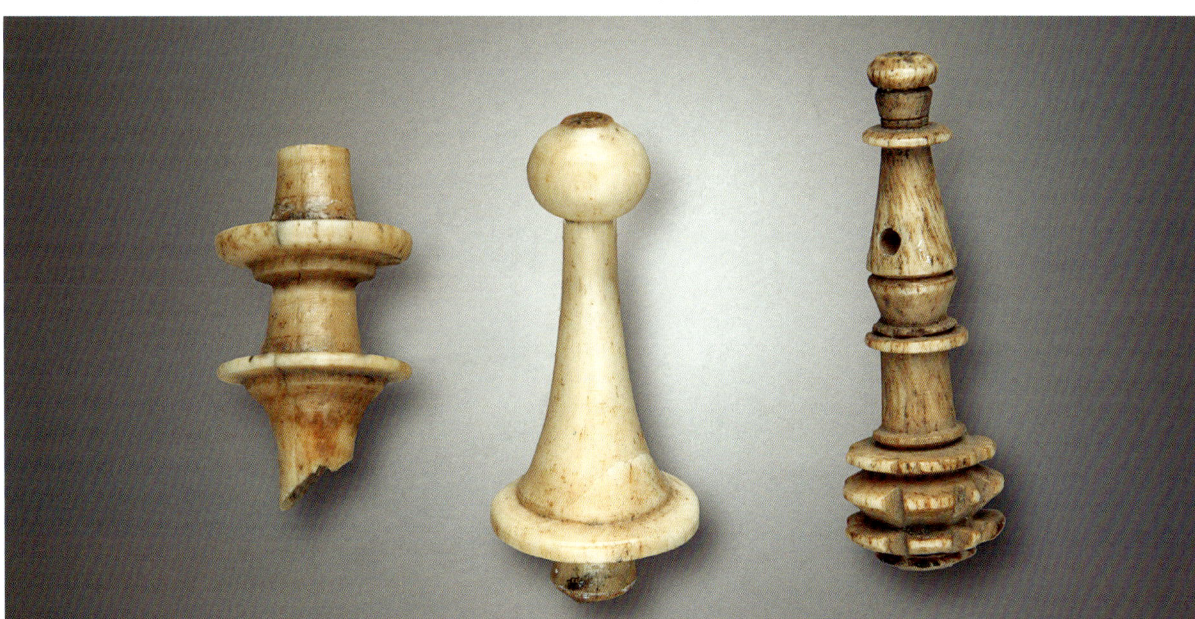

Fig. 15. Pieces of ivory. 1610–1680. Excavated from the Palace of the Governors, Santa Fe. Laboratory of Anthropology, Museum of New Mexico. Photography by Blair Clark.

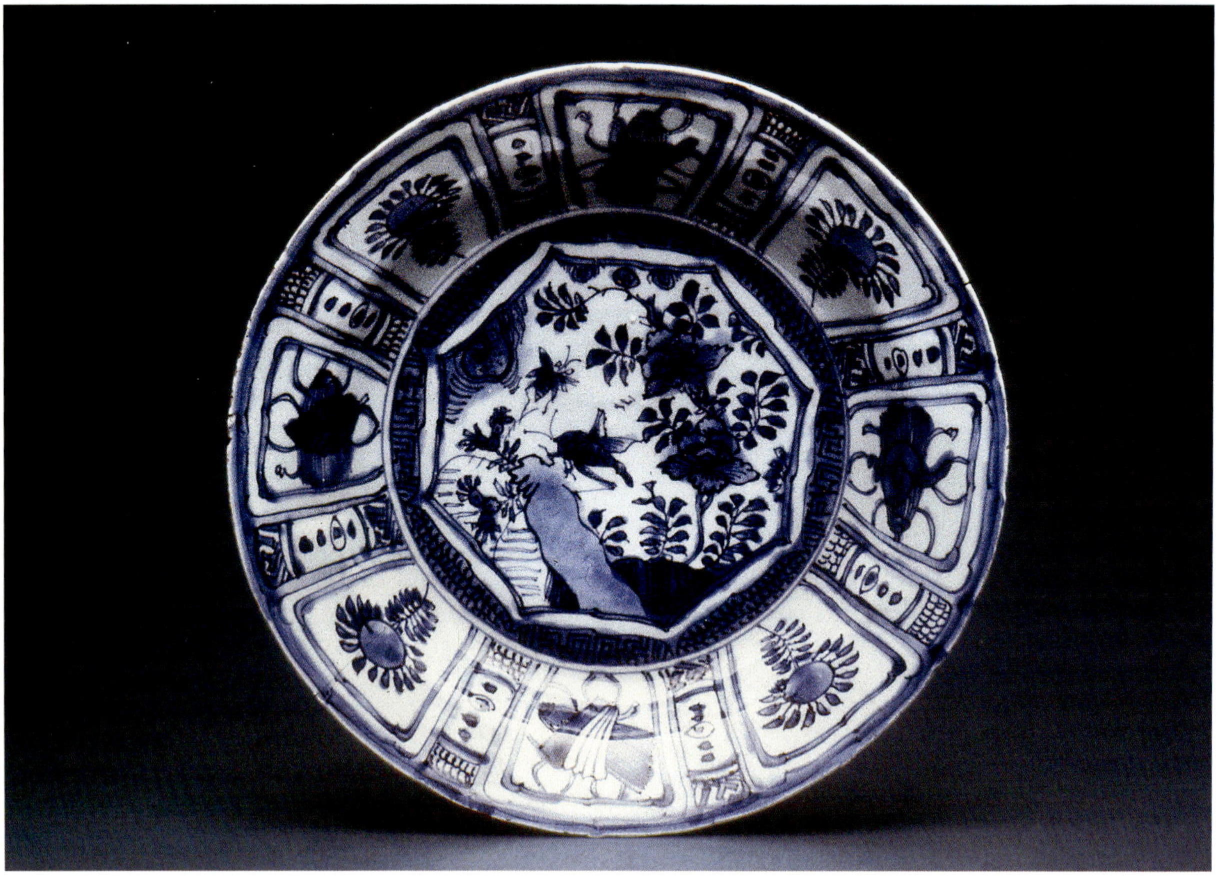

Fig. 16. Porcelain soup-plate. China, Ming Dynasty (1368–1644). Museum of International Folk Art, Santa Fe. Photography by Blair Clark.

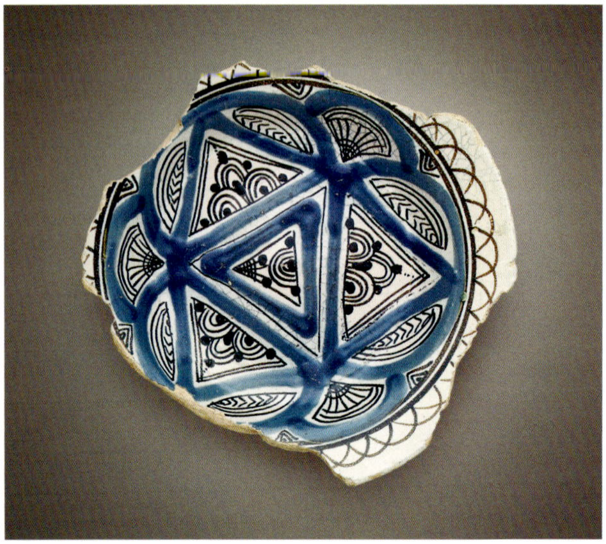

Fig. 17a. Majolica cup. Puebla Polychrome style. Puebla, Mexico, mid-17th century. Excavated at Pecos Pueblo in New Mexico. Museum of Indian Arts and Culture, Museum of New Mexico, Santa Fe (ARC#42488). Gift of Florence Lister. Photography by Blair Clark.

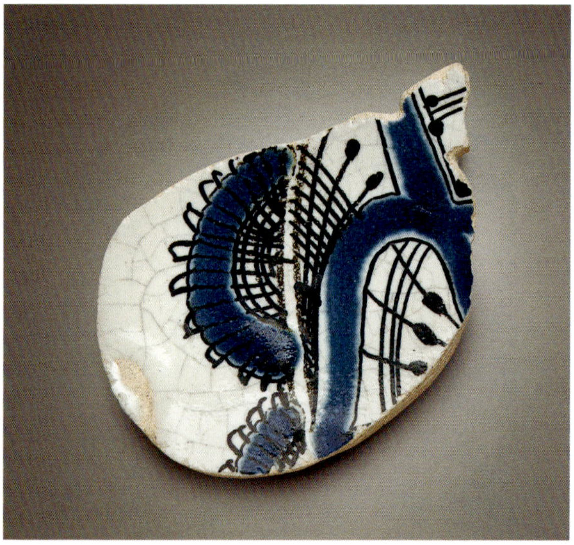

Fig. 17b. Majolica sherd. Puebla Polychrome style. Puebla, Mexico, 1600–1680. Excavated from the Palace of the Governors, Santa Fe. Museum of Indian Arts and Culture, Museum of New Mexico, Santa Fe (ARC#51628). Photography by Blair Clark.

exchange, the European soup-plate form produced in Chinese porcelain (Fig. 16) was adapted in Mexican majolica ceramics.[14] Mexican majolica with scalloped lace patterns, known today as Puebla Polychrome style, was imported by Spanish settlers to New Mexico, where it is found only in archeological sites that predate 1680, including the Palace of the Governors (Figs. 17a and b). Meanwhile, local indigenous groups in New Mexico continued their long tradition of making unglazed pottery. Some native ceramicists adapted both the soup-plate form, previously unknown in New Mexico, and the scalloped lace patterns found on majolica (Fig. 18). Examples have been excavated in the Palace of the Governors and other locations.

All objects excavated from the Palace of the Governors date before the 1680 Pueblo Indian rebellion. All written documents in New Mexico were destroyed in that revolt. However, there is a document in the Archivo General de la Nación in Mexico City that describes the household goods used by the governor of New Mexico and his wife when they lived in the Palace of the Governors in Santa Fe from 1659 to 1662.[15] Governor López de Mendizábal and his literate, Italian-born, Spanish-Irish wife Teresa de Aguilera de Roche are the same people mentioned earlier who were served chocolate every day at 3:00 in the afternoon. When López de Mendizábal's successor arrived in New Mexico, the Mendizábals were arrested and sent to Mexico City to stand trial. At the time of their arrest, their goods were confiscated and inventoried.

According to the documents, Doña Teresa had an elaborate canopy bed, which was erected in her jail cell in Santa Fe and the various cities of northern Mexico as they made the journey south. According to the inventory the bed had "a bedspread from China of embroidered yellow silk" (*colcha de china labrada de seda amarilla*) with "an old bed canopy of silk from China" (*un cielo de cama de seda de china viejísima*) (Fig. 19). She also had a chocolate chest with all of the equipment for making and serving chocolate, including a Chinese porcelain cup, a serving pot of majolica from Puebla, a *molinillo* (whisk), a silver spoon, a silver-mounted coconut cup, lacquered gourd cups (*jícaras*), and a loaf of sugar (all are seen in Fig. 2). Also, Teresa had a small chest described as being of "wood from China" (*una lendela de madera de china*). Whether this means that the chest was made in China or made of wood from China (maybe camphor) is unclear from the document. Doña Teresa also had two fans, probably Asian in origin. Most likely at least some of her long list of elaborate clothing was made from Chinese silks. Governor Mendizábal died in prison during the trial in Mexico City, and all charges against Doña Teresa were dropped. She never returned to New Mexico.

In 1680 the Pueblo Indians of New Mexico staged the most successful native rebellion in North American history. The surviving Spanish settlers fled south to El Paso del Norte (now El Paso, Texas), where they remained for twelve years until a new governor led a reconquest of the area in 1692–1693.

The Eighteenth Century in New Mexico

For the period after the Spanish resettlement of New Mexico in the 1690s, more extensive documentation is available in the form of several hundred extant wills and estate inventories.[16]

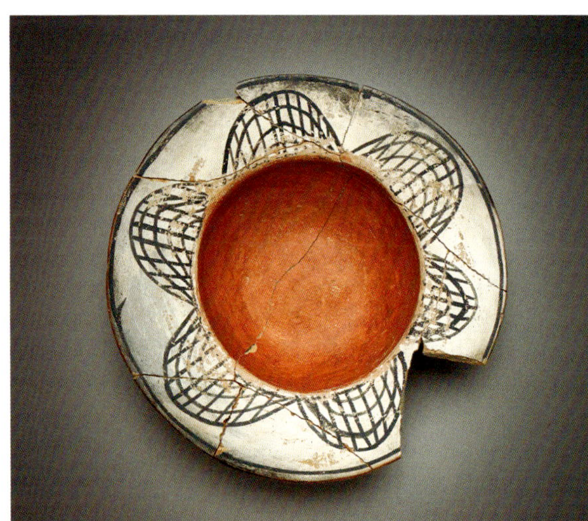

Fig. 18. Earthenware soup-plate. Tewa Indians, Tewa polychrome. Cuyamungue, New Mexico, 17th century. Laboratory of Anthropology, Museum of New Mexico, Santa Fe (1955/11). Photography by Blair Clark.

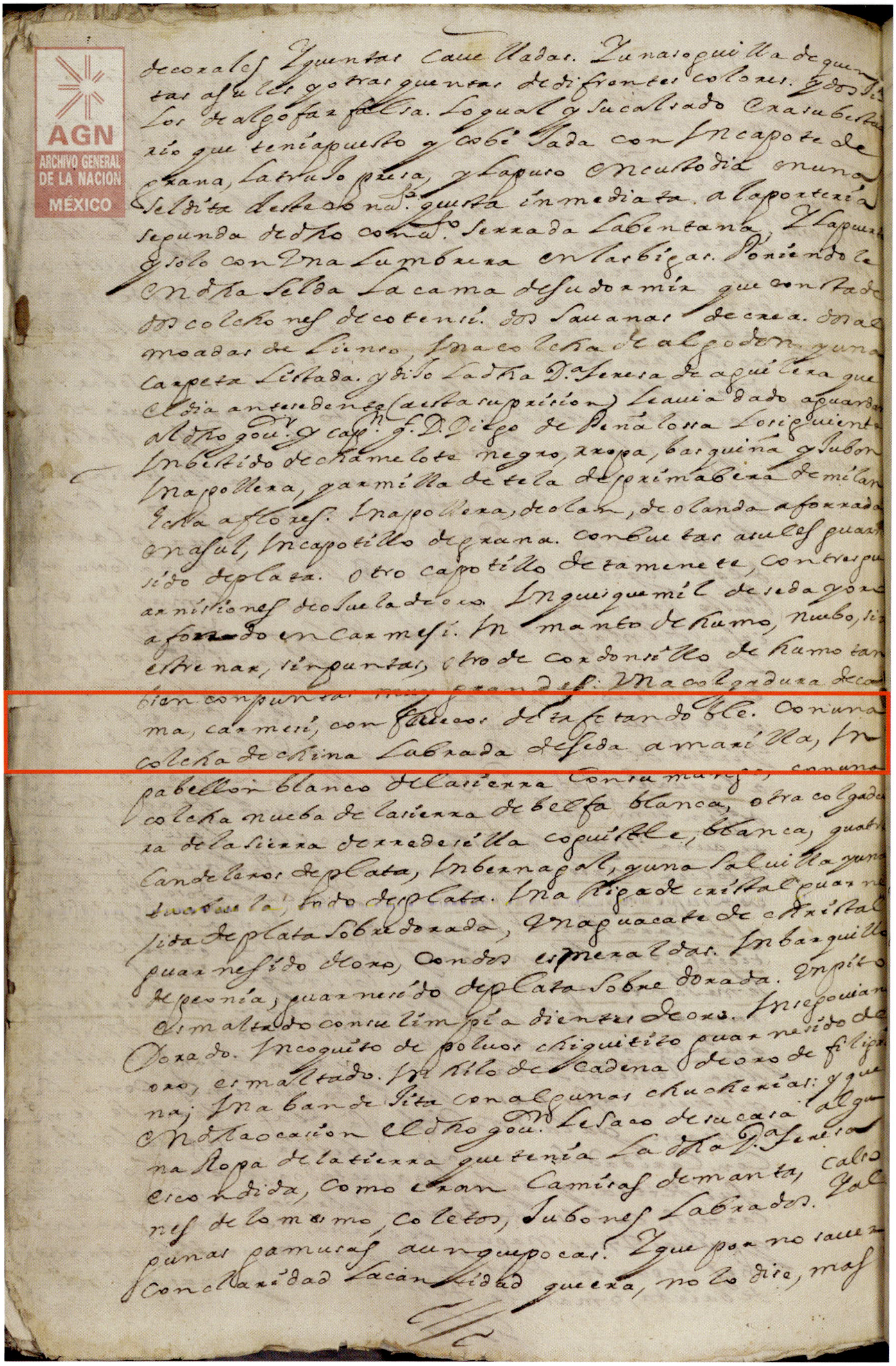

Fig. 19. Pages from inventory of possessions of Doña Teresa de Aguilera de Roche, Santa Fe, 1662. Archivo General de la Nación, Mexico City, Concurso de Peñaloza, vol. I, folios 396v and 397r.

391 2

que tambien saco de las oficina q se lleuo una espada y un
broquel. y lo firmo de su nombre con el d(ic)ho señor
curato y alguacil m(ayo)r. Ante mi. (...) doy fee

fr. Alonso de Losada
comiss(ari)o del S(an)to Off(ici)o

Doña Teresa de
Aguilera i roche

[illegible]

Passo Ante mi
(...) Salv(ado)r de guerra
notario

En la d(ic)ha Villa de Santa fe año mes y dia suso escripto
no(so)tros el Cur(a)do Juez ecl(esiástic)o y comiss(ari)o del S(an)to officio fr. Alonso de
Posada, en compañia del S(eño)r y alguacil m(ayo)r de d(ic)ho S(an)to officio
D(o)n Sal(vado)r manso, y del alferez Fran(cis)co de lion. del maese de campo
P(edr)o Lucero de godoy, y Ante el pres(en)te notario fue a la cassa
y morada, de la contenida D(oñ)a Teresa de aguilera, y roche
y serradas las puertas en conformidad de lo ordenado
y dispuesto por el yll(ustrísi)mo S(eño)r S(an)to y recto tribunal de la inq(uisici)on
hizo enbargo de todos los bienes que en d(ic)ha cassa se
hallaron pertenesientes a la persona de la d(ic)ha D(oñ)a Teresa
de aguilera. que son como se siguen

1 Primeram(en)te se le hallo una cama de granadillo, que
contiene quatro pilares los delanteros de dos quexpos. 2
sinco atrauesaños. sinq(uen)ta y ocho balaustres. treinta y
sinco perillas: chicas y las quatro son grandes. todo como
de palos de granadillo. y ocho tornillos de hierro. nube
palos, y onse tablas. de todo lo qual se compone d(ic)ha

2 Cama. con mas un colchon camero viejo

3 Mas una porselana de china y un jarro chocolatero de
la puebla

4 Mas diez y siete soacales chicos y grandes

5 Mas dos platones y sinco platos de la puebla y una
tasa de lo mismo

6 Mas un sielo de cama de seda de china bie(n) viejo

7 Mas unos chapines colorados

8 Mas dos sauanas de lana

9 Mas tres ases de cotines de la tierra labrados que hasen
cotin y medio

10 Mas una frasquera con dos o tres frascos medianos

11 Mas dos turrupiates. uno con romero y otro de alusema

12 Mas una xeringa y un asador, y cal de ueta

13 Mas un jarro chocolatero de cobre

14 Mas un almires con su mano

15 Mas una bara de tafetan rosado, usado

16 Mas un paño de manos medio labrado de morado

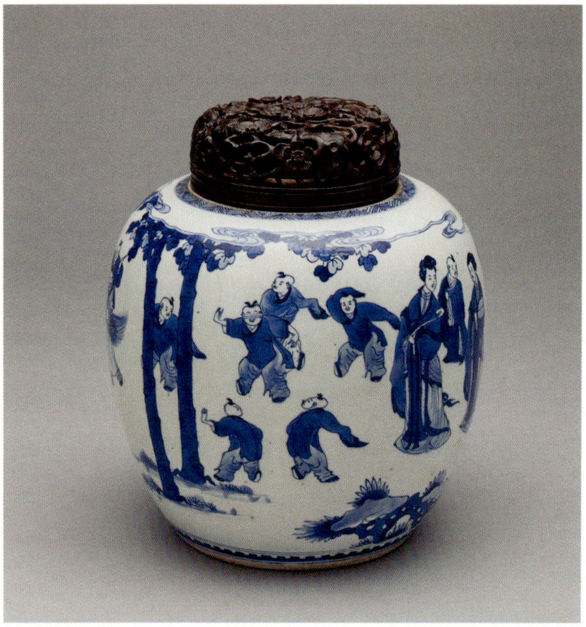

Fig. 20. Porcelain jar. China, Qing Dynasty, Kangxi Period (1662-1722). Denver Art Museum, Walter C. Mead Collection; 1933.11.

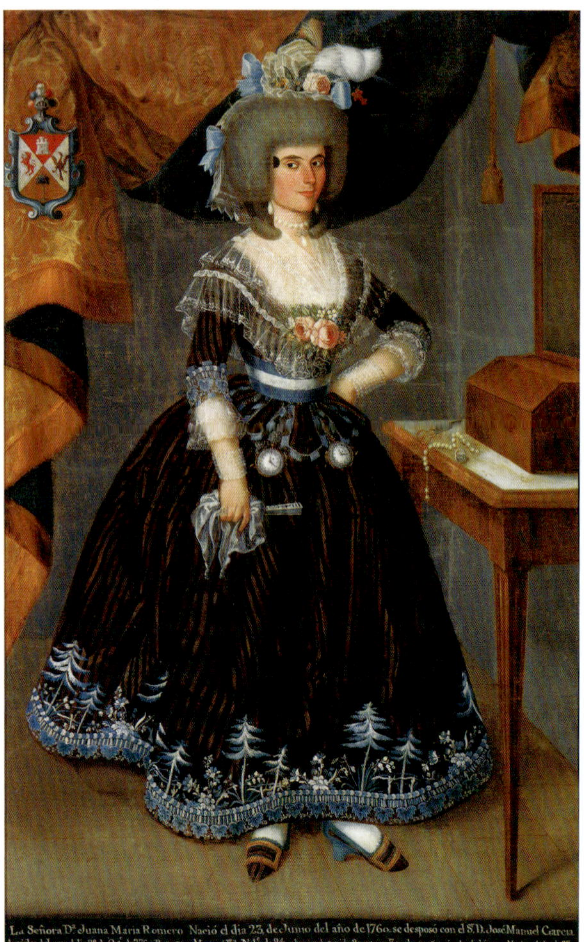

Fig. 21. Ignacio María Barreda, *Portrait of Juana María Romero*. Mexico, 1794. Courtesy of Museo Nacional de Historia, Chapultepec Castle, Mexico City (IHAH).

Although this sampling does not support broad generalizations, it does provide insight into the extent of international trade and the conflation of cultures in daily life. The documents represent a cross section of New Mexicans, from obviously wealthy individuals to much poorer citizens, as well as people of different ethnic backgrounds and professions. Extant wills include those of persons listed in the documents as Spaniards born in Spain, *creoles* (Spaniards born in Mexico), *mestizos* (half Spanish/half Indian), *coyotes* (one-quarter Spanish/three-quarters Indian), and Indians. Men and women are represented, as are blacksmiths, weavers, soldiers, artists, ranchers, farmers, millers, and merchants, among others.

In general, only goods specified in the documents as Asian in origin are mentioned here. However, in a few instances, I note goods likely to have been Asian. Again, since few objects survive from New Mexico and even fewer can be linked to specific persons, descriptions in estate inventories have been matched in the illustrations with extant examples or similar ones seen in paintings and portraits from central Mexico.

Occasionally marriage dowries of both men and women are included with the wills and estate inventories, since the value of those goods was deducted from the heir's inheritance. As a result, the 1721 dowry of Luisa Luján survives with her mother's will, providing the earliest post-Revolt documentary reference to Asian goods in New Mexico.[17] Luisa's dowry included "3 [porcelain] bowls or soup-plates from China" (*tazas calderas de china*) (see Fig. 16) and "1 large vase from China" (*un tibor de china*) (Fig. 20).[18]

In addition, Luisa had clothes of silk brocade and satin, including a jacket and hoop skirt (*pollera*) of embroidered brown brocade with silver-embroidered edging, and a black satin hoop skirt with silver edging, possibly made from imported Asian fabrics. Luisa also had "a new cape of Chinese silk tissue (or lamé) with silver trim" (*una mantellina nueba de tisú de China con sintilla de plata*). Similar examples of clothing and accessories appear in contemporaneous portraits from central Mexico, most likely manufactured of imported

Asian silks (Fig. 21). Luisa seems to have been something of a fashionista; in addition to elegant clothing she also had two hats with plumes (*una montera con plumas*; *un sombrero con plumas*), an extensive jewelry collection, silk stockings, scalloped lace gloves, and thirteen pairs of shoes, some with silver buckles and one pair with high heels.

Intriguing, but vague, references occur in the 1720s through 1740s to items that may or may not be Asian goods, including a mention in the 1727 will of Antonio Vallejos of Santa Fe, which lists "two large boxes from a foreign country, trimmed with iron."[19] These may have been similar to large trunks made in the Philippines, Malaysia, and China that survive in private collections and museums in Mexico.[20] The 1733 will of Francisco de Jesús y Espejo from Albuquerque refers to three women who owe him money for "the chinaware they went to buy."[21] Another indirect reference occurs in the will of José de Reano Tagle, who died in Santa Fe in 1743. A native of the province of Santander in northern Spain, Reano Tagle immigrated to New Mexico, where he became a successful trader.[22] He lists in his will "the goods and merchandise of Castille, China, and from this land (New Mexico) which may be found in the chests, and is set apart, the whole belonging to his wife for her expenses."[23] Unfortunately, the contents of the chests were not itemized in the estate inventory.

Drawn up in 1744, the estate inventory of Margarita Martín of the village of Rio Arriba near Santa Cruz, north of Santa Fe, lists "six medium-sized plates of Chinese porcelain" valued at 3 pesos each for a total of 18 pesos.[24] It is interesting to compare this to the value of other objects in her inventory: the six plates at 18 pesos are more valuable than her high wooden four-poster bed, valued at 10 pesos, or her painted chest from Michoacán (west Mexico) with lock and key, valued at 12 pesos. However, her "harp for playing" was still more valuable, at 40 pesos. She also had a "hoop skirt (*pollera*) of purple Piquin (Peking) cloth" and a skirt of "red Chinese silk" (Fig. 22).

Antonio Durán de Armijo had arrived in Santa Fe as a child with his brothers and their widowed mother in 1695.[25] Listed in the muster roll

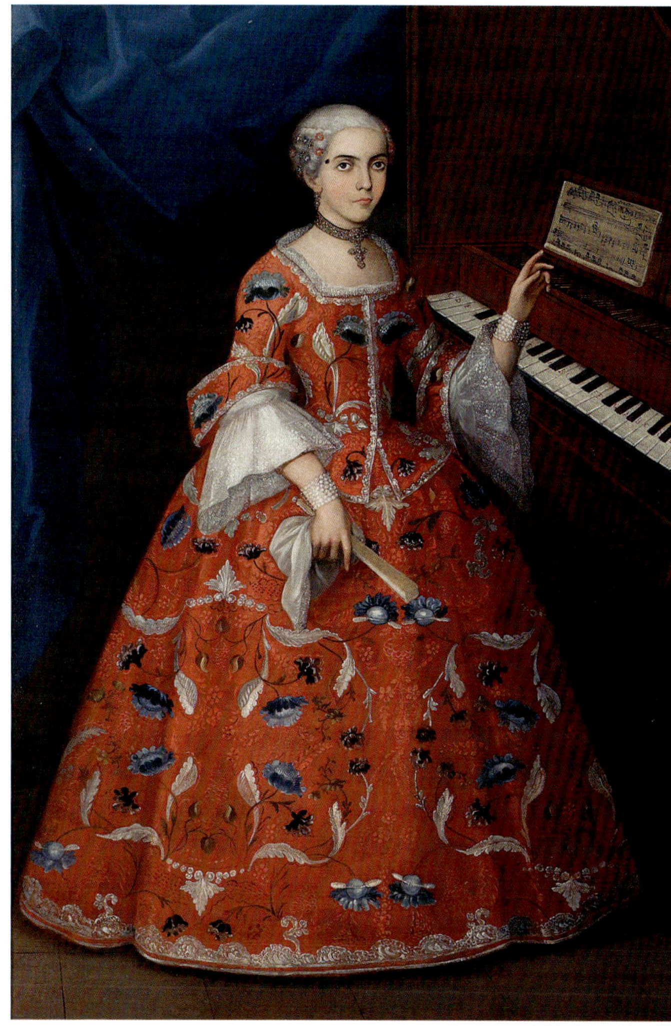

Fig. 22. Anonymous, *Woman with a Harpsichord*. Mexico, mid-18th century. Denver Art Museum, Collection of Frederick and Jan Mayer; 3.2007.

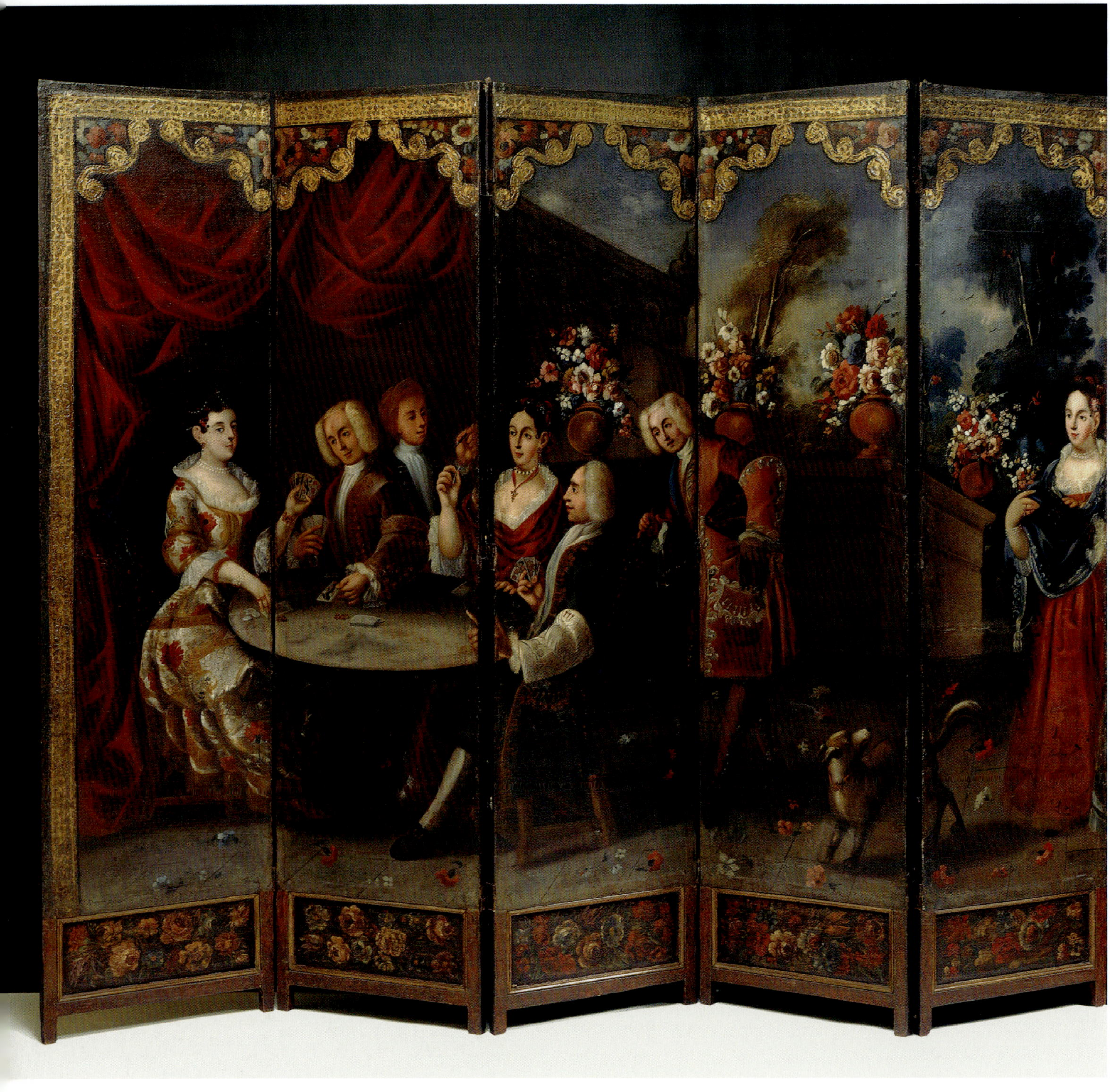

Fig. 23. Anonymous, *Garden Party on the Terrace of a Country Home*. Mexico, 1720–1730. Oil on canvas folding screen. Denver Art Museum, Gift of Frederick and Jan Mayer; 2009.759. Clothing and stockings seen here are similar to those described in New Mexican inventories.

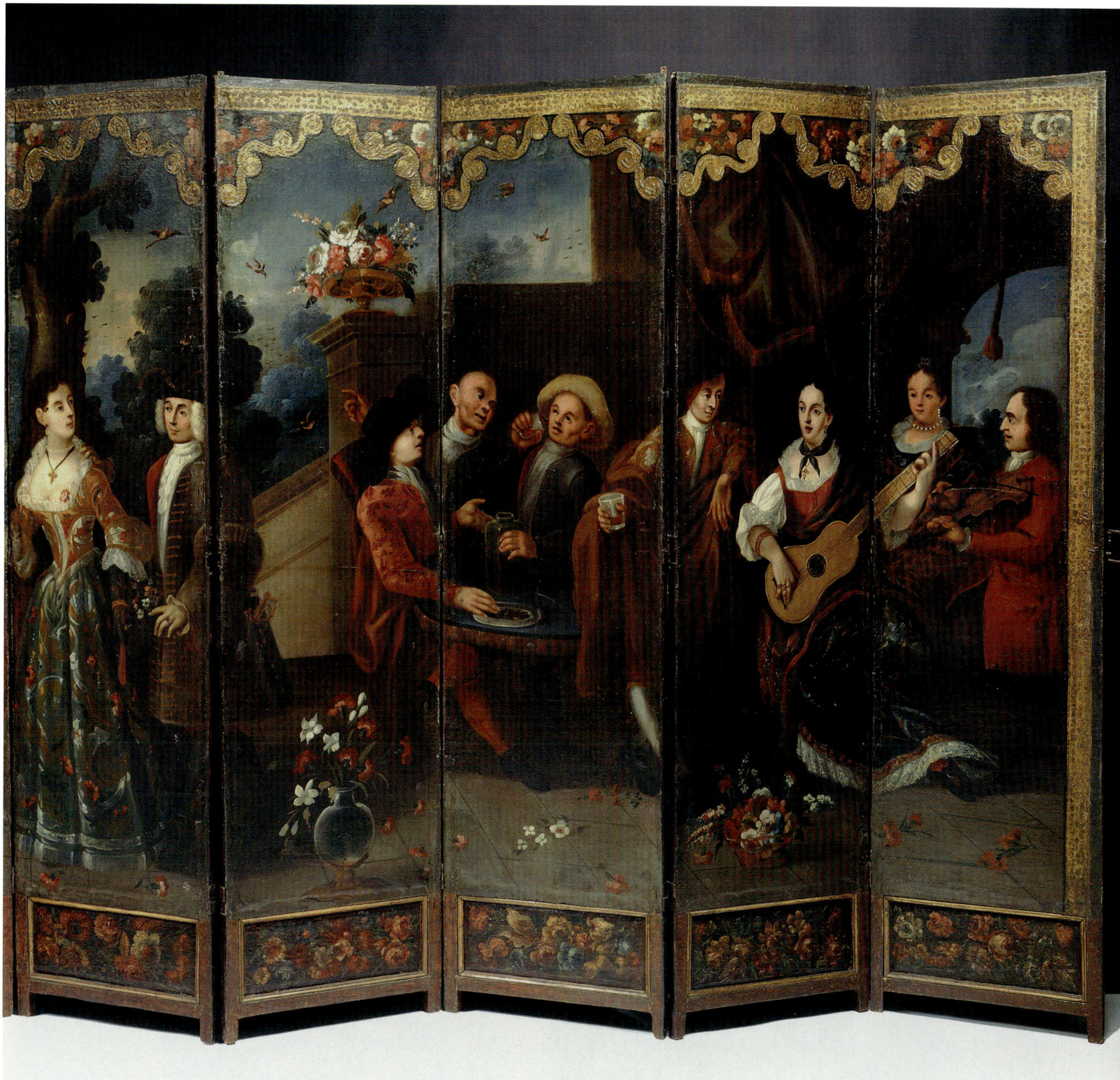

as *mestizos,* the family gave Zacatecas, Mexico, as their place of birth. Antonio became a blacksmith in Taos. When he was killed by Plains Indians in 1748, his possessions—including a two-story house of eight rooms with a portal and a balcony—were left to his only child, a minor daughter named María Gertrudes.[26] Among the goods Antonio left were two handle-less cups (*pozuelos*) and two small bowls (*tazas*) "from China."[27] Among various men's and women's clothes of silk, brocade, and linen, he also left her "10 *varas* (Spanish yards) of red Chinese silk" (*capichola de china encarmesí*) and "6 *varas* of ribbon from China woven with gold and silver" (*listón de china atizuado con oro y plata*).

In 1747, Luis García Noriega of San Antonio near Albuquerque owned two handle-less cups (*pozuelos*) of Chinese porcelain.[28] In 1749, Lugarda Quintana of Santa Cruz—daughter of the well-known New Mexican poet and musician Miguel Quintana—owned three handle-less cups (*pozuelos*), "two fine and one ordinary," implying that two were porcelain and one was majolica.[29] In 1771, Mónica Tomasa Martín of Taos owned three cups from China.[30]

When Juan Montes Vigil of Santa Fe died in 1762, he stated in his will that he owned nine (porcelain) plates from China (*platos de china*), five soup-plates (*tazas calderas*), and eight handle-less cups (*pozuelos de china*).[31] The inventory of his goods lists "5 metal plates from China, well treated, which weighed 4 pounds, valued at 32 pesos." Later in the inventory they are described as of "yellow metal," probably brass. The most intriguing references in Montes Vigil's will, however, appear in the inventory of his wife's (Nicolasa Luján's) clothing. The long list of elegant clothing (similar to some of the clothing in Figure 23) includes a green-striped dress, silk petticoat, and jacket of "Persian cloth" (*persiana*); a yellow silk short cape embroidered with turquoise, silver, and silk thread; and "an old short cape of black velvet from China" (*dengue de terziopelo negro viejo de china*). But most surprising of all, we find "one fine kimono" (*quimono fino*). Whether this was an actual kimono imported from Japan, or an imitation made in Mexico or New Mexico, or merely a name applied to some sort of robe or housecoat is unclear. In any case, it shows influence from Asia, even if merely in the language. But, as we will see, it is not the only "kimono" in New Mexico in the eighteenth century.[32]

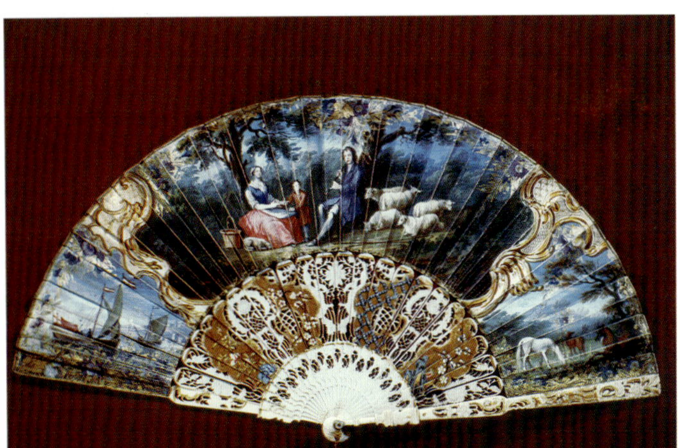

Fig. 24. Fan. China and Spain, 18th century. Paint, ivory, paper. Museo de Artes Decorativas, Madrid, Spain. Photography by Donna Pierce.

In the same year, 1762, Juana Luján died. Her primary residence was a house of twenty-four rooms on a ranch northwest of Santa Fe.[33] In addition Juana owned a farm with a house of two rooms, a garden, and planting lands at the Spanish town of Santa Cruz de la Cañada, northeast of Santa Fe. Ownership of townhouses and country estates by a single individual is a continuation of a pattern found in Spain and Mexico and is seen throughout the historical period in New Mexico. Among many other items, Juana owned a small bottle (*una botijita de china*), one plate, two bowls, and three cups, all of Chinese porcelain. Included in her inventory is a list of silk and satin clothing, some possibly Asian in origin, and accessories including "two painted ivory fans from China" (*dos abanicos pintados de china de marfil*) (Fig. 24).

When María Gertrudes Armijo died in Taos in 1776, the effects of her estate included a dozen Chinese porcelain cups and six bowls (*una dozena de pozuelos de china a 6p.; media dozena de tazas de china a 4 p.*).[34] Among the numerous items of clothing belonging to María Gertrudes were "two kimonos" (*dos quimones*), again possibly from Asia (Fig. 25).

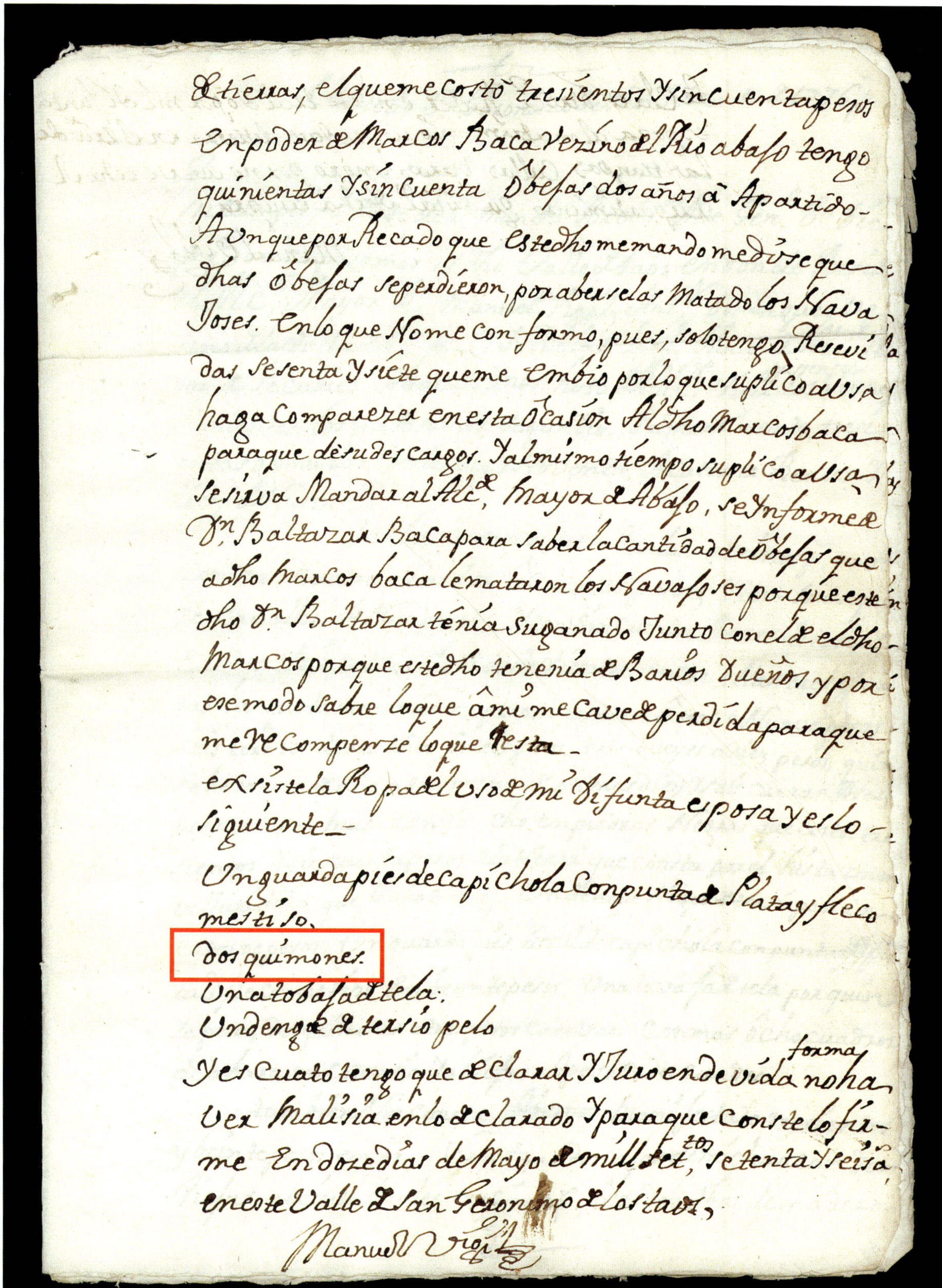

de tierras, el que me costó tresientos y sincuenta pesos
En poder de Marcos Baca vezino del Río abaxo tengo
quinientas y sincuenta obejas dos años a Apartido-
Aunque por Recado que este dho me mandó me dise que
dhas obejas se perdieron, por aberselas matado los Nava
Joses. En lo que No me conformo, pues, solo tengo Resevi
das sesenta y siete que me embió por lo que suplico a V.S.a
haga comparezer en esta ocasión Al dho Marcos baca
para que dé sus descargos. Y al mismo tiempo suplico a V.S.a
se sirva Mandar al Alcde Mayor de Abaxo, se ynforme de
Dn Baltazar Baca para saber la cantidad de obejas que
a dho Marcos baca le mataron los Navajoses porque este
dho Dn Baltazar tenía su ganado Junto con el de el dho
Marcos porque este dho tenería de Barios dueños y por
ese modo sabre lo que a mí me cave de perdida para que
me se compense lo que resta_
existe la Ropa del uso de mi difunta esposa y es lo
siguiente_
Un guardapiés de capichola con puntas de Plata y fleco
mestiso.
dos quimones.
Una tobasa de tela.
Un dengue de tersio pelo
Y es cuanto tengo que declarar y Juro en de vida forma no ha
ver malisia en lo declarado y para que conste lo fir-
me En doze días de Mayo de mill setzos setenta y seis a
en este Valle de San Geronimo de los taos,
Manuel Vigil

Fig. 25. Detail from estate inventory of María Gertrudes Armijo, Taos, 1776 (SANM I: 48, document 2, page 2 recto). Courtesy New Mexico State Records Center and Archives, Santa Fe.

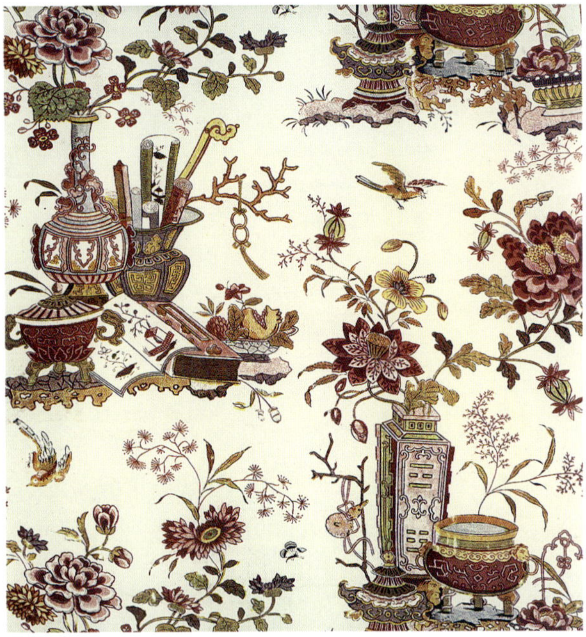

Fig. 26. Sample of East Indian chintz (*indianilla*). India, c. 1780. Block-printed cotton. From Straeten, *Toiles de Jouy*, 52, fig. 26.

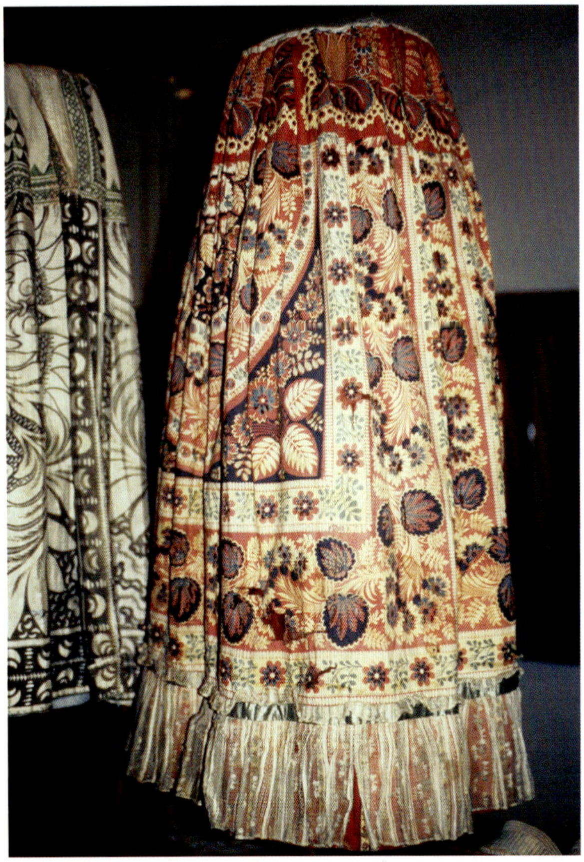

Fig. 27. Skirts made from East Indian chintz (*indianilla*). Mexico, mid-18th century. Museo José Luis Bello y González, Puebla, Mexico. Photography by Donna Pierce.

Manuel Montes Vigil of Abiquiu had an extensive estate when he died in 1780, including five small plates (*platos de china chico*) and a dozen cups of Chinese porcelain, six pieces of "Chinese ribbon," and "two mirrors from Canton."[35] In addition, the dowry of his wife (María Magdalena Valdéz) had included two kimonos (*dos Quimones*), which were still on hand. This brings us to a total of five kimonos mentioned in the documents. Vigil also had a bedspread as well as several types of bolt cloth of East Indian chintz (*7½ v. indianilla de colores fina; 6 de dicha carmina fina; 6 v. yndianilla azul;* 7½ yards of fine multicolored chintz; 6 of same, red; 6 y. of blue chintz). The word "indianilla" is the same word used in Mexico to describe printed cotton fabrics with large floral motifs imported from India, known in English as chintz (Fig. 26). These popular imports were imitated in the fabric workshops of Europe and Mexico. The material was a common fabric for women's skirts and men's housecoats in the colonial era, as seen in a few surviving examples (Fig. 27) and in *casta* paintings (Figs. 28–29). Whether the examples documented in New Mexico were truly imports from Asia or imitation cloth from Mexican textile workshops is unknown. What we do know from documentary references from the colonial period, nineteenth-century photographs, and twentieth-century folklore is that bolt chintz was used as wainscoting around the lower walls of adobe homes, as seen in a photo of an interior of a home at Isleta Indian Pueblo in the late nineteenth century (Fig. 30). It was also used for items of clothing in New Mexico. For example, María de Sena of Santa Fe had a new skirt of *indianilla* (*unas naguas de yndiania nuevas*) when her husband, Juan Antonio Fernández, died in 1784.[36]

In 1789, José Maldonado, paymaster and second lieutenant at the garrison of Santa Fe, left a surprisingly extensive list of clothing as well as "one pair of French cloth stockings" and "two pair of Chinese embroidered silk stockings" (Fig. 31).[37] In fact, most of the wills and inventories itemized here list silk stockings owned by both men and women (see Fig. 23). To cite some of the more interesting references, Manuel Montes

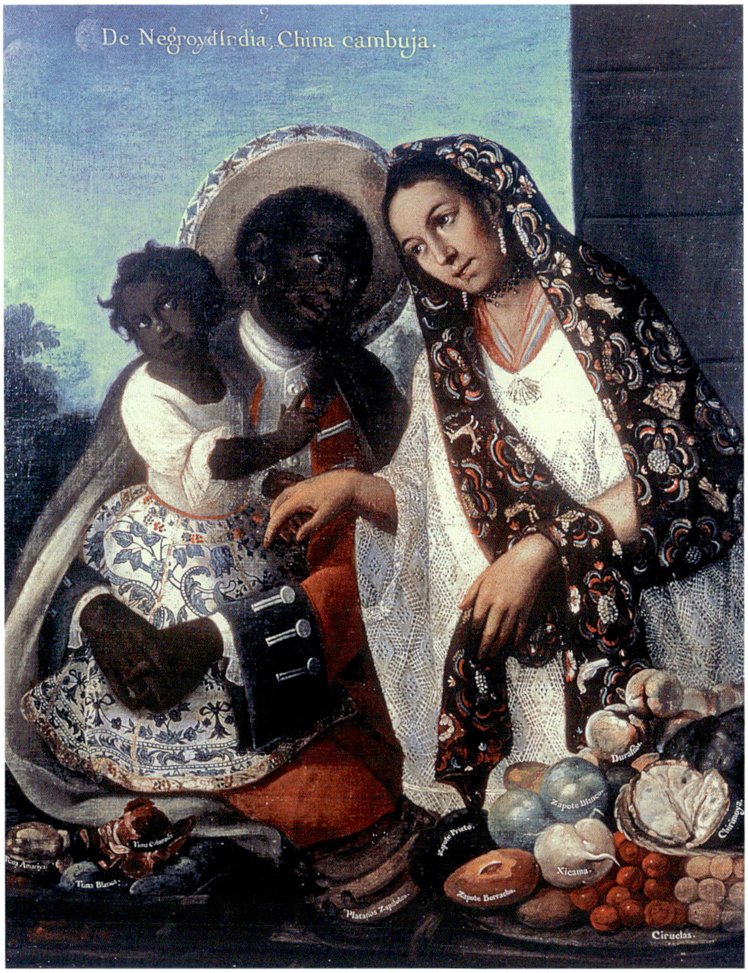

Fig. 28. Miguel Cabrera, *De Negro y India, China Cambuja*. Mexico, 1763. Museo de América, Madrid.

Fig. 29. José de Alcíbar, *From Spaniard and Black, Mulatto*. Mexico, c. 1760. Denver Art Museum: Collection of Frederick and Jan Mayer. © James Milmoe.

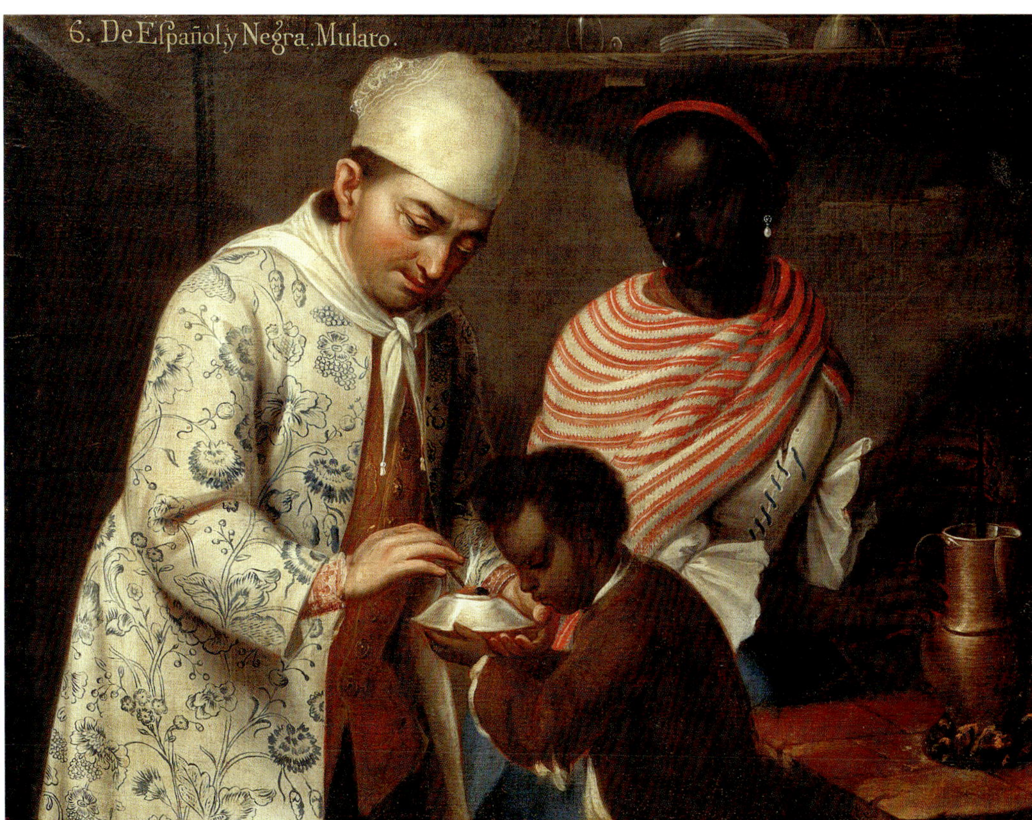

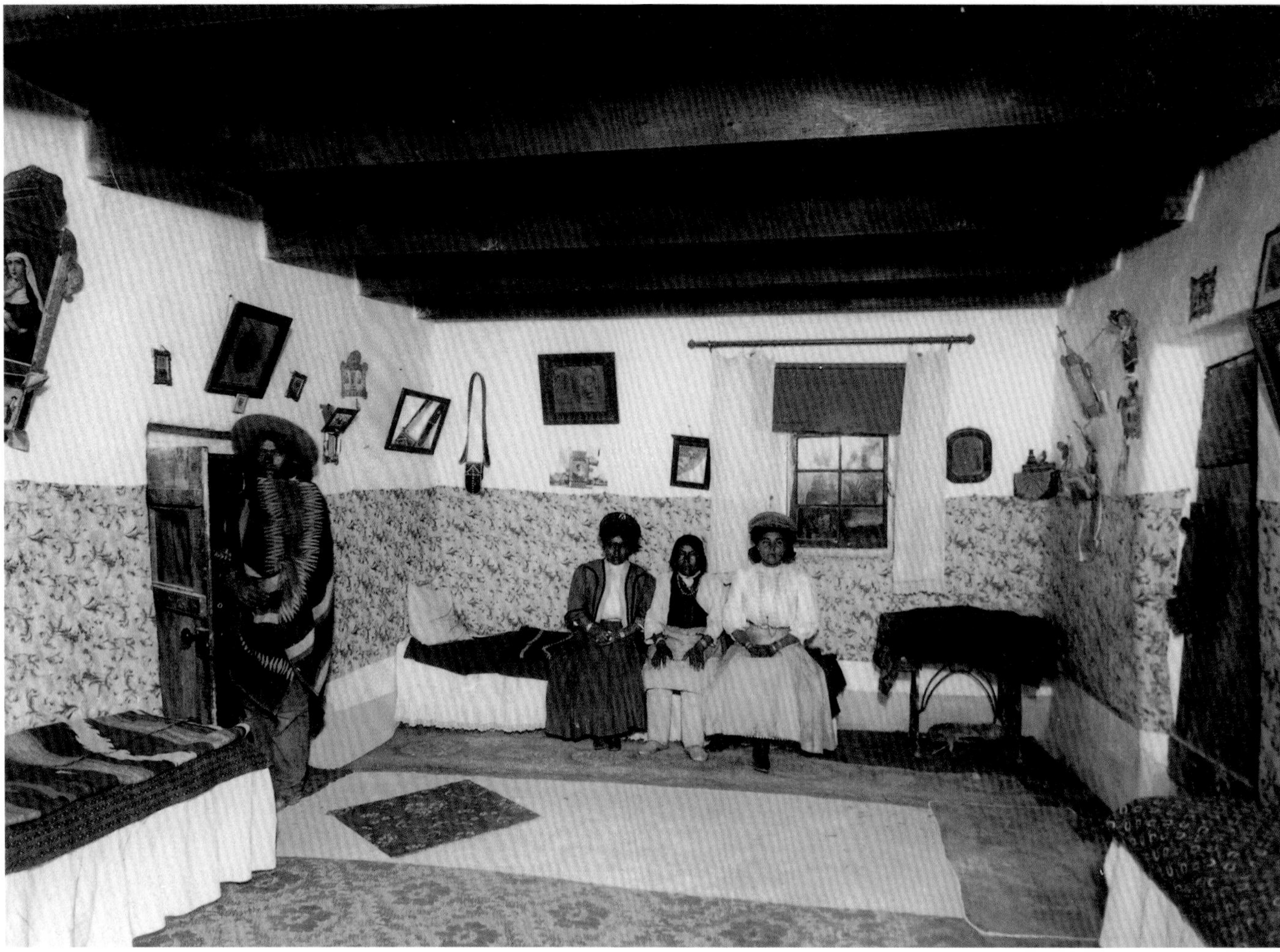

Fig. 30. Interior (showing imported chintz wainscoting), Governor Lente's house, Isleta Indian Pueblo, New Mexico. Late-19th century. Photo courtesy Museum of New Mexico Photo Archives.

Vigil of Abiquiu owned "blue silk stockings with fancy embroidery" and Mónica Tomasa Martín of Taos had "blue silk stockings embroidered with silver lace."[38] Luis Garcia Noriega of San Antonio near Albuquerque in 1747 had "a pair of black silk stockings embroidered with satin stitch valued at 25 pesos," one of the more costly items in his estate.[39] José de Reano Tagle of Santa Fe in 1743 had a pair of "embroidered silk stockings," and Antonio Tafoya Altamirano of Santa Cruz in 1744 had a pair of yellow silk stockings.[40] Such silk stockings were manufactured in China and in Europe. As Lt. Maldonado's inventory makes clear, stockings in New Mexico could have come from either place.

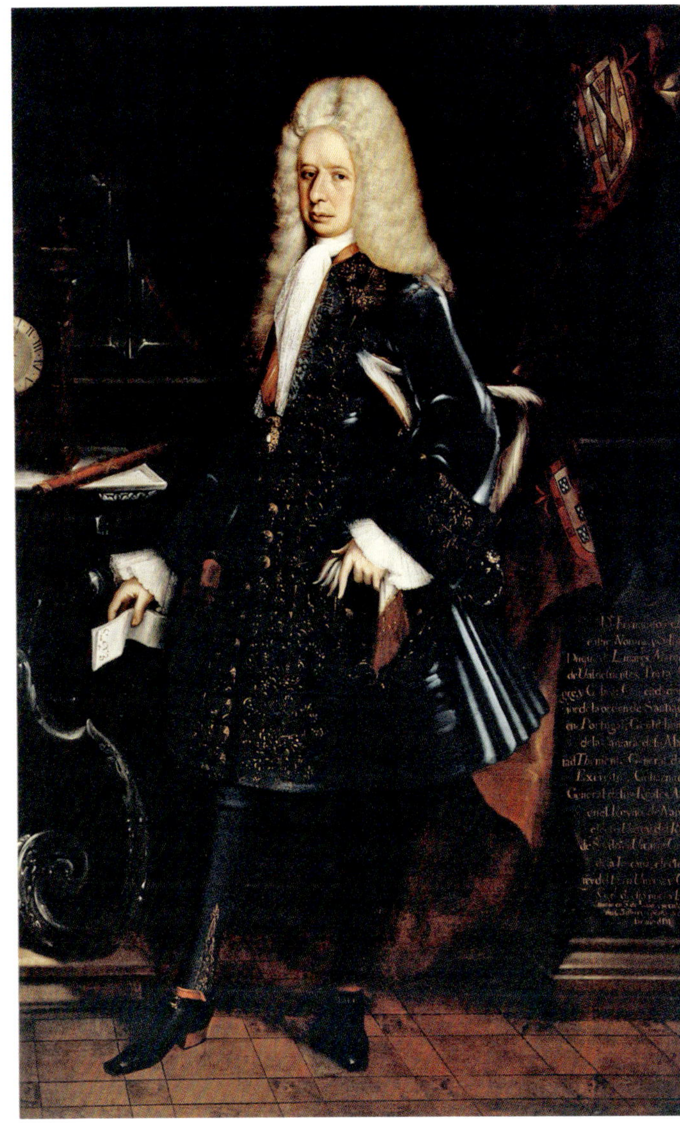

Fig. 31. Juan Rodríguez Juárez, *Portrait of the Viceroy, Duke of Linares*. Mexico, 1711. Oil on canvas. Museo Nacional de Arte, Mexico City. Note the embroidered stockings.

Merchants in New Mexico

And finally, near the end of the colonial period, Captain Manuel Delgado died in 1815 at the age of 76. Delgado had been born in Pachuca, Mexico in 1739.[41] After enlisting in the military, he was stationed at a presidio near El Paso and later at the Presidio of Santa Fe (in the Palace of the Governors), where he was second in command when he married Josefa García de Noriega in 1790. The Delgados had at least five children by the time Josefa died in 1811. In 1814, at seventy-five, he married Ana María Baca and had two more children. In addition to being a military captain, Delgado was a trader on the Camino Real to Chihuahua and Mexico City. At the time of his death he owned a house and mercantile store in downtown Santa Fe and five outlying ranches, as well as other properties and mills.

After he died intestate, the contents of Delgado's properties were inventoried and divided among his heirs.[42] The inventory begins with what must have been his store (Fig. 32a). The first items listed are bolt fabrics, with the very first being "29¾ *varas* of *yndianilla* valued at 2 pesos a *vara*," followed by "20 *varas* of the same, narrow at 9½ *reales*" (*20 Ytem angosta a 9½ r.*). These references are followed by "19 *varas* of the same from Barcelona at 13 *reales*" (*19 Ytem de Barcelona a 13 r.*), indicating that the printed calico from Barcelona, which began to be exported legally to Mexico

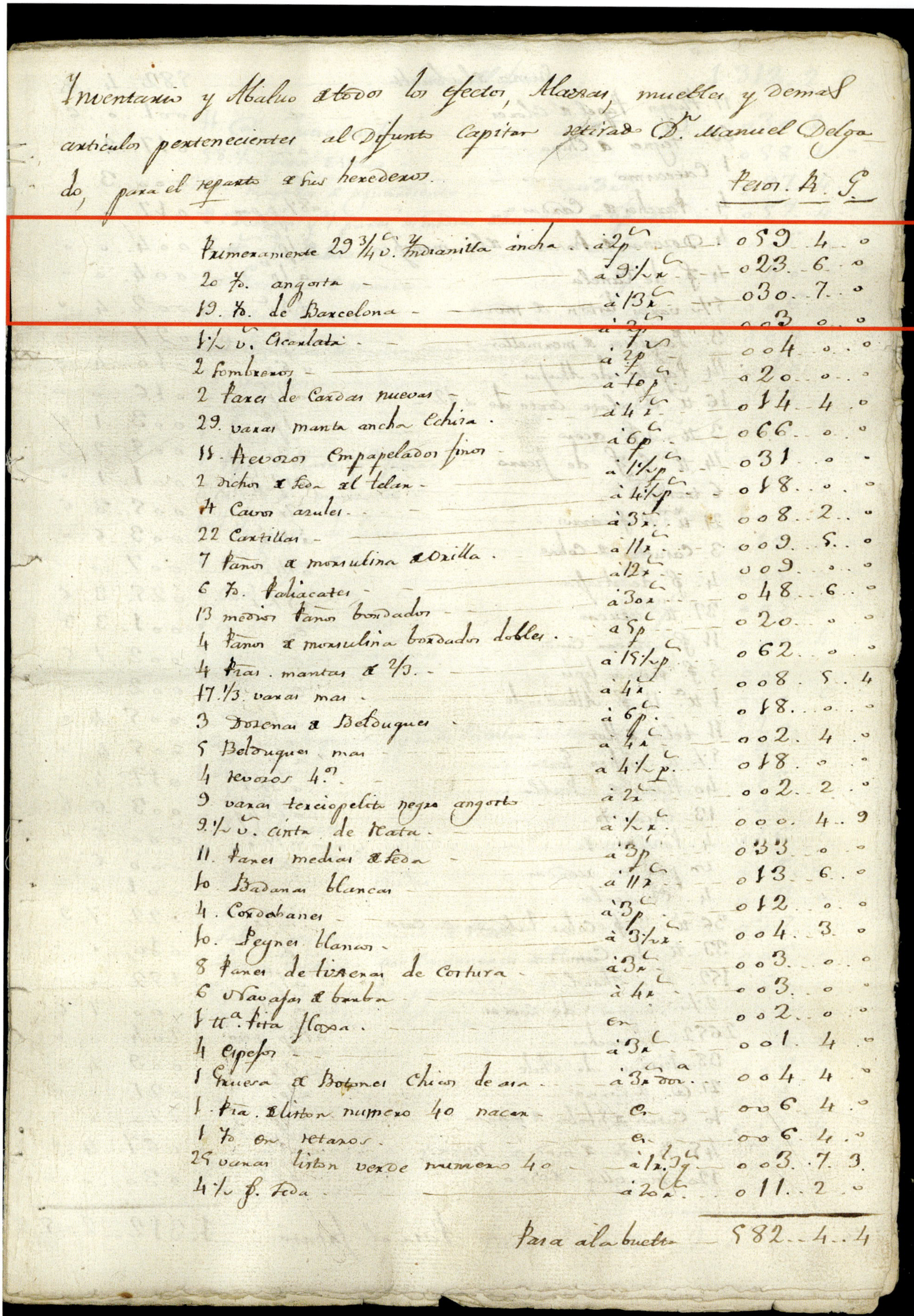

Inventario y Avaluo de todos los efectos, Marcas, muebles y demas articulos pertenecientes al Difunto Capitan retirado D.n Manuel Delgado, para el reparto de sus herederos.

		Pesos. R. G.
Primeramente 29 3/4 v. Indianilla ancha	à 2p	059. 4. 0
20 v. angosta	à 9 1/2 r	023. 6. 0
19. v. de Barcelona	à 13 r	030. 7. 0
1 1/2 v. Escarlata	à 2p	003. 0. 0
2 Sombreros	à 2p	004. 0. 0
2 pares de Cardas nuevas	à 10p	020. 0. 0
29. varas manta ancha Echiza	à 4r	014. 4. 0
11. Rebozos Empapelados finos	à 6p	066. 0. 0
2 dichos de Seda del telar	à 15 1/2 p	031. 0. 0
4 Cavos azules	à 4 1/2 p	018. 0. 0
22 Castillas	à 3r	008. 2. 0
7 paños de muselina de orilla	à 11r	009. 5. 0
6 v. Paliacates	à 12r	009. 0. 0
13 medios paños bordados	à 30r	048. 6. 0
4 paños de muselina bordados dobles	à 5p	020. 0. 0
4 pzas. mantas de 2/3	à 15 1/2 p	062. 0. 0
17 1/3 varas mas	à 4r	008. 5. 4
3 Docenas de Beldoques	à 6p	018. 0. 0
5 Beldoques mas	à 4r	002. 4. 0
4 rebozos 4os	à 4 1/2 p	018. 0. 0
9 varas terciopelito negro angosto	à 2r	002. 2. 0
9 1/2 v. cinta de plata	à 1/2 r	000. 4. 9
11. pares medias de seda	à 3p	033. 0. 0
10 Badanas blancas	à 11r	013. 6. 0
4. Cordobanes	à 3p	012. 0. 0
10. Peynes blancos	à 3 1/2 r	004. 3. 0
8 pares de tixeras de Costura	à 3r	003. 0. 0
6 Navajas de barba	à 4r	003. 0. 0
1 lb.a pita floxa	en	002. 0. 0
4 Espejos	à 3r	001. 4. 0
1 Gruesa de Botones chicos de ara	à 3r docena	004. 4. 0
1. pza. de liston numero 40 nacar	en	006. 4. 0
1 lb. en retazos	en	006. 4. 0
25 varas liston verde numero 40	à 1 1/2 g	003. 7. 3
4 1/2 lb. seda	à 20r	011. 2. 0
Para a la buelta		582. 4. 4

Fig. 32a. Page from the estate inventory of Captain Manuel Delgado, Santa Fe, 1815 (SANM I: 252, page 3 recto). Courtesy New Mexico State Records Center and Archives, Santa Fe.

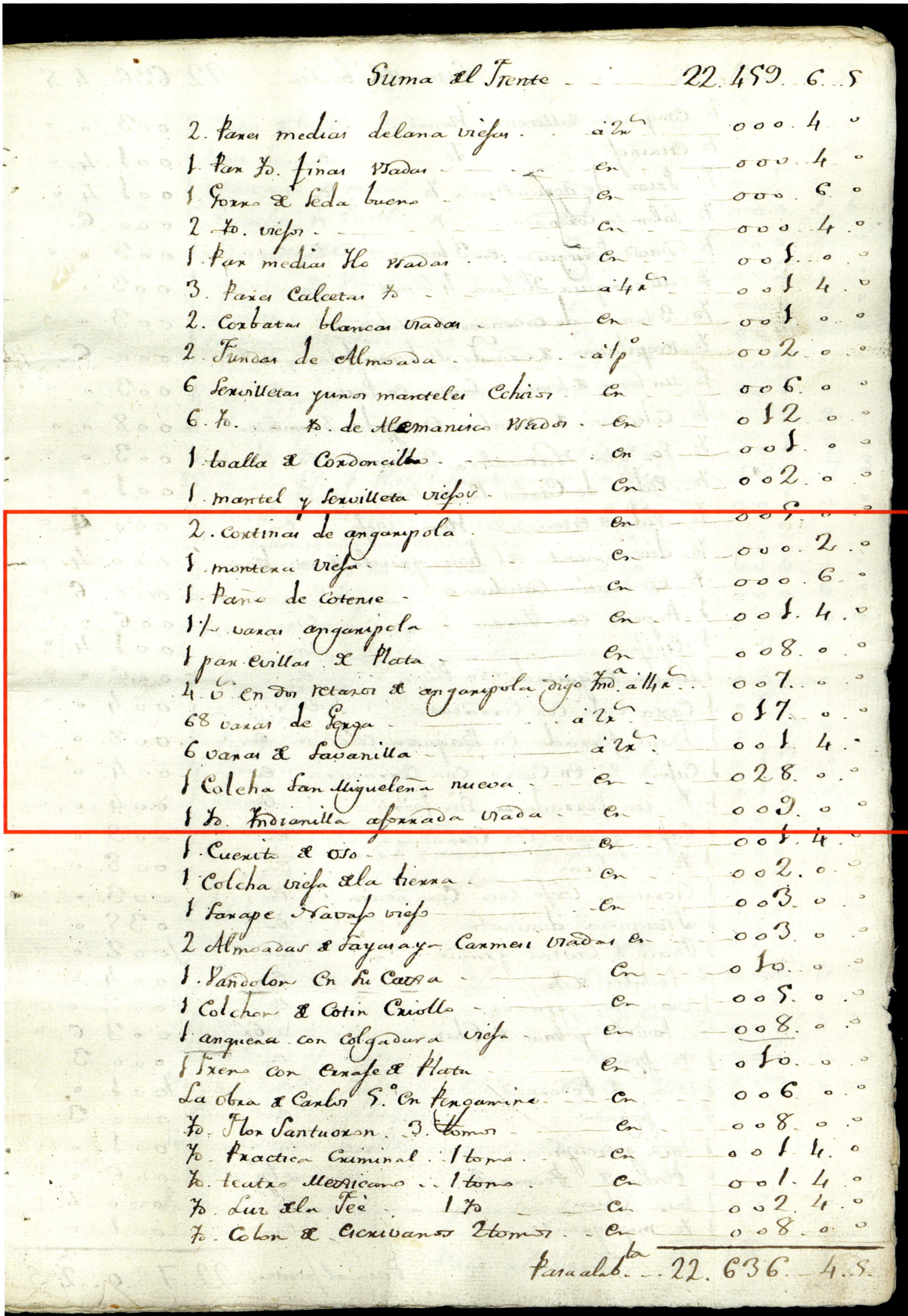

Suma del Frente		22.459. 6. 5
2. Pares medias de lana viejas	à 2rs	000. 4. 0
1 Par Id. finas usadas	en	000. 4. 0
1 Gorro de seda bueno	en	000. 6. 0
2 Id. viejos	en	000. 4. 0
1 Par medias Ho usadas	en	001. 0. 0
3. Pares Calcetas Id	à 4rs	001. 4. 0
2. Corbatas blancas usadas	en	001. 0. 0
2 Fundas de Almoada	à 1p°	002. 0. 0
6 Servilletas y unos manteles Echizos	en	006. 0. 0
6. Id. Id. de Alemanisco usados	en	012. 0. 0
1 toalla de Cordoncillo	en	001. 0. 0
1 mantel y servilleta viejos	en	002. 0. 0
2. Cortinas de anganripola	en	005. 0. 0
1 montera vieja	en	000. 2. 0
1 Paño de Cotense	en	000. 6. 0
1½ varas anganripola	en	001. 4. 0
1 par evillas de Plata	en	008. 0. 0
4 ó en dos retazos de anganripola digo 7ª	à 4rs	007. 0. 0
68 varas de Xerga	à 2rs	017. 0. 0
6 varas de Sabanilla	à 2rs	001. 4. 0
1 Colcha San Miguelena nueva	en	028. 0. 0
1 Id. Indianilla aforrada usada	en	009. 0. 0
1 Cuerito de oso	en	001. 4. 0
1 Colcha vieja de la tierra	en	002. 0. 0
1 Sarape Navajo viejo	en	003. 0. 0
2 Almoadas de Sayasaya Carmesí usadas	en	003. 0. 0
1 Vandolon en su Caxa	en	010. 0. 0
1 Colchon de Cotin Criollo	en	005. 0. 0
1 anquera con Colgadura vieja	en	008. 0. 0
1 Freno con Enfrase de Plata	en	010. 0. 0
La obra de Carlos 5° en Pergamino	en	006. 0. 0
Id. Flor Santuoron. 3. tomos	en	008. 0. 0
Id. Practica Criminal. 1 tomo	en	001. 4. 0
Id. teatro Mexicano .. 1 tomo	en	001. 4. 0
Id. Luz de la Fee 1 Id	en	002. 4. 0
Id. Colon de Escrivanos 2 tomos	en	008. 0. 0
Para ala b.ta		22.636. 4. 5.

Fig. 32b. Page from the estate inventory of Captain Manuel Delgado, Santa Fe, 1815 (SANM I: 252, page 7 recto). Courtesy New Mexico State Records Center and Archives, Santa Fe.

after 1789,[43] had reached New Mexico but was valued less than the wide East Indian version. Also listed among the goods in the store are a total of ninety-five "combs from China" (*peynes de China*), probably ivory combs such as the one excavated at the Palace of the Governors and dating from a century earlier.

Distributed among Delgado's various houses in town and on his country estates were thirteen dress suits of velvet, silk, and cashmere as well as a "jacket and waistcoat of *yndianilla*" (see Fig. 29). Delgado also owned a bedspread of lined *indianilla* (Fig. 32b). In addition to the various assorted items of the large floral-printed *indianilla* imported from eastern India, Delgado also had two wainscotings (*rodestrados*)—one 16 *varas* long by 4 *varas* wide—and two curtains made of calico, the machine-printed cotton with small floral designs, made in Europe and distinguished in the documents by the word "*angaripola*." One item reads "4 *varas* in two pieces of calico, rather (I mean), *indianilla*" (*4 varas en 2 retazos de angaripola, digo Ind.a*), making it clear the appraiser is differentiating between the two types of printed cotton (Fig. 32b). Among his personal effects, Delgado had several pairs of silk stockings that may have been Asian in origin. He also owned two pillows of red Chinese silk and six cups and bowls of Chinese porcelain.

Delgado was one of many traders on the Camino Real. In the seventeenth century, most governors of New Mexico made their fortunes cornering the lucrative business and, like Mendizábal, were accused by their successors of abuse of power and forced to endure an inquiry in Mexico City at the end of their tenure.[44] Private traders, such as Reano Tagle and Delgado, existed as well. Merchants profited from both the local New Mexican goods they shipped south (such as hides, sheep, woolen goods, and piñon nuts) and from the commodities they transported back to New Mexico from Mexico, Europe, and Asia, indicating that the northernmost outpost of the Spanish territories in the Americas actively participated in the global trade of the period by both exporting and importing goods.[45]

Conclusion

Even a cursory look at the documentary and archeological record indicates that people of all economic and social classes in New Mexico had hybrid households with a mixture of imported and local material culture. The distinction appears to have been in quantity. All excavated households, regardless of social standing, show archeological evidence of the use of local indigenous goods, particularly ceramics. Conversely, Mexican majolica and Chinese porcelains are found in excavations at Indian pueblos, though not in the quantity seen in settler households. This is not to imply that access to goods was equal, but rather to point out that all people in New Mexico were functioning in a climate of cultural exchange, even within their own households, and that international trade reached the far northern extreme of the Spanish Americas.

Of the Asian goods brought to New Mexico, the most ubiquitous type is among the most fragile: the highly valued Chinese porcelain. Fabrics, particularly Chinese silk and East Indian printed cotton (*indianilla*), are also frequently mentioned. Although not specified in the documents, many more of the textiles in New Mexico may well have been Asian in origin. In addition to the interesting references to five "kimonos" in the sampling of New Mexican wills cited above, another kimono is listed in the will of a Santa Fe woman, María Micaela Baca, in 1832, eleven years after the end of the colonial period.[46]

Although the quantity of Asian goods available on the northern frontier would not have been as abundant as in central Mexico, clearly some objects were available, or at least attainable at a cost. The extent to which Asian goods in New Mexico inspired local Spanish Colonial artists is an intriguing topic, but beyond the scope of this essay.[47] Throughout the documents from New Mexico, it is implied that ownership of "foreign" objects conferred social status. The phrases "from China," "from Córdova," or "from Michoacán," as well as "Castilian" cloth, or "Brittany" linen, or "Chinese" silk, indicate that the sources mattered, and these goods invariably bear an increased value as well. In other words, this far northern frontier "at the ends of the earth" participated not only in the international trade of the era, but also in the social value system of the global trade market.

Notes

[1] See Serge Gruzenski, *The Mestizo Mind: The Intellectual Dynamics of Colonization and Globalization* (New York and London: Routledge, 2002) and Frederick Cooper, *Colonialism in Question: Theory, Knowledge, History* (Berkeley: University of California Press, 2005). Also see Dana Leibsohn, in this volume.

[2] Portions of this article are adapted from Donna Pierce and Cordelia Thomas Snow, "Hybrid Households: A Cross Section of New Mexican Material Culture," in *Transforming Images: New Mexican Santos In-Between Worlds*, edited by Claire Farago and Donna Pierce, 101–116 (University Park, PA: Penn State Press, 2006). Also see Pierce and Snow, "A Harp for Playing: Domestic Goods Transported over the Camino Real," in *El Camino Real de Tierra Adentro* 2, compiled by Gabrielle G. Palmer and Stephen L. Fosberg, 71-86, Cultural Resources Series, no. 13 (Santa Fe: Bureau of Land Management, 1999). I would like to acknowledge here the ongoing research support from my longtime colleague and collaborator, Cordelia Thomas Snow.

[3] John L. Kessell, ed., *Remote beyond Compare: Letters of don Diego de Vargas to His Family from New Spain and New Mexico, 1675–1706*, Vargas Series 1 (Albuquerque: University of New Mexico Press, 1989), 168.

[4] For published examples mentioning Asian goods in missions and churches, see Eleanor B. Adams and Fray Angélico Chávez, translators and annotators, *The Missions of New Mexico in 1776: A Description by Fray Francisco Atanasio Domínguez with Other Contemporary Documents*, 2nd ed. (Albuquerque: University of New Mexico Press, 1956); France V. Scholes, "The Supply Service of the New Mexican Missions in the Seventeenth Century," pts. 1–3, *New Mexico Historical Review 5* (January 1930): 93–115; (April 1930): 186–210; (October 1930): 386–404; France V. Scholes and Eleanor B. Adams, "Inventories of Church Furnishings in Some of the New Mexico Missions, 1672," in *Dargan Historical Essays*, edited by William M. Dabney and Josiah C. Russell, 27–38, University of New Mexico Publications in History, no. 4 (Albuquerque: University of New Mexico Press, 1952); and Donna Pierce, "Heaven on Earth: Church Furnishings in Seventeenth-Century New Mexico," in *El Camino de Tierra Adentro* 2, compiled by Gabrielle G. Palmer and Stephen L. Fosberg, 197–208, Cultural Resources Series, no. 13 (Santa Fe: Bureau of Land Management, 1999).

[5] George P. Hammond and Agapito Rey, *Don Juan de Oñate: Colonizer of New Mexico, 1595–1628*, 2 vols. (Albuquerque: University of New Mexico Press, 1953). Also see Marc Simmons, *The Last Conquistador* (Norman: University of Oklahoma, 1991).

[6] Florence Hawley Ellis, *San Gabriel del Yunque: Window on the Prespanish Indian World* (Santa Fe: Sunstone Press, 1988) and *When Cultures Meet: Remembering San Gabriel del Yunque Oweenge* (Santa Fe: Sunstone Press, 1970). The recovered artifacts are on long-term loan from San Juan Pueblo to the Maxwell Museum of Anthropology, University of New Mexico, Albuquerque.

[7] Hammond and Rey, *Don Juan de Oñate*, 1:522–548. On August 22, 1600, Captains Juan de Gordejuela Ybarguen and Juan de Sotelo Cisneros conducted an inspection of reinforcements and supplies being sent to Oñate in San Gabriel. Cordelia Thomas Snow provides a discussion of some of the material goods imported to New Mexico in "A Headdress of Pearls: Luxury Goods Imported over the Camino Real during the Seventeenth Century," in *El Camino Real de Tierra Adentro* 1, edited by Gabrielle G. Palmer, 69–76, Cultural Resources Series, no. 11 (Santa Fe: Bureau of Land Management, 1993).

[8] Villagrá wrote an account of the Oñate expedition and settlement of New Mexico in the form of an epic poem published in Spain in 1610. See Gaspar Pérez de Villagrá, *History of New Mexico by Gaspar Pérez de Villagrá, Alcalá, 1610*, trans. Gilberto Espinosa (Los Angeles: The Quivira Society, 1933).

[9] Personal communication, Linda Shulsky Pomper, Research Associate, Metropolitan Museum of Art, New York, April 1992 and April 1993.

[10] Cordelia Thomas Snow, "The Plazas of Santa Fe, New Mexico, 1610–1776," *El Palacio* 94, no. 2 (Winter 1988): 40–51.

[11] Cordelia Thomas Snow, "A Brief History of the Palace of the Governors and a Preliminary Report on the 1974 Excavation," *El Palacio* 80, no. 3 (October 1974): 1–22. The recovered artifacts are in the collection of the Laboratory of Anthropology, Museum of New Mexico, Santa Fe.

[12] I am indebted to Linda Shulsky Pomper, Research Associate, Metropolitan Museum of Art, New York, for her generous help with the identification of these sherds and the pairings with intact pieces. Also see Linda R. Shulsky, "Chinese Porcelain in New Mexico," in *Vormen uít Vuur* 153, no. 3 (September 1994): 13-18.

[13] Unpublished document, Archivo General de la Nación, Mexico City, Inquisición 593, expediente 1, folio 60.

[14] For discussions of majolica in general—and the stylistic impact of Asian porcelains on it—see John M. Goggin, *Spanish Majolica in the New World: Types of the Sixteenth to Eighteenth Centuries,* Yale University Publications in Anthropology 72 (New Haven, 1968); Florence C. Lister and Robert H. Lister, *Andalusian Ceramics in Spain and New Spain: A Cultural Register from the Third Century B.C. to 1700* (Tucson: University of Arizona Press, 1987); Margaret Connors McQuade, *Talavera Poblana: Four Centuries of a Mexican Ceramic Tradition* (New York: The Americas Society, 1999); and Robin Farwell Gavin, Donna Pierce, and Alfonso Pleguezuelo, *Cerámica y Cultura: The Story of Spanish and Mexican Mayólica* (Albuquerque: University of New Mexico Press, 2003).

[15] Unpublished document, Archivo General de la Nación, Mexico City, Concurso de Peñaloza, v. 1, ff. 395–400. I am very grateful to Lic. Beatriz Berndt of Mexico City for her able research assistance and for acquiring publication quality scans of this document. Also, see France V. Scholes, *Church and State in New Mexico, 1610–1650* (Albuquerque: University of New Mexico, 1937) and *Troublous Times in New Mexico, 1659–1670* (Albuquerque: University of New Mexico, 1942).

[16] These unpublished estate inventories and wills are located in the New Mexico State Records Center and Archives in Santa Fe, Spanish Archives of New Mexico (SANM) I and II.

[17] Unpublished document, 1762, Juana Luján, Santa Cruz, SANM II: 556. Also see Richard Ahlborn, "The Will of a New Mexico Woman in 1762," *New Mexico Historical Review 65* (July 1990): 319–355.

[18] The phrase *taza caldera* may refer to the Asian-style soup-plates, since *taza* is usually translated as a bowl and the word *caldera* (cauldron) when used as an adjective usually refers to hot dishes such as soups or stews.

[19] Unpublished document, 1727, Antonio Vallejos, Santa Fe, SANM I: 82.

[20] Examples can be found in the Museo Franz Mayer, Mexico City. See Hector Rivero Borrell M. et al., *The Grandeur of Viceregal Mexico: Treasures from the Museo Franz Mayer*, exh. cat. (Houston: Museum of Fine Arts Houston and Museo Franz Mayer, 2002).

[21] Unpublished document, 1733, Francisco de Jesús y Espejo, Albuquerque, SANM I: 1219.

[22] Fray Angélico Chávez, *The Origins of New Mexico Families in the Spanish Colonial Period in Two Parts: The Seventeenth Century (1598–1693), and the Eighteenth Century (1693–1821)*, 1954 (Reprint Santa Fe: Museum of New Mexico Press, 1992).

[23] Unpublished documents, 1743, José de Reano Tagle, Santa Fe, SANM I: 964.

[24] Unpublished document, 1744, Margarita Martín, Santa Cruz, SANM I: 530.

[25] Clevy Lloyd Strout, "Resettlement of Santa Fe, 1695: The Newly Found Muster Roll," *New Mexico Historical Review* 53 (July 1978): 261–270; John B. Colligan, *The Juan Páez Hurtado Expedition of 1695: Fraud in Recruiting Colonists for New Mexico* (Albuquerque: University of New Mexico Press, 1995); and José Antonio Esquibel and John B. Colligan, *The Spanish Recolonization of New Mexico: An Account of the Families Recruited at Mexico City in 1693* (Albuquerque: New Mexico Genealogical Research Center, 1999). Also see Esquibel, "The Formative Era for New Mexico's Colonial Population: 1693–1700," in Farago and Pierce, *Transforming Images,* 64–79.

[26] Unpublished document, 1748, Antonio Durán de Armijo, San Gerónimo de Taos, SANM I: 240.

[27] The words *pozuelo* and *taza* are both translated as cups or small bowls. In documents I have studied in Mexico and New Mexico, *pozuelo* appears to refer to the small handle-less cups used for drinking chocolate, whereas *taza* seems to imply a small bowl. María Bonta de Pezuela concurs (personal communication, 2010). Also see María Bonta de la Pezuela, *Porcelana China de Exportación para el Mercado novohispano: La colección del Museo Nacional del Virreinato* (Mexico City: Universidad Nacional Autónoma de México, Instituto de Investigaciones Estéticas, 2008).

[28] Unpublished document, 1747, Luis García Noriega, San Antonio de Albuquerque, SANM I: 341.

[29] Unpublished document, 1749, Lugarda Quintana, Santa Cruz, SANM I, 968.

[30] Unpublished document, 1771, Mónica Tomasa Martín, Taos, SANM I: 590.

[31] Unpublished document, 1762, Juan Montes Vigil, Santa Fe, SANM I: 1055.

[32] According to Carmen Espinosa, these were "kimonos del Japón" (*Shawls, Crinolines, Filigree: The Dress and Adornment of the Women of New Mexico, 1739–1900* [El Paso: Texas Western Press, 1970], 17). However, the phrase "del Japón" does not appear in the original documents. As we will see below, other wills and inventories also mention "kimonos," but again the country of origin is not specified.

[33] Unpublished document, 1762, Juana Luján, Santa Cruz, SANM II: 556. Also see Ahlborn, "The Will of a New Mexico Woman."

[34] Unpublished document, SANM I: 48, inventory of the estate of María Gertrudes Armijo, Taos, March 26, 1776.

[35] Unpublished document, 1780, Manuel Montes Vigil, Abiquiu, SANM I: 1060.

[36] Unpublished document, 1784, Juan Antonio Fernández, Santa Fe, SANM I: 280.

[37] Unpublished document, 1789, José Maldonado, Santa Fe, SANM I: 598.

[38] Unpublished document, 1780, Manuel Montes Vigil, Abiquiu, SANM I: 1060; and unpublished document, 1771, Mónica Tomasa Martín, Taos, SANM I: 590.

[39] Unpublished document, 1747, Luis García Noriega, Albuquerque, SANM I: 341.

[40] Unpublished document, 1743, José de Reano Tagle, Santa Fe, SANM I: 964; and unpublished document, 1744, Antonio Tafoya Altamirano, Santa Cruz, SANM I: 27.

[41] Chávez, *Origins of New Mexico Families.*

[42] Unpublished document, 1815, Manuel Delgado, Santa Fe, SANM I: 252.

[43] Marta V. Vicente, *Clothing the Spanish Empire: Families and the Calico Trade in the Early Modern Atlantic World* (New York: Palgrave MacMillan, 2006), 82–83.

[44] Some of the more notable were Governors López de Mendizábal and Diego de Peñalosa. Records of their trials are in the Archivo General de la Nación in Mexico City, Inquisición 504, 593, 594; Concurso de Peñaloza; and Tierras 3268, 3283, 3286. Also see Scholes, *Church and State* and *Troublous Times.*

[45] For more information on merchants and trade see Max L. Moorhead, *New Mexico's Royal Road: Trade and Travel on the Chihuahua Trail* (Norman: University of Oklahoma Press, 1958); Christine Mather, ed., *Colonial Frontiers: Art and Life in Spanish New Mexico, The Fred Harvey Collection* (Santa Fe: Ancient City Press, 1983); Christine Preston, Douglas Preston, and José Antonio Esquibel, *The Royal Road: El Camino Real from Mexico City to Santa Fe* (Albuquerque: University of New Mexico, 1998).

[46] Unpublished document, 1832, María Micaela Baca, Santa Fe, SANM I: 144.

[47] For a cursory examination of this topic, see Pierce, "The Active Reception of International Artistic Sources in New Mexico," in Farago and Pierce, *Transforming Images,* 44–57; and Pierce, "Hybrid Households," 109.